PREFACE.

ANOTHER Guide to the English Lakes! many persons will exclaim, on first hearing of this work; and, considering the great number of Guide Books to the District already published, the Author feels that a few words of explanation are due to his readers.

Having been placed in a favourable position for ascertaining the wants of tourists, and being intimately acquainted with almost every mountain and vale, every nook and corner, in the whole district, he resolved, at the request of numerous visitors, to undertake the task of writing a Guide Book which should be as exhaustive and practical as possible, and the result of personal observation.

Although so many Guide Books are in circulation, he feels justified in adding one to the number, from the belief that there has not yet appeared a work which supplies in every respect the wants of the great majority of tourists.

For this object neither exertion nor cost has been spared.

In order to produce an accurate work, which may prove of real service to the tourist, the Author has travelled on foot over almost every inch of ground described in the following pages; and with note-book in hand has made memoranda on the spot, and written each tour whilst the subject was fresh in the memory. Although previously well acquainted with most of the district, he has made another visit to every place mentioned in the Guide, has climbed some of the highest mountains many times with the object of discovering the best road for the ascent, and has walked thousands of miles.

The book may therefore be regarded as accurate and trustworthy; and the writer believes that it will be of service not only to the stranger, but also to those familiar with the district.

Full particulars are given of the spots visible from almost every mountain in the district, and to many the repeated enumeration of names which this involves will appear undesirable. The Author has, however, after mature consideration, felt it advisable to maintain this feature, even at the risk of making the work appear dull; for he well knows that the true mountaineer takes a delight in being able to name correctly the heights which he sees; each of which is gradually invested for him with an especial characteristic, and looked upon as an old friend.

Those also who ascend a mountain occasionally will find it interesting to be able to obtain from the book information that will make clear to them, as it were, the vast panorama that meets the eye.

It should be remembered that when a day is set apart for the ascent of a mountain, the Guide Book for that day will be referred to especially for the information which it conveys respecting the particular height ascended.

The Author desires to acknowledge his obligation to those friends who have contributed the articles on Local Names, Meteorology, and Botany.

For the improvement of future editions the Author will be glad to receive corrections or suggestions from any tourist. Letters to be addressed to Henry Irwin Jenkinson, Keswick, Cumberland.

JENKINSON'S

PRACTICAL GUIDE

TO THE

ENGLISH

LAKE DISTRICT.

𝔚𝔦𝔱𝔥 𝔐𝔞𝔭𝔰.

LONDON:

EDWARD STANFORD, 6 & 7, CHARING CROSS, S.W.

—

1872.

CONTENTS.

WINDERMERE SECTION.

LANGDALE SECTION.

GRASMERE SECTION.

CONISTON SECTION.

KESWICK SECTION.

BUTTERMERE SECTION.

WASTWATER SECTION.

ULLSWATER SECTION.

INTRODUCTION.

THE Lake District is that portion of the North of England which lies to the west of the Lancaster and Carlisle Railway, and is bounded by the sea, stretching from Morecambe Bay to the Solway Firth.

It includes most of Cumberland and Westmorland, and a part of Lancashire; the southern peninsula, the Furness District, being in Lancashire, although completely isolated from the main bulk of that county.

On the summit of the Wrynose Pass are what are called the "Three Shire Stones," marking the spot where the three counties meet.

From Duddon Sands to Wrynose, the river Duddon divides Lancashire and Cumberland. From Wrynose Lancashire borders on Westmorland, the boundary following the course of the stream which flows through Little Langdale and Elterwater tarns to Windermere; then by the western shore of that lake until opposite Storrs Hall, where it crosses the lake and descends to Morecambe Bay by a small stream called the Winster. It will thus be seen that the Coniston Old Man and Wetherlam Mountains are in Lancashire, and the lakes Coniston and Esthwaite, as well as the southern part of Windermere Lake.

The boundary between Cumberland and Westmorland runs from Wrynose over Bow Fell, thence it crosses at the back of the Langdale Pikes to Dunmail Raise, and after passing along the summit of Helvellyn, it descends by the rivulet flowing through Glencoin to Ullswater,

and down the middle of that lake and by the river
Eamont to the Eden.

Most of the high and rugged mountains are in Cumberland; also the lakes Wastwater, Ennerdale, Loweswater, Buttermere, Crummock, Bassenthwaite, Derwentwater, Thirlmere, and part of Ullswater.

In Westmorland are the Langdale Pikes, the High
Street and Fairfield ranges, and the eastern side of Helvellyn; most of Windermere and Ullswater lakes, and
the whole of Haweswater, Brothers Water, Grasmere,
and Rydal lakes.

The Lake Country is not of great extent—the greatest
length or breadth of the area being about 50 miles, but
almost every inch of ground is either wild and grand,
or richly beautiful. Perhaps in no other country is
there more varied beauty in so small a space. The
tourist is enabled to pass quickly from one vale to
another, and in a few days he may take a hasty glance
at the whole. It must not, however, be supposed that
in this way justice can be done to the scenery of the
lakes. The most beautiful bits lie out of the ordinary
route of tourists, and the lover of natural scenery, and
of mountain-climbing, may spend many happy months
in visiting the hidden recesses, and scaling the innumerable peaks which are reflected in the clear waters
of the lovely lakes and tarns embosomed in every part
of the district.

The following pages are intended to meet the wants
both of those who are obliged to hasten over the ground,
and of those who make a lengthened sojourn, or visit
it many times.

The whole district has been divided into eight sections:—Windermere, Langdale, Grasmere, Coniston,
Keswick, Buttermere, Wastwater, and Ullswater; and
is illustrated with maps.

Every mountain and valley in each section, with the

carriage tours, and routes over passes, will be found fully described. This arrangement has enabled the subject to be treated in as exhaustive a manner as possible, and allows of easy reference, whilst the book will be found to be a complete guide to the tourist if he be staying for a lengthened time at any one spot in the district.

From the south and centre of England visitors generally enter the district either at Windermere Railway Station, by the Kendal and Windermere Railway, or by the Furness Railway, which skirts Morecambe Bay, and runs to the foot of Windermere Lake.

From Scotland the most direct way is to take the branch railway from Penrith to Keswick; but some tourists will take the coach from Penrith to the foot of Ullswater, sail up the lake in the steamer, and from Patterdale continue the journey to Ambleside or Keswick.

From Ireland and the Isle of Man, it is usual to land at Barrow or Whitehaven.

In the following pages the tourist is supposed to enter in the direction of Windermere Lake, and that is undoubtedly the best starting-point, as it allows of the tamest part of the country being first visited. Those, however, who adopt a different plan, will find the book meet their requirements.

Every inch of ground is rich in subjects of study, for the geologist, and botanist, and the antiquarian, will find innumerable remains of British, Roman, Saxon, and Feudal times. There is almost a total absence of legends; this, however, is amply compensated for by the halo which has been thrown around the region by a constellation of poets who have lived here, and so loved the district, as to make nearly every lake and hill, every rock and brook, the subject of verse.

The tourist who comes here for rest and change to enjoy the beauties of nature, and to be braced for future work by mountain air and exercise, will, it is hoped, find this book a useful and practical guide to a district where, "in fine vicissitude, beauty alternates with grandeur; where he will pass through stony hollows, along strait passes, traversed by torrents, overhung by high walls of rock; now winding amid broken, shaggy chasms, and huge fragments; now suddenly emerging into some emerald valley, where the streamlet collects itself into a lake, and man has again found a fair dwelling, and it seems as if Peace had established herself in the bosom of Strength."

HOW BEST TO SPEND A FLYING VISIT TO THE LAKES.

THOSE who cannot devote time for more than a flying visit to the District, are recommended to take the circular one day's tour from Ambleside, round by Coniston, Furness Abbey, and Windermere Lake.

The next day they might drive to Dungeon Gill, going by Little Langdale and returning to Ambleside by Great Langdale Valley.

Then travel by coach from Ambleside to Keswick, passing Rydal, Grasmere, and Thirlmere lakes.

From Keswick drive to Buttermere by Honister Pass and return by the vale of Lorton.

The second day's excursion from Keswick ought to be to Wastwater, by Sty Head Pass, returning by Black Sail and Scarf Gap passes, and the Newlands Vale.

Ullswater should on no account be omitted. It might be visited either from Ambleside or from Keswick. If the traveller be journeying from the S. of England to Scotland, he could visit Ullswater on his way from Keswick to Penrith. Should his intention be to leave the district again at Windermere, he could return from Keswick by way of Ullswater.

Tourists stationed at either Ambleside or Keswick, and who are anxious to visit Wastwater, but can only travel in a carriage, might arrange to take a three days' drive. Starting from Ambleside, they could pass over Wrynose and Hardknott into Eskdale, and thence to Wastwater and Calder Bridge. The second day they might proceed by way of Egremont, and the Ennerdale, Loweswater, Crummock, and Buttermere lakes, to Keswick; and on the third day return either by coach-road over Dunmail Raise, or by Ullswater and the Kirkstone Pass to Ambleside. It will not affect the interest of the tour whether this three days' drive be commenced at Ambleside or at Keswick; and it might be taken in the opposite direction to that above described.

A FOURTEEN DAYS' PEDESTRIAN TOUR.

A NUMBER of tours might be arranged for the pedestrian, commencing from different points.

This would be of little use to those who have already made a partial acquaintance with the district; and for strangers they would require to be infinitely varied to allow for differences of purse, time, and inclination.

The following fourteen days' tour will, it is hoped, be sufficiently suggestive to enable all to plan for themselves so as to meet their several requirements :—

CHARGES FOR CONVEYANCES, PONIES, AND GUIDES.

THE following scale of charges will apply over the whole district during the busy part of the season. At other times, special arrangements may occasionally be made:—

For a one-horse conveyance, 1s. per mile.

For a two-horse conveyance, 1s. 6d. per mile.

If the stage extends more than 10 miles, 1s. 4d. per mile.

The return journey with empty carriage is not charged for.

In addition to the above, the driver's charge is 5s. per day, 3d. per mile, or 6d. per hour. If the payment be by mile, no charge is made by the driver for the return journey with empty conveyance.

In long excursions it is usual to pay for the driver's refreshments, and also the horses' feed, and in all cases the hirer pays the tolls.

Ponies for mountain excursions are charged 5s. to 7s. 6d., according to the distance, and guides to the different mountains charge the same. It is in all cases better to have an understanding as to the charge before starting.

HEIGHTS OF MOUNTAINS.

	Feet.		Feet.
Scawfell Pike	3210	Branstree	2333
Scawfell	3162	Gray Crag	2331
Helvellyn	3118	Pike O'Stickle	2323
Skiddaw	3058	Pike O'Blisco	2304
Great End	2984	Yoke	2292
Bow Fell	2960	Seatallan	2266
Great Gable	2949	Carrock Fell	2174
Pillar	2927	Place Fell	2154
Hanging Knott	2903	Harter Fell (Eskdale)	2140
Fairfield	2863	Fleetwith (Honister)	2126
Blencathara	2847	Yewbarrow	2058
Crinkle Crags	2816	Wetherlam	2019
Great Dodd	2807	Herdhouse	2019
Grasmoor	2791	Causey Pike	2000
St. Sunday Crag ..	2756	High Seat	1996
Steeple	2746	Screes	1978
High Street	2663	Black Combe	1969
High Stile	2643	Maiden Moor	1887
Coniston Old Man ..	2633	Blake Fell	1878
Kirk Fell	2631	Steel Fell	1811
Haycock	2619	Lords Seat	1811
Grisedale Pike	2593	Mell Fell	1760
Glaramara	2560	Mellbreak	1676
Kidsty Pike	2560	Wansfell Pike	1597
Dow Crags	2555	Cat Bells	1482
Red Screes	2541	Silver Howe	1345
Greyfriars	2537	Low Fell	1336
Whiteside	2525	Helm Crag	1299
Harter Fell	2509	Hallin Fell	1271
Caudale Moor	2502	Wallow Crag	1234
Green Gable	2500	Latrigg	1203
High Raise	2500	Loughrigg Fell	1101
Red Pike	2479	Gummers How	1054
Ill Bell	2476	Castle Crag	900
Dale Head	2473	Orrest Head	871
High Crag	2443	Latterbarrow	803
Robinson	2417	Muncaster Fell	757
Seat Sandal	2415		
Sergeant Man	2414		
Harrison Stickle ..	2401	Ingleborough	2373
Hindscarth	2385	Crossfell	2892
Froswick	2359	Ben Nevis (Scotland)	4406
Brandreth	2344	Snowdon (Wales) ..	3590

HEIGHTS OF LAKES.

	Feet.			Feet.
Windermere	134	Brothers Water		520
Eathwaite	217	Derwentwater		238
Coniston	147	Bassenthwaite		226
Rydal	181	Buttermere		331
Grasmere	208	Crummock		321
Thirlmere	533	Loweswater		429
Ullswater	477	Ennerdale		369
Haweswater	694	Wastwater		204

HEIGHTS OF TARNS.

	Feet.		Feet.
Red	2356	Scales	—
Keppelcove	1825	Bowscale	—
Grisedale	1768	Overwater	—
Angle (Patterdale) ..	—	Little	—
Hayeswater	1383	Bleaberry (Buttermere)	—
Blea Water	1584	Floutern (Ennerdale) ..	—
Small Water	1484	Scoat (Wastdale) ..	—
Skeggles (Kentmere) ..	1017	Low (Wastdale)	—
Kentmere Reservoir ..	973	Greendale	1320
Blelham	138	Burnmoor	832
Loughrigg	308	Blea (Eskdale)	700
Elterwater	187	Devoke	766
Little Langdale	340	Angle (Bow Fell) ..	—
Blea (Langdale)	612	Sprinkling	1960
Red (Langdale)	—	Sty Head	1430
Stickle	1540	Low (Tarn Hows) ..	—
Codale	1528	Low Water (Coniston)	1786
Easedale	915	Goats Water	1646
Harrop	—	Dead	—
Blea (nr. Watendlath)	1562	Seathwaite	1210
Dock	1322	Leverswater	1350
Watendlath	847	Mockerken (Loweswater)	—
Tarn at Leaves	—	Beacon	536

HEIGHTS OF PASSES.

	Feet.			Feet.
Esk Hause	2490	Kirkstone	1481
Sticks	2450	Scarf Gap	1400
Nan Bield	2100	Hard Knott..	1291
Rossett Gill..	2002	Wrynose	1270
Gatescarth	1950	Honister	1190
Grisedale	1929	Buttermere Hause ..	1096
Black Sail	1750	Whinlatter	1043
Sty Head	1600	Dunmail Raise	783
Stake	1576		

LOCAL NAMES IN THE ENGLISH LAKE DISTRICT.

In the following pages an attempt is made to present to the reader, in as brief a form as the nature of the subject will admit of, such results of the most recent investigations in the Etymology of Place-names as bear more directly upon the region of the English Lakeland.

Something akin to the higher kind of enjoyment arising from a knowledge of geology sufficient to enable the tourist to distinguish the more striking natural features of the country through which he may be passing will, it is conceived, be derived from an acquaintance with the etymological peculiarities of the district.

No claim is put forth to much original research: beyond a knowledge of the Teutonic and Romance languages sufficient to enable the writer to follow our best northern Glossarists, he possesses no special qualifications for the task. Free use has accordingly been made of the labours of others. Among the authorities consulted may be specially named Sullivan's 'Cumberland and Westmorland, Ancient and Modern;' Ferguson's 'Northmen in Cumberland and Westmorland,' a work which no one, wishing to pursue the subject farther, should fail to peruse carefully; and the fuller and more exhaustive work of the Rev. Isaac Taylor, 'Words and Places.' McMillan & Co.

Where the writer has differed from such high authorities, he has not ventured to do so without due consideration; and where he has suggested derivations altogether new, it has not been without a full knowledge of the perils of the uncertain sea of etymology on which he launches his tiny bark. Sometimes the authorities have

been found to differ widely from each other on the derivation of a term; in such cases the etymon which, on
geographical or ethnological grounds, seemed the most
natural has been adopted. Of names of modern origin,
or of such as to an ordinary reader explain themselves,
it must be understood no notice has been taken in these
pages. The more ancient local names found in the
district now under consideration are derivable from four
principal sources, *viz.* the Celtic, Anglo-Saxon, Danish,
old Norse or Icelandic, languages. Of these it will be
seen the Celtic and Icelandic greatly preponderate over
the other two.

That the earliest known occupants of our island were
of the Celtic race seems to be generally accepted by the
philologist as well as the historian. The Celts were
divided into two main branches, which followed each
other at a considerable interval of time in their passage
across Europe from the East. Although speaking languages originally of the same stock, these languages are
said by Celtic scholars to present dialectic differences
as great as those existing between modern English and
German. The earlier comers belonged to what has been
termed the Gadhelic branch, or Hiberno-Celtic; their
language, it may be noted, still survives in the Erse of
Ireland, the Gaelic of the Scotch Highlands, and the
Manx. The other branch is known by the name of the
Cymric, or Cambro-Celtic, and their language is re-
presented by those spoken in Wales, and Brittany, in
France. From the fact that both Gadhelic and Cymric
names for the same object are found in Cumberland,
Sullivan is of opinion that tribes of both these branches
eventually penetrated into the mountainous country of
Cumberland and Westmorland. However this may be,
many of the river names, the names of some of the
loftiest mountains, as well as those of several settlements, are undoubtedly either purely Celtic or have a
strong Celtic element in their composition. The name
of the county, *Cumberland*, that of its capital, *Carlisle*;
the *Derwent, Skiddaw, Blencathara*, in the north; of the

Old Man (Coniston), the *Pen*, in Duddon, and the river *Leven*, in the south, may be cited as examples.

Whatever may be the cause, it is certain the Roman occupation left little or no impress upon the nomenclature of this remote corner of England; nor can many traces of the permanent settlement of the Anglo-Saxons be found in the inner recesses of the district—those terms more distinctively of Anglo-Saxon origin, as *mere* for lake, *beck* for river, &c., being, as a rule, referable to a later period, when the English language was either forming or formed. In the two counties of Cumberland and Westmorland there are found at the present day upwards of sixty names of places ending in the Danish suffix, *by*; but a reference to a map of the two counties will show that these names are limited to the open country, extending circularly in a border from Appleby, on the S.E., along the Cumbrian plain to Allonby, on the Solway; thence skirting the sea-coast to Moresby, near Whitehaven, and cropping out again as high up on the S.W. as Ponsonby. Forming our conclusions from data like these, we may fairly presume that the Northumbrian Danes, in those incursions into Cumbria of which history makes mention, did not settle as colonists in the region known as the Lake District. On the other hand, a glance at the map accompanying this volume will show that the prevailing names are of the Norwegian type. The suffixes—*thwaite*, of which there are more than one hundred examples in the two counties; *dale, garth, holm*, for river island; *ness, scarth, force, gill*, &c.—are distinctively Norwegian. Ferguson, in his interesting work already referred to, accounts for the presence of these names upon the supposition that towards the latter part of the tenth century bands of Norsemen, descending from the Isle of Man—where, in the course of their rovings, they had at that time fixed their head-quarters—effected a landing on the opposite coasts of Cumberland, and permanently settled in a district which would present so many natural features to remind them of their native land. In the absence of all historical confirmation of such a settlement, this theory may at first sight seem strained; but we think that a careful study of his work will do much to convert the most sceptical to the general soundness of his arguments.

CELTIC KEY-WORDS TO LOCAL NAMES IN CUMBERLAND AND WESTMORLAND.

Cam, crooked. Examples: Morecambe; Celtic, *Mor*, Great; Morecambe, great bend.

> *Sicinius.* "This is clean kam."
> *Brutus.* "Merely awry."—*Coriolanus, Act* iii., *Sc.* i.

Craig, a rock. Common in Welsh names, and in almost universal use throughout the English Lake District; but is pronounced and written *Crag*. Examples: Castle Crag, Crinkle Crag, Iron Crag.

Cwm. This word is also of frequent use in Wales to denote "a cup-shaped depression among the hills."—*Taylor*. The shepherds and foxhunters of the Cambrian mountains make common use of this term to denote a hollow or depression lying among the highest parts of the mountains. Example: Gillercoom.

> NOTE.—The Anglo-Saxon form is combe, "a low place enclosed with hills."—*Bosworth*.

D-in, a hill. Ancient hill fortresses are frequently denoted by this root. Example: Dunmallet.

Dwr, water. Gaelic and Erse, *Dur*. "Prichard gives a list of 44 ancient river names in Italy, Germany, Gaul, and Britain in which this root is found."—*Taylor*. Examples: Low*dore*, *Der*went, River Lowther, written Loder by Leland.

Llwch, Welsh for lake. Compare Scotch Loch, Irish Lough.

Llevn, smooth, an adjectival river name. Loch Leven and three rivers of the name in Scotland. Example: River Leven, flowing from Windermere.

Nant, a narrow valley or glen. Examples: Nan Bield, Nent Head.

Pen, a *head*, hence a *hill*. This is the Cymric form. The Gadhelic is Ben, Cf. Ben Nevis, &c. Examples: Pennine, the Pen, in the valley of the Duddon.

Uisgue, *water*, Gaelic and Erse. The Welsh form is gwy or wy; also wysg, a current. Examples: Esk, Esthwaite, &c.

KEY-WORDS OF ANGLO-SAXON AND DANISH ORIGIN.

Barrow, Anglo-Saxon beorg, a hill, tumulus. Bury, burg, and brough are cognate words. They all convey the notion of inclosure or protection, and since these strongholds were generally on high ground, the word came to mean a hill-fortress, corresponding to Celtic dun. Example: Underbarrow, &c.

Beck. Anglo-Saxon, Becc, a brook; Danish, baek; German, bach; Icelandic, bek (*r*). This term is used throughout the district, and is applied not only to brooks, but to principal streams. Ogilvie says it is now "obsolete in England."

By, Danish. Originally used to denote a dwelling or single farm, and is thus synonymous with Saxon *ton*, a settlement. Another form of the word is *byr*. In Iceland at the present day the name given to a farmstead is boer. Over the whole of the Lake District a cow-house is termed a byre. Cf. by-law, *i. e.* township law.

Cove, Anglo-Saxon, cofa, a cave or cove. Applied to a recess among the hills. Example: Keppel Cove.

> "It was a cove, a huge recess,
> That keeps till June, December's snow."—*Wordsworth.*

Den, Anglo-Saxon, for denu, a valley. Example: Mickleden.

Holm, Anglo-Saxon, "a river island, a green plot of ground environed with water."—*Bosworth.* This is the sense in which it is applied in the plains of Cumberland. For Holm, an island, *see* Norwegian key-words.

Mere, Anglo-Saxon, a lake; Icelandic, maere, mar, a body of water. Examples: Buttermere, &c.

Neb, Anglo-Saxon and Danish for a beak or nose; hence a rocky projection. Appears in the forms *nab*, *neb*, and *snab*. Examples: Nab Scar, Rydal; High Snab, Newlands.

Ryg, Danish for ridge or back; Anglo-Saxon, *Hriog*. Example: Loughrigg, the Rig, separating the Vale of St. John's from Naddle.

Wic. This root is found in various European languages. Latin, vicus; Erse, fich; Cymric, gwic; all signifying an abode or dwelling. *Wik*, Su Goth, a bay or creek, qù vikings or *creekers.* The Anglo-Saxons and the Scandinavians applied this root in different senses. With the former it was a station or abode on land; with the Norseman a station for ships. As a suffix, Anglo-Saxon, *wic* signifies a dwelling, station, village, or bay, according to the situation of the places. Example: Keswick, Peel Wyke.

KEY-WORDS OF NORWEGIAN ORIGIN.

Dale, Icelandic, dal (*r*), a valley. *Dala*, to depress. As a suffix this term enters largely into the composition of local names, *e. g.* Rydal, Borrowdale, &c. It is pronounced in the vernacular *dy'al*, and among the peasantry has acquired almost a *generic* force, being applied to any of the mountain valleys.

> "I want a sweetheart, an' I thowt
> Thoo mebby wad an aw,
> I'd been a bit down t' *de'al* t'neet,
> An' thowt 'at I wad caw."
> *Richardson's Cummerlan, Mak o' Talk.*

Fell, Icelandic, *fell* or *fiall*. The modern Norwegian form is fjeld, pronounced fi-ell. The Anglo-Saxon *field* is from the same root. A *fell* is a place where the ground is on the *fall;* a *field* is a piece of ground where the trees have been *felled*. Fell is used throughout the entire district as a synonym for mountain. Examples: Scawfell, Bowfell, &c.

Force. Icelandic, fors; Norwegian, foss. *Forsa*, to rush furiously. A common name in the district for a waterfall. Examples: Scale Force, Aira Force.

Garth. Icelandic, gard (*r*); Anglo-Saxon form, geard, yard, primarily a fence or hedge; hence an inclosure. Example: Gatesgarth.

Gill. Icelandic, *Gil*. A mountain ravine. A term of general use in the district. Examples: Dungeon Gill, Sour Milk Gill.

Hause or *haws*, from Icelandic and Anglo-Saxon hals, a neck or throat, a depression between two mountains. Compare Kirkstone *Pass* with Buttermere *Hause*.

Holm, Icelandic, holmi, an island. Generally on a lake or river, *e. g.* Stockholm. Examples: Rampsholme, Lingholme, on Derwentwater.

How, Icelandic, haug (*r*): a mound, a hill. Hauga, to heap up. Hence a sepulchral hill. Found all over the district, and mostly in connection with a Scandinavian proper name. Examples: Silver How, Torpenhow.

Scar. Icelandic, *sker*; Norwegian, skar. A face of rock or jagged cliff. Example: Nab Scar.

Scarth and *scarf*. Both of much the same import as scar. Examples: Hindscarth, Scarf Gap.

Seat, Icelandic, set (*r*), a dwelling or seat. The root is widely diffused over Europe. Example: Seat-oller.

Stake; Icelandic, stiaki; Anglo-Saxon, staca, a stake or pole. Example: the Stake.

Sticks; Icelandic, stiki; Anglo-Saxon, sticca; a stick. 2. A stake. Example: the Sticks.

Stickle; Icelandic, stikill; Anglo-Saxon, sticel; a sharp point or peak; hence "steep or difficult of access."—*Bosworth.* Example: Pike o' Stickle.

Tarn; Icelandic, tiorn, from taaren, to trickle; a small sheet of water. A lakelet, generally high up amongst the mountains. Examples: Sprinkling Tarn, Red Tarn.

Thwaite; Norwegian, thveit; Danish, fved. A "clearing" in a forest; land inclosed and cleared of timber. Very common as a suffix in the district, occurring about 100 times in Cumberland alone. It is often found allied with a proper name, as Ormathwaite. Sometimes the prefix used denotes the nature of the crop produced, as Applethwaite; sometimes the nature of the ground inclosed, as Stonethwaite.

LOCAL NAMES.

RIVERS.

Calder, Kel-dwr, "the wooded water."

Caldew, pron. Cawda; cawd, "cold." The village of Caldbeck stands on a branch river of the Caldew.

Derwent, Dwr-gwyn, "clear-water" (Taylor); or, from Derwyn, equivalent to the "winding river" (Ferguson). Sullivan suggests a third derivation, dur-gwent, the beautiful water. The course of the river Derwent is not tortuous. Either of the other two names would be more characteristic.

Ehen, pron. Enn. Taylor refers this to the widely-diffused Celtic root, Afon, water or river, of which he thinks it a corruption.

Esk, The river. *See* Uisque, *ante,* Celtic key-words.

Greta. A.S., grætan, to weep, cry out; Old Eng., greet, to lament, mourn, in allusion to the wailing sound of its waters over the rocky boulders in its channel. The Yorkshire Greta has also a rocky bed.

Liza or *Lissa,* probably from *lissa,* torpor, weariness (F). Cf. Eng. "lazy."

Lodore, Loyw-dwr, "clear-water," very characteristic of the stream.

Lowther. Leland writes this name "Loder." Probably the derivation identical with that of *Lodore.*

LAKES.

Buttermere, Ennerdale, and *Windermere,* are referred by Ferguson to the Scandinavian proper names, *Buthar, Einar,* and *Winder.*

Coniston, Rydal, Bassenthwaite, and *Wastwater,* evidently take their names from the valleys in which they are respectively situated.

Crummock, a corruption of Crum-beck, the name of the river flowing into it (F.).

Derwentwater, supra.

Grasmere. Ferguson says, "formerly called Gresmere or Grismere," and thinks it takes its name rather from some Northman who dwelt upon its banks than from the "grise" or wild swine which used to frequent its shores. Gris is a Norwegian proper name. The modern pronunciation in the vernacular is *Gersemere*, Anglo-Saxon, Gerse, grass, and would seem to suggest a more modern name.

Haweswater. See Hause or Haws, Norwegian key-words.

Loweswater, or Low's Water, has a modern look about it.

Thirlmere. Thorolf's Mere, from proper name Thorolf, of which Thirlmere may be a corruption, is suggested by Ferguson.

Ullswater. Ulf, a former owner of the Lake, was first baron of Greystoke. Lyulph's Tower. Norman, L'Ulf, the Wolf, a proper name.

MOUNTAINS.

Barf, one of the many forms of Barrow, burg, &c., see Anglo-Saxon key-words.

Blencathara, from Celtic Blen-y-cathern, the peak of demons.

Dodd, Icelandic, Toddi, a member or limb, hence a mountain mass attached to a larger mountain, not necessarily having a "*blunt summit*," a definition which has suggested a ludicrous etymon, *doe-headed*. Skiddaw Dodd is actually peaked. Latrigg, "Skiddaw's Cub," would answer the definition better.

Cat Bells, or *Cathbels.* No satisfactory etymon has been given. "Probably so called, from the wild cats with which it was infested (!)" F. A score of hills in the neighbourhood would be more likely to be the haunts of the wild cat than the smooth, grassy slopes of this mountain. Armstrong's 'Gaelic Dictionary' gives Cath, a combat or strife; this would convert the commonplace name Cat Bells into Cathbel, the hill of combat or *Battle*-hill.

Dolly Waggon Pike, probably from the Scandinavian proper name, Doli Wagen, the surname Doli signifying a servant (Ferguson).

Fairfield, Danish, faar, sheep, *i.e.* sheep-fell.

Great Gable, or *Gavel*, from its resemblance to the end of a house.

Haystacks. Icelandic, stack (r), a columnar rock. Hay stacks, equivalent to high rocks.

High Stile. Anglo-Saxon, stigel; English, stile; German, steil, steep.

High Street, the name of a Westmorland mountain, over the summit of which (2700 feet) the Romans constructed a road or "street." The name is obviously of a comparatively modern origin.

Helvellyn. Two derivations for this name have been suggested— Celtic, el, a height, therefore El-velin, the hill of Baal or Vèli— supposed to refer to the worship of the god Baal; or, compounded of Hill and Bell, with the addition of the definite article *inn*, which the Norse and Danish languages require to be used as a post-fix.

Knot. This is a term applied to a rocky protuberance on the side of a mountain, as Hanging Knot, Hard Knot, Eskdale.

Old Man. Celtic, Alt Maen, high rock. Corrupted into Old Man. The Old Man of Hoy is the modern name of a high rock in the Orkneys. Two rocks on the Cornish coast are called the Old Man and his Man. The " Dead Man," in Cornwall, is a corruption of the Celtic Dod-maen.

Scawfell. Icelandic, Skor, a fissure, &c., *see* Scar and Scarth, to which this root is allied. Although this is only given as a probable derivation by Ferguson, it is characteristic.

Skiddaw. This name seems to puzzle etymologists. Three widely different derivations have been given. Dr. Stukely says, " *Yscyd* (Celtic), from some fancied resemblance of the shape of this mountain to a horse-shoe." Sullivan suggests, " Sgyddau (Celtic), the Scot's mountain." Ferguson refers it to the Norse language, *viz.* Skid (*r*), signifying a separation or division, *i. e.* the divided or " twofold mountain."

Steel Fell. *See* High Stile. Su Goth., steel.

Sty Head. Anglo-Saxon, Stigan, to ascend; stig, a path, qù stig-ràp, a step-rope, *i. e.* a stirrup; Danish, sti, a ladder. The word *stee*, for ladder, is in common use in the two countries. The Sty is the ascent. Sty Head, the top of the ascent. In the same neighbourhood we have Ladder-brow, the name of the pass from Borrowdale to Watendlath.

PLACES.

Ambleside, formerly Hamelside; Hamil, a Scandinavian proper name; Icelandic, sida; Anglo-Saxon, side, used in the sense of a settlement.

Bowness. Icelandic, Bol, a dwelling; ness, a promontory. Leland writes, Bolness; Camden, Bulness. There are three places of the name in the district.

Borrowdale. *See* Barrow, burg, &c. The mountain valley, pre-eminently.

Coniston. Icelandic, Konung (*r*); Anglo-Saxon, cyning, a king, the Royal or King's Stone.

Ennerdale. Norse, proper name, Einar; more probably has some relation with the name of the river flowing out of the Lake, the Ehen. *See* River name.

Gatesgarth, Gate's Crag (three of the name in the district), and Gateswater, are all referred to Geit, goat; also a Norwegian proper name.

Keswick, Kesh, the provincial name for the water hemlock ; Anglo-Saxon, Wic or Wick, an abode, a village.   Kes(h)wick, the village or abode by the sedges.   Crosthwaite was undoubtedly the original settlement, and as the church was not founded until the 12th century, Keswick is of a later foundation.   There is no need therefore to refer this name to a Norwegian source, as Ferguson does, *viz.* Kjelsvik.

Kescadale.   Ferguson, on the authority of 'Black's Guide,' gives this as a corruption of Gatescarthdale !   The present writer suggests a more modern one, *Cascade Dale.*   At the head of Kescadale there is a fine waterfall which, in a season of rain, is visible for miles off.   Kescadale is the name given to the upper part of the *New*lands valley.

Legberthwaite.   Icelandic, Lögberg, law-mount, *see* Thwaite.   Possibly this name may have some connection with the Druids' Temple, which stands within a distance of three miles from the Vale of Legberthwaite ; the northern continuation of this valley bears the later name of St. John's.   The whole of the valley may have been anciently included under one name.

Langstrath.   Gaelic, srath, "a country confined by hills on two sides of a river."   This lonely valley corresponds to the definition exactly.   It might be a curious question for the ethnographer, as well as the etymologist, to consider why a term that is common in Scotland should be found surviving, in a solitary instance, in the English Lake District.   The valley on the opposite side of the Stake Pass bears the name of Lang*dale*.

Rydal, a name evidently due to the kind of crop produced, *viz.* rye.   *Compare* Oatlands, Biglands (barley), &c.

Seatoller.   Norwegian proper name, Oller.   The seat, *i. e.* settlement or possession of Oller (F.).

Watendlath, a name which still remains a puzzle to etymologists. Ferguson proposes Norse, Vatn-hlada, "the barn by the water."   A more modern derivation is here offered.   *Wath*, a term common in the district for "ford."   *Lath*, or *Lath*, another old English word for a barn.

> "Ic rede the king, nu her bi-foren,
>   To maken *lathes* and gaderen coren."
>   *The Story of Genesis and Exodus*, cir. tem. 1300.

Long after the lower and more fertile Borrowdale Valley was formed into settlements, this remote valley would be held as an outlying pasture, where a barn would be required for storage for fodder. Hence the terms Wath and Lath.   The small hamlet of Watendlath is · built hard upon the ford at the outlet of the tarn.   West, A.D. 1796, writes this name Watanlath.   -

P. H.

METEOROLOGY.

In our varied, fitful English climate perhaps no subject more ordinarily forms the topic of daily remark than the state of the weather. To the tourist, whose comfort and enjoyment are so much dependent upon the condition of the atmosphere of the country through which he is passing, this question of the weather becomes one of special interest. As there is an exaggerated notion that the Lake Country is characterized by an excessive rainfall when compared with other parts of England, a few remarks may not be considered out of place in a work of this kind.

The first observations on the rainfall in England were taken at Kendal and Keswick simultaneously by the celebrated Dr. John Dalton, then resident at Kendal, and Mr. Peter Crosthwaite, of Keswick. Dalton's book on meteorology, published in 1793, had numerous readers; and the results appeared so vast, that a prejudice was raised against the climate of the mountainous parts of Cumberland and Westmorland which has not altogether been removed. An accurate observer[*] has remarked :— "There is more rain in the Mountain District certainly; but, however paradoxical it may seem, there is more brilliant weather also than in plain countries, for the rain comes down more heartily, and the weather clears up more cordially there than elsewhere; and in the spots of which I have spoken, the sheltering hills, the western exposure, the clear gushing streams, the dry sunny slopes, and the splendour and cheerfulness of the scene, combine to produce a physical and mental climate such as, for an English invalid, perhaps no foreign country contains."

---

[*] Dr. Lietch, in the 'Lancet.'

A comparison of the quantity of rain which fell in the year 1848 in different localities, may be interesting:—

	Inches.		Inches.
High Street (Mountain)	48	Gatesgarth (Buttermere)	133
The Flosh (nr. Whitehaven)	28	Eskdale Head	70
Cockermouth	52	Eskdale Vale	86
Bassenthwaite	47	Wastdale Head	115
Keswick	66	Troutbeck	91
Ennerdale	97	Ambleside	76
Loweswater	76	Langdale Head	130
Kendal	60	Stonethwaite	130
Crummock Lake	98	Seathwaite	160

The number of days upon which rain fell in 1848 were: at Whitehaven, 210; at Cockermouth, 228; at Keswick, 229; at Bassenthwaite Hulls, 196; at Eskdale, 205; at Wastdale Head, 243; at Ambleside, 201; at Langdale, 212; at Seathwaite, 232; and at Stonethwaite, 242.

Dr. Dalton published a curious table of observations, which he introduced as follows:—"The late Mr. Peter Crosthwaite, of the Museum, Keswick, availed himself of his situation in the vicinity of high mountains to make observations on the height of the clouds; for which purpose he chose Skiddaw, the highest mountain in the neighbourhood, a good view of which he had from his house. By means of marks on the side of the mountain, and with the assistance of a good telescope, he could discern, to a few yards, the height of the clouds when they were below the summit, which is very often the case. Perhaps the following observations are the only ones of the kind extant, as the difficulty attending such observations in a flat country is sufficient to deter any one from making two or three daily observations for a series of years; and when the whole sky is clouded, they are quite impracticable.

"He determined, by trigonometry, the perpendicular height of Skiddaw above the level of Derwent Lake to be 1050 yards, and noted in a column in his Meteorological Journal, every morning, noon, and evening, the height of the clouds, in yards, above the level of the lake, when their height did not exceed that of Skiddaw; and when it did, he marked it as such."

The result of five years' observations was as follows; out of 5381 observations:—

10	times the clouds did not exceed 200 yards in height.					
42	times the clouds were from 100 to 200 yards high.					
62	,,	,,	,,	200 ,,	300	,,
179	,,	,,	,,	300 ,,	400	,,
374	,,	,,	,,	400 ,,	500	,,
486	,,	,,	,,	500 ,,	600	,,
416	,,	,,	,,	600 ,,	700	,,
367	,,	,,	,,	700 ,,	800	,,
410	,,	,,	,,	800 ,,	900	,,
518	,,	,,	,,	900 ,,	1000	,,
419	,,	,,	,,	1000 ,,	1050	,,
2098	,,	,,	above 1050 yards high; *i. e.*, above the height of Skiddaw.			
5381						

The observations were classified in the respective months of the year, and they show that in November, December, January, and February, the clouds are not so often above the summit of Skiddaw as in the other months. This clearly indicates the effect of cold in restraining the ascent of vapour.

The tourist who visits the country early in the season has many advantages. From the second week in May the weather is usually finer till the end of June than later on in the season. There is no better time for seeing the Lakes. The foliage has all the varied and delicate tints of early summer; the air is cool and bracing; and the views of the mountains, whether from the valleys or from their summits, are clearer than when summer is farther advanced. The tourist season might be lengthened, by a month at the beginning and a few weeks at the end, with advantage. The autumnal tints are wonderfully varied and beautiful, and not unfrequently continue till the end of October.

It has generally been supposed that the climate of the Lake District is unusually cold in winter, owing to snow being seen upon the tops of the mountains frequently. The fact is the reverse. The mountains break off the prevailing winds, and the snow seldom remains long in the valleys or on the mountains lower down than 1500 to 2000 feet above their base. Consequently the Lake Country is warmer in winter than many of the flat portions of the kingdom. Occasionally the Lakes are frozen over, when excellent recreation is afforded to residents, whilst the trains from the neighbouring counties frequently bring lovers of skating for a few days, when the scenery has a peculiar charm, and is by some considered even more romantic than at any other period of the year.

J. F. C.

GEOLOGICAL MAP OF THE ENGLISH LAKE DISTRICT.

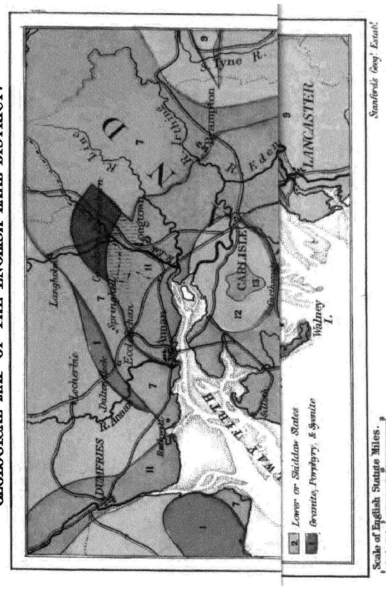

Scale of English Statute Miles.

GEOLOGY.

IF I did not believe that a deeply scientific treatise on geology would be out of place in a work like the present, and that the majority of readers would prefer a few lines free from all technicalities, and written by one who is not wedded to any popular theory, I should feel that some apology were due for the following remarks.

Moreover, differing as I do from the theories advanced by our greatest geologists, and feeling confident in my own opinions, I thought I should not be justified in allowing these pages to be used for expounding what I did not believe to be true. I was confirmed in this resolution on reading one of Professor Sedgwick's letters to Wordsworth on the Geology of the English Lake District, where, after referring to the changes which it is evident must have taken place in the Lake District during *vast intervals* of time, he says, " What has been stated requires for its comprehension no previous knowledge of geology; and any man may take the right observations, and draw the right conclusions from them, when he is once awake to the interest of those phenomena which rise up on every side of him, and seem to court his senses."

Few geologists would think of resorting to a Guide Book for information which is more properly sought for in the works of a Lyell or a Murchison. The majority of tourists are, however, not geologists; but everyone on entering this beautiful mountainous country is unconsciously led to think about the origin of those towering masses which he sees around him.

Many are the conjectures which are hazarded. Everything which it is difficult to understand is attributed by some to the Deluge, and by others to the upheaving force of internal heat. Formerly the Deluge theory was very popular, and that being found to be false, the current of opinion turned in favour of heat and volcanos, the gradual or sudden elevation of whole continents, and of each separate mountain. Even at the present day our greatest men in the geological world uphold the theory of the gradual elevation of whole continents by the agency of heat.

To account for the deposit of different strata, they say the land has been slowly pushed up from the sea and then gradually sunk again, and that this up and down movement has continued through countless ages, the same continent having slowly risen and slowly sunk many times. According to Professor Sedgwick, who himself advocates this theory, these movements are not to be explained by any known operations of nature, without a great change of physical conditions, for he says, "The valleys of Cumberland and Westmorland present phenomena not to be explained by any forces, however long continued, which are now seen to act on the surface of the country."

I have day after day thoughtfully paced the mountains of Cumberland and Westmorland, endeavouring to unravel the mystery of their origin and history. At first tacitly acknowledging, though with many misgivings, that the generally-accepted theory that the gradual rising and sinking of the land were due to the force of heat, I have been unable to reconcile that theory with facts. Like a rudderless ship in a storm, or like the individual, or the nation, that has cast off one form of religion or government before another has been found to take its place, I remained for a time undecided.

Trammelled by the generally-received notion that water is a leveller, a doctrine supported by Sir Charles Lyell, who, in the last edition of his 'Principles of Geology,' says, "The aqueous agents are incessantly labouring to reduce the inequalities of the earth's surface to a level; while the igneous are equally active in restoring the unevenness of the external crust, partly by heaping up new matter in certain localities, and partly by depressing one portion, and forcing out another, of the earth's envelope;" being puzzled, too, to account for the contortions of strata, and the elevation above the sea of mountains and continents, many were my cogitations before I could substitute a satisfactory theory for the one already rejected.

The reader must bring to the aid of the subject his imaginative faculty. He must remember that what is now dry land has been many times under the sea; that a country which is now covered with a luxuriant tropical vegetation may in past ages have been one mass of snow and ice; that this England of ours was within a very recent geological period a land of glaciers and icebergs.

For such changes to occur requires countless ages of time—a time which it is as impossible to comprehend, without bringing into play the imaginative faculty, as it is to grasp the immeasurable distances of stars, the light from some of which has not yet reached this earth, although it has been travelling millions of years.

Having expanded the mind and thrown aside exploded and contracted notions, we are now enabled, with the assistance of imagination, to apply the same gradual changes which are taking place at present, to an immeasurable past.

It is easy to conceive that an island like England, or a continent like Europe, may in some remote future, say millions of years, be gradually encroached upon by the unceasing beating sea, until it entirely vanishes under the water. But it is not so easy to conceive that what is now the bed of the ocean will, without the agency of heat, gradually appear above the water with mountains and valleys like our present continents. It is equally, at first sight, difficult to comprehend how a country which has now a tropical climate can at one time have been covered with icebergs, and how strata, contorted in every imaginable way, and lying at different angles, can have been, in that manner, deposited at the bottom of the sea. If any portion of the earth's crust be examined it will be found that such changes have undoubtedly taken place, and the English Lake District is no exception to the rule.

There are high mountains of clay slate which have been tranquilly deposited at the bottom of an ocean. The whole district is surrounded by limestone, also the deposit of an ocean bed. Above the limestone is coal, which must have been formed when the sea had left the land, and with a tropical sun. Again, the sea has encroached and covered the coal with new red sandstone. Dry land once more appears, and instead of a tropical sun we have the whole country covered with ice, like Greenland at the present day. The atmosphere becomes gradually milder, the ice vanishes from the lowlands, and is only seen at the tops of the hills and descending to the head of the glens. Year by year the climate becomes milder and the ice vanishes from its last places of retreat, and we have the climate of the present day, and nearly the same configuration of the country. These changes may, I think, be satisfactorily explained without having recourse to any but the ordinary everyday changes which are taking place on the surface of the globe.

When we study the configuration of the bed of the ocean, we presently find that instead of the water levelling the land, it is the principal cause of its unevenness. In the bed of the ocean are mountains and valleys as high and deep as those on the continents. Currents exist in almost every part of the sea, just the same as the currents in the air, one above another, sometimes flowing in opposite directions. These must have a scooping and transporting power immeasurably exceeding in its result the changes brought about by subterranean fire.

Most geologists will admit this much, and still maintain that so far as the existence of the land above the sea is concerned, water is a leveller, as it merely transports matter to the sea, and then from one to another part of the bed of the ocean, and has not the power of raising land above the sea level, which they say remains always the same.

Reasoning in this way, they have to account for the elevation of land by the agency of heat, although they are well aware that their theory will not admit of many facts being satisfactorily explained.

Professor Sedgwick says, "We are certain there have been enormous changes in the relative level of sea and land. Near the top of Ingleborough, about 2000 feet above the sea level, are beds which were once tranquilly deposited at the bottom of the sea; for they are full of well-preserved shells and corals. The highest parts of Snowdon are marked by impressions of sea shells, and similar organic spoils have been found, in some distant chains, at five times the height of any English mountains. Such changes of level, howsoever brought about, must have produced an incomparably greater transporting power than is shown in any ordinary action of the elements.

"Accordingly, in our own country, we find heaped on the flanks of the mountains, choking up the valleys, and spreading far and wide along the plains, great masses of alluvial drift, entirely unconnected with any erosion of the existing rivers. We believe that these masses were formed by the sea during periods when it was changing its level; and we sometimes (at the height of considerably more than 1000 feet) see proofs of the truth of our hypothesis, by finding sea shells of modern species imbedded in the heaps of incoherent rubbish which have been drifted over the surface.

"As far as regards the phenomena just noticed, it is a matter of indifference whether we suppose the sea to have come down from the tops of the mountains, or the mountains to have been pushed up from the bottom of the sea. The latter supposition agrees with the known powers of nature, and I know of no other intelligible cause for a change of oceanic level. Mountains are

simply the highest points of elevation, marking the
places where subterranean forces have pushed upwards
with greatest intensity, or met with least resistance."

Again, "We have the clearest proofs of great oscilla-
tions of sea level, and have a right to make use of them,
while we seek to explain some of the latest phenomena
of Geology."

In another place he says, "Before I attempt any
sketch of the older slate rocks of the Cumbrian Mountains, let me endeavour to translate into common language that chapter in the strange chronicles of the
earth of which we have been turning over the leaves
from the end to the beginning.

"*First*, then, we have the record of an ancient revolution given by the old conglomerates.

"*Secondly*, the Great Scar limestone tells us of a long
period of repose. Its coral reefs were formed in a shal-
low sea (for in such seas only do corals grow); but in
course of time it sank down, and a sea many hundred
feet deep floated over it, and spread out upon it banks
of sand and mud, and drifted vegetables washed from
the neighbouring land.

"*Thirdly*, again was a period of repose, when a second
bank of limestone, with its shells and corals, was tranquilly deposited, after which was a second subsidence,
like the former, and followed by like effects.

"These operations were six times repeated in the formation of the eastern calcareous mountains; each period
of repose and each subsidence producing a repetition of
like phenomena.

"*Fourthly* came the period of the millstone grit, when
the bays and estuaries were gradually filled up, and
marine animals ceased to leave their traces among the
waters.

"Lastly, the lagoons and estuaries were converted into
lakes and marshes; a rank tropical vegetation covered
the ground, and produced the materials of future coal-
fields. Still we are compelled to invoke the same powers
of nature; for some of our coal-fields are thousands of

feet in thickness, and I can see no intelligible means of accounting for them without the intervention of vast and repeated changes between the levels of land and water."

Professor Phillips says, "*The uplifting of the sea* is contrary to experience, and cannot be supported by evidence collected in and around the district of the lakes, for all the phenomena which have been cited in its favour seem to be more easily accounted for by the hypothesis, *the uprising of the land.* This, however, requires the additional postulate, that nearly the whole of the mountain region of the north of England, which had been uplifted prior to the new red sandstone, had again sunk prior to the era of detrital deposits. This may be allowed."

Sir Charles Lyell, in the new edition of his great work, says:—" Recent observations have disclosed to us the wonderful fact, that not only the west coast of South America, but also other large areas, some of them several thousand miles in circumference, such as Scandinavia, and certain Archipelagos in the Pacific, are slowly and insensibly rising, while other regions, such as Greenland, and parts of the Pacific and Indian oceans, in which atolls or circular coral islands abound, are as gradually sinking. That all the existing continents and submarine abysses may have originated in movements of this kind, is undeniable, for marine remains are found in rocks at almost all elevations above the sea, and the denudation which the dry land appears to have suffered, favours the idea that it was raised from the deep by movements of the earth's crust, prolonged through indefinite periods.

" Rain and rivers, aided sometimes by slow and sometimes by sudden and violent movements, have undoubtedly excavated some of the principal valleys; but there are also wide spaces which have been denuded in such a manner as can only be explained by reference to the action of waves and currents on land slowly emerging from the deep.

"It may perhaps be said that there is no analogy between the slow upheaval of broad plains or table-lands, and the manner in which we must presume all mountain chains, with their inclined strata, to have originated.

"It seems, however, that the Andes have been rising century after century, at the rate of several feet, while the Pampas on the E. have been raised only a few inches in the same time.

"Crossing from the Atlantic to the Pacific, in a line passing through Mendoza, Mr. Darwin traversed a plain 800m. broad, the eastern part of which has emerged from beneath the sea at a very modern period. The slope from the Atlantic is at first very gentle, then greater, until the traveller finds, on reaching Mendoza, that he has gained, almost insensibly, a height of 4000 feet. The mountainous district then begins suddenly, and its breadth from Mendoza to the shores of the Pacific is 120m., the average height of the principal chain being from 15,000 to 16,000 feet, without including some prominent peaks which ascend much higher. Now all we require, to explain the origin of the principal inequalities of level here described, is to imagine, first, a zone of more violent movement to the W. of Mendoza; and, secondly, to the E. of that place, an upheaving force, which died away gradually as it approached the Atlantic. In short, we are only called upon to conceive, that the region of the Andes was pushed up 4 feet at the same period in which the Pampas, near Mendoza, rose 1 foot, and the plains near the shores of the Atlantic 1 inch. In Europe, the land at the North Cape is said to ascend about 5 feet in a century; farther to the S., at the Gefle, it amounts to 2 or 3 feet in the same period, while at Stockholm it does not exceed 3 or 4 inches, and at certain points still farther S. there is no movement.

"But in what manner, it is asked, can we account for the great lateral pressure which has been exerted, not only in the Andes, Alps, and other chains, but also on the strata of many low, and nearly level countries?

"Do not the folding and fracture of the beds, the anticlinal and synclinal ridges and troughs, as they are called, and the vertical, and even sometimes the inverted position of the beds, imply an abruptness and intensity in the disturbing force wholly different in kind and energy to that which now rends the rocks during ordinary earthquakes?"

These quotations have been introduced to show the reader that our greatest geologists advocate the gradual rise and subsidence of land by the agency of heat, but at the same time, that they feel a great difficulty in accounting for various phenomena by that agency. Few thinkers will fail to observe how facts appear to be made to bend to theory, and how improbable it is that whole continents should gradually rise and sink many times; but how much more feasible is the supposition that the land remains almost stationary, and that it is the sea which gradually alternately rises and sinks. This latter theory would, no doubt, be gladly accepted, if it could be seen how the sea level could change, and how mountains and continents could appear without the agency of heat; and also how, by this means, the contortions of the strata could be accounted for.

After many months of thought on this subject, I have come to the conclusion that such is the fact; and I believe, in opposition to the great men whose names have already been mentioned, that the sea has come down from the tops of the mountains and continents, and only in exceptional cases have the mountains and continents been heaved up from the sea. After a little reasoning the reader will see, I hope, the correctness of this theory.

Let us suppose a reservoir filled with a hundred cubic feet of water. It is clear that if a foot of earth be dug out of any part of the bed, and deposited in another part, the relative level of the land and water will be changed, but the original level of the water will not be altered. This process might be continued until a hole measuring a hundred cubic feet was made below the original bed, and all the water descended into it, thus leaving the bed of the reservoir dry, and elevated to the original height of the surface of the water. It is clear that the level of the water would not alter until the last drop descended, if the earth were spread evenly over the bed, excepting that just at the last the water would first leave the part farthest from the hole into which it was descending.

Let us suppose that whilst the earth is being dug out of the hole and spread over the bed of the reservoir, currents in the water cause the earth to be deposited unevenly. It is clear that we should have a miniature of the mountains and valleys which exist at the bottom of the ocean; but as the water level would remain stationary, and there would be no upheaving force, the highest point could not be higher than the level of the water, and no dry land would appear until the whole of the hollows were filled; unless a pool or pools were left by the earth surrounding and forming hollows, and then the sheets of water left in those hollows would be as high as the surrounding land. If the sun had then to shine on the land and the pools of water, it is clear that the water in some of the pools might be evaporated and deep valleys left.

Applying this reasoning to the earth, it would seem that although the ocean currents might by scooping out the bed of the sea; and depositing the matter [in other parts, alter the relative level of earth and water, they could not alter the original level of the sea, and no mountains or continents could appear. But when we take into account the all-important fact that the earth is a round body, we presently find that we might have mountains and continents as high as those at present existing. Whilst reasoning on this subject we must not forget that relatively the greatest irregularities on the earth's surface are not more than a speck on an orange.

For the sake of further illustration let us suppose the outer crust of the globe perfectly smooth, and covered with an ocean 1000 feet deep. It is clear that the heat

from the sun would cause currents in the water which
would scoop out from one part of the bed and deposit in
other parts. If the whole of the ocean in the southern
hemisphere were, from this cause, to become 2000 feet
deep, the earthy matter thus removed would be deposited
in the northern hemisphere, and the whole of the latter
half of the globe would be dry land. The water would
first leave the north pole and gradually sink to the equator.
If, during this operation, currents also existed in the
northern hemisphere, mountains and valleys would be left;
and here and there inland seas might exist, apparently
below the sea level. In this way we should have all the
inequalities that we find on the surface of the globe:
deep valleys and high mountains in the sea corresponding with those on land. A never-ceasing change going
on throughout the globe, the water gradually leaving one
continent and overflowing another. When land appeared
above the water it would have all the irregularities of
surface, caused by currents, tides, and innumerable other
agencies. In fact, given a globe, an ocean, heat from
the sun, and immeasurable periods of time, almost everything revealed by geology is easily and quite naturally
explained.

In order to render this evident to every reader, let
us suppose the sea to batter at the South American continent until the whole land, with its high mountains,
vanishes and is transported by the currents to other
parts of the globe. Then suppose currents to scoop out
and form a deep, irregular sea-bottom where once existed
the continent,—valleys thousands of feet deep might
exist directly under where had been a mountain 20,000
feet high. All this matter would be transported to other
parts of the globe. The relative level of the sea and
land would be changed, and what had been a small,
rocky island, say where Cumberland is now, would be a
high mountain district with a large extent of lower land
around it. This change would be gradual, allowing of
the formation of such beds as the limestone and coal.
For the sake of further illustration, let us imagine the

bottom of the sea, where previously rested the South American continent, was again the scene of a deposit by ocean currents, or was filled by corals or by beds of lime or chalk, again might the Cumbrian mountains vanish beneath the water and the red sandstone be deposited.

It is easy to see that such changes would be gradual and alternating, and extend over immense periods of time.

Having explained that the principal irregularities on the surface of the earth may have been caused without the agency of heat, it is necessary, in order to establish the theory, to show that the contortions of strata do not require for their origin any upheaving force.

It is obvious that if the Lake District were now to be sunk under the sea, with mountain precipices and slopes of every imaginable shape, and after having deposited upon it volcanic matter, lime, chalk, sandstone, or any other material, the water had again to subside, after currents had in places washed away and formed precipices in the new deposit, the geologist would observe that the new strata would be infinitely contorted and lie at every possible angle. Supposing a deposit of sandstone on Skiddaw and in the Derwent Valley, it would slope down the mountain-side at every angle from one degree to ninety. In the valley and near the foot of the mountain it would be horizontal. If the whole valley were filled up to the height of the highest part of Skiddaw, then it would also lie over the summit in a horizontal layer. Supposing that the top of the mountain was again exposed to view by part of the deposit being washed away, it would appear as though the mountain had been upheaved and thrust through the sandstone, and the latter would show signs of having been tilted by that apparent movement, although in reality it was tranquilly deposited on the side of the mountain. In this way, by taking into account an infinite variety of changes, may the inclination of strata be explained without requiring the agency of an upheaving force.

It must not be inferred from the previous remarks that the existence of volcanos and internal fire is not taken into account. What I maintain is, that the effect of their action is infinitesimal when compared with the results of the operations of water. I am well aware that in the centre of the district at present under consideration, the English Lake Country, the mountains are composed principally of matter deposited by volcanos at the bottom of the ocean.

Having explained the changes in the relative positions of sea and land, a few words must now be said on the alteration of climate.

To one who hears for the first time that, within a very recent geological period, England was perennially covered with ice and snow, such a statement seems incredible and almost inexplicable.

After a little careful thought, anyone who is acquainted with the physical geography of the globe will easily explain so simple and natural a phenomenon.

In the study of geology, sight must not be lost of the changes in climate which may have been caused by gradual, almost imperceptible, alterations in the physical geography of the earth, the total result of which may be so great as to be almost incredible. The currents in the air and ocean, the tides, heat and cold, rain, rivers, volcanos and earthquakes, all are busy altering the physical geography of our earth.

We may, however, very simply, and in all probability quite accurately, account for the change in the climate of the British Isles. We have only to suppose that at a recent era the West Indian Islands were joined to the North American continent. There would then be no Gulf Stream, and England would be another Greenland.

Gradually the warm waters obtain an outlet from the Gulf of Mexico, which year by year increases. This would account for the gradual disappearance of the glaciers from our valleys. Perhaps it also explains why we have now in England hotter summers and milder winters than in former historical periods.

The reader will doubtless have been prepared by these remarks to enter into a detailed study of the geology of the district with a mind free from prejudice and preconceived ideas. With the assistance of Professor Sedgwick's letters to Wordsworth on the geology of the Lake District, we will now examine, in as cursory a manner as possible, the structure of the great mountain masses, and the surrounding plain.

The tourist, on entering the Lake Country, will be able to make a better estimate of its past geological history, and will, in all probability, entertain a true idea, if he look upon the mountains and valleys as merely the skeleton or ruin of a vast plain, originally much higher than the highest mountain now existing, and which extended to Wales, Ireland, Isle of Man, and Scotland. He must endeavour to disabuse himself of the idea that the mountains have been separately or collectively pushed up into their present position and shape by the agency of heat.

Whether the land was raised by heat or the sea gradually subsided, the fact is indisputable that the mountains and valleys were shaped by the sea currents and waves, and afterwards slightly modified by glaciers, rain, frost, heat, chemical action, and other similar agencies.

The whole of the mountains are of a slate formation, with a few slight exceptions, where granite, syenite, limestone, and old red sandstone stand at an elevation, in isolated positions. The *Skiddaw,* or *clay slate,* is the oldest of the slate series, and is probably the oldest rock in the district; and undoubtedly the oldest of the granitic and syenitic rocks are of more recent origin; and Professor Sedgwick says: "All the granites of the Lake Country are unquestionably of more recent date than the Skiddaw slate."

This rock is hardened clay which has been originally tranquilly deposited in the bed of an ocean; and Skiddaw being the principal mountain composed of it, that name has been given to it. It includes Skiddaw and Blencathara; the heights on the W. side of Bassenthwaite

Lake; Grasmoor, Grisedale Pike, Causey Pike, and neighbouring mountains; Cat Bells, Maiden Moor, Hindscarth, and Robinson surrounding Newlands; Low Fell, Mellbreak, and Blake Fell on the W. of Crummock Lake; and Dent Hill, near Egremont.

There is also an isolated portion to the S., including Black Combe mountain; and two similar strips on the E. side, one to the S.W. of Shap, and the other to the S.E. of Ullswater. In all probability the Skiddaw slate covered the whole of the Lake Country prior to the deposit of the green slate.

Lead, copper, barytes, and cobalt have been found in it; but although the slaty cleavage runs through a part of the rock, good slate is rarely produced.

Fossils, principally graptolites, are occasionally to be discovered in the natural bedding. The mountains comprised in the district of this rock in general present smooth, sloping sides, though there are two or three fine exceptions.

Green Slate.—The highest and most rugged mountains are in the centre of the district, and are composed of green slate and porphyry, a rock which consists principally of volcanic ashes deposited in the bed of the sea. Sometimes the ashes have resembled fine mud, and at other times the particles have been larger and angular. The volcanic eruptions appear to have been at irregular intervals, allowing for deposits of layers of silt and other matter; but no organic remains have been found. The aqueous deposits seem to have been too often interrupted by igneous action to permit the growth of shell beds and coral banks. It is probable, however, that fossils may yet be discovered in some part of these rocks. In this series are extensive copper and lead mines, the former at Coniston, and the latter in Patterdale; and in Borrowdale is the famous plumbago mine, which is now closed. Slate is extensively worked in Honister Crag, and at Borrowdale, Patterdale, and Coniston. In many places amongst the green slate rocks, and sometimes on the tops of the mountains, are small deposits of iron ore,

d

a fact which appears to indicate that the whole of the district was, at one period, covered with red sandstone, which was afterwards washed by the sea from the mountainous part.

Just as we find isolated portions of the Skiddaw slate away from the main bulk of that rock, so do we find an isolated strip of the green slate on the N. side of the Skiddaw range of mountains, commencing near Cockermouth, and extending past Uldale, to Hesket-Newmarket, and the Carrock Fell, and including the hill named Binsey. This appears to point to the conclusion that at one time the green slate covered Skiddaw and neighbouring mountains, and was afterwards washed away.

The reader will observe that as the green slate was deposited in the sea at successive intervals, it is natural to expect traces of lime and sandstone. Accordingly we find that the beds of plutonic silt generally effervesce briskly when first plunged in acids, from which we may imply the presence of lime; and they are sometimes cellular, probably from the lime having been taken away by water. In the S. of the district is a narrow band of limestone, called by geologists Coniston Limestone, which stretches from the Duddon Valley, near Broughton-in-Furness, to near Shap Wells, in a line passing the head of Coniston and Windermere lakes, and across the Troutbeck, Kentmere, and Long Sleddale valleys.

The limestone is rich in fossils. It rests on the green or middle slate series, and above it are the *upper slates*. These latter consist of bands of dark fossiliferous, flaggy slates, called Coniston flags, Coniston grits, Ireleth slates, &c., which alternate with layers of sandy and argillaceous deposits. They occupy most of the Lake Country south of the band of Coniston Limestone, and surround the Windermere, Esthwaite, and Coniston lakes.

In isolated positions in the divisions of the slate series of rocks, *viz.* the lower (Skiddaw, or clay-slate), the middle (green slate), and the upper (the Coniston flags,

&c.), are granites of Skiddaw, Eskdale, and Shap, and varieties of syenites.*

Skiddaw granite is a compound of quartz, light-coloured felspar, and black mica. It appears between Blencathara and Skiddaw, in the bed of the river Caldew, and in Syningill. Professor Phillips says: "It is the lowest rock of the whole district, though probably of the most recent origin; for the veins which issue from it into some of the incumbent slaty beds may be regarded as proof of its having been in a state of fusion since the date of their deposition."

Professor Sedgwick says: "I can offer no proof that it is older than the beautiful syenite of Carrock, or the granite of Eskdale, or the red syenite of Ennerdale and Buttermere."

Shap granite is a compound of grey and reddish felspar, quartz, and dark mica, in grains of small or moderate size; but amidst there are scattered large and fine crystals of reddish felspar, one inch or even more in length. It breaks out at the base of the upper division of the slates, and occupies a small area in a position between the upper and lower slates. It is now extensively quarried and polished, large works having been erected near the railway at Shap.

Eskdale granite is a compound of felspar, quartz, and silvery mica; but in some portion of it there is no mica, and it becomes a large-grained "binary" granite, composed of felspar and quartz. It occupies a large area, and forms most of the rugged hills on both sides of the rivers Esk and Mite. Iron ore has been found in it, and a mine is now being worked near to the hamlet of Boot.

The *syenite of Carrock Fell* is contiguous to the Skiddaw granite. It is composed of felspar (red or pale green), quartz, and hornblende. In places are dis-

---

* *Granite* is formed by the union of *quartz, felspar,* and *mica;* when the *mica* is replaced by *hornblende* the rock becomes a *syenite.* Any rock is called a *porphyry* which has a nearly uniform base studded with crystals.

d 2

seminated through its mass crystals of hyperthene and oxide of iron.

The *syenite and porphyritic rocks of the Vale of St. John* rest between the middle and lower slates, and include the northern part of the Naddle Fell, and the ground stretching from the Threlkeld railway station to the Wanthwaite Crags.

The *syenite of Red Pike and Ennerdale* is composed of red felspar, with quartz interspersed, and a variable admixture of a soft greenish or yellowish mineral. Rarely distinct hornblende is observable. It is situated between the middle and lower slates, and includes Red Pike, overlooking Buttermere, Herdhouse, and other heights around Ennerdale Lake, and extends to the feet of the Haycock and Seatallan mountains.

Most geologists look upon the granites and syenites as igneous rocks; but I am inclined to think that the day is not far distant when a different explanation will be given of the origin of this class of rocks.

It appears to me deserving of notice that in the Lake Country they generally occupy a position between the middle and lower slates, and I often ask myself, may not the bed of the ocean have been here and there covered with sandstone during the periodic deposition of the volcanic matter of the green slate series, and may not the sandstone have been pushed by the volcanic matter to the side of the clay slate, and there been changed by the action of heat and water to its present syenitic and granitic character? In this way we may in all probability satisfactorily account for the numerous dykes of syenitic and granitic porphyry which are to be found in different parts of the district.

Old Red Sandstone.—Resting on the slate series is the old red sandstone, which is intermixed with rolled masses of slaty rocks, and is found only in a few localities. It appears near Kirkby Lonsdale, Sedbergh, and Shap; but its longest area is on the N.E. side of Ullswater Lake, commencing at Pooley Bridge, and including the hills Dunmallet and Mell Fell, the latter rising to a height of 1760 feet above the sea. Near Shap it may be seen between the limestone and the slates. It is supposed to have been deposited after the slate rocks had attained solidity, and had been scooped into deep valleys. Although it now occupies only a small area in the Lake District, it probably was at one time much more extensively spread, and was afterwards washed away by ocean currents.

Mountain Limestone.—Above the old red sandstone is the mountain limestone, which almost encircles the whole of the Lake district. According to Professor Sedgwick, "It requires little effort of imagination to conceive that all the great patches of limestone, now marked on this part of our geological maps, were once united." It stretches from Egremont, past Cleator, Cockermouth, Caldbeck, Greystoke, and Shap, to Kirkby Lonsdale, and Kendal. In the S. of the district it embraces the heights of Underbarrow, Whitbarrow, and Witherslack. By the sea-coast at Grange it forms beautiful cliffs and terraces, and crosses over the Leven Sands to Dalton-in-Furness. A small patch lies on the opposite side of the Duddon Sands, close to Holborn Hill. Fewer mineral veins are found in the mountain limestone surrounding the lakes than in the same rock in other parts of Britain; but this is amply compensated for by the rich deposit of iron ore (hæmatite) which is found in the fissures and hollows of the limestone at Cleator, near Egremont, and near Dalton and Ulverston in Furness.

The geologist who has entered the limestone caverns of Yorkshire and Derbyshire, and there observed the formation of the stalagmites and stalactites, will have no difficulty in accounting for the deposit of the " kidney ore." In all probability the new red sandstone covered the limestone, and the waters of the sea, saturated with red oxide of iron, filtered through the fissures and caves of the limestone and filled them gradually with metallic matter held in partial solution. The reader will remember that in a previous page it was stated that the same kind of ore is found near the tops of the highest mountains, from which it was inferred that the sandstone had at one time covered the whole district.

Coal.—The coal formation rests on the mountain limestone, and stretches along the W. coast from White-haven to beyond Maryport. At Whitehaven the mines extend far beneath the sea. The whole deposit once consisted of alternations of sand and finely-laminated mud, with countless fragments of drifted vegetable, sometimes single, sometimes matted together in thick and widely-extended beds. Occasionally the plants are upright in posture, and so entire that they seem not to have been drifted from the spots on which they grew; in such cases the coal-beds become the indications of forests and bogs submerged in bygone ages during the changes of level between land and water. In course of time the drifted sand-beds became sandstone; the mud became slaty clay or shale; the vegetable fossils were bituminized; and the whole formation passed into the condition in which we now see it.

In the upper part of this group (as exhibited in different parts of the North of England) there are no marine remains; but it contains some beds of shells belonging to fresh-water genera. All the plants are of extinct species; many of them of extinct genera; and they are of forms which indicate a high tropical tem-perature.

Among them are coniferous trees, like those in some of the South Sea Islands; gigantic reeds; tree ferns; enormous creeping plants with sharp pinnated leaves (*Stigmariæ*); trees with fluted stems; and many other strange but beautiful forms of vegetable life, seemingly pushed to rankness and luxuriance by great heat and moisture. It is in vain to speculate on the exact dura-tion of the carboniferous epoch; but we are sure that it lasted through a vast period of time.

New Red Sandstone.—This is the newest formation of the country under notice; for wherever it is asso-ciated with other deposits it is always found to rest

upon them. It fills all the lower part of the basin of
the Eden, from the neighbourhood of Brough to the
shores of the Solway Firth. At Maryport it is cut off
by the coal measures; but it reappears at St. Bees
Head, and strikes along the coast to the estuary of the
Duddon and the western promontories of Low Furness;
and it is seen in a few spots on the shores of Morecambe
Bay. In some parts of this long coast range it seems to
have been entirely washed away, and in other places it
is covered by enormous heaps of diluvial drift, the colour
of which is derived from the abraded fragments of red
sandstone.

If we cross to the other side of Morecambe Bay, we
meet with the same great formation on the coast of
Lancashire; and it may then be traced, through the plains
of Cheshire, to the great red central plain stretching
across our island from the mouth of the Tees to the
mouth of the Severn.

Glacial Era.—Frequent mention has been made in
this work of the evidences of a past glacial era which
everywhere meet the eye of the visitor who has had his
attention called to the subject.

In the valleys, and high up on the sides of the mountains, the rocks are observed to be smooth, rounded, and
scratched. Perched blocks of stone, often of a nature
differing from the rocks on which they rest, and which
evidently have been carried from their parent rock over
hill and dale, are to be seen on every hand.

Heaps of loose stones, terminal moraines, are found in
scores of places; and near the head of almost every
glen are round grass-covered mounds, some of which are
partly washed away by the streamlets, and exhibit a
mass of boulders and loose earth. These were evidently
formed when the glaciers were being melted, and are
composed of the stones and earthy matter which fell
upon the ice from the neighbouring mountains. The
hollows in which rest many of the most picturesque tarns
have evidently been formed by the last and smallest
glaciers which descended the mountain precipices,

scooped out the hollows, and formed embankments on the opposite side. Blocks of Eskdale granite have been transported to the plains of Lancashire and Cheshire; and also blocks of the Shap granite have been carried to the eastern coast of Yorkshire. Undoubtedly they have been borne to those places by ice, but whether on icebergs or glaciers is doubtful. Most of the English Lakes occupy ground anciently covered by immense glaciers, and those lovely sheets of water are gradually diminishing in size, being filled up by matter washed from the neighbouring plains and mountains.

Derwentwater and Bassenthwaite undoubtedly formed, at one time, a lake about 10m. long, and the river Greta, and other tributaries to the Derwent River have brought down matter which has formed the level land in the Keswick Vale.

In like manner have other lakes been separated, such as Buttermere and Crummock. In some places ancient lakes and tarns have existed where are now only swamp and bog. It is probable that future geologists may be able to estimate the time which has elapsed since the glacial era, by observing the average quantity of matter annually deposited in the lakes and tarns, and then measuring the quantity already accumulated.

Considering the small changes which the weather has effected on the rounded and grooved rocks, and on the erratic blocks of granite found away from the district, lying bare on the surface; and the existence in every glen of round grassy mounds which often have preserved the shape they took when originally deposited, we come to the conclusion that the sea has not covered this district since the glacial era, and that that era was comparatively recent.

H. I. J.

BOTANY.

THE variety of soil that characterizes the Lake District, the elevation, and degree of temperature, produce a corresponding variety of plants. Of these, perhaps the most interesting to the tourist are the ferns, a complete list of which is included in the following Table, as well as the rarer plants found in the district.

NATURAL ORDER.

RANUNCULACEÆ.

Botanical Name.	Common Name.	Habitat.	Time of Flowering.
Caltha palustris . . .	Marsh marigold . .	Margins of lakes .	March to May.
Ranunculus aquatilis .	Buttercup	Derwent Lake . .	May to Aug.
„ circinatus .	„	Bassenthwaite Lake.	„ „
„ fluitans .	„	Derwent Lake . .	
„ Lenormandi	„	Common in ditches .	June to Aug.
„ hederaceus	Ivy-leaved ranunculus		May to Aug.
„ Lingua	Spearwort	St. John's Vale . .	July to Sept.
Thalictrum alpinum .	Meadowrue . . .	Helvellyn. . . .	July to Aug.
„ majus .	„	Lodore	„ „
„ minus . .	„	Derwent Lake . .	„ „
„ flavum. .	„	Moist meadows . .	„ „
Trollius europæus .	Globeflower . . .	Margins of lakes .	June to Aug.
Aquilegia vulgaris. .	Columbine	Rampsholm Island .	May to June

PAPAVERACEÆ.

Meconopsis cambrica .	Welsh poppy . . .	Moist glens, West-morland . . .	June.
Glaucinium luteum	Horned „ . . .	Seashore, near Ul-verston . . .	June to Oct.

SOLANEÆ.

Hyoscyamus niger . .	Henbane	Near Ulverston . .	June to Aug.
Atropa belladonna . .	Deadly nightshade .	Humphrey Head and Arnside . . .	„ „
Solanum dulcamara . .	Bittersweet . . .	Cartmel	„ „

RHAMNEÆ.

Rhamnus catharticus .	Buckthorn	Carke and Cartmel .	May to July.
„ frangula . .	Berry-bearing alder, or dogwood . . .	„ „ .	May to June.

NATURAL ORDER.

CRASSULACEÆ.

Botanical Name.	Common Name.	Habitat.	Time of Flowering.
Sedum Rhodiola . .	Roseroot	Helvellyn . . .	May to Aug.
„ anglicum . .	„	Castlehead . . .	June to Aug.
„ Telephinium .	Orpine	Hedge-banks & copses	July to Aug.

LINEÆ.

Linum catharticum .	Purging flax . . .	Common in pastures	June to Sept.
Radiola millegrana .	Allseed	Near Keswick . .	July to Aug.

UMBELLIFERÆ.

Hydrocotyle vulgaris .	Pennywort . . .	Marshes and bogs .	May to Aug.
Meum athamanticum .	Spignel	Elevated pastures .	June to July.
Cicuta virosa . . .	Water-hemlock . .	In brooks (common)	July to Aug.
Myrrhis odorata . .	Cicely	Near Keswick . .	May to June.

JUNCEÆ.

Juncus filiformis . .	Rush	Margins of lakes. .	July to Aug.
„ triglumis . .	„	Bogs	„ „
„ maritimus . .	„	Capeshead, Ulverston	„ „
Luzula campestris . .	Woodrush	Mosses	April to June.
„ Forsteri. . .	„	Whitbarrow & Lodore	„ „
„ spicata . . .	„	Westmorland . .	July.

ONAGRARIEÆ.

Circæa alpina . . .	Enchanter's nightshade	Near Keswick . .	July to Aug.
Epilobium alsinifolium	Willow herb . . .	Spongy rills . . .	July.
„ angustifolium	Rosebay	Shap	July to Aug.

ORCHIDEÆ.

Cephalanthera ensifolia	Helleborine . . .	Rondsea, Cartmel .	May to June.
„ grandiflora	White Helleborine .	Holker Woods . .	
Epipactis latifolia . .	Helleborine . . .	Near Keswick . .	July to Aug.
Habenaria albida . .	Orchis	Watendlath . . .	June to Aug.
„ bifolia . .	Butterfly orchis . .	Bassenthwaite Lake	„ „
„ viridis . .	Frog „ . .	Watendlath . . .	„ „
Listeria Nidus avis .	Bird's-nest „ . .	Great Wood, Keswick	June to July.
Ophrys apifera . . .	Bee „ . .	Woods at Witherslack	
„ muscifera . .	Fly „ . .	„ „	May to July.
Orchis latifolia . . .	Marsh „ . .	Borrowdale . . .	June to July.
„ pyramidalis. .	Orchis	Pastures	June to Aug.

LEGUMINOSÆ.

Astragalus glycyphillos	Milkvetch	Humphrey Head, Cartmel . . .	June to Sept.
Hippocrepis comosa .	Horseshoevetch . .	Hampsfield Fell . .	May to Aug.
Lotus major . . .	Bird's-foot trefoil. .	Moist meadows and roadsides . . .	July to Aug.
Ulex europæus. . .	Whin, gorse, furze .	Common	Feb., March, Aug., Sept.
„ nanus	„ „ „	„	July to Nov.

NATURAL ORDER.

ROSACEÆ.

Botanical Name.	Common Name.	Habitat.	Time of Flowering.
Alchemilla alpina . . .	Lady's mantle . .	Skiddaw	June to Aug.
Agrimonia Eupatoria .	Agrimony	Ormathwaite, Keswick . . .	„ „
Poterium sanguisorba.	Salad Burnet . . .	Scout Scar . . .	„ „
„ officinale. .	Great „	Isthmus, Keswick .	„ „
Rubus chamæmorus .	Cloudberry	Peaty moors. . .	June to July.
„ saxatilis . .	Bramble	Keswick	„ „
„ Idæus . . .	Raspberry	Common in woods .	June to Aug.
Spiræa ulmaria. . .	Meadowsweet . . .	Common	„ „
„ salicifolia . .	Dropwort	Moist plantations (not indigenous) .	July to Aug.

ERICACEÆ.

Arctostaphylos Uva Ursi	Bearberry	Grasmoor . . .	May to July.
Vaccinium Vitis Idæa	Cowberry	Helvellyn, Scawfell.	June to July.
„ myrtillus .	Bilberry	Common	April to June.
Oxycoccos palustris .	Cranberry	Witherslack mosses.	August.
Pyrola secunda. . .	Wintergreen . . .	Near Keswick (rare)	July.

NYMPHÆACEÆ.

Nuphar luteum . .	Yellow water-lily .	Common in lakes .	June to Aug.
Nymphæa alba. . .	White „ .	In the large lakes .	„ „

LILIACEÆ.

Colchicum autumnale .	Meadow saffron . .	Thornthwaite . .	Aug. to Oct.
Paris quadrifolia . .	Herb Paris	Near Ambleside. .	May to June.
Convallaria majalis .	Lily of the valley. .	Waltham Wood, Cartmel . . .	„ „

CAMPANULACEÆ.

Campanula glomerata .	Campanula. . . .	Isthmus, Keswick .	Sept. to Oct.
„ latifolia .	„	Common	July to Aug.
„ Trachelium	Nettle-leaved campanula	Woods and copses .	Sept. to Oct.
Lobelia dortmanna .	Lobelia	Common in the lakes	July to Aug.

CANNABINEÆ.

Humulus lupulus . .	Hop	Lake Road, Keswick	July to Aug.

PLUMBAGINEÆ.

Armeria vulgaris . .	Seapink	Seashore at Humphrey Head . .	April to Oct.

CRUCIFERÆ.

Arabis petræa . . .	Rock cress	Scawfell	June to Aug.
Hesperis matronalis .	Dames-violet . . .	Bassenthwaite . .	May to July.
Lepidium Smithii . .	Cress	Fields and roadsides.	April to Aug.

NATURAL ORDER.

BORRAGINEÆ.

Botanical Name.	Common Name.	Habitat.	Time of Flowering.
Anchusa sempivirens .	Alkanet	Pooley Bridge . .	May to June.
Mysotis palustris . .	Forget-me-not. . .	Near Keswick . .	May to July.
„ repeus. . .	Scorpion grass . . .	Skiddaw and Helvellyn	June to Aug.

PRIMULACEÆ.

Anagallis tenella . .	Bay pimpernel . .	Lodore	July to Aug.
Primula farinosa . .	Bird's-eye primrose .	Lothwaite, St. John's Vale	June to July.

ARISTOLOCHIEÆ.

Asarum europæum .	Asarabacca . . .	Keswick	May.

GERANIACEÆ.

Geranium columbinum	Cranesbill	Cartmel	June to July.
„ pyrenaicum .	„	Meadows	June to Aug.
„ sylvaticum .	„	Common near Keswick	June to July.
Impatiens noli me tangere	Yellow balsam . .	Great Wood, Keswick	July to Sept.

COMPOSITÆ.

Artemisia absinthium.	Wormwood . . .	Cartmel	Aug. to Sept.
Hieracium alpinum .	Hawkweed . . .	Helvellyn . . .	July to Aug.
„ nigrescens .	„	Cumberland . . .	Aug. to Sept.
Saussarea alpina . .	„	Scawfell	August,
Senecio saracenicus .	„	Near Keswick . .	July to Aug.
Serratula tinctoria . .	Sawwort . . .	Cartmel	August.

RUBIACEÆ.

Galium boreale . .	Bedstraw	Moist rocks . . .	June to Aug.
„ aparine . .	Cleavers	Common	June to July.

DROSERACEÆ.

Drosera rotundifolia .	Sundew	Bogs and heaths . .	July to Aug.
„ longifolia . .	„	Shoulthwaite Moss .	„ „

SALICINEÆ.

Salix herbacea . . .	Dwarf willow . . .	Skiddaw	June.

CAPRIFOLIACEÆ.

Sambucus ebulus . .	Dwarf elder . . .	Near Keswick (rare)	July to Aug.

HYPERICINEÆ.

Hypericum androsæmum	St. John's wort . .	Newby Bridge . .	July to Aug.
Hypericum elodes . .	„ „ . .	Shoulthwaite Moss .	„ „

NATURAL ORDER.

DIOSCOREÆ.

Botanical Name.	Common Name.	Habitat.	Time of Flowering.
Tamus communis . .	Black briony . .	Cartmel	May to June.

LENTIBULARINEÆ.

Pinguicula vulgaris .	Butterwort. . . .	Common	May to July.
Utricularia minor . .	„	Pools and ditches .	June to Sept.
„ vulgaris .	„	Derwent Lake . .	July to Aug.

VALERIANEÆ.

Valeriana dioica . .	Valerian	Bogs at Witherslack	May to June.
„ officinalis .	Cats Valerian . . .	Wet meadows and near streams . .	June to Aug.

VIOLACEÆ.

Viola odorata . . .	Sweet violet . . .	Thornthwaite . .	April to July.
„ hirta	Violet	Dry soils . . .	April to June.
„ palustris . . .	„	Swamps and bogs .	April to July.
„ lutea	Heartsease . . .	Near Keswick . .	May to Sept.

GENTIANEÆ.

Menyanthes trifoliata .	Bogbean	Derwent Lake . .	May to July.

FUMARIACEÆ.

Corydalis solida . .	Solid-rooted corydalis	Borrowdale . . .	April to May.

MYRICACEÆ.

Myrica gale. . . .	Sweet gale, bog myrtle	Common in bogs .	May to July.

AMARYLLIDEÆ.

Narcissus pseudo— narcissus	Daffodil.	Lord's Island, Derwent Lake . . .	Mar. to April.

URTICEÆ.

Parietaria officinalis .	Pellitory	Walls at Wraysholme Tower, Furness Abbey . .	June to Oct.

CARYOPHYLLEÆ.

Cerastium alpinum .	Mousear, chickweed .	Helvellyn . . .	June to Aug.

CELASTRINEÆ.

Eunonymus europæus.	Spindletree. . . .	Grange in Cartmel .	May to June.

LABIATÆ.

Scutellaria minor . .	Skullcap	Margins of lakes (rare)	July to Oct.

MALVACEÆ.

Malva moschata . .	Mallow.	Near Keswick . .	July to Aug.

NATURAL ORDER.

PLANTAGINEÆ.

Botanical Name.	Common Name.	Habitat.	Time of Flowering.
Littorella lacustris . .	Shore weed . . .	Margins of lakes. .	August.

POLYGONEÆ.

Oxyria reniformis . .	Mountain sorrel . .	Helvellyn. . . .	July to Aug.
Polygonium viviparum	Bistort	Mountain pastures and wet rocks . .	June to Aug.
„ hydropiper	Waterpepper . . .	Watery places . .	Aug. to Sept.

TYPHACEÆ.

Typha latifolia . . .	Bullrush	Holker mosses . .	July to Aug.
„ angustifolia .	„	Ditches	July.

CHENIPODIACEÆ.

Salicornia herbacea. .	Marsh samphire . .	Seashore (common).	Aug. to Sept.

GRAMINEÆ.

Agrostis vulgaris var- pumilla	Bent	Common	June to Sept.
Phragmites communis.	Reed	In most lakes . .	July to Aug.
Sesleria cærulea . .	Sesleria.	Grangein, Cartmel .	April to June.

SAXIFRAGEÆ.

Saxifraga oppositifolia	Saxifrage	Helvellyn . . .	April to May.
„ nivalis . .	„	„ . . .	July to Aug.
„ stellaris . .	„	Mountain streams .	June to July.
„ aizoides . .	„	„ „ .	
„ tridactylites.	„	Greystoke, on walls.	April to June.
„ hypnoides .	„	Wet places on moun- tains	May to July.

OROBANCHEÆ.

Lathræa squamaria .	Toothwort	On roots, chiefly of hazel	April to May.

CYPERACEÆ.

Cladium mariscus . .	Cotton grass . . .	Bogs	July to Aug.

DIPSACEÆ.

Dipsacus sylvestris .	Teasel	Seatoller	Aug. to Sept.

CONIFERÆ.

Juniperus communis .	Juniper	Open hill sides, com- mon.	May to June.

NATURAL ORDER.

FILICES (Ferns).

Botanical Name.	Common Name.	Habitat.	Time of Fruiting.
Hymenophyllum uni-laterale (Wilsoni) .	Filmy fern . . .	Lodore Fall . . .	June to July.
Pteris aquilina . . .	Brake or bracken . .	Common	July to Aug.
Cryptogramme crispa .	Parsley fern, rockbrake	Barrow, Castlerigg .	June to July.
Lomaria Spicant (Blechnum boreale).	Hardfern	Ullock Moss . . .	July to Aug.
Asplenium ruta-mu-raria	Spleenwort . . .	Near Keswick . .	June to Oct.
Asplenium septentrio-nale	Forked spleenwort .	Thornthwaite . .	„　　　„
Asplenium alternifo-lium	Alternate spleenwort.	„　　　. .	„　　　„
Asplenium tricho-manes	Common maidenhair spleenwort . . .	Falcon Crag . . .	May to Oct.
Asplenium viride . .	Green spleenwort. .	Shoulthwaite, Scandal Bridge . . .	June to Sept.
„　　　marinum .	Sea spleenwort . .	St. Bees Rocks . .	„　　　„
„　　adiantum nigrum	Black maidenhair spleenwort . . .	Castle Crag . . .	June to Oct.
Athrium Filix fœmina	Common lady fern .	Keswick Park . .	July to Aug.
Ceterach officinarum .	Scaly spleenwort . .	St. Bees, Whitbarrow	April to Sept.
Scolopendrium vulgare	Hartstongue . . .	Castle Crag, Thorn-thwaite. . . .	July to Aug.
Woodsia ilvensis . .	Oblong woodsia . .	Helvellyn . . .	July to Sept.
Crystopteris Fragili .	Bladderfern . . .	Borrowdale . . .	July to Aug.
„　　montana .	Mountain bladderfern	Whitbarrow . . .	„　　　„
„　　Dentata .	Brittle bladderfern .	Raffa Bridge . . .	„　　　„
„　　angustata.	„　　„　„	Castlerigg . . .	„　　　„
Aspidium lonchitis .	Hollyfern	Helvellyn . . .	June to Aug.
„　　lobatum .	Common prickly shieldfern . . .	Castlecrag . . .	July to Aug.
„　　angulare .	Soft prickly shieldfern	Keswick Park . .	„　　　„
Nephrodium Filixmas	Male fern	Common	„　　　„
„　　spinulosum	Crested buckler fern .	Portinscale . . .	Aug. to Sept.
„　　dilatatum.	Broad „　　„	Keswick Park . .	„　　　„
„　　rigidum .	Rigid „　　„	Hutton Roof Crags .	July to Aug.
„　　Oreopteris	Mountain „　　„	Newlands . . .	„　　　„
Polypodium vulgare .	Common polypody .	Castlehead . . .	June to Sept.
„　　Phegopteris	Beech fern	Wallowcrag . . .	June to Aug.
„　　Dryopteris	Oak „　　. . . .	Wallowcrag, Brathay Woods . . .	July to Aug.
„　　Calcareum	Limestone polypody .	Newbiggin Wood, Whitbarrow . .	„　　　„
Osmunda regalis . .	Royal fern . . : .	Holker Mosses, Bas-senthwaite. . .	June to Aug.
Ophioglossum vulgatum	Adder's tongue . .	Portinscale . . .	May to July.
Botrychium Lunaria .	Moonwort	Latrigg	June to Aug.

NATURAL ORDER.

LYCOPODIACEÆ (CLUB MOSSES).

Botanical Name.	Common Name.	Habitat.	Time of Fruiting.
Lycopodium Clavatum	Common club-moss .	Causey Pike . . .	July to Aug.
„ Alpinum.	Savin-leaved club-moss	„ „ . . .	„ „
„ inundatum	Marsh „	Under Falcon Crag .	„ „
„ Selago .	Fir „	Causey Pike . . .	June to Aug.
Selaginella selaginoides	Prickly mountain-moss	Mountain bogs . .	July to Aug.
Isoetes lacustris . .	Quillwort	Bottoms of lakes. .	May to July.

MARSILEACEÆ.

Pilularia globulifera .	Pillwort	Margins of lakes . .	June to Aug.

J. H.

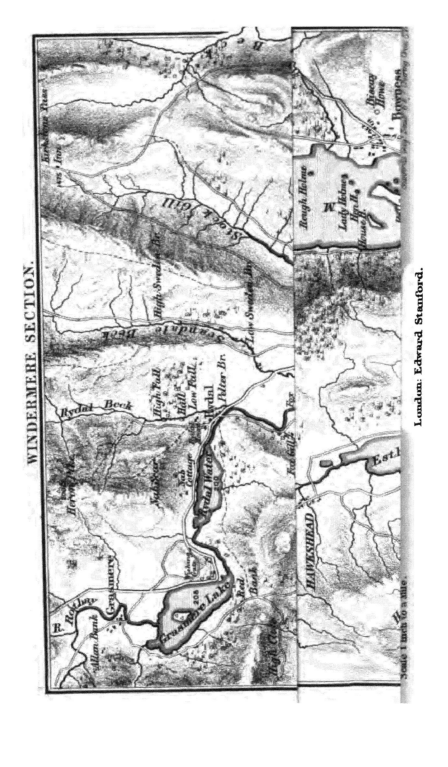

WINDERMERE SECTION.

London: Edward Stanford.

PRACTICAL GUIDE

ENGLISH LAKE DISTRICT.

WINDERMERE SECTION.

WINDERMERE AND BOWNESS.

THE tourist who enters the Lake District by the railway which runs from Oxenholme Junction and Kendal to the Windermere station, ought, if possible, to remain some time at Windermere village, or at Bowness, which is 1½m. distant from the Windermere station. Both places are charmingly situated, in the midst of a cheerful, well-timbered tract of country. Many of the excursions which may be taken from Ambleside as a centre, might be made almost equally well from these places. They are the best points from which to visit the Long Sleddale, Kentmere, Troutbeck, and Rusland vales, but rather inconvenient for the ascent of the higher mountains, with the exception of High Street.

Windermere village is 1m. from the lake by road, though only ½m. by footpath, and 5m. from Ambleside. It stands on elevated ground at the foot of Orrest Head. Before the railway was constructed it was a small hamlet, called Birthwaite. Mansions and picturesque cottages are seen peeping out of the woods on every hand. *Rigg's Hotel*, which is close to the station, is one of the largest and best hotels in the district. It stands on an eminence, and commands lovely views of Windermere Lake. There are two other hotels, the Queen's and the Elleray, both comfortable; and private lodging-houses are numerous. Omnibuses from the hotels in Bowness meet the trains; fare, 6d. a head. A conveyance from

B

Low Wood Hotel, 3m. distant, also meets the trains,
and coaches leave the station, and Rigg's Hotel, two or
three times every day, for Ambleside, Grasmere, and
Keswick.

There is a coach every morning during the summer
for (Ullswater Lake) Patterdale.

Elleray, formerly the residence of Professor Wilson
(Christopher North), is a few hundred yards from the
station.   The old house has been pulled down and
replaced by a more modern structure,

There are few spots in England abounding with more
rich and varied scenery than is to be met with around
Windermere village.   The tourist who cannot arrange
to stay here any length of time, ought by all means to
devote five minutes to walking up a lane a few yards
to the right of Rigg's Hotel.   It ascends Orrest Head,
and reveals most of Windermere Lake in all its beauty,
with its wooded islands, bays, and neighbouring undulating hills.   He will feel reluctant to hurry from a
scene so fair, and will probably be induced to continue
the walk to the top of

Orrest Head (871).—The whole climb will occupy
only 10 or 15 minutes.   The prospect is one of great
magnificence.   Windermere is seen from end to end, and
its cluster of islets appears to be within a stone's throw.
To the S. and S.E. are arms of the sea in the midst of
low outlying hills.   To the N. the straggling village
of Troutbeck is seen resting on the side of Wansfell
Pike, beyond which are Red Screes and Fairfield, and
to the W. are many wild and lofty peaks.   The Coniston Old Man and Wetherlam are very prominent, with
Black Combe to the left, and to the right the depression
of the Wrynose Pass.   At the head of the Langdale
Vale are the Langdale Pikes, Bow Fell, and Crinkle
Crags, with Scawfell Pike, Great End, and Great Gable
beyond, and in front Oxenfell and Lingmoor.   Between
Loughrigg and Nab Scar is Helm Crag, the famous
Lion and Lamb, rising out of the Grasmere Vale.

Bowness is a favourite resting place.   It stands in a

pleasant bay on the shore of Windermere Lake, and commands excellent views of the upper reach of the lake, with the heights of Fairfield, Langdale Pikes, and Coniston Old Man. It contains 1415 inhabitants. There are many good hotels. The three principal are (Cloudsdale's) Crown Hotel, (Scott's) Royal Hotel, and (Scott's) Old England Hotel. There are also the Stag's Head, and the Commercial Hotel.

The steam-yachts, which ply many times a day the year round, all call here. There are plenty of excellent pleasure-boats, and the tourist will find few things more agreeable than a row amongst the bays and islands on a fine, hot summer's day. Belle Isle is the largest island. It contains a private residence, and visitors are not allowed to land. They may, however, spend many delightful hours in visiting and rambling on the numerous smaller islets. The charge for boat is 1s. per hour, and for boat and boatman 1s. 6d. per hour. The *Ferry* is ¾m. distant. A pleasant footpath leads to it across the fields.

There are several spots near the town where fine views of the lake are to be obtained, Biscay How and Brant Fell being among the principal.

The *Church* is an ancient structure, and contains a fine stained-glass window, which is said to have originally belonged to Furness Abbey.

A coach leaves the town every morning during the tourist season for (Ullswater Lake) Patterdale, by the vale of Troutbeck and Kirkstone Pass.

AMBLESIDE.

The market town of Ambleside contains 1988 inhabitants. It stands nearly 1m. from the head of Windermere Lake, in an attractive situation, at the foot of Wansfell Pike. A small stream, the Stockgill, from the Stockdale Glen, flows past it, and enters the river Rothay. Ambleside is the best centre in the south of the district from which to commence excursions, and

visitors usually make it their head-quarters for a short
time.   It is well supplied with hotels, the principal of
which are the Salutation, the Queen's, and the White
Lion.   The Waterhead Hotel is a comfortable house on
the margin of the lake, close to the pier.   The Low
Wood Hotel, 2m. from Ambleside, stands on the eastern
shore of the lake, surrounded by plantations, and is one
of the most pleasantly-located and best-frequented
houses in the district.   The town is full of private
lodging-houses.   Omnibuses go many times a day to
the head of the lake and to Grasmere, and coaches leave
two or three times daily for Windermere railway station
and for Keswick.   There are two churches; the new
one, St. Mary's, stands conspicuously in the centre of
the valley.   Ambleside is supposed to have been a
Roman station.   Some fragments of tesselated pave-
ment, urns, and other relics, have been dug up in a field
near the head of the lake.

**Walk to the New Church (St. Mary's), and back
by "The Knoll."**—As soon as apartments have been
obtained at the hotel, the tourist ought to take this walk,
of not more than 1m.   It combines a series of pleasing
views, and will enable him to gain a good knowledge of
the neighbouring vales and mountains.

Passing under the covered way close to the Queen's
Hotel, a lane leads to St. Mary's Church.   From the
rocks in the churchyard a good view is had of the
meadows and woods of the vale of Rothay.   The lower
part of Loughrigg Fell is close at hand, with Loughrigg
Brow, the conspicuous mansion of the Rev. C. D. Bell,
standing in a prominent position on one of the rocky
knolls at the side of the hill.   A long range is seen
extending from Nab Scar, past Heron Pike and Great
Rigg, to the summit of Fairfield, below which is the deep
hollow of the Rydal Glen.   To the right of Rydal is the
Scandale Fell (called on the Rydal side, Rydal Fell),
with High Pike overlooking the Scandale Glen, which
is bounded on its E. side by Red Screes.

On leaving the church, follow the footpath through

the fields in the direction of Loughrigg Brow. A few
rocky hillocks are passed, giving evidence of the
smoothing action of ancient glaciers. A small wooden
bridge crosses the Stockgill Beck at the point where it
enters the Rothay River. Miller Bridge is reached, and
the Scandale Beck is seen flowing into the river. Avoid
crossing Miller Bridge, and return to the town by
another path through the fields. The ivy-covered house
passed on the left is " The Knoll," the residence of
Miss Martineau. The Grasmere road is entered a few
yards from Ambleside.

Stockgill Force.—The Stockgill Force is a few hundred yards from the town. The way to it lies through
the stable-yard of the Salutation Hotel, and by a foot-
path which goes through a picturesque plantation by
the side of the stream.

It is a pleasant fall, with a broken leap of 70 feet;
but it may be well to observe here that most of the falls
in the Lake District are small, and seldom realize the
expectations of those who visit them. During a dry
season many of the falls are mere trickling rills, but the
tourist is recommended not to pass them by unheeded, as
he will miss some picturesque and perfect bits of scenery.

**To head of Windermere Lake, and back by
Rothay Bridge.**—The head of the lake is ¾m. from
Ambleside, and it is reached by following the Kendal
road, which skirts the base of Wansfell.

Omnibuses run to meet the steamers many times
during the day. The charge is 6d. each person. The
return ride the same day being free.

Pleasant views are obtained all the way. Loughrigg,
Nab Scar, Fairfield and Scandale fells, are in sight,
and gradually Oxenfell and Wetherlam appear. Just
before the lake is reached, the mountains at the head
of the Brathay and Langdale vales present a picturesque appearance.

From the beach Clappersgate is seen pleasantly
situated at the base of Loughrigg.

Wray Castle is a fine object on the opposite shore,

under the Furness Fells and Latterbarrow. This beautiful mansion is a modern structure, the residence of James Dawson, Esq., M.D., of Liverpool. It was meant to resemble a feudal fortress of the Middle Ages, but without moat and rampart.

Leaving the boat landing-place, take the road which winds to the left, at the head of the lake. Presently Clappersgate again appears, and the Brathay Church is a prominent object in the Brathay Vale. Loughrigg gradually hides the Langdale and Coniston heights. Ambleside is seen resting at the foot of Wansfell, and at the end of a shoulder of Red Screes. The heights of Nab Scar, Fairfield, and Scandale Fell, are also fine, prominent, bulky masses. From this point a good idea is gained of the situation of the Rydal, Scandale, and Stockdale glens. At a turn in the road two footpaths branch to the right. One leads past the St. Mary's Church, and the other into the road leading from the town to the lake. A few yards farther Rothay Bridge is reached, which stands midway between Ambleside and Clappersgate, ½m. from each place.

Boat on Windermere.—Windermere Lake is 10½m. long, and 1m. broad in its widest part, 134 feet above the level of the sea, and it varies in depth from 90 feet to 220 feet. There are only two or three tiny islets in its upper or lower end, but near the centre, opposite Bowness, is a cluster of about a dozen, the largest of which is Belle Isle, containing 30 acres. Most of the others are very diminutive, but all are more or less wooded, and add considerably to the picturesque beauty of the lake.

Numerous bays and promontories diversify the shores. The hills which surround the lake are not high, varying from 500 to 1000 feet, and are in most parts covered with wood, and free from anything approaching the stern or majestic. The lower part is comparatively tame, and has much the appearance of a river, but at the higher end it widens considerably, and at a short distance bare and lofty hills rise on every hand.

A few yards from the head of the lake the rivers Brathay and Rothay unite their waters, and then enter the lake near the boat landing-stage.

The Brathay receives the drainage from the Langdale vales and Wrynose, and the tarns Blea, Little Langdale, Stickle, Elterwater, and Loughrigg. The sources of the Rothay are the Dunmail Raise Pass and Easedale Vale; and the tarns Codale and Easedale. It flows through Grasmere and Rydal lakes, and is joined by tributaries from the Rydal, Scandale, and Stockdale glens.

On the W. side of Windermere, streams enter from Esth'waite Water and Blelham Tarn; on the E. side from Troutbeck Vale.

The river Leven flows out of the lake past Newby Bridge, and to the Ulverston Sands in Morecambe Bay.

A pleasure-boat ought to be hired and some of the bays visited. The Pull Wyke Bay, on the western shore, is a most charming and secluded nook.* Good fishing can also be had. The lake contains perch, pike, trout, and char. The char frequent the deepest part of the lake, and are generally taken by nets, and afterwards prepared and sold in pots. It is said that the char go up the Brathay River to spawn, while all the trout go up the Rothay.

When on the lake, ever-varying prospects are had of the surrounding heights. The Fairfield range is in one direction, and in another are seen the Langdale, Bow Fell, and Coniston mountains.

Scandale Glen.—Of many tourists staying at Ambleside, the Scandale Glen will be a favourite haunt. It is a secluded and pleasing spot, and entered after a few minutes' walk. A few yards below the old church at Ambleside take the left-hand road; then avoid all turns to the right. This road, or rather lane, is bounded by stone walls, and commands good views of the head of Windermere Lake; the Coniston, Crinkle Crags, Bow

* The charge for a boat is 1s. per hour, and for boat and boatman 1s. 6d. per hour. A boat for the day is 5s., and with boatman, 10s.

Fell, and Langdale mountains; with Wansfell Pike,
Loughrigg, and Nab Scar close at hand. The Scandale
Beck is soon heard, and occasionally seen, tumbling
musically down the wooded dell on the left. When the
tourist reaches the Sweden Bridge, the rustic and picturesque little arch which spans the beck about half-way
up the glen, and 1½m. from Ambleside, he will probably
be tempted to cross it, and return by a rough and rather
wet path, which leads through the wood. Many times
will he be induced to step down to the bank of the
torrent, where, alone and shaded from the sun, he may
gaze with delight on the lively little stream, which
descends charmingly along a rocky, uneven bed. On
reaching the lower bridge, near a reservoir, cross to a
farm-house, and follow a lane to Ambleside. The whole
distance is 3m., and will be found to be a delightful stroll.

Those who have seen the Kirkstone Pass would enjoy
reaching Patterdale from Ambleside by walking up the
Scandale Glen, and over the fell at the head, leaving Low
Hart Crag on the left, and descending by the course of
a streamlet, with High Hartsop Dodd on the left, and
Kelsey Chimney on the right. The Kirkstone road
would be entered a short distance from Brothers Water.

**To Rydal and Back, by Fox Howe and Pelter
Bridge.** — This excursion can be taken in a carriage,
but few will desire to hurry through such a charming
sylvan district. It is a delightful walk of not more
than 3m. Follow the footpath which leads to St. Mary's
Church, and through the fields to Miller Bridge. A
carriage road is entered which runs at the base of
Loughrigg, by the side of the river Rothay, and commands a pleasing view of the vale, and of Ambleside
and the neighbouring hills. Fox Howe is the first
house which is passed. It stands close to the road on
the right hand. It is the residence of Mrs. Arnold, the
widow of that great and good man, the late Dr. Arnold,
of Rugby, who came here during many vacations, to
enjoy the beauties of the scenery, and to brace himself
for future labours. The pretty dell in which nestles

Fox Gill, at the foot of a wooded side of Loughrigg, is passed on the left, and a few yards below are seen some stepping-stones in the river, which lead across to a farm-house, and to the coach-road. By taking advantage of this path the walk may be shortened ½m. Few will, however, wish to do so. They will proceed a few yards farther and cross the Rothay at Pelter Bridge, close to Rydal village, which is charmingly situated at the foot of Nab Scar.

Rydal Park is directly opposite, with Rydal Hall in the midst. Rydal Mount and Rydal Falls may be visited. See page 25. On returning by the coach road the Rydal Beck is crossed, and pleasant bits of scenery are had all the way to Ambleside. By looking back occasionally most charming and ever-varying views are obtained of wooded knolls and the high mountain range of Fairfield.

Ascent of Wansfell Pike (1597). — Wansfell Pike stands at the back of Ambleside to the S.E. It is without any very characteristic features, and of moderate elevation. The ascent is easy, and the prospect pleasing. The distance from Ambleside to the top of the mountain and back again is 4½m., and the time occupied will be two hours.

Wansfell Pike may be ascended in three ways. The best plan is to go through the stable-yard of the Salutation Hotel, and follow the rugged cart-road which runs near the side of Stockgill Beck and Force. If the fall be visited, the road can be re-entered about 30 yards to the right of the torrent. A direct ascent can be made from the fall without having more than one wall to scramble over.

Another plan, and one practicable for ponies, is to follow the Windermere road for about 200 yards from the Salutation Hotel, and then enter the first road branching to the left. This leads past the gas-works and narrows to a rugged lane. At a single out-building on the right pass through a gate, cross a small field, go through another gate, and ascend to the top of a small rock. From this point gates will be found enabling the walls to be passed and the summit to be reached.

A third route, also practicable for ponies, is found by continuing along the Windermere road until within a short distance of the lake. Here enter the lane on the left, which gradually ascends the hill. After passing a solitary house the lane becomes very rugged. The open fell is soon reached, and an interesting ascent is made to the top. This is the most circuitous, though perhaps the most pleasant, route. Windermere Lake is in sight during the greater part of the walk. Some persons will prefer the lake bursting suddenly in sight on attaining the top of the mountain, which is the case when the climb is made from Stockgill Fall.

From the summit Windermere is seen from end to end, in all its beauty, with its cluster of wooded islands in its centre. A wide expanse of sea is visible, with inlets which branch into the different parts of the undulating tract of country to the S. Grasmere and Rydal lakes are observed sending their waters by the Rothay to join its sister river, the Brathay, which discloses the position of Elterwater Tarn. Blelham Tarn lies fully exposed near the head of Windermere. At the feet of the spectator are the Rothay, Brathay, and Stockdale vales, with Ambleside, Clappersgate, Rydal, and Rydal Hall, charmingly situated in the midst of wood and meadow. The highest house in England, at the top of the Kirkstone Pass, is a distinct object. To the right of it are the heights Caudale Moor, Thornthwaite Crag, High Street, Froswick, Ill Bell, Yoke, and Applethwaite Common. To the left, Red Screes, Scandale Fell, Rydal Head, Fairfield, Great Rigg, and Nab Scar. On the farther side of the Grasmere Vale are Ullscarf, Sergeant Man, Silver Howe, Pavey Ark, and then the unmistakable Langdale Pikes. The white streak to the right of Silver Howe is Sour Milk Force. Beyond Loughrigg are Lingmoor, Pike O'Blisco, Crinkle Crags, Scawfell, Bow Fell, and Great End; with Scawfell Pike peeping over Bow Fell, a little to the right of the summit. On the left of the Wrynose Pass depression are the Carrs, Wetherlam, Coniston Old Man, and Black Combe, with the lower heights of Oxenfell and the Furness Fells in front.

Ascent of Loughrigg Fell (1101).—Loughrigg Fell will in all probability be a favourite resort of those who remain for any length of time at Ambleside. It has a fine long uneven top, covered with gorse and rocky hillocks, and commands most enchanting prospects, which are ever varying as the pedestrian rambles in perfect seclusion from point to point. The highest peak is the part of the mountain farthest from Ambleside, which overlooks Red Bank and Grasmere. There are many ways of ascent. The three best are from Clappersgate, Loughrigg Brow, and Fox Gill. At Clappersgate a path runs up the hill from a point in the village nearly opposite Brathay Bridge. The Fox Gill ascent is commenced just behind Fox Howe. The route by Loughrigg Brow is the most direct. A path will be found mounting the hill behind the mansion, which is perched so conspicuously on a rocky knoll by the side of Loughrigg. It passes a farm-house, and then enters the open fell. Arrived at this point the tourist will prefer rambling and picking his way to the top of the different rocky knobs, where he may one minute obtain a view of Windermere, and the next, by slightly changing his position, see the Langdale Vale, or Grasmere and Rydal Water.

For a description of the view from the highest point, see page 84.

Circular Tour by Coniston, Furness Abbey, and Windermere Lake.—This is the cheapest excursion in the Lake District. It enables a large extent of ground to be passed over quickly—ground which most tourists are anxious to hasten from to the more rugged scenery amongst the loftier mountains. The tickets are now issued under conditions which will allow the tourist either to hurry over the ground, or to make a more lengthened stay. When properly explored, much of the comparatively level country in the Furness district is discovered to be very beautiful, and it contains many places of great interest.

Tickets, which are 10s. first class, and 7s. second class, for the whole tour, can be obtained at Ambleside, Bowness, Coniston, Lake Side, Furness Abbey, and Ulverston; and at a little difference in price they can also be had at any station on the Furness Railway, between Carnforth and Whitehaven. They are available for seven days, and the tourist is allowed to accomplish the whole journey in one day, or to break the journey as often as he likes during the week. If a ticket be taken, say, at Ambleside, it includes char-à-banc to Coniston, train thence to Furness Abbey, and to the Lake Side Station, at the foot of Windermere, and steamer up Windermere Lake.

The tourist might stay a night in Coniston, explore the Duddon or climb the Old Man, and resume the journey at Coniston or Broughton; stay again at Furness Abbey, or at any other station, and visit Barrow, Grange, and other places, then proceed to Lake Side; and so on during the whole round, only being careful to return to Ambleside within the seven days, or the ticket would be forfeited.

Of course when a *détour* is made, and ground is traversed which is out of the circuit, the ticket will be useless until the regular journey is resumed.

It is advisable to sail *up* Windermere Lake, and therefore let us suppose the journey to be commenced by taking the char-à-banc from Ambleside to Coniston.

At Clappersgate, a village 1m. from Ambleside, and prettily situated at the foot of Loughrigg, the road crosses the Brathay Bridge and passes through a wooded district at the head of Pull Wyke Bay. It then bends to the right and mounts a rising ground, allowing of fine retrospective views of Ambleside and the neighbouring mountains. 3m. from Ambleside, on the brow of the hill, is the Barn Gates Inn. From this point the road runs through a wild upland country, and commands a view of Hawkshead and Esthwaite Water. Presently Coniston Old Man, and Wetherlam appear, and the road descends steeply through ground thickly covered with timber. At one place a glimpse is caught of the whole of Coniston Lake. After passing Water-head House, the residence of J. G. Marshall, Esq., which is surrounded by beautiful woods, the head of the lake is skirted, and the Waterhead Hotel is reached.

Coniston is sometimes entered from Ambleside by following the road for Little Langdale until within ½m. of Colwith Bridge. See page 20. After continuing for 2m. or 3m. along the base of Oxenfell, a descent is made into Yewdale, a beautiful cultivated glen, famous for its venerable yew. The heath-crowned crags surrounding this glen are strikingly beautiful. Tarn Hows, where a much-admired prospect is obtained, stands on the left. The opening into the Tilberthwaite Glen is left behind, and Coniston is reached after passing along the base of some picturesque cliffs.

The Waterhead Hotel is a first-class house. The Crown Hotel, a few hundred yards distant, is also large and comfortable.

Coniston Lake is 6m. long and ½m. broad. It is 147 feet above the sea, and its greatest depth is 164 feet. It abounds with char, trout, and perch, and contains two islets, Peel Isle and Fir Isle. It is a lovely sheet of water when seen from some points of view, but to those who look at it from the western side only it will be rather disappointing. The three best stations are, at the foot of the lake, on its eastern side, and from near Tarn Hows. A steam gondola plies up and down the lake two or three times a day; but tourists who intend visiting Furness Abbey, and arriving at Ambleside the same evening, will be obliged to relinquish this tempting excursion. They will, no doubt, on seeing the presiding genius of the place, the Old Man mountain, desire to come here at some future time to explore some of the recesses of his weather-beaten sides. Those who can spare a few days are recommended to break the journey, and before proceeding climb the Old Man, Wetherlam, and Black Combe, and walk up the Duddon Valley.

Furness Abbey.—Tourists generally take the train for Furness Abbey after remaining an hour at Coniston. The railway between Coniston and Broughton passes through a dark heath-covered tract of country, which completely hides the lake. On leaving Broughton, the shore of the Duddon Estuary is skirted, and some lime-quarries, iron-ore mines, and furnaces, are passed before the train enters the charming dell in which the abbey is situated. The railway station, hotel, and the abbey ruins, are all close together. Everything is neat and comfortable, and made to correspond as much as possible with the character of the place. The Furness Abbey Hotel is an excellent house, fitted up in a style to harmonize with the surrounding associations. During the tourist season there are tables d'hôte at 2 P.M. and 6 P.M. Visitors are allowed free access to the grounds. The ruins, now the property of the Duke of Devonshire, are finer than any ruins in Britain, except Fountains Abbey, in Yorkshire. The abbey was founded by Stephen, Earl of Montaigne and Boulogne, afterwards king of England, in the reign of Henry I., 1127. The monks originally came from Savigny, in Normandy, and were of the Benedictine order, but afterwards became Cistercians. This abbey was a mother institution, having under it Calder Abbey, in Cumberland, Rushin Abbey, in the Isle of Man, Fermor Abbey, in Ireland, and Byland, near Malton, in Yorkshire, and five other monasteries. It was richly endowed by Stephen, and from time to time it received gifts from opulent persons resident in the neighbourhood. Extraordinary powers were conferred upon the abbot, which were formally ratified by twelve English monarchs. He was a sort of king; both in civil and ecclesiastical rule he was supreme over the whole of the Furness district, extending from the Duddon to Windermere. For a period of 400 years the abbots succeeded one another in unlimited sway over this district, enjoying privileges conferred in no other part of the country.

All the people were vassals, and all mesne lords did homage and;fealty "to be true to them against all men, excepting the king." Every tenant was bound to furnish a man and horse fully equipped for the Border wars and for the protection of the coast.

Barrow.—This busy, thriving town is situated 2m. from Furness Abbey. It contains a population of 18,245, and stands in a peninsula where, in the early part of the present century, there was only one house. The discovery of iron ore in the Furness district has been the cause of this rapid change. Extensive steel works have been erected. Walney Island, 10m. in length, serves as a natural breakwater. Docks have been made, adapted for vessels of all sizes. Steamers sail almost daily for Ireland and the Isle of Man. The principal hotels are the Sun, Imperial, and Royal.

Peel Castle, now a ruin, which was built by the monks of Furness, stands on an island near Peel Pier.

Ulverston is 7m. from Furness Abbey. It is an old-fashioned market town, the modern capital of Lower Furness. Population, 7607. Dalton was, at one period, the metropolis of the district. The principal hotels are the Sun, Queen, and Braddyll's Arms. Upon Hoad Hill, close to the town, has been erected a monument to the memory of Sir John Barrow, for many years Secretary to the Admiralty, and native of this town.

Swarth Moor Hall, 1m. from Ulverston, was formerly the residence of George Fox, the founder of the Society of Friends. A place of worship here, having over the door Fox's initials, and the year 1688; was the first meeting-house erected by the Quakers.

Conishead Priory, the residence of H. W. Askew, Esq., is a magnificent mansion built on the site of an ancient priory. It is 2m. from Ulverston, and the grounds extend to the shore of Morecambe Bay. It has been called the "Paradise of Furness."

Gleaston Castle stands 2m. E. of Furness Abbey. Some of the towers are nearly entire, but of the interior nothing remains. It is pleasantly situated.

Holker Hall, on the opposite side of the estuary of the Leven, about 5m. from Ulverston, is a seat of the Duke of Devonshire. It contains a fine collection of paintings. The grounds, which slope down to the water's edge, are richly wooded, and well stocked with deer.

Grange is 10m. from Ulverston by railway. A coach leaves it for Newby Bridge every morning during the summer season, distance 7m. The Grange Hotel is large and beautifully situated, close to the railway and the sea shore. At the village are other hotels and numerous lodging-houses. This is fast becoming a favourite watering-place. It is a small Ventnor or Torquay, perched in a warm nook on the north-west coast of England.

Levens Hall, the seat of the Hon. Mrs. Howard, ought to be visited whilst the tourist is staying at Grange. It is a venerable mansion, and stands amidst tall aged trees, on the E. side of the river Kent. It may also be reached conveniently from Kendal. The park is well stocked with deer. The gardens were planned by Beaumont, gardener to James II., who is said to have designed Hampton Court Gardens. They are laid out in the old Dutch style. The trees are cut and twisted about in most fantastic shapes. In the interior of the house are some interesting pictures, tapestry, and oak carvings. The carved decorations of one room are said to have cost at least 3000*l*.

Lancaster.—Before the tourist leaves Grange, he will probably pay a short visit to Lancaster. Population, 17,245. *Lancaster Castle* is a magnificent building, formerly the residence of John of Gaunt, Duke of Lancaster. The assize courts are held here, and it is a place of imprisonment for defaulters under the County Court Act. The handsome bridge over the Lune also deserves inspection. The principal hotels are the King's Arms, Queens, and Commercial.

On resuming the circular tour from Furness Abbey the traveller passes by train through Dalton and Ulverston, and then by the shore of the Leven Estuary and

wooded banks of the Leven River to the Lake Side
Station, at the foot of Windermere. Here are the Lake
Side Hotel and a Refreshment Room.

If the weather be fine, the day's excursion will be most
agreeably terminated by a sail in the steam-yacht, up this
lovely sheet of water.

Near the foot of the lake, on either side, are low
copse-clad hills, the highest point being Gummers
How, directly opposite the station; and at the back of
the hotel is Finsthwaite Height, upon which has been
erected a pleasure-house. From the pier are seen Fairfield, Red Screes, and Wansfell Pike.

Soon after starting, Ill Bell and High Street appear,
and Blake Holme Isle is passed. A part of Helvellyn
comes into view, Silver Holme Isle being left behind.
Storrs Hall, the residence of the Rev. T. Staniforth, is
a pleasant object in a deep bay on the right. Scott,
Wordsworth, Southey, Canning, and Professor Wilson,
met here as the guests of the then proprietor, Mr.
Bolton. The voyager will picture in his mind the
happy days when these celebrated men met, and Windermere glittered with all her sails in honour of the
" Great Northern Minstrel."

When Ling Holme Isle and Storrs Hall are left in
the rear, the Ferry promontory, Belle Isle, and The
Nab appear to run across the lake and terminate it.
In front are the wooded heights of Orrest Head, with
Bowness and Windermere at its feet. The Station-
house is seen perched amongst the wood on the side
of the hill on the left. After passing the Ferry Hotel
and a few islets, and rounding the Nab promontory,
the lower part of the lake disappears, and a capital
view is had up to the head, with Fairfield, Loughrigg,
and Wansfell Pike in the background. The steamer
calls at Bowness, and then passes the islets Hen Holme,
House Holme, Lady Holme, and Rough Holme. Rigg's
Hotel, Elleray, and the Abbey, are seen peeping from·
beneath the trees at the foot of Orrest Head; and on
proceeding a little farther the Furness Fells are passed,

c

and Wray Castle appears.   Calgarth Hall is on the right, the residence of the late Dr. Watson, Bishop of Llandaff, and Ecclerigg, the mansion occupied by R. L. Watson, Esq., the grandson of the bishop.

Lofty heights now advance to view on the left at every step with magical effect.   First come the Langdale Pikes, and then Glaramara, Great Gable, Great End, Bow Fell, Scawfell, Crinkle Crags, Wetherlam, and Coniston Old. Man.   Beneath these are Silver Howe, Lingmoor, Pike O'Blisco, and Oxenfell.

The Low Wood Hotel is on the eastern shore, and a few yards above it Dove's Nest is observed to be prettily perched on the side of Wansfell.   It was for a few months the home of Mrs. Hemans.

After rounding a headland, Ambleside appears to be close at hand, pleasantly situated beneath Fairfield and Wansfell.

Excursion.—Ambleside to (Dungeon Gill) Langdale.

Skelwith Bridge, 3m.; Colwith Bridge, 4½m.; Blea Tarn, 8m.; Dungeon Gill, 11m.; Grasmere, 18m.; Ambleside, 22m.

This is the best carriage excursion that can be taken from Ambleside, and it is not inferior to any other in the Lake District, with the exception of the Buttermere Excursion from Keswick.

The distance from Ambleside to Dungeon Gill, by the most direct road, is 8m., passing Loughrigg Tarn and through the Great Langdale Valley.

Tourists are, however, recommended to take the route above indicated, going by Blea Tarn and returning by Grasmere.

Sometimes travellers who have already visited Grasmere, will return direct from Langdale, and thus shorten the journey by 2m.

One mile from Ambleside is passed the pleasant village of Clappersgate, a few yards beyond which stands the Brathay Church, picturesquely situated on the opposite bank of the river Brathay.   The road continues for some distance by the edge of the river, and skirts the side of Loughrigg. On turning round a sharp corner, the river is seen winding through green meadows, and the hamlet of Skelwith Bridge makes a pleasing picture at the feet of low wooded heights, with lofty mountains in the background.

Skelwith Force.—On arriving at the small inn at Skelwith Bridge, strangers usually leave the conveyance for a few minutes and visit the Skelwith Force which is 200 yards farther up the river. Without any charge a guide will accompany the party from the inn. A small gate, which is generally locked, has to be passed through before a descent can be made to the rocks in the bed of the river.

There is a public footpath on the north bank of the river, which leads past the fall to Elterwater village, but we do not feel justified in advising the guide to be dispensed with, and half a dozen yards of ground to be trespassed over. The Skelwith Force is not one of great beauty. There is a large body of water which descends 16 or 20 feet between a gap in the rock about 12 feet wide. Being near the road to Coniston and Langdale, it is often visited, although there are many far superior cascades in the district which are rarely seen. The best view of the force is had by crossing the bridge and taking through the second gate on the right. After threading through some coppice-wood, the tourist gains the rocks on the S. side of the stream. Here the fall, with wood on either side, and the Langdale Pikes in full view beyond, form a picturesque bit of scenery.

On leaving Skelwith Bridge, the road slightly ascends, and then *Elterwater Tarn* comes in view on the right. This lakelet looks mean and insignificant; a poor representative of the wild and solitary tarns up in the hills. It contains trout and pike.

Grand views are now obtained on every side of pleasing groups of wild and lofty mountains.

Directly in front are fine outlines of hills, ranging height above height to the summit of Coniston Old

Man, Wetherlam, and the Carrs. To the right of the Wrynose Pass depression stand Pike O'Blisco and the Crinkle Crags. The nearer height is Lingmoor, and to the right of it are the Langdale Pikes and Silver Howe. Over the Red Bank Pass are seen Helvellyn, Seat Sandal, and Fairfield. On the right is Loughrigg, and in the background, Wansfell Pike, Ill Bell, and Froswick.

A mile beyond Skelwith Bridge the road branches to the right, and descends to Colwith Bridge. The direct road leads through Yewdale to Coniston.

Colwith Force.—At the Colwith Bridge is a farm-house, where a guide may be obtained, without charge, to Colwith Force, which is a few yards farther up the stream, and is reached by a locked door. The best view is had by walking from the bridge on the S. side of the stream; but this involves a return the same way. The cascade is of no great height. It tumbles wildly over rocks into a picturesque dell, and is well worth a visit, though inferior to some others in the district. Wetherlam is a fine object in the background. The road is again entered a few yards above the fall, and the carriage will be there in waiting.

A pleasant district is now passed through, in which is situated Little Langdale village and tarn. In every part are small knolls, some green, others formed of bare rock or covered with trees, and rising above these are lofty heights, Wetherlam and the Carrs being the principal. The left-hand fells, strewn with débris of slate quarries, hide the beautiful glen of Tilberthwaite.

The *Little Langdale Tarn*, which is in sight, is perhaps the most uninteresting of all the lakelets, being an ordinary sheet of water in a low marshy ground, and although Wetherlam and other hills are not remote, they are too far to give a pleasing effect. It contains trout.

When beyond the tarn the road skirts the base of Lingmoor, the hill which separates the Little Langdale and Great Langdale vales. Fell Foot, the farm-house half hid by yew trees, is passed on the left, and the

Wrynose road is seen ascending to the Three Shire Stones.

The tourist is now in the midst of scenery described in Wordsworth's 'Excursion,' and will presently reach the abode of the "*Solitary*" of that poem. The road is steep and rugged, and passes through a wild tract, with Lingmoor on the right and Blake Crag on the left. The Langdale Pikes, those

> " Two huge peaks
> That from some other vale peer into this,"

gradually advance to view with magical effect, and then stand nobly at the head of the valley. From no other point do they present so fine an appearance. After the traveller has passed the " steep ascent,"

> " Behold !
> Beneath his feet, a little lowly vale,
> A lowly vale, and yet uplifted high
> Among the mountains ; even as if the spot
> Had been, from eldest time, by wish of theirs
> So placed,—to be shut out from all the world !   •
> Urn-like it was in shape, deep as an urn ;
> With rocks encompassed, save that to the south
> Was one small opening, where a heath-clad ridge
> Supplied a boundary less abrupt and close—
> A quiet, treeless nook, with two green fields,
> A liquid pool, that glittered in the sun,
> And one bare dwelling ; one abode, no more !
> It seemed the home of poverty and toil,
> Though not of want : the little fields, made green
> By husbandry of many thrifty years,
> Paid cheerful tribute to the moorland house.
> There crows the cock, single in his domain ;
> The small birds find in spring no thicket there
> To shroud them ; only from the neighbouring vales
> The cuckoo, straggling up to the hill tops,
> Shouteth faint tidings of some gladder place."

These words were written on the supposition that the spectator was looking down upon the valley, not from

the road, but from one of its elevated sides.   The stranger
will also observe that the vale is no longer a "treeless
nook," there being now fir and larch plantations.   The

"One bare dwelling; one abode, no more,"

is seen at the foot of the vertical cliff called Side Pike.
Blea Tarn has not a particularly interesting appearance,
but the whole vale looks secluded and pleasing.   The
tarn contains trout.   Langdale Pikes peer into the
valley at one end, and Wetherlam on the other.   Blake
Crag is a fine object rising above the dark fir-trees which
border the opposite shore.

When descending, a capital echo, perhaps the best to
be met with in the district, will be discovered.

Just before arriving at the house, Great End, Bow
Fell, Crinkle Crags, and Pike O'Blisco appear.

From the house the road gradually ascends, and the
vale from this point has a dark and bleak appearance.
Most tourists will feel a relief when a view is had down
into the vale head of Langdale, which is divided by the
Band into the Mickleden and Oxendale glens.   A steep
descent is made by a stony, winding road, to the Wall
End farm, and presently the Old Dungeon Gill Hotel is
seen at the feet of the Langdale Pikes.

On the left, at the head of Mickleden, is Rossett Gill
Pass, leading to Scawfell Pike and to Wastwater; and
on the right the Stake Pass, conducting to Borrowdale
and Keswick.   After passing the farm-house, and crossing the valley, the hotel is reached, and 1m. farther
down, at Millbeck, is the New Dungeon Gill Hotel.
Both houses are pleasantly situated and comfortable.
The lower house occupies an especially favoured situation
at the foot of a number of fine rocks, close to the cleft
in which is the Dungeon Gill Fall.   A little to the right
of the cleft is the Millgill stream, tumbling over ledges
of rock, and forming pleasing cascades in its descent
from Stickle Tarn, which lies hidden in the hollow
above, at the foot of the fine cliff of Pavey Ark.   The
Dungeon Gill Fall will be visited whilst luncheon is pre-

paring. It is a few hundred yards behind the hotel.
There is not much water, but it has a perpendicular fall
of about 90 feet, and is deeply recessed in the hill, with
vertical walls of cliff on either hand. In one place two
stones, which appear to have got wedged at the top of
the cliffs, form a natural weird-like bridge across the
ravine, and a few surrounding shrubs give them a picturesque appearance.

On leaving the inn the road runs down the Great
Langdale Valley, with Lingmoor on the right and Silver
Howe on the left. Many times will the tourist look
wistfully back into the fine vale head, which is bounded
by Pike O'Blisco, Crinkle Crags, Bow Fell, and the
ever-pleasing cliffs of the Langdale Pikes. After passing Thrang slate-quarry, and the romantic hamlet of
Chapel Stile, the road branches, at a point directly
opposite the Elterwater village and gunpowder works.
The left-hand road mounts the hill, runs by High Close
and Red Bank to Grasmere, and commands excellent
views. The direct road goes past Loughrigg Tarn to
Ambleside. At the tarn a road strikes off for Red Bank,
and there meets the road from Chapel Stile. It is
somewhat more circuitous, but not so steep as the other.

Loughrigg Tarn is seen whichever route be taken.
This lakelet lies in a quiet and fertile spot, environed
by green meadows, at the base of the rocky, wooded
side of Loughrigg Fell. It contains pike and perch.

High Close, the large mansion near to Red Bank, is
the residence of W. Balm, Esq. From the dilapidated
seat, which has the words "Rest and be thankful" carved
on it, and which stands by the roadside a few yards
from the house, is obtained what has been said to be
"the finest view in Westmorland." Immediately the
descent is commenced, charming prospects are had of
the lake and vale of Grasmere and the surrounding
mountains. Owing to the steepness of the road the
tourist's attention is very much distracted, and therefore
he is recommended to leave the carriage at High Close,
walk over Red Bank, a little to the left of the pass, and

meet the carriage again on the western shore of Grasmere Lake.

During the walk Rydal Lake will be seen to the right
beyond Grasmere, and rising from its shore is Nab Scar,
the end of the long ridge which culminates in Fairfield.
The coach-road to Keswick is observed winding up the
Dunmail Raise Pass between Seat Sandal and Steel Fell.
The rocky summit of Helm Crag, the famous " Lion and
the Lamb," forms a prominent feature to the left of the
village.

Grasmere Lake is little more than 1m. long, and
its greatest breadth is not quite ½m. It is 208 feet
above the sea, and its greatest depth is 180 feet. A
single green isle of about 4 acres lies in its centre.
This has a clump of black firs and a grey barn upon it,
and is used as grazing ground for cattle.

The Prince of Wales Hotel is a large, first-class
house, delightfully situated on the margin of the lake.
In the village is the Red Lion, a good and commodious
hotel; and half a mile distant, on the coach-road, stands
the Swan, which is comfortable, and noted for having
been the point whence Scott, Wordsworth, and Southey
commenced the ascent of Helvellyn. A small house at
Town End, near the Prince of Wales Hotel, was occupied by Wordsworth for eight years, and afterwards for
a time by De Quincey. Wordsworth removed to Allan
Bank, which stands on an eminence behind the village,
and this he quitted in 1813 for Rydal Mount.

Before the tourist leaves the beautiful vale of Grasmere he will visit the *Church*—the church of the 'Excursion.' In a corner of the burying-ground, close to the
river, are the graves of Wordsworth and his family, and
of Hartley Coleridge.

After passing the Prince of Wales Hotel the road
skirts the lake, with Loughrigg in front, and the single
green isle fully displayed. On rounding a wooded knoll
Nab Scar appears, and the margin of *Rydal Lake* is
traversed. This is one of the most diminutive of the
lakes, being only ½m. long by scarcely ⅛m. broad. It is

200 feet above the sea; its greatest depth is 54 feet.
On its shores is a diversity of meadow, wood, and cliff.
It contains two or three wooded islets, upon one of
which was a heronry until within the last two years.
From some points of view on the opposite shore it looks
very beautiful, but it is nowhere seen to advantage from
the main road.

Nab Cottage, the ivy-covered house standing close to
the lake by the roadside, was formerly the residence of
Hartley Coleridge, and it was here that he died. The
tourist now arrives at the charming village of Rydal,
where are situated Rydal Hall, the seat of General Le
Fleming, and Rydal Mount, for many years the residence
of Wordsworth.

Rydal Falls are at the back of the hall, and to visit
them it is necessary to obtain a guide at the cottage
below the church. No charge is made, but, of course,
few will allow such services to be rendered without
offering a small acknowledgment. There are two falls,
an upper and a lower. The walk from one to the other
is nearly ½m. They are both small, but very beautiful.
The lower one is most admired. It is beheld through a
window in an old summer-house, and appears like a
picture set in a frame.

Rydal Mount stands on a slight acclivity a few yards
above the church, in a quiet, secluded nook. It is a
simple, unpretending edifice, almost concealed by trees
and shrubs. This was the poet's residence for thirty-
seven years, and here he died on the 23rd April, 1850,
having attained his eightieth year. The house does
not contain any furniture which belonged to Wordsworth, and is not occupied by any of his relatives. A
beautiful view is obtained from the grassy mound in
front, a portion of Windermere being visible over the
lovely wooded Vale of Rothay.

From Rydal to Ambleside, a distance of 1½m., the
scenery is charming.

Ambleside to (Ullswater Lake) Patterdale.

Top of Kirkstone Pass, 3m.; Patterdale (Ullswater Hotel), 10m.;
Top of Kirkstone Pass, 17m.; Ambleside, 20m.

Ullswater is generally visited either from Ambleside
district or from Keswick. Tourists who enter the Lake
Country at Windermere, and intend to leave it at the
same place, in order to save time will sometimes go to
Keswick by coach over Dunmail Raise Pass, and return
viâ Patterdale and the Kirkstone Pass, to Ambleside or
Windermere.

During the tourist season a coach leaves Ambleside
for Patterdale every morning (Sundays excepted) at
10 A.M. Unfortunately, owing to this coach having to
run in connection with the steamers on both the Windermere and Ullswater lakes, it is pushed for time, and
has to return by the route taken in the morning. A
much better drive may be taken by extending the
journey 4m., and returning by the vale of Troutbeck.
If the tourist desires to include a visit to the Troutbeck
Vale, and does not wish to hire a private conveyance,
he can go either to Bowness or to Windermere Station,
and there obtain a coach for Patterdale, which both
goes and returns by Troutbeck.

The road from Ambleside to the Kirkstone Pass
(1481) runs in front of the Salutation Hotel, and then
branches to the right, passing the old church. It is in
places very steep, and winds along the side of the fell,
which is an offshoot of Red Screes. At some distance
below, on the right, flows the Stockgill stream, on the
opposite side of which is Wansfell Pike. There is
nothing of interest directly in front, but a retrospective
view includes the head of Windermere Lake, Blelham
Tarn, and the Coniston and Langdale mountains. On
gaining a high part of the road, the house at the top of
the pass comes in sight; on the left of which is Red
Screes, and on the right Caudale Moor. Yoke, Ill Bell,
and Froswick, the beginning of the High Street range,
are seen standing to the right on the opposite side of

the Troutbeck Vale, and the Roman Road may be traced a few yards below their tops.

The inn near the summit of the pass (The Traveller's Rest), is said to be the highest inhabited house in England. It is 1475 feet above the sea.

When descending into Patterdale, Place Fell appears, and on the left is passed the stone which

"Gives to the savage pass its name."

It is not like a kirk from this side, but when seen from a point half-way down the pass it assumes that shape. During the descent Brothers Water is in sight, and a part of the Patterdale Valley, with Place Fell rising from it, and a portion of Mell Fell in the distance. On the right is Caudale Fell, which sends a branch to the north called Low Hartsop Dodd. A cove is observed high up on the side of Red Screes. The height branching to the north from this is called Kelsey Chimney. Gradually the small glen of Caiston opens to view on the left, with High Hartsop Dodd opposite. The latter hides the Hartsop Park Vale and Dovedale. When at the foot of the pass, Hartsop Hall is seen on the left, near an old lead mine (it is now merely an ordinary farm-house), and a view is had up Hartsop Park. Dovedale lies out of sight higher up, but the Dove Crag is a fine object at the head of the glen. Greenup End and a part of Fairfield can also be seen. A little roadside inn, the Cross Keys, is passed on the left, and from this point the Dove Crags and neighbouring rocks look extremely wild and picturesque. At the inn, pedestrians benighted, and unable to reach Patterdale, may obtain a clean and comfortable bed.

The road now skirts the shore of *Brothers Water*, which is said to have received its name from two brothers having been drowned in it. Its length is ¼m., and extreme breadth less than ⅛m. It is 520 feet above the sea, and its greatest depth is 72 feet. It is well stocked with trout. The hamlet of Hartsop is seen to the right, and a fine view is had of Low Hartsop Dodd, Gray Crag, and part of High Street. The stream, which flows through Hartsop, has its source in Hayeswater Tarn, which lies in a secluded recess 2m. distant. The road now crosses the Goldrill Beck a few yards below Brothers Water. A rearward view discloses a fine grouping of the hills which have been passed.

After rounding a shoulder of the ridge which separates Dovedale and Deepdale, a peep is had up the latter glen to the wild eastern side of Fairfield. The road then skirts the end of an offshoot of St. Sunday Crag, which separates the Deepdale and Grisedale glens, and on turning sharply round a rock, the village of Patterdale is reached, and a glimpse is caught of the head of Ullswater Lake. At the village are two hotels, the Patterdale Hotel, a large, excellent house, and the White Lion, a small, but comfortable inn.

The village stands in a green cultivated vale, a few hundred yards from the head of the lake. The coach goes 1m. farther down the valley to the Ullswater Hotel, a first-class house situated in a pleasant position on the shore of the lake. Upon leaving the village, the church, a modern structure, is passed, and a glance is had up the Grisedale Glen. Wild rocks and coves on the eastern side of Dolly Waggon Pike and Helvellyn stand nobly at the head, and a part of the famous Striding Edge is visible. After crossing the Grisedale Beck, and passing the beautifully-wooded grounds of Patterdale Hall, the residence of W. Marshall, Esq., the road skirts the margin of the lake. Place Fell rises almost sheer from the opposite shore, and presents a beautifully-coloured front. Tourists who have heard of the transcendent attractiveness of Ullswater, and who, during this drive, see it for the first time, will, in all probability, be much disappointed, for to do justice to the lake it ought to be approached from the lower end, or from Gowbarrow Park. This feeling will, however, be temporary, and wear away, when the lake is seen from other points of view.

The Ullswater Hotel is on the margin of the lake, at

the bottom of Glenridding, a glen containing some large lead mines which are worth visiting. Perhaps there is no hotel in the Lake District more favourably situated. The scenery all around is rich and varied. The whole vale is finely wooded, and the mountains at its head are picturesquely grouped. The view from the windows of the hotel, of the green grass sloping to the water's edge, and the peaceful lake with its wooded shores and tiny islets, is extremely beautiful.

The pier from which the steam-yacht sails is on the hotel grounds, and few tourists will fail to avail themselves of a sail to the foot of the lake and back again. The times of sailing are 10.20 A.M., 2 P.M., and 5 P.M.; arriving at 10.5 A.M., 12.50 P.M., and 4.15 P.M. Fares, 2s. 6d. and 1s. 6d. The boats, after calling at How Town, land passengers at about ½m. from Pooley Bridge, whence coaches run to meet the trains at Penrith.

Ullswater Lake is 9m. long; greatest breadth, ½m.; height above the sea, 477 feet; and greatest depth, 218 feet. It zigzags and forms three reaches extending from Patterdale to Pooley Bridge. The lowest reach is 3m. long, and is terminated by Hallin Fell and the Skelly Neb promontory, on which is Mr. Marshall's mansion of Hallsteads. The middle reach is 4m. long, and ends at the Silver Hill promontory and the House Holm Island. The upper reach is the most beautiful; it is 2m. long, and it contains two or three pretty islets. Ullswater has a gracefulness and richness which is unsurpassed. Some put it even before Derwentwater, and in many respects it is worthy of the first place. If we may be allowed the simile, Ullswater may be likened to the graceful and accomplished belle of the ball-room, attired in rich flowing dress, and Derwentwater to the beautiful loving matron, a pleasant companion in all the various moods of life.

The coaches generally arrive at the hotel at 12 noon, and as the steamer does not sail until 2 P.M., there is time for a row in a pleasure-boat down to Lyulph's Tower, where a landing may be effected for Aira Force.

Lyulph's Tower is a castellated building covered with ivy. It was built as a shooting-box by a Duke of Norfolk, and is said to stand on the site of an old tower which belonged to the first Baron of Greystoke. It was bequeathed to the Howards, to whom it now belongs. The park is stocked with deer. *Aira Force* is in a pretty dell a few yards from the tower. The stream falls 80 feet, between two rugged rocks. Two rustic bridges span the chasm, the one above, the other below, and command full views of the fall. A guide can be procured from the tower. Aira Force is the scene of the tale which is the subject of Wordsworth's poem, "The Somnambulist."

> " List, ye who pass by Lyulph's Tower
> At eve, how softly then
> Doth Aira Force, that torrent hoarse,
> Speak from the woody glen!
> Fit music for a solemn vale!
> And holier seems the ground
> To him who catches on the gale
> The spirit of a mournful tale
> Embodied in the sound."

The " mournful tale " may be here briefly told. In a castle on the site of Lyulph's Tower there dwelt a beautiful lady named Emma, betrothed to a knight, Sir Eglamour. This knight being absent on his travels longer than the lady anticipated, her mind became affected, so that she used to walk in her sleep to the holly bower in Aira stream, where she had last parted from her lover. On the evening of the knight's return home he saw her there, at first believing it a phantom of his imagination; and, going up quietly, he touched her. She immediately awoke and fell shrieking into the stream; the knight plunged in and saved her, but only in time for her to die in his arms. It is futher said that he built a cell at the edge of the fall, and lived there in solitude, shunning all intercourse with the world.

If Aira Force be not visited, two hours may be pleasantly spent by taking a boat across the lake to Blowick Bay, and then walking by a footpath on the side of Place Fell. The views obtained from this path are perhaps unsurpassed in beauty by any other prospects in the Lake District. The whole of Patterdale, with Brothers Water, and the upper reach of Ullswater, are spread at the feet of the spectator. The Glencoin, Glenridding, Grisedale, Deepdale, and Glaiston glens are seen to branch away to the W., to the base of the rugged cliffs on the east side of Helvellyn and Fairfield. The tourist will descend into the valley and cross the Goldrill Beck close to the Patterdale village, 1m. from the Ullswater Hotel.

On a fine evening the return drive will be very enjoyable. The aspects of mountain scenery vary greatly with the time of day, and the heights as seen from a fresh point of view will present a novel appearance.

As soon as the village is passed, Caudale Moor and Low Hartsop Dodd stand in front, with the wild and solitary glen of Thrasthwaite Mouth on their left. When beyond the Deepdale Glen, the Kirkstone Pass appears, with Red Screes and Kelsey Chimney on the right of it; and on the left of Thrasthwaite Mouth the Gray Crag is a fine object. After crossing Goldrill Beck, a portion of High Street will be seen in the distance over Hartsop village. High Hartsop Dodd and Dove Crag gradually appear on the right. The road now skirts Brothers Water, and after passing the Cross Keys Inn, commences the ascent of the Kirkstone Pass. Those who are fond of a good walk might here leave the conveyance, go up the Caiston Glen, and descend by the Scandale Glen to Ambleside.

The ascent to the top of Kirksotne Pass is very toilsome and rather dreary. On either side are hills, bare of rocks, and strewn with loose stones; but near the top the Red Screes become more wild. The stone, which looks like a kirk, is an interesting object most of the way up; but it loses all its charms when closely inspected. On gaining the summit of the pass, Blelham

Turn, the upper part of Windermere, and a strip of the sea are seen. A few yards below the inn, the road branches on the right to Ambleside, and descends on the left into the *Vale of Troutbeck*. If the latter route be followed, the Ill Bell range of hills and the beautiful vale of Troutbeck gradually appear. When about 3m. from the top of the pass, the road makes a sudden turn, and, almost as by magic, Windermere is revealed, with its wooded bays and cluster of islands. It winds gracefully round a number of low hills, grouped most symmetrically. In the foreground is the Vale of Troutbeck, and some well-timbered ground. This is certainly one of the most beautiful and highly-finished bits of scenery to be met with in any country.

The tourist now passes through the picturesque village of Troutbeck, of which Professor Wilson writes :—" The cottages stand for the most part in clusters of twos and threes, with here and there what in Scotland is called a clachan,—many a sma' town within the ae lang town; but where, in all broad Scotland, is a wide, long, scattered congregation of rural dwellings, all dropped down where the painter and the poet would have wished to plant them,—on knolls and in dells, on banks and braes, and below tree-crested rocks,—and all bound together, in picturesque confusion, by old groves of ash, oak, and sycamore, and by flower gardens and fruit orchards, rich as those of the Hesperides."

In the village are two comfortable inns, ' The Mortal Man ' and ' The Queen's Head.' The former name was derived from a humorous signboard which formerly hung over the door, on which were depicted the portraits of two well-known characters in the vale, and below were the following lines :—

> " ' O ! Mortal Man, that liv'st on bread,
> How comes thy nose to be so red ? '
> ' Thou silly ass, that looks so pale,
> It comes of drinking Birkett's ale ! ' "

From Troutbeck the road skirts the base of Wansfell

to Low Wood, and thence to Ambleside. Before arriving at Low Wood, a view is had, of which Professor Wilson writes:—" There is not such another prospect in all England. The lake has much the character of a river, without losing its own. The islands are seen almost lying together in a cluster; below which all is loveliness and beauty; above, all majesty and grandeur. Bold or gentle promontories break all the banks into frequent bays, seldom without a cottage or cottages embowered in trees; and, while the landscape is of a sylvan kind, parts of it are so laden with woods, that you see only here and there a wreath of smoke, but no houses, and could almost believe that you are gazing on the primeval forests."

Ambleside to Kendal, and back by the Long Sleddale, Kentmere, and Troutbeck Valleys.

Kendal, 13m.; Head of Long Sleddale, 23m.; Kentmere, 25m.; Troutbeck, 29m.; Ambleside, 33m.

A pleasant day's excursion may be had by taking the train from Windermere to Kendal, going thence up the Long Sleddale Valley, and returning to Ambleside by crossing over the fells to Kentmere, and from Kentmere to Troutbeck and Windermere. The whole journey is practicable for carriages.

Kendal is the principal market-town in Westmorland, although Appleby is the ancient county-town. It is situated on the river Kent, contains 13,446 inhabitants, and sends one member to Parliament. The principal hotels are the King's Arms, the Commercial, and the Crown. The town is built of mountain limestone, which abounds in fossils, and is obtained in great abundance from the neighbouring fells. This material is quarried out in large blocks, and being susceptible of a high polish, is also extensively used in the manufacture of chimney-pieces. Kendal is of great antiquity, but has now a modern appearance. Formerly it was famous for the manufacture of a coarse woollen cloth called "Kendal Green," mentioned in many of the works

D

of our old writers, and in the old ballad minstrelsy.
This cloth is no longer made, and the principal
articles manufactured are blankets, railway wrappers,
and carpets.

The *Parish Church* deserves a visit. It is an ancient
Gothic structure with five aisles, and contains curious
monuments and epitaphs. At the E. end are three private chapels, which belonged to the neighbouring families
of the Stricklands, the Bellinghams, and the Parrs.

The *Natural History Society's Museum* is also worthy
of notice. It contains a collection of antiquities, of
natural history, and of fossils from the neighbouring
limestone. No charge is made for admittance, but an
order must be obtained from a member of the Society.

Kendal Castle, the seat of the ancient Barons of
Kendal, and the birthplace of Catharine Parr, the last
Queen of Henry VIII., is now a ruin comprising only
four broken towers, and part of the outer wall. It
stands on a grassy knoll on the E. side of the town, and
commands a pleasing and extensive prospect.

Watercrook, 1m. from Kendal, where some relics have
been found, is supposed to have been a Roman station.

Upon a large artificial mound opposite the Castle, on
the W. side of the town, is an obelisk in commemoration
of the revolution of 1688. The mound is believed to be
of Saxon origin, and to have been one of those hills upon
which justice was administered.

About 1½m. S.W. of the town is an escarpment of
limestone rock which contains numerous fossils, and
commands a striking view of the southern part of the
Lake District.

On leaving Kendal for the *Long Sleddale Valley*, the
turnpike-road which leads to Penrith and Carlisle must
be followed for 4½m. This ground is not very interesting until the river Sprint is seen below on the left,
flowing from Long Sleddale, the deep, narrow valley
into which the tourist passes by a branch road descending the hill. At the bobbin-mill a small bridge spans
the stream; but the traveller, instead of crossing it,

must follow the road up the valley, having the beck on his left hand. When the writer first entered this vale, he was surprised on being informed by a resident that it did not contain a single public-house, shop, or trades-man. It is free from the intrusion of art, but lacks the wild grandeur of some of the other valleys. A few cottages embowered by trees lie scattered over the vale. The stream flows through meadows in a smooth, un-interesting course, and on the sides of the low heath-covered hills are here and there patches of rock and wood. At the head of the dale Goat Scar is very pro-minent, exhibiting a bleakness which forcibly contrasts with the tamer scenery through which the tourist is travelling. The church is passed, and the highest houses at Sadgill Bridge, 10m. from Kendal, are reached. At Little London, ½m. below Sadgill, the geologist will be interested by following the right-hand streamlet for a few hundred yards to a lime kiln. Here is exposed a thin bed of limestone, which can be traced all the way across the fells to the W. of Coniston.

Those who have time, and desire an interesting walk through a wildly-picturesque district, ought to add 6m. to the day's excursion, and ascend the Gatescarth Pass (1950) at the head of the glen. The track can be seen from Sadgill. It is a rough cart-road which passes between Harter Fell and Branstree, and descends to Mardale Green and Haweswater. When a short distance down the pass on the Mardale side, Small Water Tarn and the Nan Bield Pass (2100) may be reached by cross-ing to the W., directly under the rocky front of Harter Fell. A most interesting walk leads down from the Nan Bield Pass, by the side of the Reservoir, to the Kentmere village. The scenery at the head of Kent-mere is wild and striking. If this delightful mountain walk be considered too fatiguing, the tourist may cross from Sadgill to Kentmere village by following a rough cart-road, which leads over the heath-covered hill sepa-rating the Long Sleddale and Kentmere vales. When ascending from Long Sleddale the stratum of limestone is observed in the gill on the left. During the descent into *Kentmere*, fine views are had of the Ill Bell and High Street ranges of hills, which stand at the head of the valley. The Low Bridge Inn is reached without difficulty. It stands close to the river Kent, and within a few yards of the church. From the inn a road leads down the valley to Staveley, along a flat, uninteresting tract of country. The lower part of Kentmere being very tame, offers quite a contrast to the noble and picturesque scenery at its upper end.

On leaving the inn and passing the church, the tourist, before proceeding farther, ought to stroll to Kentmere Hall, which stands a few hundred yards to the left, the birthplace of Bernard Gilpin, one of the Reformers, who was known as "The Apostle of the North." Close to the hall is an ancient ivy-covered tower. It is a picturesque object, and can be ascended by winding stone steps. From the church a cart-road leads under some fine crags, ascends the hill, passes a few limestone rocks, and crosses the flat moorland tract to the Troutbeck Vale. Mountains to the W. gradually appear, and then the Troutbeck village is seen seated on the side of Wansfell Pike. The valley is crossed, and Ambleside entered by Low Wood.

Drive round Windermere Lake.

Wray Castle, 3m.; Ferry Hotel, 7m.; Newby Bridge, 14m.; Beech Hill, 18½m.; Bowness, 22m.; Ambleside, 28m.

A good carriage-road runs round Windermere Lake, which, in some places, skirts the shore, and never considerably diverges from it.

The southern half of the lake, between the Ferry and Newby Bridge, is not very interesting, and therefore most tourists will cross at the Ferry, and thus shorten the journey to 14m.

Leave Ambleside by the Clappersgate road. After crossing the bridge which spans the Rothay, the pleasant little village of Clappersgate is reached. Here turn to the left and cross the Brathay Bridge. The road now passes through a well-timbered district, at the head of Pull Wyke Bay, and then branches at the point where a guide-post directs to Coniston and to Hawkshead. Take the Hawkshead road, to the left. Glimpses are caught at different points of the Langdale Pikes and Coniston Mountains. A few hundred yards farther the road again branches; the one to the right leading to Hawkshead. The left-hand road, which must be followed, leads to Wray Castle. Near to the Castle, on the opposite side of the road, is seen *Blelham Tarn*. It contains trout, but is not a very picturesque sheet of water. Here the Coniston and Wetherlam heights are conspicuous, and looking in the opposite direction the Rydal, Scandale and Stockdale vales are spread out to view. The road now slightly ascends, and at the little church connected with Wray Castle, it is well to leave the main road and pass through a gate on the left into a car-road which leads to the shore of the lake. It is a private way, but the public are allowed the use of it. When the lake is reached, Low Wood Hotel is directly opposite, and presently, on looking up the lake, a good view is had of Wray Castle and of Ambleside, at the foot of the Fairfield range. The road keeps at the very edge of the lake, and on passing through a gate, Bowness comes in sight in front; and on the left, at the foot of Orrest Head, Windermere village, Rigg's Hotel, and Elleray. It is a charming drive all the way from Wray Castle to the Ferry, the road being close to the water, and at the base of a thickly-wooded hill. On reaching the point opposite Belle Isle, and a lot of smaller islands, which break the lake into a number of pretty bays, a retrospective view includes Troutbeck Vale, with the small hill called the Tongue, in the centre of the vale, and Ill Bell on the right of it. Presently the Ferry promontory is reached, where stands the Ferry Hotel, a snug place to loiter a while. It commands fine views up and down the lake. A pleasure-house, called the Station, accessible by a short and agreeable walk from the inn, commands

a view of nearly the entire surface of the lake, and
has windows coloured with stained glass, to show the
appearance of the landscape at the several seasons of the
year. . The steam ferry-boat conveys passengers, horses,
and carriages to the opposite promontory, called the
Nab, ½m. from Bowness. The charges are :—For foot
passengers, 2d.; for horse and two-wheeled carriage, 1s.;
for horse and four-wheeled carriage, 2s.; for two horses
and four-wheeled carriage, 3s.

On leaving the Ferry, the main road leads to Esthwaite Water and Hawkshead. Another road, which
must be followed, branches to the left and takes through
a wood by the side of the lake.

Storrs Hall is seen opposite. The Sawrey Beck is
crossed, and shortly afterwards the Cunsey Beck which
flows from Esthwaite Water. The road then traverses
a copse-wood tract, occasionally near, and at other times
some distance from, the lake, but without passing anything of particular interest. The hills are comparatively
dwarfed. At the foot of the lake stand the Lake Side
Railway Station and Hotel, and 1m. farther down is the
village of Newby Bridge, which contains a large, comfortable hotel, the Swan. The bridge spans the river
Leven. This sylvan retreat has been less frequented
since the construction of the railway, the station being
1m. distant. A Waltonian could hardly desire a better
resting-place. It is surrounded by low, wooded hills,
with which the scenery on the river banks happily
harmonizes. A tower on the Finsthwaite Height, close
by, is worth a visit. It commands a good view. The
key is kept at the hotel. A coach leaves every afternoon
during the summer for Grange, 7m. distant. Carriages
can be hired at either the Lake Side Hotel, or at Newby
Bridge.

After crossing the bridge, the tourist must follow the
road, and avoid all turns to the right. Presently the
mountains at the head of the Troutbeck, Scandale, and
Rydal glens, appear in perspective. The road for 2 or 3m.
continues an up-and-down course a little above the shore

of the lake, through copse and brushwood, at the base of Gummer's How, and the Cartmell Fells; allowing of occasional glimpses at the lake, the Coniston range, and 'the mountains standing near the head of the lake. When the little roadside inn, at the foot of Beech Hill, is reached, the Langdale Pikes and Bow Fell appear.

During the whole journey the Furness Fells on the opposite side present a pleasant foreground to the jagged mountains in the distance. After passing Storrs Hall, and arriving opposite the Ferry, a view is had up to the head of the lake, with the wooded islands in the foreground, and in the distance the heights of the Rydal and Troutbeck vales. Just before reaching Bowness, a good prospect may be obtained by mounting Brant Fell, a small height on the right. When descending to the town, Cloudsdale's Crown Hotel is passed. Strangers are permitted to enter the grounds in front of the house, and they ought, on no account, to omit taking advantage of this privilege. The views from the terrace, and from the large comfortable coffee-room, are very pleasing. For some distance after leaving Bowness the road is shaded by trees, and is separated from the lake by a breadth of one or two green fields. After passing Millerground Bay, where a foot-path from Windermere Station touches the lake, the road makes a steep ascent to the top of the Miller Brow. Here a splendid view is gained of nearly the whole of the lake, with the mountains from Coniston Old Man to Fairfield, the Langdale Pikes being especially well defined. A few yards farther stands The Priory, the residence of W. Carr, Esq., a modern elegant mansion; and then Cook's House, a well-known place, where four roads meet, *viz.* from Bowness, Ambleside, Windermere Station, and the Troutbeck Vale. An old-fashioned farm-house, called Cook's House, which occupied this site, has recently been pulled down. The road now runs at some distance from the lake, and Scawfell Pike, Great End, and Great Gable appear.

At Troutbeck Bridge, a village situated on the stream

which flows from the vale of that name, is the Sun Hotel, a comfortable roadside house. Calgarth Hall, the residence of the late Dr. Watson, Bishop of Llandaff; and Ecclerigg, the residence of R. L. Watson, Esq., the grandson of the Bishop, are passed on the left, and the lake is again met at the Low Wood Hotel. Here good views are had of the distant hills, and Wray Castle is a prominent and pleasing object on the opposite shore.

A few yards beyond Low Wood is Dove's Nest, perched under Wansfell. It was for a few months the home of the poet, Mrs. Hemans, and in writing to a friend, she says, " I am so delighted with the spot that I scarcely know how I shall leave it. The situation is one of deepest retirement; but the bright lake before me, with all its fairy barks and sails glancing like ' things of life' over its blue water, prevents the solitude from being overshadowed by anything like sadness." A pleasant walk of 2m. farther leads past Waterhead to Ambleside.

Excursion to the Rusland and Grisedale Vales, and to Hawkshead and Esthwaite Water.

Rusland, 4½m.; Force Mills, 6m.; Satterthwaite, 7m.; Grisedale, 8m.; Hawkshead, 11m.; The Ferry, 16m.

An agreeable day's outing may be had by sailing down the lake to Newby Bridge, and going thence up the Rusland and Grisedale vales to Hawkshead and Esthwaite Water. The ground is richly wooded, and the scenery calm and peaceful.

From the Swan Inn, at Newby Bridge, enter the road having the river on the left, and cross the railway. About 1m. from the village, a road turns to the right for Finsthwaite, and another road leads to the left. Keep straight forward for another ½m. until an arm of the sea, the Greenodd Sands, and the monument at Ulverston are visible. Here branch to the right. The road now runs high up along the side of a hill, with the beautiful vale of Rusland on the left, and in the distance the Coniston and Wetherlam mountains. The hills close at hand are not very high, but they are charmingly diversified with rock, copse-wood, and a variety of trees, principally Scotch firs and yews. The breast of Yew-barrow, which is skirted by the road, is perhaps more beautiful than anything of the kind in the Lake District.

A remarkably fine row of about 100 large beech trees is passed, and then a descent is made into the vale of Rusland. The road crosses the valley to Rusland Hall. When at the Hall, take the left-hand road. On crossing the beck and passing the church, the road ascends a low moorland fell, and commands a view of rocky undu-lating hills covered with copse-wood and larches. A descent is quickly made to a charming hamlet called Force Mills, which contains some bobbin-works. The tourist will be attracted by a waterfall, which tumbles over a series of wide picturesque ledges of rock, half hid by the surrounding foliage. There is not a large body of water, except after heavy rains.

The traveller has now the choice of routes. Hawks-head can be reached in two ways, either by the Grise-dale Vale or the Dale Park Glen. Both are beautiful. The former is the nearer way, but the latter allows of the south shore of the Esthwaite Water being traversed.

To reach Grisedale, Satterthwaite has to be passed through. It is a cheerful-looking village, containing a church, and situated in a peaceful vale, surrounded by low, well-wooded hills.

Grisedale is 1m. distant, and is equally charming. A steep path leads to the top of Hawkshead Moor, and then a capital view is had of many high mountains to the N. and W. On descending a few yards Esthwaite Lake appears immediately below, and presently *Hawks-head* is reached, a quaint and picturesque little market-town, with an excellent inn, the Red Lion. The Church is a prominent object, on an eminence which commands a pleasing view of the lake and vale. Here is a Free Grammar School, founded in 1585 by Edwin Sandys, Archbishop of York. Some years ago this was a far-famed school, and at one time contained 120 pupils. The poet Wordsworth, and his brother Dr. Wordsworth,

were educated here.   Till the end of his life the poet
cherished fond recollections of Hawkshead and the
scenes around it.

Esthwaite Water is 2m. long, ½m. broad, 217 ft. above
the sea level; and its greatest depth is 80 ft.   A carriage-
road goes round it.   The scenery is purely pastoral;
green fields, plantations, and farm-houses give to the
valley a pleasant, cheerful aspect.   Lofty distant mountains peer from other vales into this, and, by reminding
the resident of sternness and sterility, help to impress
a feeling of happy contentedness.

A pool near the N. end of the lake is said to have contained a floating islet, upon which grew a few trees.   The
islet, which only moved about before a strong breeze,
has of late become attached to the shore.   An old in-
habitant informed the writer that he remembers it
getting fixed to the side many years ago, and how he
assisted setting it afloat again, by tying ropes to the
trees and pulling it from the shore.   Esthwaite Water
is the scene of Wordsworth's fine description in the
'Prelude' of skating by moonlight.   .

Tourists who are fond of fishing and quiet rural
seclusion, ought to take up their abode here for some
little time.   For such persons Hawkshead is very suitable.
At the inn may be had comfortable lodgings and good
food at a reasonable rate.   The lake is well stocked with
trout, pike, perch, and eels; and in Watson Tyson, an
old resident, a genuine representative of Isaac Walton
will be found, who knows the neighbourhood well, and
who will be happy to act as cicerone.

The distance from Hawkshead to Ambleside is 5m., to
Coniston 4m., and to the Ferry on Windermere 5m.

The road to the Ferry runs by the side of the lake,
and mount some high ground at Sawrey, where a pleasant
view is obtained of most of Windermere Lake.   A quick
descent leads to the Ferry Hotel, and at Bowness the
steamer may be gained for Ambleside.

Hawkshead is often visited by tourists, who drive from
Bowness to Coniston, a distance of 9m.

Ambleside to Nab Scar (1300), Fairfield (2863), Rydal Head (2698), Dove Crag (2500), and Red Screes (2540).

Rydal, 1½m.; Nab Scar, 3m.; Fairfield, 6m.; Dove.Crag, 7½m.; Red Screes, 10m.; Ambleside, 14m. Time, 7 hours.

This is the best mountain excursion which can be taken by visitors stationed at Ambleside, and it is one of the most enjoyable to be had in the Lake District. Those who think the whole round too laborious, may shorten the journey by descending along the height dividing the Rydal and Scandale glens, or a descent may be made into either of those glens. Those who dare not attempt Fairfield, should endeavour to ascend Nab Scar, from whence a fine view is to be gained. All who are capable of a good mountain climb are, however, strongly recommended to undertake the whole journey, in the order hereafter described. First ascending Nab Scar, and walking along the top of the ridge to Fairfield, then passing over Rydal Head and Dove Crag, the heights at the head of the Rydal and Scandale glens, to the summit of Red Screes, whence a descent may be made into the Kirkstone road, a short distance from Ambleside.

This expedition is pleasantly commenced by following the coach-road to Rydal village. When 1m. from Ambleside, a view is had up Rydal Park to the summit of Fairfield, and the whole ridge is in sight from Nab Scar. After passing Pelter Bridge, take the wide, clean carriage-road on the right, which leads by the Church, Rydal Hall, and Rydal Mount. When 100 yards beyond Rydal Mount bend to the left round a farm-building, and mount the fell between stone walls. The end of Nab Scar is seen directly above. Windermere Lake comes in sight at once, and remains visible during almost the whole journey.

Having passed over some wooden railing and a stone-step stile, the walls end. Here walk some 30 yards to the left until under a rock, and a charming view will be obtained of Rydal Lake, and part of Grasmere Lake,

with the Coniston, Crinkle Crags, and Bow Fell mountains in the distance. A toilsome climb up a steep
grassy slope, with the Rydal Glen in sight on the right,
lands the tourist on the rocky end of Nab Scar, where
he will see the Windermere, Esthwaite, Coniston, Rydal,
and Grasmere lakes; Elterwater Tarn, and portions of
Blelham and Easedale tarns, with arms of the sea. The
lovely village of Grasmere lies immediately below. In
the distance are numerous mountains, with Harrison
Stickle, one of the Langdale Pikes, and Pavey Ark, very
distinct, just to the right and in front of Bow Fell.

A wall has now to be scrambled over, a slight depression crossed, and another climb leads to the top of
Heron Pike (2000). Here the pedestrian will be joined
by any fellow-traveller who may be on horseback.
Owing to the obstruction of stone walls, horses cannot
get to the top of the end of Nab Scar. They have to
continue for ½m. along the road which runs up the
Rydal Glen, until at a gate the walls are passed. Then
an ascent has to be made to the left, where another gate
leads through some wire fencing, and the top of the
ridge is gained, and the horses can reach Fairfield from
thence, and return by the Scandale Fell. From the
point now attained Fairfield is observed at the left-hand
side of the head of Rydal Glen, and the whole way to
the top is in view. A slight descent has to be made, and
then a rise over Great Rigg, and again a drop of a few
feet, before the summit is reached. To the left of Fairfield are observed Seat Sandal, and Dolly Waggon Pike,
which is a part of the Helvellyn range; and to the right,
Rydal Head, Scandale Fell, Red Screes, and Wansfell
Pike. Scawfell Pike, Great End, and Grisedale Pike,
are also seen. During the remainder of this exhilarating
ascent the tourist is favoured with grand and ever-varying prospects. Most of the lakes and mountains already
enumerated are in sight, and other heights appear at
every step. On attaining the top of Great Rigg, the
wild cliffs on the E. side of Helvellyn range present
themselves, with the peaked summit of Catchedecam

peering over the narrow ridge of the famous Striding Edge.

High Street and Ill Bell rise on the right; and on the left, Great Gable, Pillar, High Stile, the mountain cluster surrounding Newlands Vale, and a part of Skiddaw.

On reaching the cairn situated on the broad, flat top of Fairfield, if the atmosphere be clear, the tourist will soon forget the toil of the ascent on beholding the glorious *coup d'œil* spread all around.

Glittering in the sun in the hollows of the low ranges of hills to the S. are Windermere, Esthwaite, Coniston, Blelham, Elterwater, and numerous inlets of the sea. By changing the position a few yards, a part of Grasmere is seen, and nestling amongst the hills to the right, are the Easedale and Codale tarns. The Wetherlam and Coniston group of mountains show to great advantage.

The distant heights are Crinkle Crags, Bow Fell, Scawfell Pikes, Great End, Great Gable, Steeple, Pillar, High Stile, Dale Head, Hindscarth, Maiden Moor, Whiteless Pike, Grasmoor, Whiteside, Grisedale Pike, and Causey Pike; and below are Lingmoor, Pike O'Blisco, Silver Howe, Langdale Pikes, Sergeant Man,. High Raise, Glaramara, Ullscarf, Helm Crag, Steel Fell, and Seat Sandal.

Standing at the cairn overlooking the wild E. side of Fairfield, a view is had down the Deepdale Glen. In the distance are the Yorkshire Hills, and in front the High Street range, the Martindale Fells, Angle Tarn, Place Fell, St. Sunday Crag, Caudale Moor, Gray Crag, Froswick, Ill Bell, Red Screes, and Wansfell Pike.

It is well to walk a few yards to the N. to obtain a grand view of the wild cliffs and coves on the E. side of Helvellyn and Dolly Waggon Pike, with Striding Edge and Catchedecam. In the hollow on the left may be seen Grisedale Tarn, and down the Grisedale Glen, behind St. Sunday Crag, a strip of Ullswater Lake is visible.

Retracing one's steps to the cairns, the return journey

must be commenced with Rydal Glen on the right and
Deepdale Glen on the left.   After passing a rocky part,
a descent is made to a depression called the "Step,"
from whence, on the right hand, a view is had of Rydal,
and the whole of Nab Scar and Fairfield ridge; and on
the left, of the wild, rocky part of Deepdale.   From this,
or the next hollow, a further descent might be made into
Rydal, and sometimes tourists ascend Fairfield by that
route.   Another ascent leads to the rocky, bare top of
what on the Ambleside side is called Rydal Head, and
on the Patterdale side, Greenhow End.   Beautiful views
are had all the way.   The lakes to the S. are fully
displayed, and wild mountains completely encircle the
traveller.   On descending this height a dilapidated stone
wall will be seen, which runs along the heights, and will
act as a good guide for the next part of the journey.
After another gradual rise, the top of Dove Crag is
gained, and by making a *détour* of a few yards to the
left Brothers Water and parts of Ullswater are seen,
and a view is had into the wild glen of Dovedale.
Having quitted the cairn on the summit of Dove Crag,
the wall bends to the right, and runs along the ridge
between the Scandale and Rydal glens.   .

The tourist who is tired, and who does not wish to
ascend the Red Screes (and from this point they look
rather formidable, rising on the farther side of a considerable depression), must follow the wall.   Either side
of it may be taken, but perhaps the better way is to have
it on the right with a view into the Scandale Glen, as on
the Rydal side walls branch from the main wall, and a gate
in one of them is sometimes locked.   Horsemen are pre-
vented by a wall from ascending Red Screes, and therefore at this point they will be obliged to commence the
descent.   Ambleside is seen at the foot of the ridge, and
good views are had all the way.   When half-way down, a
descent may be made into the pleasant glen of Scandale,
and the beck crossed at Sweden Bridge; or the ridge
may be traversed its whole length, and the beck crossed
at the lower bridge, close to the reservoir.

Pedestrians who wish to include a visit to Red Screes must descend to the hollow at the head of Scandale Glen, leave the rocky knob of Low Hart Crag on the left, and then follow the course of a wall, running up the side of the Red Screes, until it joins another wall. During the ascent Brothers Water is seen on the left, and a wild, noble array of heights gradually comes into view on every side.

Having scaled the wall, the tourist will be pleased to learn that the stiffest bit of the mountain has just been overcome, and now an easy, gradual ascent, with an inclination to the left, leads to the summit. Fortunately the prospect from the well-built cairn amply repays for the toil of the ascent.

A wide extent of sea opens to the S. The whole length of Windermere is seen, and most charming it looks, with its cluster of islands in the centre. Coniston and Blelham bear it company, and in the retrospect are Brothers Water and a strip of Ullswater. The Kirkstone Pass is immediately below, with Caudale Moor rising sheer on its opposite side. A fine group of hills are to the E., beginning with Mell Fell, and ending with Wansfell Pike, and including Place Fell, Martindale Fells, High Street, Kidsty Pike, Harter Fell, Froswick, Ill Bell, and in the distance the Yorkshire Hills. To the S.W. Coniston Old Man and Wetherlam Range are as usual very prominent.

Beyond the Wrynose Pass stands Harter Fell, in Eskdale, and to the right of it Crinkle Crags, Bow Fell, Scawfell, Mickledore Chasm, Scawfell Pikes, and Great End; and in front of these Pike O'Blisco, Lingmoor, Silver Howe, Langdale Pikes, Sergeant Man, High Raise, and Nab Scar. In the distance to the W. stand, unmistakably, the Great Gable, Pillar, High Stile, and Grasmoor. To the N. are the wild, craggy sides of Dove Crags, Fairfield, St. Sunday Crag, and the Helvellyn range; and in the distance the summit of Blencathara is seen

During the descent Grasmere and Rydal are visible on

the right, and splendid views are had all the way down.
A stone wall and then a wire fencing has to be crossed.
By inclining to the left the Kirkstone road may be
entered, a short distance from Ambleside.

**Ambleside to Penrith, by the Roman Road along
the top of the Ill Bell and High Street Range.**—
Most visitors look upon this range of mountains with
particular interest, owing to there being on the top
traces of what is supposed to have been a Roman road.
The track, or road, is clearly defined in some places
upon, and in other places near, the top of the mountain
ridge, for a distance of at least 15m. The tourist who
takes the walk above indicated will admit that, however
dubious he may be about the track having been at one
time a good solid Roman road, it has in former ages
been used by persons who have travelled from the
Windermere to the Penrith district, and that as the
ground presents no insuperable obstacle, the idea of the
Roman road is quite feasible.

High Street may be ascended from Ambleside by
going to the top of the Kirkstone Pass, and then
climbing Caudale Moor; and following a wall which
descends to the depression at the head of the Troutbeck
Vale, mounts the Thornthwaite Crag, and thence runs
along the summit level to the top of High Street.

Another way of ascent is from the E. side of the
upper part of the vale of Troutbeck. This point is
reached either by going past Low Wood and the Troutbeck village and church to the highest farm-house,
which is seated at the foot of Troutbeck Tongue; or
by taking the rough cart-road which runs past Stockgill Force, by the side of Wansfell Pike, and then crossing the head of Troutbeck Vale, behind the Tongue.
On arriving at this point, a deeply-scarred ravine will
be seen descending from Ill Bell, and a grass road
observed slanting up the side of Froswick. By following this track the ascent can be made without difficulty.

Those who desire to traverse the whole range in the
direction of the Roman road, may shorten the excur-

sion in many ways hereafter mentioned, should they find the walk to be too laborious.

The journey is best commenced from the church in the vale of Troutbeck. A few hundred yards beyond the church, pass through a gate on the right, and follow a cart-road which crosses the stream, and takes to a farm-house seated at the foot of Applethwaite Common. Then pursue a rough cart-track to another farm-house, ½ m. farther up the valley. When a few yards beyond the latter building, pass through a wall at a gate, and commence a long gradual ascent to the top of the mountain called Yoke. At the head of the vale is seen the Thornthwaite Hause depression, leading over to Thrasthwaite Mouth and Patterdale. On the left of it is Caudale Moor, and on the right Thornthwaite Crag. Between the latter height and Yoke are seen the tops of Froswick and Ill Bell. During the ascent Red Screes and Wansfell Pike are the near heights on the left, and in the distance gradually appear Langdale Pikes, Scawfell Pikes, Bow Fell, Crinkle Crags, Wetherlam, Coniston Old Man, and Black Combe. Windermere is a beautiful object at the foot of the Troutbeck Valley. About two-thirds of the way up, an old slate quarry is passed.

On gaining the top of Yoke (2292) a wide expanse of sea is visible, and to the E. the Yorkshire Hills. In addition to these heights, the Great Gable and the Pillar appear to the right, and beyond the Langdale Pikes. Between Red Screes and Caudale Moor are Dove Crag, Fairfield, Dolly Waggon Pike, Helvellyn, and St. Sunday Crag. The Kentmere Vale is close below on the right hand, with Harter Fell on the opposite side of it; and the Nan Bield Pass depression, Lingmell End, and High Street at its head.

Continuing along the summit ridge, the Kentmere Reservoir appears underneath. The Roman road can be traced on the W. side of Yoke and Ill Bell, a few yards below the summit. A slight depression is passed over, with a fine cove visible on the right, and then a short steep climb lands the traveller on the round

E

conical top of Ill Bell (2476), where are three well-built cairns.

From this point the vale of Troutbeck and the Windermere Lake constitute a remarkably beautiful picture. The small sheet of water is Blelham Tarn. The whole of the above-named mountains are in sight, and in addition Blencathara appears to the N., with its finely-ridged front; and the Cross Fell range in the distance, over the Nan Bield Pass. The Mickledore Chasm, separating Scawfell and Scawfell Pike, is very distinct.

Descending to the hollow between Ill Bell and Froswick, a fine view is gained into the head of Kentmere, and of the wild, rocky side of Ill Bell. On the left is the upper part of Troutbeck. The Roman road is entered for a few yards, and then it can be seen winding to the left, diverging from the top of Froswick (2359). After a gradual ascent the latter height is gained, and the prospect is much the same as from Ill Bell, besides a pretty peep at the upper end of Ullswater Lake, over the Thornthwaite Hause depression. After another slight descent, and then a gradual mount, the top of Thornthwaite Crag is gained. Here, when a wall is reached, it is well for the tourist to incline to the left until he arrive at a large obeliskal cairn. From this point a good view is had of Helvellyn, Fairfield; and the other heights to the W. of Patterdale. If the traveller desires to return to Ambleside, or descend to Patterdale, he may follow the wall down to the hollow of the Thornthwaite Hause; then descend the Thrasthwaite Mouth Glen to Patterdale, or by Troutbeck and round the N. end of Wansfell Pike to Ambleside. By following the wall, an ascent might be made from Thornthwaite Hause to Caudale Moor, and then by descending to the Kirkstone Pass, either Ambleside or Patterdale can be reached.

On leaving the cairn and walking to the E., in the direction of the wall and some wire fencing, another wall is quickly gained, which runs over the summit of High Street (2663).

Should the tourist walk in a S.E. direction from this point, he may descend to Mardale Green and Haweswater by the Nan Bield Pass and Small Water.

From High Street the prospect is extensive and magnificent. To the E. is a wide expanse of plain, bounded by the Cross Fell range, and close to are Branstree and Harter Fell. To the S., Froswick, Ill Bell, and Yoke present their wild eastern sides, and stand prominently and alone. Much of the sea is visible, and Windermere looks most charming. To the W. is a grand array of heights stretching from Black Combe and Coniston Old Man to Blencathara; including Crinkle Crags, Bow Fell, Scawfell, Scawfell Pikes, Great End, Great Gable, Red Screes, Langdale Pikes, Dove Crag, Fairfield, Dolly Waggon Pike, Helvellyn, St. Sunday Crag, Striding and Swirrel Edges, Catchedecam, Great Dodd, and part of Skiddaw. On scaling the wall, and walking a few yards on the W. side of it, Gray Crag and Place Fell appear, and Hayeswater is seen directly below. A few yards on the E. side, Haweswater is visible.

On leaving this height, Windermere Lake, the sea, and some of the heights to the S. disappear. When a slight descent is made, a fine view is had down Riggindale to Mardale Green, with Kidsty Pike close to on its northern side. The Roman road is here distinctly traced on the W. side of the wall. At the lowest point in the depression, there is a gate in the wall where a steep descent on the E. side leads down Riggindale to Mardale Green and Haweswater; and on the W. another descent, not so steep, leads to Hayeswater and Patterdale. If the direction of the wall be followed for a few yards farther, a descent might be made by the pony track to either Patterdale or Haweswater.

Continuing on the summit level, the wall disappears, a slight ascent is made, and presently pleasing views are had of the Martindale Fells and Glens, and of parts of Ullswater Lake. The Rampsgill Glen is close below, on the left. The traveller will, in all probability, catch a sight of some of the wild red deer which frequent

these hills. During the whole walk there is a multitudinous array of heights on the left; Helvellyn and
Fairfield being especially wild, and Blencathara very
characteristic. Skiddaw is to the left of the latter
mountain, but on this side it does not show to advantage. When a height, crowned with a cairn, is crossed,
a shoulder is seen to branch to the right. Down the
hollow on the left of it, the Measand Beck flows to
Haweswater. Another wall is now reached, which runs
along the summit ridge. In order to avoid boggy
ground, it is well to pass through a gate and have the
wall on the right. The wall continues on the top for
more than 1m., and then winds and descends to the left.
By following its course the tourist may drop into Fusedale Glen, and reach the pleasant little hamlet of How
Town, which contains a good inn, and rests at the
bottom of the glen close to Ullswater.

Tourists from How Town to Haweswater generally
cross over here, and descend into the hollow, through
which flows the Measand Beck.

Those who keep on the top must aim for a small stone
building, visible about 1m. in front. It is reached after
a heavy walk over ground which in places is wet and
boggy. Here are traces of the Roman road. The
mountains which have been in sight behind and on the
left all the way, now gradually disappear, and a wide
expanse of level cultivated country is spread in front.
The houses at Penrith are pretty objects on the side of
the Beacon Hill. A gradual descent must be made at
the back of Swarth Fell, over a heath-covered tract,
aiming in the direction of Penrith, until Pooley Bridge
is seen on the left, at the foot of Ullswater Lake.

From this point, by inclining to the right, the road
from Lowther Castle to Penrith may be entered. To
reach Pooley Bridge, descend to the left by the side of
a wall, and a pleasant little ravine, until a farm-house is
reached. The road is entered ½m. from Pooley Bridge
and 5m. from Penrith.

Ambleside to Wastwater, by Carriage, over Wrynose and Hardknott.

Fell Foot, 7m.; Cockley Beck Bridge, 11m.; Boot, 16m.; Strands, 24m.; Wastdale Head, 30m.

Tourists who take this drive, generally proceed from Wastwater to Calder Bridge, and thence to Keswick, and make a three days' circular tour.

The road from Ambleside to Fell Foot is given in the excursion to Dungeon Gill. See page 18.

When the tourist reaches farm-house at Fell Foot, which is encircled by yew trees, let him follow the road leading close past the front of it, being careful not to continue on the road which leads by the side of Lingmoor to Blea Tarn. Over Wrynose and Hardknott the old Pack-horse track from Kendal to Whitehaven formerly ran, and the house at Fell Foot was then an inn. It is said that when the cavalcade on returning was seen descending the pass, the bread was kneaded and put into the oven and made ready by the time the men and horses reached the house. The story will hint to strangers that the ascent is long and toilsome. The road winds round the end of Blake Crag. On the left is a deep hollow, with a rill trickling from it, on the opposite side of which is Rough Crag, almost completely hiding Wetherlam. At the top of the pass (1270) is a small heap of stones, called the "Three Shire Stones," which marks the spot where Cumberland, Westmorland, and Lancashire meet. Some one, apparently a Lancastrian, has erected an upright slab, and has had "Lancashire" cut into it on one side, and on the other the initials W. F., and date 1816. The road, in descending, runs down a long uninteresting waste, by the side of a brawling beck. The path over the Hardknott is seen in front, zigzagging near to a deep, dark gully, and to the left of it stands Harter Fell. At Cockley Beck Bridge is a farm-house, where the stranger may obtain comfortable lodgings. Here the summit of Scawfell Pike is seen.

During the ascent of Hardknott (1291) the upper part
of the Duddon Valley is in sight; and, when the summit
is gained, a prospect is had of the rich green valley of
Eskdale, and its finely-grouped hills, with the sea in the
distance. When half-way down the pass, at the point
where a slight elevation hides the valley, it is well to
walk to the right for a hundred yards. Here are the
remains of what is supposed to have been a Roman fortress, now called by the country people "Hardknott
Castle,"

" . . . . . that lone camp on Hardknott's height,
    Whose guardians bent the knee to Jove and Mars."

All that remains is an enclosure of about 300 feet square,
surrounded by loose stones, with heaps of stones in the
centre, and apparently at the corners the remains of
towers.

When below the castle, pedestrians ought to make a
détour and follow the course of the river up the valley
for about 1½m., until a bridge is reached, which spans
the brook at the point where it branches into two
streamlets, one flowing from Bow Fell, and the other
from the Scawfell range. Here are the Esk Falls.
Both rivulets are worth exploring, but especially that
on the left hand. A short distance beyond the bridge a
capital view is had from a round grass-covered hill, close
to the left-hand stream. There is, perhaps, no place in
the district where the mountains look more wild. Scawfell, Scawfell Pikes, Hanging Knott, Bow Fell, and
Crinkle Crags make a grand display. On returning to
the road, the opposite bank of the river may be traversed.
After descending Hardknott, Bow Fell is seen on the
right. 1½m. down the valley is the Wool Pack Inn, a
snug little baiting-place, and 1m. farther is the hamlet
of Boot, which contains a small clean inn, the Masons'
Arms. It will be observed that the rocks around are
composed of granite, and that close to Boot is an iron-ore
mine. The ore is obtained from an irregular vein in
the granite. A short distance beyond Boot, at a school-

house, a road branches to the left, which crosses the river and valley, and leads to Dalegarth Hall and Stanley Gill Fall. When on the bridge, a notice will be seen on a gate to the right, directing visitors to a cottage where a guide and the key can be had for the waterfall. No charge is made, but it is usual to give the guide 1s. The Hall, a dilapidated building, now used as a farm-house, and the surrounding grounds, belong to Mr. Stanley, of Ponsonby Hall, near Calder Bridge. The *Stanley Gill Fall* is generally considered to be the most beautiful waterfall in the whole district. The grounds are well laid out, and the view, from one of the summer-houses is exceedingly beautiful. The fall has a leap of about 60 feet. There is not a great body of water, but the narrow wooded ravine is charmingly picturesque. The crags are composed of granite, and covered with larch, pine, and a variety of other trees and shrubs. After visiting the fall and regaining the road, the King of Prussia Inn is passed, 1½m. farther down the valley.

Eskdale is now left and Miterdale entered. Lovely views are had of the Muncaster Fells, the sea and the bay of Ravenglass, where the Esk, Mite, and Irt flow into the sea. The Bower House Inn is passed, and then the river Irt is reached at Santon Bridge. Instead of crossing the bridge, the road to the right must be taken, which leads to Strands, 2m. distant. The mountains round Wastwater gradually come in sight, and present a noble appearance. After crossing the river Irt, the road divides, the right-hand branch leading to the lake, and the other to the hamlet of Strands, where are two humble but clean inns, the Strands Inn and the Strands Hotel. The lake is 1m. distant. Strands is pleasantly situated, and from the green are seen the mountains Buckbarrow, Middle Fell, Yewbarrow, Great Gable, Lingmell, Scawfell, and the Screes.

Leaving the Strands, the woods are entered which surround Wastdale Hall, the residence of John Musgrave, Esq.

Hawl Gill, a red-coloured ravine, is observed on the

side of the Screes. It is a remarkably fine ravine, enclosed by rocky sides of granite, and ought to be explored by those who remain a night at Strands.

When passing the Hall, the tourist should ask permission at the lodge to walk about 200 yards in the grounds to a slightly-elevated plot close to the foot of the lake, whence is had a prospect surpassingly grand and beautiful. The lake lies close at the feet of the spectator, and the whole of it is spread to view, with the Screes seen in all their grandeur, and right noble and impressive they look. The mountains at the head of the lake are finely grouped, Great Gable being in front, and flanked on the left by Yewbarrow and Kirk Fell, and on the right by Lingmell. After passing the Hall, the road skirts the shore of the lake along its whole length. The cliffs of the Screes look wild and imposing, rising sheer from the opposite side of the water, and the shingle from the granitic and syenitic rocks gives to the mountain a pleasing variety of colour.

Gradually, as the glen is approached, the grand mountains at its head present an imposing appearance. To see Wastwater, the Screes, and Wastdale Head, properly, the tourist must undoubtedly approach them from the Strands. In no other way can they be properly appreciated.

At Wastdale Head, 1m. beyond the head of the lake, the traveller will reach a small inn, and near it are two or three farm-houses.

Ascent of Scawfell Pike (3210), Great Gable (2949), and Bow Fell (2960), from Ambleside.—Scawfell Pike and Great Gable are best ascended from Keswick, but Bow Fell, which is one of the finest mountains in the district, ought to be visited during the sojourn of the tourist at one or other of the resting-places near Windermere. The ascent is commenced from Langdale (Dungeon Gill), and that is also the point of departure for Scawfell or Great Gable, if it be decided to visit them before going to Keswick.

Windermere to Keswick by Coach.

Ambleside, 5m.—fare, 1s. 6d.; Grasmere, 9m.—fare, 2s. 6d.;
Wythburn, 13m.—fare, 3s. 6d.; Keswick, 21½m.—fare, 5s. 6d.

The above fares do not include the coachman's fee,
and extra charge is made for seats inside the coach.

Two coaches leave Windermere railway station and
Rigg's Hotel every day during the year for Keswick, but
during the tourist season extra coaches are run.

Immediately upon leaving the station Elleray is seen
on the right. The College, and the mansion called the
Abbey, are passed on the left, and shortly afterwards
the hamlet of Troutbeck Bridge. After passing Calgarth
Hall, the residence of the late Dr. Watson, Bishop of
Llandaff, and traversing a well-timbered district, the road
skirts the shore of Windermere Lake, and lofty moun-
tains appear to the W., including Coniston Old Man,
Wetherlam, Crinkle Crags, Bow Fell, and the Langdale
Pikes, the latter being especially prominent and fine.

Wray Castle is a beautiful object on the opposite
shore. A few yards beyond the Low Wood Hotel,
Dove's Nest is seen on the right, in a nook on the side
of Wansfell Pike. It was for a short time the residence
of Mrs. Hemans.

A pleasant view is had down the lake, and at the head
are seen Loughrigg Fell, Nab Scar, and Fairfield. 1m.
from the lake, Ambleside is reached. On leaving
Ambleside the road runs through the charming vale of
Rothay. The Knoll, Miss Martineau's residence, is on
the left, behind a plain building; and Fox Howe, the
residence of Mrs. Arnold, the widow of Dr. Arnold, of
Rugby, is seen at the base of Loughrigg Fell. Rydal
Park is on the right, and in the midst of it stands Rydal
Hall, the seat of General Le Fleming. At the pretty
little village a glimpse is caught of Rydal Mount, where
Wordsworth spent many years of the latter part of his life.

The Rydal Lake is now skirted, with the rocky front
of Nab Scar overhanging on the right, and Loughrigg
Fell on the opposite side. Silver Howe and Sergeant

Man appear in front, and the Crinkle Crags peep over Red Bank. At the ivy-covered cottage by the road close to the lake, Hartley Coleridge resided for many years.

A sharp turn is now made round a wooded knoll, and Grasmere Lake and Vale burst into view, with Fairfield, Seat Sandal, Dunmail Raise Pass, Steel Fell, and Helm Crag in front. The rocks on the summit of the latter mountain present the appearance of a lion and a lamb. The shore of the lake is skirted for a short distance, and the Prince of Wales Hotel reached. From this point a road runs direct to the Swan Inn, leaving the Grasmere village a short distance on the left. The coaches run round by the village to the Red Lion Hotel, and pass close by the church, where are interred the remains of Wordsworth and his family, and of Hartley Coleridge.

Leaving the Swan Inn, the road makes a tedious ascent to the summit of Dunmail Raise Pass, which is 783 feet above the sea.

Here a wall, which descends Steel Fell on the left, crosses the pass, and ascends Seat Sandal on the right, marks the boundary between Cumberland and Westmorland. A heap of stones by the roadside near to the boundary-wall is supposed to have been raised by Edmund, King of England, to commemorate the defeat and death of Dunmail, the last King of Cumbria. A view is now obtained of Thirlmere Lake, with Helvellyn on the right, and part of Skiddaw in the distance. Some promontories on the western side of the lake gradually appear, and look like islands.

Presently the small inn and church at Wythburn are reached.

> " Here, traveller, pause and think, and duly think,
> 　　What happy, holy thoughts may heavenward rise,
> 　Whilst thou and thy good steed together drink,
> ·　　Beneath this little portion of the skies.

> " See ! on one side a humble house of prayer,
> 　　Where Silence dwells, a maid immaculate,
> 　Save when the Sabbath and the priest are there,
> 　　And some few hungry souls for manna wait.

" Humble it is, and meek, and very low,
　And speaks its purpose by a single bell :
　But God Himself, and He alone, can know
　　If spiry temples please Him half so well." *

Leaving the Nag's Head Inn at Wythburn, the eastern shore of the lake is skirted for nearly 2m.

Thirlmere Lake is 3m. long, and scarcely more than ¼m. in breadth. It is 533 feet above the sea, and its greatest depth is 108 feet. It is well stocked with trout, but the public are not allowed boats upon it. About 1m. from the northern end, it contracts to within a few feet, and is crossed by a picturesque foot-bridge close to Armboth House. From the western shore rise beautiful irregular rocks, the principal of which are Raven Crag, and Fisher Crag; and the E. side is flanked by the bulky mass of Helvellyn. The best views of this lake are obtained from the western shore, and from some points it is exceedingly lovely.

After the road takes a slight elevation, and bends from the lake, Blencathara comes in sight, presenting a fine ridgy front at the far end of the vale of St. John. The King's Head Inn, at Thirlspot, in Legberthwaite, is passed, and then a near view is had of the far-famed Castle Rock, the fairy castle of Sir Walter Scott's ' Bridal of Triermain.' For the next 3m. the road runs through the rather uninteresting vale of Naddle, but on gaining the brow of the slightly-elevated ground of Castle Rigg, the most lovely vale of Derwent is spread to view, with Keswick town, and portions of Bassenthwaite and Derwentwater lakes immediately at the feet of the traveller. Skiddaw and Blencathara are fine objects, and the western mountains surrounding Newlands and Buttermere present grand and varied outlines. A steep descent is made to the town, and the coach is driven up in turns to one or other of the hotels, and then it runs to the Keswick Hotel and railway station.

* Hartley Coleridge.

LANGDALE SECTION.

LANGDALE (DUNGEON GILL).

NEAR the fine vale head of Langdale are two large and comfortable hotels, the New Dungeon Gill Hotel and the Old Dungeon Gill Hotel. The latter is the highest up the vale, and the former is close to the Dungeon Gill Fall. This is a pleasant, secluded spot, and at a convenient distance from Ambleside, Grasmere, Coniston, Wastwater, and Borrowdale. It is a good starting-point for many fine mountain excursions. Mackereth, at the lower house, is a second Ritson; and Bennett, at the higher house, is an excellent guide.

Ascent of the Langdale Pikes from Dungeon Gill. —The Langdale Pikes are so conspicuous from Windermere, and are seen from so many other parts of the district, that the first object of every visitor to Langdale, after seeing the Fall, will be to ascend these celebrated peaks.

They are neither so high nor so massive as many other mountains, but probably no other heights in the district are more familiar to the tourist. They consist of Harrison Stickle (2401), and Pike O'Stickle (2323).

Pedestrians may follow the course of the Mill Gill torrent to Stickle Tarn, and then climb up the hollow between Harrison Stickle and Pavey Ark.

Another plan, if on foot, is to climb by a grass-covered track up the slope between Mill Gill and Dungeon Gill. The path gradually bears to the left until near the Dungeon Gill cleft. It then winds round, and in the rear of a crag which has hitherto appeared directly in front. Harrison Stickle is now seen. A grass plateau has to be crossed, with the Mill Gill stream in sight on the right, and Windermere, Elterwater, and Loughrigg behind. The Old Man and Wetherlam are also very

distinct in the distance. Without descending to Stickle Tarn, which is seen below on the right, bear round the cliffs of Harrison Stickle, and scramble up the sloping depression between that height and Pavey Ark. The latter cliffs overhang the tarn, and present a fine appearance when seen from this point. When the steep part is conquered, a gradual inclination to the left will land the tourist on the summit of Harrison Stickle.

The easiest ascent is by the pony-track, which, after leading from the hotel to the Dungeon Gill Fall, ascends with the fall and chasm on the right. A peep at the point where the two stones form the bridge will be interesting. It is said that Wordsworth loved to cross this most dangerous and romantic causeway; but visitors will do well not to follow his example. A good path winds up the hill, and when some distance from the fall, it bends from the stream and overlooks the Old Dungeon Gill Hotel. It then winds to the right, round rocks, and again the gill ravine is seen. On attaining a small plateau, Windermere Lake and Blea Tarn appear. Wetherlam has been in sight all the way up, but now Coniston Old Man rears its head. When the Langdale Valley, with Bow Fell, Crinkle Crags, and Pike O'Blisco appear, an inclination must be made to the right. After rounding a few rocks, a wet plateau is reached, and Harrison Stickle stands boldly in front, separated by a deep ravine from the rocks leading to Pike O'Stickle. A good view is now had of Elterwater, Windermere, and Blea Tarn, with the mountains Fairfield and Ill Bell, and the Yorkshire Hills in the distance. After crossing the wet plateau, a romantic walk may be taken by keeping close to the ravine. The path is very narrow, and there is a steep descent into the gill, which is wild and craggy. The walk is only practicable for good mountaineers. The pony-track passes round the S. side of the rocks which stand on the left of the ravine. On rounding these rocks, Esthwaite Water is seen and strips of the sea. After crossing a little boggy and hillocky ground, at the source of the Dun-

geon Gill stream, a short but steep ascent leads to
the summit of Harrison Stickle. Pike O'Stickle is to
the left, and can easily be visited before ascending
Harrison Stickle. The left-hand cliffs might be scaled,
but the easiest course is to keep close below them.
Pike O'Stickle is unmistakable, being round like a huge
haycock. It will be seen from many parts of the Lake
District subsequently visited, and will be looked upon
as an old friend, so that the little labour of the ascent
ought not to be shirked. The view is good, though not
equal to what it would be if the mountain were a few
feet higher, the near hills hiding. much of the prospect.
To the N. is Skiddaw and a part of Blancathara. Cat
Bell range is visible to Dale Head, beyond which are
Grasmoor, Grisedale Pike, and the top of Causey Pike.
Glaramara runs from Esk Hause all along the W. side
of the hollow in which lies the Longstrath Valley, and
over it are High Crag, Green Gable, and Great Gable,
the latter standing out more boldly and prominently
than its neighbour-heights. Then comes the mass, con-
sisting of Great End, Scawfell Pike, Hanging Knott,
Bow Fell, and Crinkle Crags; with Rossett Gill and the
Stake Pass immediately below. To the S. are Lingmoor,
Pike O'Blisco, Wetherlam, and the Coniston Old Man
range; Blea, Elterwater, and Loughrigg tarns; Windermere, and Esthwaite lakes, and arms of the sea. To the
E. is Harrison Stickle, and beyond are Helvellyn, Dolly
Waggon Pike, St. Sunday Crag, Seat Sandal, Fairfield,
Red Screes, and High Street; and the lower heights of
Silver Howe, Loughrigg, and Wansfell Pike.

A 20 minutes' walk leads from Pike O'Stickle to the
top of Harrison Stickle, and then Stickle Tarn is seen
close below the foot of the fine cliff called Pavey Ark.
The mountains in view from this height are for the most
part the same as those seen from Pike O'Stickle; Black
Combe, Helm Crag, Steel Fell, Nab Scar, and a few
others being also visible.

If a descent be made to Grasmere, keep Pavey Ark at
some distance on the right, and cross a wet, rocky table-

land, called Thunacar Knott, from whence Bassenthwaite Lake is seen. Make in the direction of High Raise and Sergeant Man. The latter has a prominent cairn on a round peak. If it be not intended to go over these heights, descend to a hollow on the right. After crossing the rivulet which flows into Stickle Tarn, pass close by a sheepcot, and proceed along the base of Sergeant Man, without either descending or mounting any more than can be avoided. Thread amongst the hillocks until Stickle Tarn is seen on the right, with Pavey Ark and Harrison Stickle rising from its shore, and in the distance the Coniston Mountains. Now ascend a little on the left, just above a rock which is seen in front with two small and curiously-fixed stones upon it. On crossing a few yards of rough ground, Codale Tarn is observed below, and immediately afterwards Easedale Tarn. Take in the direction of Codale Tarn, cross a rill, go to the tarn, and descend to Easedale Tarn, in the rear of a small knob, keeping the streamlet which descends from Codale Tarn on the right. From this point either shore may be traversed, but it is desirable to keep to the N. in order to avoid wet ground. Grasmere is then reached without difficulty.

Those who wish to visit the summits of High Raise (2500) and Sergeant Man (2414), in the descent from the Langdale Pikes to Grasmere, must, after leaving Thunacar Knott, instead of descending into the hollow on the right, traverse a wet grassy table-land. A long and rather tedious walk leads gradually to the summit of High Raise, from whence there is a fine view of many wild and lofty hills. A walk over a grass-covered plateau, which, after heavy rains, is wet and disagreeable, leads to the rocky peaked summit of Sergeant Man. Immediately below lies Stickle Tarn, and farther distant are seen Rydal, Windermere, and Esthwaite lakes, and Elterwater and Loughrigg tarns.

The deep hollows and heights from Pavey Ark and Harrison Stickle to the Coniston Mountains look wild and beautiful. On the right are Crinkle Crags, Bow

Fell, Scawfell Pikes, Hanging Knott, Great End, Glaramara, and Great Gable. To the N. and E. are Skiddaw, Blancathara, Ullscarf, Helvellyn, St. Sunday Crag, Seat Sandal, Fairfield, Helm Crag, Nab Scar, Silver Howe, Loughrigg, Wansfell Pike, Scandale Fell, and Ill Bell.

The descent is over rough ground. It may be made to Codale Tarn, and thence to Easedale Tarn, or along the rocks on the N. side of the latter sheet of water.

Ascent of Scawfell Pike (3210) from Langdale.— Proceed to the head of the valley; ascend by Rossett Gill, and follow the track past Angle Tarn to the top of Esk Hause. See p. 72.

For the remaining part of the ascent refer to p. 194, where the route is described in detail.

Ascent of Great Gable (2949) from Langdale.— The foot of the mountain must be reached by going up Rossett Gill, and past Angle Tarn, Esk Hause, and Sprinkling Tarn to the top of the Sty Head Pass. The route is described at p. 72. For the ascent from Sty Head Pass, see p. 198.

Ascent of Bow Fell (2960) from Langdale.—Bow Fell is one of the highest and most rugged mountains in the district. On every side it presents perpendicular cliffs, and its bare, peaked summit is composed of wild rocks and huge detached blocks. It may be ascended from Esk Hause, or from Angle Tarn, but the best route is up Oxendale from Langdale. This way presents no difficulty, and a pony may be taken to within a few yards of the summit.

Pass through a gate close to the bridge in front of the Old Dungeon Gill Hotel (the higher hotel), and follow a cart-track by fields to the highest farm-house in the vale. The house stands at the foot of the Band, the hill which separates Oxendale and Mickleden. During the walk Crinkle Crags are visible at the head of Oxendale. Pike O'Blisco is on the left, and on the right the Langdale Pikes. Bow Fell is seen over the Band. The course of the Oxendale Beck may be followed, but the easier plan is to continue round the base of the Band, just above the highest wall.

When a little way up the glen, the stream is seen to separate into three torrents, which descend deep ravines. Down Browney Gill flows the water from Red Tarn, which lies behind Pike O'Blisco. Crinkle Gill is the one directly in front, descending from Crinkle Crags. Hell Gill is to the right, in the rear of the Band, and its course has to be followed. Either side of the streamlet is available, but it is well to keep it on the left hand. A green sloping hill is seen to separate Hell Gill from Crinkle Gill, and it may tempt some strangers to cross the torrent at a small wooden foot-bridge, and ascend the green slope, which they will discover to be deceptive, and require harder work than they expected. The better plan is to keep on the side of the Band, and reach Hell Gill after passing over the top of a water-worn combe. Below the ravine is the Hell Gill Fall, a fine mountain cascade which has a descent of not less than 150 feet. The ravine is exceedingly wild and romantic. It is a deep, dark dell, with a stream flowing along a rugged bed, and huge cliffs on either side, partly covered with ling, shrubs, and stumpy trees. Right through the gill is visible a part of Bow Fell. The tourist must climb to the summit of the cleft, and then follow the rill until the depression is gained between Bow Fell and Crinkle Crags, where are three pools of water, called the Three Tarns.

From this point Bow Fell appears rugged and precipitous. A good view is had of Scawfell and Scawfell Pikes, with Mickledore Chasm between them. Eskdale lies below, and farther distant are Birker Moor, Black Combe, Devoke Water, and the sea at Ravenglass. The tourist must make his ascent direct from the pools, and after passing some interesting rocks on the right hand, a gradual inclination to the left will lead him to the summit, which is crowned with a large cairn.

The prospect that now opens before him is one of

F

great extent and magnificence. Bow Fell appears to
stand in the centre of a tumultuous array of huge
mountain heights. It has a wild, desolate summit,
covered with bare rocks and large blocks of stone. The
Duddon, Esk, Langdale, and Longstrath valleys appear
to radiate from Bow Fell as from a centre. To the N.
are Skiddaw and Blencathara; to the left of Skiddaw
the Solway Firth, and the cluster of mountains, including Grasmoor, Grisedale Pike, Causey Pike, Maiden
Moor, Dale Head, and Robinson. Immediately at the
feet of the spectator is the Longstrath Glen, with Glaramara on the left of it, and on the right Bull and
Eagle Crags, and the flat top which commences with
High Seat, and includes Ullscarf, High Raise, and Sergeant Man, and ends with the Langdale Pikes, which
stand close to, and present a fine rocky front. A long
range of hills starts near Blencathara, and runs to Windermere, including Helvellyn, St. Sunday Crag, Fairfield, High Street, Ill Bell, Red Screes, and Wansfell
Pike. The green fields of Great Langdale are in sight,
surrounded by Silver Howe, Loughrigg Fell, Lingmoor, and Pike O'Blisco. Windermere Lake, Esthwaite
Water, and Loughrigg Tarn are pleasant objects in an
undulating and cultivated country. Beyond the near
heights of Crinkle Crags are Wetherlam, the Carrs,
Coniston Old Man, Grey Friars, Dow Crag, and Walney
Scar. To the right of these are the Duddon River and
Estuary, Devoke Water, Esk River, and the sea at Ra-
venglass; with the heights Birker Moor, Black Combe,
Harter Fell, and Muncaster Fells. The wildest and
most bulky masses are to the W., and include Scawfell,
Scawfell Pikes, Great End, Hanging Knott, Pillar, Great
Gable, Green Gable, and Brandreth.

A descent may be made on the N.W. side of the
mountain, by Ewer Gap to Angle Tarn, or over Hanging Knott to Esk Hause.

Those who do not adopt either of these routes, or
return by Hell Gill, may have an agreeable walk over
Crinkle Crags. See p. 67.

Ascent of Crinkle Crags (2816), **from Langdale.—**
Crinkle Crags stand at the head of Langdale, and rise
out of the Oxendale Glen. They are fine serrated
heights, and prominent objects from the Ambleside
district. The mode of ascent is the same as that for
Bow Fell until the Three Tarns are reached. Here bend
to the left, climb the Shelter Crags, and thread in an up-
and-down course amongst the bare, rugged rocks. The
views on either hand are extensive, embracing much wild
and beautiful scenery. Looking back, Bow Fell presents
some fine perpendicular cliffs, and the Scawfell range
is most imposing. During the walk on the uneven tops
some hard work may be avoided by keeping a little on
the Eskdale side; but this is not advisable, as the views
into Oxendale and Langdale are very fine. At one point
the tourist will be specially delighted with a peep down
a deep gorge, with a wild mass of hills in the foreground,
and in the distance Wetherlam and Coniston Old Man.
The summit is covered with bare rocks, rendering the
mountain a fit companion for Bow Fell and the Scawfell
Pikes.

Standing at the cairn on the highest point, the spectator will see at his feet the Esk, Duddon, and Langdale
vales; the stream in the latter meandering beautifully
through green fields to Windermere Lake, which catches
the eye in two places. Esthwaite Water, Rydal Lake,
and Devoke Water are in sight, also a large extent of the
sea. To the S. are the Coniston Mountains, Birker Moor,
and Black Combe. Turning in an opposite direction,
are Skiddaw and Blencathara; to the E. the Helvellyn,
Fairfield, and High Street ranges, with the Yorkshire
Hills in the distance; whilst nearer is a group of smaller
heights, amongst which the Langdale Pikes are particularly noticeable, presenting a fine bold escarpment of
rock. On the Eskdale side stand the wild masses of
Bow Fell, Hanging Knott, Great End, Scawfell Pike,
and Scawfell.

During the descent the tourist passes over some precipitous crags on the S. end of the mountain, and catches

F 2

glimpses from time to time of fine romantic scenery.
From the last rock the Langdale Valley reveals a perfect
picture of beauty, every tree and house appearing to be
placed for the purpose of beautifying the vale and har-
monizing with the surrounding scenery.   The stream
takes a serpentine course through green fields and red-
coloured arable land, and the valley makes a beautiful
curve round Lingmoor and Silver Howe.   After leaving
the last rocky height and arriving at a flat tract, where
there are some pools of water, incline to the left, and
descend into Oxendale by the side of an interesting
ravine.

Ascent of Pike O'Blisco (2304), from Langdale.—
This hill may be ascended from Wall End farm-house by
following the Kettle Gill streamlet, or from Oxendale by
Browney Gill and Red Tarn.   Perhaps the better plan
is to ascend by the latter route and return by the
former.   When Red Tarn is reached, it proves to be a
poor representative of its namesake under Helvellyn.
From its shore Pike O'Blisco presents a rather formidable appearance.   It is covered with ledges of rock and
loose stones, which are partly clothed with heather.

When on the top the spectator has spread at his feet the
beautiful Langdale Valley and the more distant vale of
Rothay.   Windermere and the cultivated country surrounding it present a charming appearance.   From this
point Esthwaite Water is also a pretty object; and Rydal
Lake and Stickle Tarns are in view.   Beyond the level
country rise the Yorkshire Hills.   The Langdale Pikes
appear to be within a stone's-throw, and Skiddaw assumes
its best appearance, all its southern recesses and offshoots
being displayed.   The ranges of Helvellyn, Fairfield,
High Street, and Ill Bell are prominent; in front of
which are Steel Fell, Silver Howe, Loughrigg, Lingmoor,
and Oxenfell.   To the N.W. are Glaramara, Grasmoor,
a part of Scawfell Pike, Bow Fell, and Crinkle Crags,
the latter looking remarkably wild.   To the S. are Black
Combe, Birker Moor, and the Coniston range, with strips
of the sea.

In descending, the tourist will have to pick his way for some distance amongst bare ledges of rock, and then a smooth slope is reached, with a streamlet, which leads to the Wall End farm in Langdale.

Crinkle Gill.—Crinkle Gill, in Oxendale, at the head of Langdale, is wild and picturesque; and is perhaps unequalled in its way, unless it be by Piers Gill in Wastdale. To do justice to its hidden grandeur the visitor ought to clamber up its rugged bed to the very head of the chasm, from whence exit may be made without difficulty. It is soon reached after passing the highest house in the valley.

On entering the Oxendale Glen, cross the stream, keeping it on the right while ascending for a short distance, and then drop into the gill.

The pedestrian walks up a rough stony bed, down which falls a streamlet, in places forming pretty cascades, but there is never more water than may be easily passed over. Upon entering the fissure he finds himself in a secluded recess, with wild cliffs towering on every hand, one above another, in picturesque confusion, to the summit of the Crinkle Crags, which are 2816 feet high.

Gradually, as he wends his way up this wild gill, the rocks increase in grandeur, and near the top the scene is magnificent in the extreme.

On the return journey either Hell Gill or Browney Gill may be visited. The former lies to the right, and the latter to the left of Crinkle Gill.

Langdale (Dungeon Gill) to Coniston, by Blea Tarn and Tilberthwaite Glen, 8m.—Follow the road which crosses the valley opposite the higher hotel (the Old Dungeon Gill Hotel). It passes the Wall End farm-house, mounts in a winding course round the end of Lingmoor, and descends into the Little Langdale Glen to Blea Tarn. During the ascent a capital view is had into the Mickleden and Oxendale glens, at the head of Great Langdale, and the Langdale Pikes, Bow Fell, and Crinkle Crags present a noble appearance.

On entering Little Langdale Glen by this side it looks a dark, bleak spot, but after the traveller has passed the solitary house near the tarn the view becomes more pleasing. Wetherlam comes into view, and the Blake Crag on the opposite shore of the tarn, and the Langdale Pikes in the rear, are pleasing objects. A descent is made by the side of Lingmoor to the farmhouse, surrounded by yew trees, at Fell Foot. The path for Coniston may be seen running along the side of the fells in front, just above some slate *débris*. On entering the road which leads from Ambleside past Fell Foot to Eskdale, by the Wrynose and Hardknott passes, bend to the right, and after proceeding a few yards, enter the lane which branches to the left. It crosses the vale and mounts round the end of an offshoot of Wetherlam. Little Langdale Tarn lies close below on the left, looking very meagre. A number of hills come in sight to the E., including Loughrigg Fell, Wansfell Pike, and the ranges of Ill Bell, Red Screes, and Fairfield. After passing some ground covered with rocky hillocks, and strewn with slate *débris*, a descent is made into the lovely little glen of Tilberthwaite.

At a farm-house here the tourist may obtain oatcake and a glass of good milk. After passing successively some cottages, a slate quarry, and a copper mine, the road runs above a pretty brawling stream, and then enters Yewdale, near the famous Yew Tree. Here the rocky hills on every hand are very fine, in part covered with heather, and beautifully coloured. Inclining to the right, the base of the Yewdale Crags is skirted, and Coniston is quickly reached.

Langdale (Dungeon Gill) to Keswick, by the Stake Pass.

Top of Stake Pass, 3m.; Rosthwaite, 8m.; Keswick, 14m.

Leaving either of the Dungeon Gill hotels, the course of the stream must be followed until the head of the valley be reached. On the left are the heights Pike O'Blisco, Crinkle Crags, and Bow Fell; and on the right Pike O'Stickle. A low ridge is seen at the head of the valley, on the left of which is Rossett Gill Pass, and on the right the Stake Pass. The latter is the one which must be taken, and the path is distinctly traced by the side of a streamlet. From the summit (1576) Bow Fell and the surrounding eminences look extremely wild, and in the distance portions of the Coniston Old Man range present themselves. The path continues for about a mile over a piece of desolate ground, covered with hillocks and morass. When the Longstrath Valley appears, the mountain seen on the left of it is Glaramara, and on the right the high ridge, including High Raise and White Stones; and terminating with Bull and Eagle crags. Skiddaw stands in the distance.

During the descent, a streamlet on the right hand, which forms some pretty cascades, must be crossed by a wooden bridge near its junction with the Longstrath Beck. The source of the beck is Angle Tarn, about 2m. distant, at the foot of Bow Fell and Hanging Knott. After passing the bridge a foot-track will be found on the eastern side of the valley. With many this glen is a favourite, owing to its wild and secluded character. It does not contain a single dwelling, and scarcely a tree. After travelling along half its length, and rounding a slightly projecting hill, a perched stone stands very prominent, and the Bull and Eagle crags tower grandly on the right.

The Longstrath Beck must be crossed at another wooden bridge, a short distance past Eagle Crag; and a rough, stony cart-road leads thence to Stonethwaite and Rosthwaite. The road between Borrowdale and Keswick is given at page 143.

Langdale (Dungeon Gill) to Wastdale Head, by Rossett Gill.

Top of Rossett Gill, 4m.;   Top of Esk Hause, 5m.;   Top of Sty Head Pass, 6½m.;   Wastdale Head, 9m.

During this journey the tourist is conducted through some of the wildest scenery in the district.

A pony can go the whole distance. As far as the top of Esk Hause the route is the same as that taken by travellers who ascend Scawfell Pike, or Great Gable, from the Windermere district.

On leaving the New Dungeon Gill Hotel, take the road which leads up the valley. When opposite the old hotel, cross the bridge, and enter a path at the back of the house. This point may be reached from the Waterfall, by following a green lane at the foot of the rocks.

The valley at its upper end becomes divided by the Band into two small glens. Oxendale is on the left, with Crinkle Crags at the head of it, and Mickleden on the right, from which rise the fine cliffs of the lofty mountain Bow Fell. The Langdale Pikes are passed on the right; the Pike O'Stickle presenting a bold escarpment, and looking like a huge petrified haycock. At the head of the glen is a low height which appears to debar the passage. A path by the side of the right-hand rill leads over the Stake Pass to Borrowdale and Keswick.

Rossett Gill, which the tourist has now to scale, is the cleft on the left, close to Bow Fell.

After traversing some soft green turf, a few small heaps of moraine matter are reached, which have evidently been deposited by some of the last glaciers which descended Bow Fell. From a sheepcot at the head of the glen, incline to the left, and follow the direction of the streamlet.

No mistake can be made, if it be noted that the Stake Pass is by the second rill from Pike O'Stickle, and Rossett Gill is on the left, by a wider watercourse than the others. When the point is reached where the steepest part of the ascent commences, Bow Fell is directly over-head on the left, presenting a sternly grand appearance.

Pedestrians may keep close to the ravine, having it on the right until three-fourths of the way up; then scale the rest by the course of the rocky bed of the stream, which is usually nearly dry. Ponies have to take a more circuitous course along the breast of Bow Fell. The path is ill-defined, and equestrians taking this route will require a guide.

Rossett Gill Pass is the steepest in the Lake District, and a little hard work has to be done by the climber. It is 2002 feet high. When the top is gained, Great End appears peeping over Esk Hause. The long ridge stretching away to the right is Glaramara. Blenca-thara is visible in the distance. Nearer, are some fine rocks on the sides of Bow Fell and Hanging Knott; below which, at the feet of the spectator, is Angle Tarn, calm and lovely in its solitude. It contains perch. It is one of the most attractive of the many charming mirrors which lie in these mountain fastnesses, reflect-ing in their bright, calm surface the noble heights around them. A true lover of nature who wanders about in this beautiful district will gradually become inspired by a kind of affection for these mountain tarns; and if he be a follower of Isaac Walton, many quiet and happy days may he spend on their shores under the shadow of the overhanging rocks.

After crossing the stream, just where it issues from the tarn, the path alternately mounts and descends an uneven ground for another mile to the top of Esk Hause. The track in places is difficult to trace; but the tourist cannot go wrong if he bear in mind that below, on the right, is the Longstrath Glen, and on the left the cliffs of Hanging Knott.

Allen Crags, the beginning of the Glaramara range, is to the right of Esk Hause, and Great End is seen rising above the pass. On gaining the summit of the Hause (2490), several fine heights appear upon the W. Great Gable is a prominent object directly in front, separated

from Green Gable by a deep, wide scar; and on the left
of it are Kirk Fell and the Pillar.   Grasmoor, and the
mountains surrounding the Newlands Vale, stand at a
greater distance to the right.   On looking back, Windermere is seen, and the Langdale Pikes will, as usual,
attract the eye (see page 194).

A descent is made, by the side of a red-coloured ravine,
to the front of Great End, which is one of the largest
and noblest of the vertical cliffs to be met with in the
district.   Skiddaw, Blencathara, and Derwentwater presently appear to the right, looking very beautiful (see
page 193).

When the ravine turns to the right, the path leaves it,
and presently passes by Sprinkling Tarn.   The streamlet
is crossed just where it quits the tarn, and as it flows to
Sty Head Tarn, the course is obvious.   When a little
way down, cross the brook again, and then keep it on
the right, gradually leaving it when near to the Sty
Head Pass (1600).

Sty Head Tarn is seen below, and without touching its
shore the track leads to the left, and enters the path
which runs from Keswick and Borrowdale to Wastdale
Head.   The wild bulky masses of Lingmell, Scawfell
Pikes, and Great End present an impressive appearance.
The houses and green fields of the secluded little glen of
Wastdale appear below at the foot of Yewbarrow, and a
glimpse of the sea is caught in the distance.   The descent is steep, and by a stony path (see page 161).

**Langdale (Dungeon Gill) to Grasmere, by Stickle,
Codale, and Easedale Tarns, 6m.**—Cross the brook,
after going through the first gate behind the. hotel.
The direction of the Mill Gill Fall and stream must be
followed to Stickle Tarn.   Tourists who visit the
Dungeon Gill Fall, and then commence the ascent to
the tarn, may round the shoulder which divides the
Dungeon Gill and the Mill Gill streams, and thus reach
the latter.   Cascades tumbling over picturesque ledges
of rock will be observed during the ascent.   The heights
on either side are wild, and in front rises Harrison

Stickle. A retrospective view includes Great Langdale Valley, with Windermere in the distance.

On nearing the tarn, the grand cliff of Pavey Ark comes sharply into view. There are few finer effects than this sudden appearance. Pavey Ark will compete for pre-eminence with the most noted vertical cliffs in the district. It rises a sheer precipice from the beautiful and secluded Stickle Tarn. This tarn is famous for its trout. Either shore may be skirted to the point where the water enters the lakelet. Here is seen, on the left, the peaked summit of Sergeant Man, and on the right a grassy plot, in a degree free of rocks, whilst between the two the ground is covered with rocks and hillocks. Mount the latter, and presently Codale and Easedale tarns, and the Grasmere Vale, will be seen below, and in the distance the Helvellyn and Fairfield ranges.

Aim for Codale Tarn, and follow the rill which issues from it and flows into Easedale Tarn. Either shore of the latter may be traversed. From the hut a path leads by Sour Milk Gill Force to Easedale and Grasmere.

Langdale (Dungeon Gill) to Grasmere, by Blindtarn Moss.

With pony, or on foot. Distance, 4½m.

If the rivulet in the rear of the hotel be crossed, a way will be found along the fell side, behind the highest wall, until the track crossing the hill is reached. To avoid all chance of error, it is advisable to take the main road down the valley for ½m., and when opposite the third farm-house, cross to it by a cart-track which passes through a field.

This point may also be reached by taking the road in front of the hotel, and at the bridge which crosses the Mill Gill stream, entering the cart-road on the left. Then pass through a gate on the right, and after threading through one or two fields along a cart-track, a road will lead to the third house.

In the rear of the house a lane leads a short distance up the hill. When the lane terminates, two enclosures must be crossed, and the walls passed through at openings.

The track is now gained which goes over the hill, and has been visible all the way from the hotel. It runs along the first grassy part from Dungeon Gill. The ascent is short, and rather steep. When the top is reached, the Coniston and other high mountains disappear, and Helvellyn, Seat Sandal, and Fairfield, come into view. About 200 yards of level ground have to be crossed before the descent begins. Helm Crag and the Easedale and Grasmere vales are seen below. A rill, descending into the hollow called Blindtarn Moss, must be kept on the left for a short distance; then bear to the right and make for the point where the water descends into Easedale. Yew Crag is on the left, and under it the ground is very wet and boggy. The water during its fall to Easedale Valley makes one or two cascades, and its course must be followed until a cottage is reached. The path is then attained which leads by the side of Easedale Beck to the Grasmere road.

Langdale (Dungeon Gill) to Grasmere, by Meg's Gill and the Rifle Targets.

Time, 1¼ hour.   Distance, 4½m.

Follow the road in front of the hotel. More than 1m. distant it makes two sharp turns, and passes close to a farm-house, situated at the foot of the fell. Here go through the gate which crosses the road, and then commence mounting the hill on the left. Keep by the side of a wall until close to a semi-detached rocky knob. Pass in the rear of this, and continue along an uneven track of ground with rocks above, and the valley and slate-quarries below. Elterwater and Windermere are seen in front. On arriving at the deep ravine called Meg's Gill, the path rises steeply, and crosses the torrent above some miniature cascades.

It then winds round a small hill and attains the summit of the pass whence Grasmere and Rydal come into view. An easy descent is now made by the rifle targets, and when a wall appears, it must be kept on the right for some distance; then a short lane conducts to the road, at the point where it passes the boat landings, on Grasmere Lake, and the church and village are close at hand.

GRASMERE SECTION.

GRASMERE.

THE peaceful vale of Grasmere, with its lovely lake and
green emerald isle, is a little gem in the diadem of the
Lake District. The tourist ought, if possible, to remain
here a few days. It is a telegraph station. There are
three good hotels—The Prince of Wales, a large house,
which stands in a delightful situation on the margin of
the lake; the Red Lion, in the village; and the Swan,
on the side of the coach-road, ½m. distant. There are
also numerous lodging-houses. Wordsworth, who, it
will be remembered, lived here for many years, has made
almost every rock and nook in the neighbourhood the
subject of song.

Many persons will enjoy spending a quiet Sunday at
Grasmere, and, after attending the church, hallowed by
so many associations, and visiting the poet's grave, will
delight to saunter in the neighbourhood with ' The Excursion' as a companion, or a volume of the lyrical
poems.

Loughrigg Terrace.—A most interesting and pleasing excursion may be had by following the Loughrigg
Terrace road to Rydal, and returning by the Wishing
Gate. The distance is 6m., and a pony can go the whole
way.

From the Grasmere church follow the road leading to
Silver Howe, and by the boat landing-place. It runs
between stone walls along the base of the hill, and at a
short distance above the shore of the lake. Some houses,
pleasantly situated in the midst of wood, are passed, and
occasional glimpses are had of the lake and the vale of
Grasmere. A few yards before the top of the Red Bank
Pass is attained, a lane on the left must be entered,
which continues along the N. side of Loughrigg. It is

however, advisable to extend the walk ¼m. to a seat bearing the inscription, "Rest and be thankful!" This seat, which is now much decayed, stands 20 yards beyond High Close House, and is reached by following the right-hand road at the top of the pass. It commands a pleasing prospect, embracing Windermere Lake, with Wray Castle prominent on its shore, and the Elterwater and Loughrigg tarns, the Great Langdale Valley, the Langdale Pikes, Coniston range of mountains and the lower heights, Lingmoor, Oxenfell, and Loughrigg.

Returning to the lane above mentioned, the open side of Loughrigg Fell is entered, just above the point where the water leaves the Grasmere Lake, and a most lovely prospect is revealed. The lake, with its single green island, the church and village, and houses picturesquely situated at the feet of the surrounding hills, all combine to form a pleasant picture.

The road runs along the side of the hill at some distance above the stream, and on rounding a slight projection Rydal Lake is spread to view, with Rydal Park and Scandale Fells in the background. Here a stone step-stile leads over the wall into a plantation, and a narrow rough path conducts to a wooden foot-bridge which crosses the river. Tourists who wish to shorten the walk might follow this path, and enter the main road a mile from Grasmere. On passing the above-mentioned stile the road descends to the shore of Rydal Lake. The ivy-covered house opposite is Nab Cottage, formerly the residence of Hartley Coleridge. When the lake is passed another stone step-stile leads into a plantation, where there is a path which conducts to a small foot-bridge spanning the river.

Without entering the wood, a cart-road may be followed, and the river crossed at Pelter Bridge, which stands a few hundred yards lower down the stream. There is a road leading to Ambleside on each side. As soon as the stream is crossed, the tourist finds himself in the sylvan vale of Rothay, at the charming village of

Rydal, where, before returning, he can visit Rydal Mount and Rydal Falls. See page 25.

On leaving the village a foot-track, commanding good views, may be taken at the back of Rydal Mount, under the rocky end of Nab Scar. The main road skirts the lake, and passes Nab Cottage. At some slate-quarries two roads branch to the right, and take over the rocky knob called Whitemoss Howe. The first road allows of the best views. The Wishing Gate—the subject of one of Wordsworth's poems—is the great attraction of the second, or middle, road. It is said to have been the popular belief that any wish formed or expressed here would be fulfilled. The old gate, with the "moss-grown bar," has been replaced by one which is now covered with the initials of tourists :—

> " . . . even the stranger from afar,
> Reclining on this moss-grown bar,
> Unknowing and unknown,
> The infection of the ground partakes,
> Longing for his beloved, who makes
> All happiness her own."

The view from this point is good, but not deserving of the lavish praises which it has often received. A short distance farther a descent is made, a few houses passed, and the main road entered close to the Prince of Wales Hotel.

Grasmere to Easedale Tarn.—The best short walk from Grasmere, and one which no tourist ought to neglect, is that to Easedale Tarn, situated in a wild and secluded mountain recess, 2½m. from Grasmere. A pony can go the whole journey; carriages only half way. Leaving the village at the Red Lion Hotel, follow the second road on the left, and on arriving by the side of Easedale Beck, take over the foot-bridge, and through the fields, having the stream on the right. The carriage-road passes the bridge, and makes a little longer circuit, through the fields, to the last farm-house in Easedale, which is as far as the carriage can be taken, and here a bridge crosses the stream, and the foot-path is re-entered. The ascent is made along a rough winding way by following the course of the streamlet on the right which issues from Easedale Tarn, and forms the foaming cataract called Sour Milk Gill Force. This is a fine fall; but owing to the want of wood and overhanging rocks, it reminds the on-looker of the beauty which is bold and showy, rather than of that which is modest and refined. The surrounding scenery is wild and beautiful. Erratic blocks and smooth rocks on every side are mute evidences of a past era of glacial action. On looking back, houses half hidden by trees stand in every nook and corner of the valley, and in the distance Nab Scar, Loughrigg, and Wansfell Pike are seen. On arriving at the top of the fall the Helm Crag range is well displayed, and on the right a low ridge hides the Far Easedale Glen. The jagged clump of rocks on the N. end of Helm Crag forms what looks like a mortar, and a pianoforte from the opposite side; and those on the S., which are not so distinct, form the Lion and the Lamb. Over the hollow to the left of Helm Crag are seen Fairfield and Seat Sandal, between which is the Grisedale Pass. After winding a little to the left, another short climb leads to the hollow where lies *Easedale Tarn*. Many persons will be annoyed on finding a small hut erected in this mountain nook, which retreat seems dedicated to solitary, pleasing reverie. Refreshments are provided by the person in charge of the hut, and a boat can be hired for a row, or a little trout fishing on the tarn. The charge for boat is 1s. per hour, and 5s. per day. From the shore of the tarn rises an amphitheatre of wild, rocky precipices, Tarn Crag lying on the right, and Blake Crag directly in front, with Sergeant Man farther back. A large number of moraine heaps are on each side of the water, and the ground near the shore is rich in detached blocks.

Codale Tarn, containing trout, lies out of sight in a hollow behind a small knoll, at the head of the glen, and the rill which issues from it is seen to descend the rocks

G

and flow into Easedale Tarn. If it be visited, a pleasing
deviation on returning may be made by descending into
the Far Easedale Glen. Another pleasant return route
is had by climbing Silver Howe, and descending near to
Grasmere Lake.

Walk over Allan Bank and Wray Breast (900).—
This is a pleasant walk of 2m., and will occupy an hour
or more.

Proceed along the road which strikes N.W. from the
Red Lion Hotel, and pass through a gate which leads
into the grounds of Allan Bank House, for a time the
residence of Wordsworth. When opposite the house,
follow the cart-road branching to the right, and leading to a farmstead, which leave on the right, and continue round the plantation, along a rough road, passing
through two gates. During the ascent, good views are
had of Easedale, Sour Milk Gill, and the head of Grasmere Vale. Having rounded the plantation, turn to the
left, and walk through an opening between stone walls.

Another clump of larch trees is seen higher up the
side of Silver Howe. On reaching the rocky knolls
which constitute the highest part of Allan Bank and
Wray Breast, a most lovely prospect is obtained of the
lake and the vale of Grasmere.

When viewed on a calm summer's evening, a more
peaceful and contented scene it is impossible to imagine.
In descending, return by the same route for a few yards;
then bend to the left under Silver Howe, and cross the
Wray Gill rivulet. A lane is found which enters the
road at the boat landing-place, a few hundred yards
from the church.

Ascent of Silver Howe (1345) from Grasmere.—
Silver Howe is the mountain which stands between the
Easedale and Langdale vales. Like all other heights
which claim to be ascended from Grasmere, a pony can
travel to the top. The ascent is commenced immediately
after leaving the village, without any extent of level
ground having to be traversed.

Follow the road described above, to the rear of Allan

Bank House. When past the first plantation, ascend behind the second, and bear well to the right. A small ravine will be found on the left, which must not be crossed until at a point higher up the hill, where it almost disappears. The summit of Silver Howe is now seen a little distant on the left, and the ascent is easy.

A capital view is had of Grasmere, Rydal, and Windermere lakes, and of Loughrigg and Elterwater tarns. A slight glimpse is caught of Coniston Lake at the end of a knob branching from the Coniston Mountains. Grasmere vale and village look, as usual, extremely beautiful. Wray Castle is a very distinct object, on the western shore of Windermere. Blencathara peers over the Dunmail Raise Pass. To the left of the pass are Helm Crag, Steel Fell, Ullscarf, Sergeant Man, Pavey Ark, Langdale Pikes, Bow Fell, Crinkle Crags, Pike O'Stickle, Lingmoor, and the Coniston Mountains. Between Coniston and Ambleside are Oxenfell and a great number of minor ridges. The circle is completed with Loughrigg, Wansfell Pike, Ill Bell, Scandale, Nab Scar, Rydal Head, Fairfield, Grisedale Pass, Seat Sandal, Dolly Waggon Pike, and Helvellyn.

In descending, walk in a southern direction until a gradual slope on the left conducts to the rifle targets. Pass these, and continue under the cliffs, and above the highest wall, until a lane leads to the road close to the lake, at the boat landing-place. The journey is 3½m., and will occupy from one hour and a half to two hours.

Ascent of Butter Crags (1200).—Butter Crags are on the Grasmere side of Nab Scar, to the S. of Above Beck Gill, and the Swan Inn.

The best plan is to start from the Prince of Wales Hotel and return by the Swan Hotel, or *vice versâ*; making a circuit of 4m. The journey will occupy two hours. Follow the road which mounts the hill, called Whitemoss, at the back of the Prince of Wales Hotel, and at a plot of hollow waste ground bend to the left and mount the hill by a steep rough track between

stone fences. On passing through a gate the open fell-
side is reached, and a good view is had of Grasmere
Lake and a part of Rydal Lake. A few yards farther,
Grasmere and Easedale vales are in sight, and look
charming. Following the direction of the left-hand wall
a small sheet of water is found resting behind a wooded
knoll. The inhabitants of Grasmere sometimes call this
Alcock's Tarn, and at other times Harwood's Tarn. It
is partly natural, partly artificial. It formerly belonged
to Mr. Alcock, and has since been purchased by Mr.
Harwood, who keeps a boat upon it. The ground in
which it is situated is enclosed by a wall, and therefore
the tourist is recommended to pass the gate and continue
on the fell side with the wall on the left. Presently the
bare part of Butter Crags is reached, and a lovely view
had of the lake and valley; Easedale, Greenburn, and
Dunmail Raise; and the heights Red Bank, Silver
Howe, Sergeant Man, Helm Crag, and Steel Fell; with
many mountains in the background. The Above Beck
Gill is below, on the right, and a track will be found
descending to it. The stream is pretty, and will interest
the tourist whilst he is following its course to the main
road close to the Swan Inn.

Ascent of Loughrigg Fell (1101), from Grasmere.—
Follow the cart-road to the top of Red Bank Pass.
There enter the left-hand road, which leads to Loughrigg
Tarn. On descending about 20 yards from the top of
the pass commence mounting the hill on the left by the
side of a wall. The top of the mountain is very uneven,
and consists of rough hillocks and deep hollows.

From the different points on the summit are seen parts
of the Lakes Windermere, Esthwaite, Grasmere, and Ry-
dal; and the tarns Elterwater, Loughrigg, and Blelham.
To the N. are the Grasmere Vale and the Dunmail Raise
Pass, on the left of which stand Steel Fell, Helm Crag,
Silver Howe, Ullscarf, Sergeant Man, and the Langdale
Pikes. Rising out of the Langdale Glen are Bow Fell,
Crinkle Crags, Pike O'Blisco, and Lingmoor; to the left
of which is the bulky mass consisting of Wetherlam and

the Coniston Old Man range. Oxenfell and a number of other small heights occupy the whole of the ground to the S. At the foot of Wansfell Pike, Ambleside lies peacefully. The mountains to the E. are Ill Bell, Scandale Fell, Rydal Fell, Nab Scar, Fairfield, Dolly Waggon Pike, and Seat Sandal.

A descent may be made to the terrace road, or to Rydal, Ambleside, or Loughrigg Tarn. Should the tourist return direct to Grasmere the whole journey will be 4½ m., and will occupy one and a half to two hours.

Ascent of Helm Crag (1299) and Steel Fell (1811), from Grasmere.—Helm Crag is one of the most noted mountains in the district. Many will climb to the summit to have a closer inspection of those mysterious rocks which form shapes so fantastic as at times to resemble a lion and a lamb, a mortar throwing shells, an old lady, and an astrologer.

The Lion and the Lamb are unmistakable when the mountain is seen from many points in the Grasmere Vale, and on looking from Dunmail Raise, the Mortar is quite perfect.

Wordsworth speaks of "the ancient woman seated on Helm Crag," and in the ' Waggoner' he says:—

> "The Astrologer, sage Sidrophel,
> Where at his desk and book he sits,
> Puzzling on high his curious wits;
> He whose domain is held in common
> With no one but the Ancient Woman,
> Cowering beside her rifted cell,
> As if intent on magic spell;
> Dread pair, that, spite wind and weather,
> Still sit upon Helm Crag together."

The walk from Helm Crag to Steel Fell, along the tops which surround the Greenburn Valley, is one which will not be found too much for the ordinary pedestrian.

Helm Crag is most conveniently ascended by following the road towards Easedale from the village, and turning off to the right, directly under some wild and beautiful rocks, called Jackdaw Crags.

For a short distance the tourist must climb by the side of a wall, and when the wall begins to descend, incline to the left. On attaining the summit he will experience a little difficulty in deciding which rocks among the chaotic mass are those giving rise to the whimsical comparisons, when seen from below. On examination he will probably discover that the rocks which assume the appearance of the Lion and the Lamb are distinct, and at some distance from those forming the Mortar.

After exploring the dark hollows of this crater-like summit, the prospect, though not so commanding as from higher ground, is found to be very beautiful. The lovely vale of Grasmere, with the lake and village, and houses dotted here and there along the sides of the mountains, present a charming picture of rural peace. Over Loughrigg Fell and Red Bank are seen portions of the lakes Windermere and Esthwaite; and to the W. most of Easedale Tarn is visible. Silver Howe, Sergeant Man, Ullscarf, and Steel Fell, present a grand natural circus stretching from the lake to Dunmail Raise; and to the E. are Helvellyn, Seat Sandal, Fairfield, and Nab Scar.

After descending a little, some uneven rocks, called the Carrs, have to be crossed. The Greenburn Glen and Steel Fell are on the right, and on the left the Far Easedale Glen, with the Langdale Pikes peering beyond Sergeant Man. If the whole journey to Steel Fell be considered too fatiguing, a descent may be made either into Far Easedale or Greenburn.

Far Easedale is described at page 101.

The Greenburn Glen is small, without a single habitation, and destitute of trees. The hills which surround it are finely grouped and coloured, and the glen presents to the visitor an idea of tranquil beauty. Like all similar parts of the district, it contains many small, rounded heaps, the result of glacial action. At one place the stream flows down some steep rocks, and forms a rather wild fall.

Pedestrians who keep the tops will, on arriving at the highest point of the Carrs, have spread to view Grasmere Lake and Vale, and part of Windermere Lake. The Ullscarf ridge is seen stretching along the far side of the hollow of Wythburn Head, and the lowest part on the right of White Stones and Sergeant Man is the pass over to Borrowdale by Greenup Gill.

A tract of boggy ground has now to be crossed in rounding the head of the Greenburn Vale, and 1m. of rather monotonous ground must be traversed. To pass the vale head, bear to the right, being careful not to make too great a descent.

When half-way along the ridge on the N. side of Greenburn, the prospect gradually becomes more interesting. Windermere and Grasmere lakes, and the mountains of Coniston and Langdale appear to the S. ; and to the N., Wythburn, Thirlmere Lake, Helvellyn, vale of St. John, with its famous Castle Rock, Blencathara, and Skiddaw. A gradual ascent is made to the top of Steel Fell, where there is a tolerably good prospect. The most beautiful bit is to the N., including the green fields at Wythburn, two parts of Thirlmere, with the Great Howe, Naddle Fell, Raven Crag, and the vale of St. John; and in the background, Blencathara and Skiddaw. The long flat tops of Ullscarf, White Stones, and High Raise, stretch rather monotonously from Thirlmere Lake to the Langdale Pikes, with parts of Glaramara and Great Gable peering over the lowest part. Then appear Pike O'Blisco, Lingmoor, and the Coniston Mountains. Nearer are Helm Crag with its rocky top well in view, Grasmere Lake and Vale, Windermere and Esthwaite lakes, and the heights of Silver Howe and Oxenfell. To the E. are Nab Scar, Fairfield, Seat Sandal, St. Sunday Crag, Dolly Waggon Pike, and Helvellyn.

The tourist will experience no difficulty in descending to Grasmere, or to the top of the Dunmail Raise Pass.

Ascent of Seat Sandal (2415), **from Grasmere.—** Seat Sandal is the mountain which stands between the Dunmail Raise and Grisedale passes. It may be ascended from the top of either of these passes, but the best plan is to start from the path just above the Tongue Gill Fall. An easy gradual ascent leads to the summit, where a very superior view is obtained.

Grasmere vale and lake are close at the feet of the spectator, and more distant are Windermere, Esthwaite, and Coniston lakes, with many arms of the sea; also Blelham, Easedale, and Harrop Tarns. A grand array of mountains is visible, including Coniston range, Black Combe, Pike O'Blisco, Crinkle Crags, Bow Fell, Great End, Scawfell Pikes, Glaramara, Great Gable, Green Gable, Steeple, Pillar, Red Pike, High Stile, Dale Head, Hindscarth, Maiden Moor, Grasmoor, Causey Pike, Grisedale Pike, Whiteside, Lord's Seat, and Skiddaw. The nearer heights in front of these are Loughrigg, Oxenfell, Silver Howe, Lingmoor, Helm Crag, Steel Fell, Langdale Pikes, Sergeant Man, High Raise, Ullscarf, and High Seat. To the E. are Helvellyn, Dolly Waggon Pike, an extent of level country, the town of Penrith, Crossfell range of hills, Little Mell Fell, the second reach of Ullswater, Birk Fell, Place Fell, St. Sunday Crag, and Fairfield. By walking a few yards to the E. of the wall, Grisedale Tarn comes in sight. The descent may be made on any side of the mountain.

Ascent of Heron Pike (2000) **and Nab Scar** (1300) **from Grasmere.—**By the houses behind the Prince of Wales Hotel enter the road which ascends the Whitemoss Howe. Follow it for a few yards, and at two yew trees branch to the left, and pass a hollow waste bit of ground. Gradually ascend, with a wall on the left, along a rugged path. The lake and then the village come into view, and presently the Windermere and Coniston lakes, the town of Bowness, Elterwater Tarn, and fine ranges of mountains in the W. When in the rear of a clump of trees and a sheet of water, strike up the hill on the right and make for the highest point. The path presents no difficulty. When the summit ridge is attained, Windermere looks very beautiful, with the towns of Ambleside and Bowness on its shores. Grasmere and Easedale are immediately below on the right, and in front are the waters Esthwaite, Coniston, Blelham, and Elterwater.

Most tourists, when descending, will wish to visit Rydal, and walk thence to Grasmere. They must scale the wall, and incline to the left, when near the end of the hill. Rydal Lake, with its islets, looks beautiful when seen from this point. About half-way down, a plot of ground between two walls is crossed, and a cart-road, which runs up Rydal Glen, is entered near to Rydal Mount and The Hall.

The distance thence to Grasmere is 2½m., and the whole journey is 6m. With ponies a descent must be made into Rydal Glen, in the rear of the wall which runs up the fell.

Ascent of Fairfield (2863) from Grasmere.—Those who do not visit Fairfield from Ambleside may ascend it from Grasmere. The summit, which commands one of the finest prospects in the lake country, is reached after a comparatively easy walk of 3m., and the double journey will occupy three and a half hours.

The ascent may be made from the top of the Grisedale Pass, or from a point a short distance nearer Grasmere, at the head of the Tongue Gill stream. Some persons may choose to go to Rydal, and walk up the whole length of Nab Scar and Fairfield, following in the track of tourists who go from Ambleside.

The easiest course, however, and the one usually adopted, is to take the road which quits the highway at right angles, close to the Swan Inn. After walking a few yards, a lane branches to the right, and another to the left, near a house. Keep straight forward, having the house and the brook close by on the right, and another house on the left. Pass through a gate, leave the brook, and bend to the left, up a lane with a wall on either side. The walls soon diverge, and a very steep ascent is made

along a smooth grassy slope, by following in a tortuous
path, keeping in the direction of the right-hand wall.
A small gate will be observed in a corner of the wall,
on the left, which must be avoided.   When the steep
part of the journey is accomplished, a lovely prospect is
unfolded: Grasmere Lake and valley lying immediately
below, environed by Loughrigg, Silver Howe, and Helm
Crag; and in the distance are the Coniston and Langdale mountains.   After another easy ascent, the walls
are left behind, and an inclination is made to the left;
the ravine being close below on the right.   Continuing
up a green, smooth part of the mountain, a glance is
caught of Easedale Tarn, with the Sour Milk Gill stream
flowing from it; and on looking back a small sheet of
water is observed in the rear of Butter Crags, with
Esthwaite Lake beyond.   When nearing the head of the
ravine it is advisable, in order to avoid any descent, to
incline to the left, and scale the rocks in the rear of
Stone Arthur.   The ponies are generally taken directly
under these; but the view northwards is then missed.
Elterwater Tarn is now seen over Red Bank.   The
Coniston Mountains are very prominent, and gradually
Coniston Lake is displayed.   On the left are the Grisedale and Dunmail Raise passes, and the heights, Steel
Fell, Seat Sandal, Dolly Waggon Pike, and Helvellyn.
Over a low part of Fairfield gradually appear Scandale
Fells, Wansfell Pike, and Windermere Lake, the latter
being especially lovely.   The summit of Fairfield is
concealed by the lower height of Great Rigg, which is
in front.   Presently a fine peep is obtained over the
eastern side into Rydal Glen.   Just before the last
climb is commenced, glorious views are had of the steep
ridges on the eastern side of Helvellyn, with Catchedecam peering over Striding Edge, and the Grisedale
Tarn is seen lying at the base of Seat Sandal.   Rydal
Head is now fully displayed, and a part of the High
Street range and Ill Bell appear.

A smooth, gentle slope leads to the summit, the view
from which is given at p. 45.

An easy descent may be made to Grisedale Tarn, and
to the top of Grisedale Pass, by making in the direction
of Seat Sandal. After descending a few feet, incline to
the right, until a wall is reached, which runs down the
mountain, crosses the pass, and ascends Seat Sandal.
The tarn is seen a few feet below. A track will be
found rounding the base of Seat Sandal, and leading to
Grasmere without difficulty.

Another easy descent is made by leaving the Grisedale Pass a short distance on the right, and following
the course of the Tongue Gill rivulet, which flows from
the pass to Grasmere. Some tourists will pursue the
whole length of the mountain, and over Nab Scar to
Rydal; others will keep on the tops round Rydal Head,
and descend by the Scandale Glen.

The narrow ridge connecting Fairfield with St. Sunday Crag may tempt good mountaineers, and will not
be found impracticable.

Ascent of Helvellyn (3118), from Grasmere.

Grisedale Tarn, 3m.; Summit of Helvellyn, 6½m.; Wythburn, 9m.;
Grasmere, 13m.

Helvellyn is generally visited by tourists staying at
either Grasmere, Patterdale, or Keswick, but it is more
frequently ascended from Grasmere than from the two
other places. Ponies can be taken to the summit without difficulty. The time required for the ascent is about
three hours, and the descent to Wythburn will occupy
one hour. The easiest descent is to the Nag's Head
Inn at Wythburn, and carriages may be sent there to
be in readiness for the remaining 4m. of the return
journey.

Wythburn is the nearest starting-point for the ascent
of the mountain, but if it is selected by the tourist, it
will not be advisable to return by the same route, as,
by so doing, much of the best scenery will be missed.
Leaving the famous Swan Inn, whence Wordsworth,
Southey, and Scott once started for the ascent of Hel-

vellyn, the Keswick road must be followed for nearly
½m., until a point is reached, indicated by an ivy-covered
cottage on the right, and a small mill on the left.

Turn to the right along the path at the N. side of
the cottage. In the Tongue Gill stream, on the right,
there is a pleasing waterfall which will well repay a
visit.

Where the stream divides and flows along both sides
of a small hill which stands directly in front, between
Seat Sandal and Fairfield, proceed by the side of the left-
hand stream, and make for the top of some rocks, at the
side of Seat Sandal, near to the Grisedale Pass. Care
must be taken not to ascend to the summit of Seat
Sandal, a mistake sometimes fallen into. When on the
rocks the tourist will pause to observe the view. Grasmere, as usual, looks very beautiful, and in the distance
there is the sea and the Coniston Lake. The mountains
Wetherlam and Coniston Old Man are prominent; and
to the right of them are Pike O'Blisco, Crinkle Crags,
Harrison Stickle, and the peaked summit of Bow Fell.
The near heights are Lingmoor, Silver Howe, Helm
Crag, Sergeant Man, and Steel Fell.

Rounding the S.E. base of Seat Sandal a pretty stream
is seen flowing from the pass by the side of Fairfield to
Grasmere, and another sharp ascent brings the traveller
to a wall which runs down Seat Sandal, crosses the
summit of the pass (1929), and ascends Fairfield. Passing through an opening in the wall the Grisedale Tarn
is seen lying a few yards below, beautiful and solitary,
and environed by Fairfield, Seat Sandal, and Dolly
Waggon Pike, an offshoot of Helvellyn. To the left, in
the distance, stands a cluster of mountain tops, consisting of Grasmoor, Whiteside, Causey Pike, and Grisedale
Pike; and looking back the whole length of Coniston
Lake is visible.

After walking a few yards; with the tarn on the left, a
peep is had down the Grisedale Valley, with St. Sunday
Crag on the right, and a portion of Ullswater below.
Having crossed the stream near where it issues from the

tarn, the zigzag path must be taken which leads up
the side of Dolly Waggon Pike to Helvellyn. Here is
encountered the hardest climb of the whole journey.
At one place, near where six stakes are fixed in the
ground, there is no path for a few yards, but by inclining to the right it is presently reached again without
difficulty. After arriving on Dolly Waggon Pike a view
is obtained down the Grisedale Valley, and the path
continues along the eastern edge of the mountain, with
the precipices and coves on the right, and on the left a
grassy, sloping table-land.

Ullswater, Windermere, Esthwaite, Coniston, Easedale
Tarn, and the Sea, are now in prospect, and during the
remaining two miles' walk along the tops, the views are
extremely fine, more especially of the deep hollows and
perpendicular precipices on the eastern edge of the
mountain.

The tourist will be apt to exclaim with Scott, "The
mighty Helvellyn," for it is only by traversing its whole
length that the greatness of its mass can be realized.
The Striding Edge will recall to the mind the fate of
Charles Gough, a young lover of nature, who, in the
spring of 1805, met with an accident which caused his
death, whilst he was walking along the ridge. He was
attempting to climb Helvellyn from Patterdale, after a
fall of snow had partially concealed the path, and rendered it dangerous. It could never be ascertained
whether he was killed by his fall, or perished from
hunger. Three months elapsed before the body was
found, and then it was watched over by a faithful dog
which Mr. Gough had with him at the time of the
accident. His remains were interred in the burial
ground of the Friends' Meeting House at Tirril, near
Penrith.

The following lines of Wordsworth and Scott will
probably help to impress more forcibly upon the mind
of the tourist the scenery of this " savage place " :—

" A barking sound the shepherd hears,
A cry as of a dog or fox;
He halts, and searches with his eyes
Among the scatter'd rocks:
And now at distance can discern
A stirring in a brake of fern;
And instantly a dog is seen
Glancing from that covert green.

" The dog is not of mountain breed;
Its motions, too, are wild and shy;
With something, as the shepherd thinks,
Unusual in its cry:
Nor is there any one in sight
All round, in hollow or on height;
Nor shout, nor whistle strikes his ear;—
What is the creature doing here?

" It was a cove, a huge recess,
That keeps till June December's snow;
A lofty precipice in front,
A silent tarn below!
Far in the bosom of Helvellyn,
Remote from public road or dwelling,
Pathway, or cultivated land;
From trace of human foot or hand.

" There sometimes doth a leaping fish
Send through the tarn a lonely cheer;
The crags repeat the raven's croak,
In symphony austere;
Thither the rainbow comes—the cloud—
And mists that spread the flying shroud;
And sunbeams: and the sounding blast,
That, if it could, would hurry past,
But that enormous barrier binds it fast.

" Not free from boding thoughts, a while
The shepherd stood; then makes his way
Towards the dog, o'er rocks and stones,
As quickly as he may;
Nor far had gone before he found
A human skeleton on the ground;
The appall'd discoverer with a sigh
Looks round, to learn the history.

" From these abrupt and perilous rocks
   The man had fallen, that place of fear !
At length upon the shepherd's mind
   It breaks, and all is clear :
He instantly recall'd the name,
And who he was, and whence he came ;
Remember'd, too, the very day
On which the traveller pass'd this way.

" But hear a wonder, for whose sake
   This lamentable tale I tell !
A lasting monument of words
   This wonder merits well.
The dog, which still was hovering nigh,
Repeating the same timid cry,
This dog had been through three months' space
A dweller in that savage place.

" Yes, proof was plain that since the day
   On which the traveller thus had died
The dog had watch'd about the spot,
   Or by his master's side :
How nourish'd here through such long time
He knows, who gave that love sublime,
And gave that strength of feeling, great
Above all human estimate."— *Wordsworth.*

" I climbed the dark brow of the mighty Helvellyn,
   Lakes and mountains beneath me gleamed misty and wide ,
All was still, save, by fits, when the eagle was yelling,
   And starting around me the echoes replied.
On the right, Striding Edge round the Red Tarn was bending,
And Catchedecam its left verge was defending,
One huge nameless rock in front was impending,
   When I marked the sad spot where the wanderer died.

" Dark green was that spot, 'mid the brown mountain-heather,
   Where the Pilgrim of Nature lay stretched in decay,
Like the corpse of an outcast abandoned to weather,
   Till the mountain winds wasted the tenantless clay.
Not yet quite deserted, though lonely extended,
For, faithful in death, his mute favourite attended,
The much-loved remains of his master defended,
   And chased the hill-fox and the raven away.

" How long did'st thou think that this silence was slumber?
    When the wind waved his garments how oft didst thou start?
How many long days and long nights didst thou number,
    Ere he faded before thee, the friend of thy heart?
And, O! was it meet, that no requiem read o'er him,
No mother to weep, and no friend to deplore him;
And thou, little guardian, alone stretched before him,
    Unhonoured the pilgrim from life should depart?

" When a Prince to the fate of a Peasant has yielded,
    The tapestry waves dark round the dim-lighted hall,
With scutcheons of silver the coffin is shielded,
    And the pages stand mute by the canopied pall:
Through the courts at deep midnight, the torches are gleaming;
In the proudly arched chapel the banners are beaming;
Far adown the long aisle sacred music is streaming,
    Lamenting a chief of the people should fall.

" But meeter for thee, gentle lover of nature,
    To lay down thy head like the meek mountain lamb,
When, wildered, he drops from some rock high in stature,
    And draws his last breath by the side of his dam.
And more stately thy couch by this desert lake lying,
Thy obsequies sung by the grey plover flying,
With but one faithful friend to witness thy dying,
    In the arms of Helvellyn and Catchedecam."—*Scott.*

The highest part of the mountain overhangs Red
Tarn, and the view is very extensive. The Striding
Edge on the S., and the Swirrel Edge, with the pointed
top of Catchedecam, on the N. side of Red Tarn, are
grand objects. Over Swirrel Edge is Keppel Cove Tarn,
and to the N. of the different heights of the Helvellyn
range are Blencathara and Skiddaw. To the left of
Skiddaw is the Solway Firth; but the northern part
of Helvellyn hides Thirlmere and Bassenthwaite lakes,
although by walking a few yards a view of them can be
had. To the E., in the plain, is Penrith, and beyond is
the Crossfell range. The middle and lower reaches of
Ullswater look very beautiful, and to the right of Place
Fell, Angle Tarn glitters in the sun. To the S.E. are
High Street, Ill Bell, Caudale Moor, Red Screes, St.

Sunday Crag, Fairfield, and in the distance Ingleborough Mountain.

Over Dolly Waggon Pike are the lakes Windermere, Esthwaite, and Coniston, and strips of the sea. Then come Wetherlam, Coniston Old Man, Black Combe, Pike O'Blisco, Crinkle Crags, Bow Fell, Scawfell Pikes, Great End, Lingmell, and the Sty Head Pass depression. Below these are Helm Crag, Steel Fell, Silver Howe, Lingmoor, Harrison Stickle, High Raise, Ullscarf, Glaramara, and Harrop Tarn. To the right of the Sty Head Pass are Great Gable, Green Gable, Kirk Fell, Brandreth, and Honister Crag; and above them the Pillar, Steeple, and Yewbarrow. High Crag, High Stile, and Red Pike are well defined. Derwentwater is concealed, but to the W. of it are the Newlands Mountains, Maiden Moor, Dale Head, Hindscarth, and Robinson; and Grasmoor, Grisedale Pike, and Causey Pike are prominent.

After descending a few hundred yards to the opening on the left, which affords a view of the Grisedale Valley, and of the S. side of Striding Edge, the path striking to the right, and running S.W., is the one which must be taken, if it be intended to descend to Wythburn.

Some tourists who may be accustomed to mountaineering will, perhaps, from this point, take due W. direct down the mountain, along by the side of a streamlet, and arrive at the inn at Wythburn by the quickest and most direct route.

About half-way down the mountain there is no path for a short distance, but by avoiding descending too soon into the hollow on the right, the path will be regained, and then there is no further difficulty. Thirlmere Lake gradually comes in view, and very beautiful it looks with Raven Crag and Skiddaw in the background.

Ascent of Helvellyn (3118), from Wythburn.—Although other paths to Helvellyn are more interesting than that from Wythburn, many tourists may find it convenient to start from this place. The distance to the top is 2½m.

H

The ascent is commenced after passing through a gate on the Keswick side of the Nag's Head Inn. Continue for a few yards with a wall on the right, and on the left the stream, which is seen forming some small cascades higher up the mountain. The route to be taken is at the base of a rock, which will be observed overhead to the S., and must be kept on the right hand. Leave the stream, and bend in the direction of the wall. The rocky summit of Helm Crag peeps over Dunmail Raise on the left of Steel Fell. Thirlmere Lake also meets the eye, with Skiddaw in the background.

At a small gate pass through the wall, and a good zigzag path rounds a shoulder of the mountain, and enters a combe with a few rocks in front, and a rill trickling from them. A part of Harrop Tarn is now seen, and some hill-tops to the W., over the Armboth Fells. The path leads from the rivulet, and mounts close to the left of the right-hand rock. On attaining this elevation, it winds to the left, along a bit of stony ground, and gradually ascends with the ravine kept at some distance on the left. The Coniston and Langdale mountains, and many western heights, reveal themselves at every step.

By continuing the ascent, with a slight inclination to the left, the point is reached whence a view is had down the eastern precipice into the Grisedale Glen; and then, by keeping the cliff line on the right, and walking due N. for a short distance, with Red Tarn below, the cairn on the summit is reached, the prospect from which is given at page 96.

Grasmere to Patterdale, by the Grisedale Pass.— The distance from the Prince of Wales Hotel, Grasmere, to the Ullswater Hotel, Patterdale, is 8m. The journey is one of the most charming and romantic in the Lake District, and must be travelled with pony or on foot. The route, as far as the Grisedale Tarn, is the same as that taken in ascending Helvellyn.

At an ivy-covered cottage, ½m. from the Swan Inn, on the road leading over Dunmail Raise, a track is entered

which follows the course of the Tongue Gill stream.
This torrent, for some distance, flows along a ravine a
few feet below, on the right, and in one place it forms
a pretty cascade, which the tourist ought not to omit
descending expressly to see.

Where the stream branches and flows along both sides
of a small hill standing directly in front, between Seat
Sandal and Fairfield, tourists must follow the left-hand
rivulet, and climb to the top of some rocks at the side
of Seat Sandal, near to the Grisedale Pass, and then continue round the S.E. base of the mountain.

Pedestrians may arrive at this point by climbing the
low hill, and passing *under* the rocks. A short distance
farther the top of the pass is attained; height above the
sea, 1929 feet.

During the ascent pleasing views are had of Grasmere
and Coniston lakes, of an arm of the sea, and of many
lofty and rugged mountains. On passing through an
opening in a wall Grisedale Tarn is observed lying a few
feet below, in a secluded situation, and surrounded by
Seat Sandal, Dolly Waggon Pike, and Fairfield. Crossing the stream where it leaves the tarn, the descent into
the Grisedale Glen is commenced. On the right is the
fine mountain of St. Sunday Crag, connected by a narrow ridge with Fairfield, and on the left are some bold
and frowning rocks, called Tarn Crags. Looking down
the valley, a glimpse is caught of Ullswater Lake, with
Birk Fell rising from the shore.

The stream must be kept at some distance on the
right, and a stony path will be found directly under the
left-hand rocks. Birk Fell and Place Fell gradually
advance to view at the bottom of the valley; St. Sunday
Crag shows a steep front on the right, and the precipices of Dolly Waggon Pike, with the Helvellyn range
on the left, open up new beauties at every step. About
half-way down the pass stands a small building, which
has been erected by Mr. Marshall, of Patterdale Hall,
as a luncheon-house for the accommodation of his
visitors whilst climbing the mountains. Here a rivulet

issues from the Ruthwaite Cove. Disregarding a path
on the other side of the glen, keep the stream on the
right for some distance farther. Here the water tumbles over ledges of rock, and forms some beautiful cascades. On passing Eagle Crag and a lead mine, which
is now closed, go through a gate, close to a miner's dilapidated hut. From this point either side of the valley
may be traversed. The best plan is to bend to the right,
and cross the stream at a bridge, where the tourist, on
looking back, will have presented to his gaze dark
frowning rocks and lofty precipices, wild and desolate
in the extreme. Few scenes in the district are wilder or
grander than this. At the first farm-house, avoid a path
which leads across the beck. Keeping the stream on the
left, some fields are now crossed, and then the road passes
through a beautifully-wooded part, with the Grisedale
Beck below, murmuring musically along a rough bed
strewn with large boulders. Patterdale Hall presently
appears amongst the trees, and a glimpse is caught of
the higher reach of Ullswater. Place Fell presents a
beautifully-coloured front, with slate-quarries at its base.
On entering the road in Patterdale, turn to the left, pass
the fine grounds of Patterdale Hall, and at a bridge, a
road to the right leads past the church to the Patterdale
Hotel and to the village; and the direct road takes to
the Ullswater Hotel, situated 1m. distant, on the margin
of the lake.

**Grasmere to Keswick, by Far Easedale Valley,
Greenup Gill, and Borrowdale.** Distance, 14m.—Leave
Grasmere by the road to Easedale Tarn, and take a
branch road on the right, which runs along the S.W.
side of Helm Crag. This mountain range must be
kept close on the right all the way up the Far Easedale Valley. Sour Milk Gill will be observed at some
distance on the left. Its stream flows from Easedale
Tarn. The rocky ridge running from Sour Milk Gill to
Helm Crag hides Far Easedale, but the road winds
past the rocks, and then enters the valley by the side
of the stream. Here the tourist finds himself in a

quiet secluded recess, bare of trees, with hills and rocks
on either side, and loose boulders strewn in every part.
A pleasant resort on a summer's day for those who enjoy

" The peace that dwells among the lonely hills."

When the road ends, the tourist may take either side of
the stream, walking sometimes close to its bank, and at
other times at a little distance, in order to avoid wet,
marshy ground. A low ridge runs almost across the
valley and divides it into two parts, the water having
cut for itself a course through the rock. When at the
foot of the low rising ground where the stream divides,
cross the left-hand rivulet and climb the hill, which is in
front. Then take up a narrow depression with a rill
trickling down it, and a few bare rocks on the left.
After passing a detached rock which has a small tree
growing on it, the top of the ridge is reached and the
head of the valley is entered, down which flows a
streamlet to Wythburn. On the left are craggy heights,
and in front, and to the right, a low range of smooth
sloping hills. Cross the valley, and wind round the
base of the rocky heights, keeping them close on the left.
Climb a depression at the head of the valley in a N.W.
direction, passing immediately under a low precipitous
rock.

Looking down the valley the Helvellyn range is in
sight. When the top of the pass is reached, there is a
grand view of Bassenthwaite Lake, Skiddaw, Newlands
Mountains, Honister Crag, and a number of other high
and rugged mountains.

Take in a direct line with Bassenthwaite Lake, N.W.,
for a short distance. The near, long, rugged height on
the opposite side of Longstrath Valley is Glaramara.
Presently the head of the Greenup Valley is seen on the
left, and also the low ridge which separates it from the
Longstrath Valley, ending in Eagle Crag. When
the streamlet is seen flowing from the head of the
Greenup Valley, round the base of Eagle Crag, commence a short steep descent, with a knoll on the left-

hand. Here a large number of rounded heaps of terminal moraine matter give a weird-like aspect to the place, and make it very interesting to the geological student.

The streamlet, which must be kept on the left hand, forms some pretty falls. After passing Eagle Crag, and the opening to the Longstrath Valley, another ½m. brings to a bridge which leads to Stonethwaite hamlet; and 1m. farther is the village of Rosthwaite.

For the remaining 6m. to Keswick, see page 143.

Grasmere to Langdale (Dungeon Gill), by Easedale, Codale, and Stickle Tarns, 6m.—This excursion is not fatiguing, and there are few which include in so small a space scenery of so varied and high an order.

The route to Easedale Tarn is given at page 80.

At the head of the tarn, and at the end of the Tarn Crag ridge, close under Sergeant Man, is a small rocky knob, down both sides of which trickles a rill. Codale Tarn lies at the back of this knob, and the right-hand rill issues from it. The ascent may be made by taking either side of Easedale Tarn; then aim to the right, for the first bit of grassy ground to the left of Tarn Crag, and at the back of the knob, leaving the latter on the left.

The course of the stream which enters Easedale, may, however, be followed, and the ascent made directly under the knoll; then an inclination to the right leads to the tarn, which is small, and lies in a secluded situation. This ascent is more wild and romantic, but requires somewhat harder work.

From Codale Tarn cross the rivulet, which flows down the S.W. side of Sergeant Man, just beneath where a few dwarfed trees are seen growing in the ravine. Some rocks rise in front, and an inclination may be made either to the right or to the left.

The shortest way is to the left, but by climbing to the right a better view is had of Sergeant Man and High Raise. The difference in distance is only a few hundred yards. The ground between Codale Tarn and Stickle

Tarn is composed of rocky hillocks and boggy hollows. On arriving at the top, the descent is at once commenced, and Stickle Tarn is seen below lying at the base of Pavey Ark and Harrison Stickle. The Crinkle Crags, Pike O'Blisco, Lingmoor, and Wetherlam are also in sight, with Esthwaite and Windermere lakes.

Looking back, are Codale and Easedale tarns, Grasmere Vale, and the summits of Helvellyn, Seat Sandal, Fairfield, and Ill Bell.

On reaching the tarn, the Pavey Ark rock—a lofty perpendicular precipice—is perhaps most advantageously seen when the tourist walks directly under it. A slight depression separates it from Harrison Stickle. The tarn is large, and during dry seasons it is used as a reservoir for the Elterwater Powder Works, and a small embankment has been constructed where the water makes its exit. Following the course of the stream, called Stickle Gill, and sometimes Mill Gill, either side may be taken. When about half-way down, the water forms two or three good cascades.

The Langdale Valley, with Elterwater Tarn and also part of Windermere Lake and Loughrigg Tarn, come in sight, all beautifully timbered.

Lingmoor hides Little Langdale. The New Dungeon Gill Hotel is immediately below. If the descent be made with the stream on the left, the cleft in which is the Dungeon Gill fall will be observed after rounding the right-hand rock, and by following a path some yards the fall may be visited. An easy descent leads to the hotel. There is another hotel (the Old Dungeon Gill Hotel) nearly 1m. higher up the valley.

Grasmere to Langdale (Dungeon Gill), by Blindtarn Moss.

With pony, or on foot. Distance, 4½m. Time, 1½ or 2 hours.

Leave Grasmere by the Easedale road, and cross the Easedale Beck at the foot-bridge; then keep the stream on the right for nearly ½m., and turn through the fields

to the solitary cottage on the left.   The Blindtarn Gill
stream will have been noticed descending the hill more
than ¼m. to the left of Sour Milk Gill Force, and it
passes close by the cottage.

This house was occupied upwards of 40 years ago by a
peasant family named Green; the parents were unhap-
pily lost in a snowstorm one winter's evening when
crossing from Langdale.   It is worthy of remark that
all the fatal accidents which are known to have occurred
on the mountains in the Lake District have resulted
from snow and ice, or winter's storms.

After passing the house, the course of the brook must
be followed.   Either side of the gill can be taken.   It
contains two or three small falls.   When the wet, flat
hollow is reached, incline to the left, and keep the mossy
ground below on the right.   In front, to the W., are the
Yew Crags, and on the left of these a slight depression,
with a rill trickling from it.   Make for the depression,
and after a quarter of an hour's ascent the summit level
is attained.   On looking back, Helm Crag, Steel Fell,
Helvellyn, and Fairfield are in sight; and, after crossing
several yards of level ground, the Langdale Valley and
the Coniston and Langdale mountains burst into view,
with Lingmoor directly opposite.   Leaving the rocks at
a short distance to the right, a winding track will be
found conducting down the hill to a wall.   Passing
through two gates and two enclosed plots of ground, a
rough cart-road leads to a farm-house, where another
road leads up the valley to within ¼m. of Dungeon Gill
Hotel.   To avoid mistake, it is recommended to cross a
field along a cart-track in front of the farm-house, and
enter the main road.

Some tourists may prefer continuing along the side of
the fell, close above the highest wall; but the ground is
rough and uneven, and there is no well-defined track.

Grasmere to Langdale (Dungeon Gill), by the Rifle Targets and Meg's Gill.

Time, 1½ hour. Distance, 4½m.

Follow the road which leaves the church in the direction of Silver Howe. At the boat-landings turn up the steep, narrow lane opposite. When the lane terminates incline a little to the left, and ascend until above the highest wall which skirts the fell at the base of Silver Howe. During the ascent Grasmere Vale, and the Grasmere and Rydal lakes, with the neighbouring heights, are seen to great advantage. When the wall begins to descend, strike to the right along a green path, which passes by the Rifle Butts, and mounts close under the rocky end of Silver Howe. When on the summit level, the head of Windermere Lake and the Wetherlam and Coniston mountains come into view; and presently appear Loughrigg and Elterwater tarns and the Langdale Valley, with a number of slate-quarries on the side of Lingmoor. Here the tourist will see a hill on the right crowned with a cairn. The path rounds under this hill, and at first the descent appears to be into an impracticable hollow; but after going down a few yards all danger disappears, and the track will be seen to cross the head of the Meg's Gill ravine just above the small cascades. It then descends a few yards and bends to the right, continuing over some uneven ground, with rocks above and the valley and slate-quarries below.

Presently Bow Fell and the Langdale Pikes appear, and at the base of the latter the New Dungeon Gill Hotel. A few hundred yards in front stands a semi-detached rock. Pass in the rear of this, over a grassy ridge, and descend with a wall on the left until the road is entered at a farm-house. The hotel is 1¼m. farther up the valley.

Grasmere to Dungeon Gill, by Dow Bank.—This route is a little nearer, but steeper, than that by Hunting Stile. It allows of a view of Grasmere and Rydal lakes together, and on this account it will be preferred by some tourists.

Follow the road on the W. side of the lake until a streamlet enters the lake from the end of Silver Howe, and some cottages stand on the right. Pass through a gate, and take the path which mounts the hill behind the cottages. When in the rear of the latter, bend to the right, cross a small rill, and have another streamlet on the right hand—the path is along a steep rugged lane. When through a gate, the open fell-side is reached. The track is then marked out by a plantation on the left, and on the right the stream, with Silver Howe above. A lovely view is gained of Grasmere and Rydal lakes. A gate and a stone step-stile lead through a wall, and the summit of the pass is presently attained, the rifle targets being at some distance on the right. An easy descent leads into Langdale near to Chapel Stile, which is 2½m. from Dungeon Gill.

Grasmere to Dungeon Gill, by Hunting Stile, 5m.— This is the easiest of the many routes from Grasmere to Langdale. The journey can be accomplished on horseback, but carriages must be taken a short distance farther round, by Red Bank and High Close.

Follow the road on the W. side of the lake until at the point where stands a house on the left. Here take the carriage-road branching to the right. A few yards farther, this road leads to a pleasantly-situated villa. A rough lane, fenced in by stone walls, continues straight on, and mounts the hill. On passing through a gate and entering the open green slope, incline to the right, and pursue the course of a small stream. Pleasing views are had of Grasmere Lake and Vale, and presently, on going through another gate, the top of the pass is attained, and on the other side appear Wetherlam, Coniston Old Man, Oxenfell, Elterwater, Wray Castle, and part of Windermere Lake. Immediately in front is the beginning of the Langdale Valley, with Elterwater village and gunpowder works at the foot of the S. end of Lingmoor.

After descending a few yards, the road is entered which runs from Red Bank, and then the Chapel Stile village and church are passed. Here is a small public-house, in front of which the higher road leads to Thrang slate-quarries. The lower road must be followed. On continuing up the vale, the New Dungeon Gill Hotel is in sight all the way, situated at the foot of the Langdale Pikes, which are very prominent. Mill Gill Force is the waterfall on the right of the hotel. The Dungeon Gill Fall is situated in the fissure a little more to the left, and close in rear of the hotel. At the head of the glen are Bow Fell and Crinkle Crags, and on the left Lingmoor: part of Silver Howe stands on the right.

Wythburn to Keswick, *viâ* Harrop, Blea, Dock, and Watendlath Tarns.

Harrop Tarn, 1m.; Blea Tarn, 2m.; Watendlath Tarn, 4m.; Keswick, 9m.

Cross the Wythburn Beck at a wooden bridge behind the Nag's Head Inn, and pass through the fields, and over stone walls to a large detached rock, which is well smoothed and rounded.

If the walls be considered insuperable obstacles, a circuitous cart-road will lead to some farm-houses at the foot of the rock. If the tourist be walking over Dunmail Raise Pass, and does not wish to visit the inn at Wythburn, he can enter a cart-road which strikes to the left a few yards below the summit of the pass, and after going by three farm-houses, he will reach the smooth rock just mentioned.

A zigzag path must be taken, having on the right the stream which issues from Harrop Tarn, on reaching which, cross the stream at some stepping-stones. The tarn is not interesting, being ill-defined, and scarcely deserving a more dignified appellation than that of a mountain pool; but the surrounding rocks are wild, and give some interest to the place. The tarn contains trout. The landlord at the Nag's Head Inn supplies a boat.

Keep the tarn on the left, and make for the N. side of

a semi-detached rock, which is in front, immediately under the highest and most precipitous rocks at the head of the tarn. The only mistake which can well be made here is that of walking too much to the right—to the N.W. instead of to the S.W.

The stream which flows from the W. must be kept on the left, and on arriving at the point where the western mountains come into view, Blea Tarn will presently be seen below. It is a large sheet of water with well-marked shores, but lacking the overhanging rocks which add such charms to most tarns. It contains trout and perch. On its northern side is a large morass, most disagreeable to the tourist. To avoid this it is recommended to walk by the southern shore, and cross the stream about 80 yards after it has left the tarn. Then walk almost due N., taking heed not to descend into the valley on the left, through which the stream flows from Blea Tarn to Watendlath Tarn.

The western mountains are now very prominent, and the Pillar, Great Gable, and Bow Fell look like monarchs of the hills. Bassenthwaite and a strip of the head of Derwentwater are in sight. Keep in the direction of these lakes, and when the tarn and hamlet of Watendlath are seen in the valley on the left, descend to a wall and walk by the side of it until it terminates. Here a descent must be made to the hamlet, a ravine and some trees lying to the left.

If it be intended to visit Dock Tarn, which is situated amongst wild heath-covered rocks to the S., about half-way between the Blea and Watendlath tarns, the tourist must, after ascending from Harrop Tarn, round the base of Coldbarrow Fell, keeping Blea Tarn well to the right. Care must be taken not to descend too far into the valley along which winds the stream flowing from Blea Tarn to Watendlath. The fells which have to be crossed are very uneven, and in places covered with bog. As soon as the Eagle Crag and the Longstrath Valley appear to the S., incline to the right, and make for a rocky knoll with a small cairn upon it. Here Dock

Tarn is seen below, and also a little of Borrowdale Valley. The tarn is small and contains an islet. It is rarely visited, and is little known, but with some tourists it is a favourite. It contains perch. The water from it flows to Stonethwaite in Borrowdale. After noting the position of the Watendlath Valley, keep due N., in the direction of Skiddaw, and when Watendlath Tarn comes in view, make a direct descent to it, and pass along by its western side to the hamlet.

The road between Watendlath and Keswick is described at page 155.

Armboth to Keswick, by Watendlath.

Watendlath, 2½m.; Keswick, 7½m.

The Fisher Gill, which runs down the fell at the back of Armboth House, must be ascended, and either side of the ravine can be taken.

At the top of the fell a wall is encountered; and if the tourist climb on the N. side of the stream, he must pass through a gate 100 yards distant from the stream on the right, leading through a sheepfold; but if he climb on the S. side of the ravine, he will pass through the wall at a gate about 200 yards from the stream on the left. After passing the wall the course of the rivulet must be followed for a short distance; and before reaching the few trees that overhang its banks, incline to the right, in order to avoid some wet, peaty ground. A small hill in front, with a heap of stones on the top of it, must be ascended, having during the climb some peat stacks on the left. The Borrowdale Mountains now appear. Continue almost due W., slightly inclining to the left, and presently a path is seen winding over the low range of hills between Watendlath and Rosthwaite. Walk in a direct line with this path, and when the tarn and hamlet of Watendlath meet the eye below, descend direct to the buildings, having on the left a stream clothed with a few trees. For a description of the road between Watendlath and Keswick, refer to page 155.

CONISTON SECTION.

CONISTON.

CONISTON is a pretty village, pleasantly situated at the foot of the Old Man and of Wetherlam, and near the head of the lake.

It is a telegraph and railway station. The Waterhead and Crown Hotels are large, well-conducted establishments, and there are also one or two small inns, and some private lodging-houses. The surrounding country is in places richly sylvan and remarkably beautiful.

Some delightful excursions may be made to the neighbouring hills and vales.

Tarn Hows.—A delightful walk of three or more miles may be had by following the road which branches to the left, about ½m. from the Waterhead Hotel, and close to Mr. Marshall's residence.

The tourist travels up a pleasant wooded dell, with fine retrospective views of Coniston Lake. Perhaps from no point does this water look more lovely. After leaving the Tarn Hows farm-house on the left, ascend some high ground on the right, where rests a pretty tarn of irregular shape. The tourist who has leisure will enjoy wandering here for hours, and at every step he will have pleasing and ever-varying prospects. He may descend into Yewdale on the left, or follow a path which runs to the right, and enters the Ambleside and Hawkshead road, about 2m. from Coniston.

Drive round Coniston Lake, 14m.—A road runs all round the lake. On the western side there is little to interest the traveller, but fine views are obtained when approaching the mountains by the eastern shore. Following the road which runs a little below the railway station, Coniston Hall, with its ivied chimneys, is seen on

CONISTON SECTION.

Scale 1 Inch to a Mile

London: Edward Stanford.

Stanford's Geog.¹ Estab.ᵗ 6&7, Charing Cross S.W.

the left. It was once the residence of the Le Flemings, the owners of Rydal Hall.

Just before Torver is reached, Walney Scar, Dow Crags, and the Old Man come in sight on the right. Torver is a straggling village, containing a railway station and a church. Here the road crosses the railway, and conducts across the fells in the direction of the lake. When the shore is gained, by looking back, a view is had up the lake, and the Fairfield range of mountains is seen in the distance. The Dow Crags and Old Man are also visible. Peel Island is directly opposite. The road skirts the shore, and passes along rocky hillocks to the Lake Bank Hotel, a good-sized comfortable house, which stands perched on an elevated piece of ground, close to the foot of the lake. It commands a capital view of the whole lake, with Helvellyn and Fairfield ranges in the background. The Old Man, Wetherlam, and Dow Crags are included in the prospect. From the neighbouring heights of Backbarrow and the Beacon extensive views are to be had. The gondola pier is close to the hotel.

Pleasure-boats can be hired, and there is good fishing in the lake and river; also in a small tarn, called the Beacon, which lies amongst the adjacent hills. The road crosses the river Crake, about ¾m. farther down, by the Bowder Bridge, and then it runs to the village of Nibthwaite, situated close to the foot of the lake, on the E. side.

Pedestrians may save 1½m. by taking a boat, and rowing across to this point. The road traverses the eastern margin of the lake, passing through copse-wood, at the base of a low range of hills. Walney Scar, Dow Crags, Coniston Old Man, and Wetherlam, are prominent objects on the opposite side of the water. The scenery is pleasant all the way, but the view is especially charming when the upper end of the lake is visible. On arriving near to Fir Isle, a pretty wooded islet, which is only a few yards from the mainland, a most charming prospect is revealed. The upper end of the lake is seen, beautifully wooded, with the houses about Coniston peeping above the trees. The Yewdale Fells rise behind the woods, exhibiting a pleasing diversity of colour. In the distance are the Helvellyn and Fairfield ranges. The Coniston Mountains, with their rocks and coves, are spread to view from end to end. No houses are passed for more than 5m.; but during the last mile of the circuit there are some mansions, well situated, one of which was for a time the residence of Mr. Tennyson, the Poet Laureate. Mr. Ruskin, the art-critic, has recently made Coniston his summer residence.

The road makes a gradual rise near the close of the journey, the shore being left at some little distance. A good view is obtained, Coniston gleaming very prettily on the opposite shore.

Ascent of Coniston Old Man (2633) from Coniston. —The Coniston range of mountains, if properly explored, will be found to be remarkably wild and beautiful. On every side are large weather-beaten recesses, in some of which lie deep, lovely tarns.

Visitors whose sojourn is protracted at Coniston may have many a pleasant day's ramble in exploring the deep solitudes of this grand mass of hills, and those who are fond of the "gentle craft" will find excellent sport, as all the tarns are well stocked with trout, and in Seathwaite Tarn and Goats Water are both trout and char.

These mountains are composed of green slate, in which are many veins of copper and some fine roofing material.

The Old Man Mountain, the loftiest height, branches to the S.E., and from it run the Carrs and Greyfriars, in a N.W. direction, to the Wrynose Pass. To the N. branches Wetherlam, and to the S. the Dow Crags and Walney Scar. The ascent is sometimes commenced by following the Walney Scar road for about ½m., until the open fell is reached. The most interesting route, however, is by the regular pony-track, turning round the Black Bull Inn, and mounting by the side of a foaming torrent, which brings down discoloured water from the copper-mines, to which it is a romantic walk. The mines are picturesquely situated in a secluded place at the foot of some wild recesses of the Old Man and Wetherlam. Should the mountain not be ascended, this spot will well repay a visit. Some 120 men are employed at the mines, which are the largest copper works in the district. The visitor can at any time inspect the crushing and washing operations, and at the office he can obtain permission to go underground.

Here cross the streamlet, and make by a winding path to the slate-quarry, distinctly seen half-way up the mountain. From the quarry walk to the right for a few yards, until the dark secluded hollow is reached in which rests Low Water.

This lakelet lies at the foot of a grand amphitheatre of wild vertical cliffs, on the top of which is seen the well-built cairn, marking the highest point of the Old Man. The geological student will notice on every hand grooved and rounded rocks, the result of glacial action.

After leaving the tarn, Levers Water is seen on looking back. It is a large sheet, lying in a hollow between Coniston Old Man and Wetherlam, and is the source of the stream which flows past the copper-mines.

A second and higher slate-quarry is soon reached, and at every step the view becomes more extensive. Coniston Lake, which is visible from end to end, is a beautiful object.

After a few more minutes' hard work, the summit is gained, and an exquisite prospect is unveiled. Close to the spectator are the Carrs, Wetherlam, and Dow Crags, and the wild hollows in which rest Low Water, Levers Water, Dead Tarn, Goats Water, and Seathwaite Tarn; the three first of these tarns are visible, and Goats Water may be seen by descending a few yards on the S. side of the mountain.

To the N.W., Scawfell, Scawfell Pikes, Bow Fell, and Crinkle Crags present a bulky, rugged aspect. Looking in the direction of the Carrs are Glaramara, Skiddaw, Langdale Pikes, Stickle Tarn, High Raise, Blencathara, and Helvellyn.

I

To the right of Wetherlam rise Fairfield, High Street,
and Ill Bell, and numerous smaller heights.   To the E.
are seen Windermere, Esthwaite, and Coniston lakes,
the Tarn Hows, a wide extent of sea, and a large undulating tract of country reaching to Ingleborough Mountain.   Turning to the S. and S.W., are Walney Scar,
Black Combe, Birker Moor, Harter Fell, Hardknott, the
smooth side of the Screes, and the Haycock.   The eye
turns with pleasure from the hills, and surveys a glorious
expanse of sea.   The Isle of Man and Wales are distinctly visible, if the atmosphere be cloudless.

There are many ways by which the return journey
may be varied, and the veritable mountaineer will be in
high spirits at the prospect of the glorious walks which
he may have on these lofty summits.

Continuing on the topmost ridge, with Low Tarn deep
below on the right, and Goats Water on the left, a
point on the Carrs is gained whence are seen Levers
Water on one side, and Seathwaite Tarn on the other.
By descending to the ridge at the head of Levers
Water, the tourist may climb Wetherlam, and then descend to the copper-mines, or, on the opposite side, to
the Tilberthwaite Glen.   Another fine excursion is had
by crossing from the Carrs to the Dow Crags, with
Goats Water on the left and Seathwaite Tarn on the
right, and then descending by Walney Scar.

A third route is to continue over the Carrs to the top
of the Wrynose Pass.

Those who descend direct to the mines should cross
the bridge which spans the torrent ½m. below, and thus
obtain some beautiful retrospective views before reaching
Coniston.

Ascent of Black Combe (1969).—This mountain rises
from the shore of the Irish Sea, and stands at the S. end
of the Lake District, away from the loftier peaks.   It is
composed of the Skiddaw or clay slate.   Being in the
outskirts of the district, it is little visited, although it
commands one of the most extensive prospects to be obtained from any height.

Tourists who remain any time at Coniston ought to devote a day to this mountain, and ascend it from Silecroft railway station, the distance to the summit being 4m., and thence descend to Broughton, a distance of 6m. Others may prefer scaling it from Broughton or from Bootle.

The distance by railway from Coniston to Silecroft is 15m. Close to the railway station at Silecroft is the Royal Albert Hotel. On leaving the railway station, aim for a farm-house at the foot of the first hollow in the mountain. Climb by the rill which trickles down the hollow, and then bend to the right. A long gradual climb over smooth ground leads to the top. During the walk the tourist will, in all probability, be refreshed by a healthy sea breeze. When the summit is reached, the sea is close at the feet of the spectator, and a wide stretch of its silvery surface is visible, extending from beyond St. Bees Head to the coast of Wales. The Scotch and Welsh mountains and the Isle of Man are distinctly apparent when the atmosphere is clear, and it is reported that occasionally a part of Ireland can be discerned.

Turning from the sea, the level country to the W. is spread out as if on a map; and eastward are the Furness Fells, with the Yorkshire Hills in the perspective. The Coniston Old Man range, Birker Moor, and Harter Fell are close at hand; and to the right of the Old Man are seen the Ill Bell and High Street range; and to the left, Helvellyn, and also a number of jagged heights, including Crinkle Crags, Bow Fell, Hanging Knott, Scawfell Pikes, Scawfell, Great Gable, Kirk Fell, Pillar, Steeple, Haycock, Seatallan, and the Screes. In the far distance, between Great Gable and Kirk Fell, a part of Skiddaw is visible.

It is advisable to walk northwards, on the top of the mountain, for some distance, and then to descend on the right to the little cultivated vale of Swinside, where there is a perfect Druidical Circle, 90 yards in circumference, and containing 50 moderate sized stones.

The distance thence to Broughton is 4m.

I 2

Duddon Valley. — Tourists staying any length of time at Coniston ought to devote a day to the Duddon Valley, and saunter leisurely up the vale with Wordsworth's 'Sonnets to the Duddon' in hand.

Wordsworth follows the river Duddon from the source to the sea; but a better plan is to track its course in the opposite direction.

The tourist ought to travel by railway from Coniston to Broughton-in-Furness. The latter is a small clean town containing two good hotels, the Old King's Head and the New King's Head, where a conveyance or horses can be hired. Near to the town is Broughton Tower, an embattled mansion commanding a charming and extensive view.

The river Duddon has its source near the Wrynose Pass, a distance of 14m. from Broughton. It may be as well to remind the stranger that the stream divides Cumberland from Lancashire; and that on the W. (the Cumberland side) the whole of the land is in the township of Ulpha, while on the Lancashire side the township of Dunnerdale stretches up the valley for 5m. from Broughton, there joining the township of Seathwaite, which continues as far as the Wrynose Pass.

Five miles and a-half from Broughton are the Ulpha Kirk and a small inn called The Traveller's Rest; but the tourist must not expect to find a town or village, the houses being scattered all the way up the valley.

Two and a-half miles from Ulpha Kirk, and on the opposite side of the river, is the Seathwaite church, close to which stands the Newfield Inn. Here there is no village, Newfield being merely the name of the inn, which was formerly only a farm-house.

In other pages of this work the reader will find full particulars relating to the beautiful scenery and to the places of interest in this valley.

On leaving the Newfield Inn, Coniston may be reached by crossing over the Walney Scar road; or the journey may be continued to the head of the valley and over the Wrynose Pass. A better plan is to follow the Seathwaite

Beck to the romantic recess in which lies imbedded Seathwaite Tarn, and then cross over to Goats Water, or climb the Old Man Mountain.

Coniston to (Dungeon Gill) Langdale, by Tilberthwaite Glen and Blea Tarn, 8m.—After leaving the Waterhead Hotel in the direction of Coniston, take the first road on the right. It runs up Yewdale at the base of a fine rocky escarpment. Enter the first road which branches to the left and slightly ascends. It leaves Yewdale and enters Tilberthwaite. The fine tinted rocks of Holme Fell and Raven Crag, on the opposite side of the torrent, are pleasing objects. The Tilberthwaite Glen is small, but highly picturesque and full of wild beauty. After passing in succession a copper-mine, a slate-quarry, and a row of cottages, a farm-house is reached, where the traveller can obtain good milk and biscuits.

The road now makes a steep ascent, and leaves the glen. Ill Bell, Fairfield, and Helvellyn ranges come in sight, and presently the Langdale Pikes, and on the right are hillocks strewn with slate *débris*. After threading amongst heath-covered rocks, a descent is made to Fell Foot, and the Little Langdale Tarn is seen lying below at the base of Lingmoor. A cluster of yew trees half conceals the farm-house at Fell Foot. A winding path is discerned ascending the Wrynose Pass. When the road is entered close to the yew trees, walk to the right for a few yards. The path is now gained which leads through Little Langdale, by the side of Lingmoor, and past Blea Tarn to Dungeon Gill. See p. 21. Some distance may be saved by climbing the hill from Blea Tarn, with Side Pike on the left, and then descending direct to the New Dungeon Gill Hotel. By this means a remarkably good position is obtained for seeing the Langdale Pikes.

Coniston to Wastdale Head, by Walney Scar, Birker Moor, and Burnmoor Tarn.

Newfield, 5m.; Ulpha, 7½m.; Boot, 13½m.; Wastdale Head, 19m.

The Walney Scar road mounts the hill in the rear of the Coniston railway station, and rounds the E. end of the Old Man. It commands fine views of Coniston Lake, the Ill Bell range of mountains, the rocks and hollows of Wetherlam, and Coniston Old Man.

When the tourist gains the open fell-side, he must follow a rough track which runs along the smooth grassy ground close to the foot of the mountain, and avoid entering a cart-track which branches to the right, and leads to some slate-quarries. On getting in the rear of the Old Man, the Dow Crags appear, and present a wild aspect. At their feet, out of sight, lies Goats Water Tarn, and in a small hollow higher up on the left, close to some slate *débris*, is a small sheet of water, called Dead Tarn. The Walney Scar path is observed ascending in a winding course to the left of the slate-quarry. The tedium of the ascent is relieved by a view of Coniston Lake, the Furness Fells and a wide expanse of sea, including Duddon Sands and Morecambe Bay. On attaining the top of Walney Scar (2000), a great part of the Duddon Valley is spread at the feet of the spectator; and on the opposite side of the vale is the long range of comparatively low heights, stretching from Black Combe, over Birker Moor, to Harter Fell and Hardknott, and over these a large tract of sea is visible. The bulky mass of the Scawfell Mountains is very prominent, and to the left of it are the Steeple, Haycock, and other heights. The hollow wherein rests Seathwaite Tarn, and from which flows the Seathwaite Beck, is observed high up in the Old Man range. The path winds to within a few yards of a slate-quarry, and then bends to the right, and descends into Seathwaite, a sweet, secluded vale, which seems to be entirely separated by low rocky hills from the larger valley of the Duddon. The Seathwaite Church and the Newfield Inn are 1m, farther down, and in travelling to them the tourist will pass through some picturesque scenery, rock, wood, and water forming a happy combination. It is the most charming bit which is to be met with in the Duddon Valley, and is equal to anything of the kind in the Lake District.

Those who are anxious to reach Eskdale and Wastdale Head in the most expeditious way, might enter the road which branches to the right ½m. before arriving at the Newfield Inn, at the point where a guidepost directs to Langdale, Coniston, and Broughton. By following the Langdale road for a short distance, until a sight is obtained of the Duddon River, and then crossing the stream at some stepping-stones, the fell is ascended by the side of a ravine, down which flows a streamlet. During the ascent it is advisable to step a few yards to the left, in order to see a fine cascade called Gill Spout. It has a fall of more than 200 feet, broken into three leaps. After passing a few green fields and the Grass Gars farm-house, in order to avoid wet, boggy ground, bend to the right, and skirt the base of Harter Fell. A well-defined peat-track will be found leading down by the side of the mountain. The Esk Valley is gained close to the foot of the Hardknott Pass, and 1m. from the Wool-pack Inn. Some adventurous travellers will cross the wet tract on Birker Moor, and descend into Eskdale, directly opposite the Wool-pack, or a little farther down, by the Low Birker Pool and Birker Force.

Eskdale, of course, may be reached from the foot of Walney Scar, by proceeding up the Duddon Valley, and crossing over Hardknott.

From the Wool-pack the most direct course to Wastdale is by a track which ascends the hill at the back of the house. After passing through a wall, the open fell is entered. Keep by the side of the left-hand wall, and after walking a short distance, quit it, and mount the hill by a peat-road, which leads to Eel Tarn. This is a small lakelet containing trout and perch, and it lies in a wild, heath-covered moor. Another similar sheet of water, called Stony Tarn, lies out of sight amongst the rocks, a few hundred yards distant to the E. From Eel Tarn the tourist must aim for the hollow between Scawfell and the Screes, with the Pillar and Great Gable direct in the front. The stream which flows from Burnmoor Tarn is crossed at a small wooden bridge, and then the path is entered which leads from Boot to Wastdale Head.

Tourists who walk from Walney Scar to Wastdale, by the route above indicated, ought not to leave the Duddon Valley without first occupying half an hour in a walk to Newfield Inn and back, and thus visiting the church, and seeing the beautiful scenery in the neighbourhood. The Newfield Inn is clean and comfortable, and delightfully situated close to the junction of the Duddon River and the Seathwaite Beck.

Not many yards from the inn, are the " Steppingstones," the subject of two of Wordsworth's sonnets :—

" . . . . Here the Child
Puts, when the high-swoln Flood runs fierce and wild,
His budding courage to the proof; and here
Declining Manhood learns to note the sly
And sure encroachments of infirmity,
Thinking how fast time runs, life's end how near ! "

" Not so that Pair whose youthful spirits dance
With prompt emotion, urging them to pass ;
A sweet confusion checks the Shepherd-lass ;
Blushing she eyes the dizzy flood askance ;
To stop ashamed—too timid to advance ;
She ventures once again—another pause !
His outstretched hand He tauntingly withdraws—
She sues for help with piteous utterance !
Chidden she chides again ; the thrilling touch
Both feel, when he renews the wished-for aid :
Ah ! if their fluttering hearts should stir too much,
Should beat too strongly, both may be betrayed.
The frolic Loves who, from yon high rock, see
The struggle, clap their wings for victory ! "

The Seathwaite Church, and pleasant little parsonage,

are only a few yards from the inn. Here the "Wonderful Robert Walker" dwelt, and officiated as curate for sixty-seven years.

> "Such priest as Chaucer sang in fervent lays;
> Such as the heaven-taught skill of Herbert drew;
> And tender Goldsmith crowned with deathless praise!"

In the churchyard is his grave. A plain stone slab records that he died on the 25th June, 1802, in the ninety-third year of his age. His character is given in the 7th Book of Wordsworth's 'Excursion.'

> "In this one Man is shown a temperance—proof
> Against all trials; industry severe
> And constant as the motion of the day;
> Stern self-denial round him spread, with shade
> That might be deemed forbidding, did not there
> All generous feelings flourish and rejoice;
> Forbearance, charity in deed and thought,
> And resolution competent to take
> Out of the bosom of simplicity
> All that her holy customs recommend,
> And the best ages of the world prescribe.
> —Preaching, administering, in every work
> Of his sublime vocation, in the walks
> Of worldly intercourse between man and man,
> And in his humble dwelling, he appears
> A labourer, with moral virtue girt,
> With spiritual graces, like a glory, crowned."
>
>   *   *   *   *   *
>
>   "And him, the *Wonderful*,
> Our simple shepherds, speaking from the heart,
> Deservedly have styled.—From his abode
> In a dependent chapelry, that lies
> Behind yon hill, a poor and rugged wild,
> Which in his soul he lovingly embraced,
> And having once espoused, would never quit;
> Hither, ere long, that lowly, great, good Man
> Will be conveyed. An unelaborate stone
> May cover him; and by its help, perchance,
> A century shall hear his name pronounced,
> With images attendant on the sound."

The value of his curacy, when he entered upon it, was 5*l*. per annum, with a cottage. He married shortly afterwards, and his wife brought him a fortune of 40*l*. He had twelve children, of whom eight lived, and these he respectably educated, and made one of the sons a clergyman. Besides acting as parish priest, he was schoolmaster and doctor; made wills and wrote letters for his parishioners; assisted for hire in hay-making and sheepshearing, spun wool, and made his own clothing. There being no public-house, he sold ale of his own brewing. He was munificent in his hospitality and generous to the needy, and is said to have died worth 2000*l*., although his income from his curacy never exceeded 50*l*. per annum.

From Newfield Inn to The Traveller's Rest, at Ulpha, is 2½m. Pleasant bits of scenery are had all the way down the valley. The latter inn offers homely but clean accommodation. Before crossing Birker Moor, the tourist ought to visit Ulpha Church, the subject of one of Wordsworth's sonnets. It is perched on a rock by the side of the river Duddon, and is reached after a pleasant stroll of a few hundred yards from the inn.

> " How sweet were leisure! could it yield no more
>   Than 'mid that wave-washed Churchyard to recline,
>   From pastoral graves extracting thoughts divine;
> Or there to pace, and mark the summits hoar
>   Of distant moon-lit mountains faintly shine,
> Soothed by the unseen River's gentle roar."

From Ulpha the road to Eskdale lies over a desolate moor abounding in peat. It ascends the hill close behind the inn, and leaves Hesk Fell on the left. Gradually the Duddon hills disappear in the rear, and in front rise the Pillar, Kirk Fell, Scawfell, and Scawfell Pikes.

Harter Fell is a pleasant object on the right. At the foot of Hesk Fell are a few farm-houses and green fields, to which a road branches on the left. About 3m. from Ulpha a road turns off to the right, leading past Stanley Gill Fall and Dalegarth Hall to the village of Boot, in Eskdale. The direct road passes within a short distance of Devoke Water, and enters Eskdale near the King of Prussia Inn, 2m. below Boot.

Devoke Water is 2½m. in circumference, with a rocky islet in its centre. It is well stocked with trout, perch, and eels. To obtain a view of it, the tourist must walk a few hundred yards to the left of the road. Close to this lakelet are some heaps of stones, which extend 300 yards one way and 100 the other. They are called "The ancient city of Barnscar," and are supposed to be the remains of a Danish town.

Most travellers will follow the road which bears to the right, on the top of Birker Moor, and descends to Dalegarth Hall. It passes two farm-houses, and then allows of a beautiful view up Eskdale. After leaving the open moor, some wooded ground is entered, and out of sight, in a ravine a short distance on the right, is Stanley Gill Fall. At the house, close to the old dilapidated hall, a guide may be obtained for the fall.

The hamlet of Boot is 1m. distant, on the opposite side of the valley. Here is a small inn, called the Mason's Arms. From Boot to Wastdale Head, the path crosses heath-covered ground in the direction of the stream which flows from Burnmoor Tarn. This stream is reached by following the road at the back of the inn, and entering the open fell.

Upon the hill to the left, on the farther side of which is the small glen of Miterdale, are a number of small stone circles, and a tiny sheet of water, called Blea Tarn.

During the walk to Burnmoor Tarn, fine views are obtained of Eskdale and the surrounding mountains. In front rise Scawfell, Great Gable, Kirk Fell, and the Pillar. To the left is the smooth side of the Screes Mountain. Burnmoor Tarn is a large cheerless sheet of water, lying in the midst of a bleak moor. A gamekeeper's house stands near to its shore, on the brow of the hill.

After crossing the stream, just where it issues from the tarn, the path bends slightly to the left, and then again to the right, and descends to Wastdale Head, behind the highest wall, along some rough, stony ground.

During the descent, the lake is in sight, and the lofty mountains at the head of the glen present a noble appearance.

When the valley is entered, all traces of the path are lost. After threading along ground partly covered with rough stones, and resembling the dry bed of a torrent, with here and there a few shrubs, the beck is crossed at a wooden foot-bridge near to the head of the lake, and the road is gained which leads to the inn.

Coniston to Wastwater, *via* **Drigg or Seascale.—** Wastwater may be reached from Coniston by taking a carriage through Yewdale and Tilberthwaite to Fell Foot, and thence by Wrynose and Hardknott, see page 53. A more expeditious mode is to travel by railway to Drigg or Seascale, and there hire a conveyance for the remaining 12m. to Wastdale Head, at the upper end; or 6m. to Strands, near the foot of the lake. By railway the tourist will pass Millom and Muncaster castles.

Millom Castle is situated ½m. from Holborn Hill, a maritime village at the foot of Black Combe, and was formerly the residence of the Huddlestones. It is now occupied as a farm-house. A considerable portion is roofless, and the massive walls are clothed with ivy. It was never of great extent.

Muncaster Castle is 1m. from Ravenglass station. It is the seat of the ancient family of the Penningtons. Lord Muncaster, its present owner, is M.P. for the Western Division of Cumberland. The mansion is principally modern, only a tower of the ancient castle remaining. It is situated on a height, amidst fine woods, and commands views of great beauty.

A glass cup, called "The Luck of Muncaster," was given by Henry VI. to Sir John Pennington, after the Battle of Hexham, in 1464. It is said that the king was met, on his flight, by some shepherds in Eskdale, and conducted by them to the castle. The glass is carefully preserved as a precious heirloom, and a harbinger of the family's fortunes.

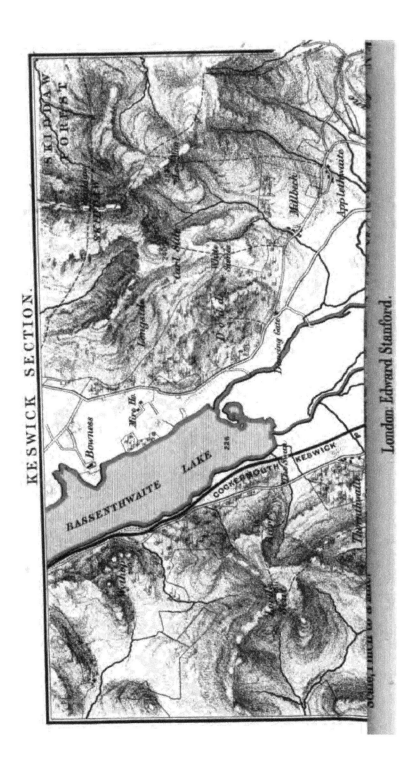

KESWICK SECTION.

London: Edward Stanford.

KESWICK SECTION.

KESWICK.

THE market town of Keswick contains 2777 inhabitants. It is the best centre from which to visit most of the wildest scenery in the Lake District. Although it is little more than ½m. from Derwentwater, the most beautiful of lakes, and is surrounded by a glorious assemblage of mountains, and rests at the foot of Skiddaw, which is, perhaps, the grandest mountain in Great Britain, the town itself, if compared with most places of fashionable resort, may rather disappoint the tourist on his first entrance, but this feeling soon wears off.

It contains many private houses pleasantly situated for the accommodation of visitors, and there are many excellent hotels in the town and neighbourhood, suitable for every class.

In the town are the Royal Oak, Queen's, King's Arms, George, Atkinson's Lake Hotel, Shearman's Station Hotel, Gill's Hotel, Skiddaw Temperance Hotel, and Jeffery's Temperance Hotel; all good and comfortable.

At the railway station, ¼m. distant, is situated the Keswick Hotel. It is one of the largest hotels in the north of England, and commands excellent views of the surrounding mountains.

At the foot of the lake, and about 1m. from Keswick, in the pretty village of Portinscale, are two large hotels, the Derwentwater Hotel and the Tower Hotel. The Derwentwater Hotel is very commodious and well managed; the grounds in front command pleasant views, and extend to the lake, where there are boats belonging to the establishment. The Tower Hotel is quite new, and extensive lake and mountain prospects are to be had from its windows.

The Lodore Hotel, situated on the eastern margin of the lake, 3m. from Keswick, and behind which is the

Lodore Fall, has been considerably enlarged, and is now a handsome structure. It has the advantage of most picturesque views of lake and mountains.

About ½m. beyond Lodore is the Borrowdale Hotel, a large, new house, very comfortable, and in a fine situation, near the head of the lake, and at the entrance to Borrowdale Valley.

At Rosthwaite, in Borrowdale, 6m. from Keswick, are the Royal Oak and Scawfell Hotels, both clean and cosey.

Private lodgings may also be obtained at Portinscale and Grange villages, the Borrowdale and Newlands valleys, and at Armboth House on Thirlmere Lake.

In describing the following excursions the tourist is supposed to be located in Keswick, and, of course, if he be staying at some hotel outside the town, he must make slight alterations in his travelling arrangements.

Soon after arriving at Keswick, it is well to walk down the main street, to the bridge crossing the river Greta, where a good view may be had of *Greta Hall*, standing to the right, on a slight elevation, and almost surrounded by trees. The poet Southey lived here from 1803 until his death, in 1843. He is buried in *Crosthwaite Churchyard*, ½m. to the N. of Keswick, which is reached by continuing along the road over the bridge.

The church was restored in 1845 by James Stanger, Esq., at a cost of 4000*l.* It contains a monument erected to the Laureate's memory, consisting of a pedestal of Caen stone, on which reposes a full-length figure, cut in white marble by Lough, and which cost 1100*l.*, raised by private subscription among his friends and admirers. The inscription (a poetical one) was written by Wordsworth. In the chancel of the church is a monument of Sir John Radcliffe, Kt., an ancestor of the Earls of Derwentwater, and Dame Alice, his wife, recumbent, in alabaster, and a bronze of the family arms with a black-letter inscription. There is also an ancient baptismal font, curiously carved with emblematical designs, and bearing the arms of Edward III. In one of the windows is preserved some stained glass, said to be from Furness Abbey, representing St. Anthony with bell and book. Before quitting the church some visitors will be glad to ascend the tower, where a good view is obtained of the surrounding vale. The person in attendance expects and generally receives a trifle: a portion of such receipts assists in paying the organist's salary.

A very pleasant walk of about ½m. may be had on returning to Keswick, by strolling past the school buildings close to the churchyard, and along a lane leading into the Portinscale road. Before arriving at the bridge spanning the river Derwent, take a foot-path on the left, leading through a meadow called Howray. This walk was a favourite with Southey. The mountains are seen magnificently grouped all around, forming a vast circular range. On the N. is the huge but graceful mass of Skiddaw, supported by Latrigg. On the E. Wallow Crag, with Bleaberry Fell beyond, and to the S. the Borrowdale Mountains. The Newlands and Coledale Mountains on the W. are especially well grouped when seen from this point. The road is again entered at Greta Bridge, and after crossing the stream, tourists will visit the PENCIL MANUFACTORY on the right, where they will be initiated into many of the mysteries of the staple trade of Keswick. The celebrated Borrowdale Lead Mine is situated 9m. from Keswick, at Seathwaite, in Borrowdale. The lead, or plumbago, locally termed "wad," which was found in the mine, is the best material ever discovered for making lead pencils. At one time the mine yielded enormous profits, and there were especial Acts of Parliament for its protection; but one or two companies who worked it some years ago were not successful, and the mine has now been closed for about thirteen years. The plumbago is not found in regular veins, but occurs in lumps or nodules, in the fissures of the slate-rock, the lumps varying from 1 oz. to 50 lbs.; and in working the mine a fortune might be lost or made without any previous certainty. Some people believe the mine is practically all but exhausted. The firms in Keswick have a quantity

of the real Borrowdale lead in reserve, which they use
very sparingly.   An inferior kind of plumbago is obtained from other countries, principally Mexico, and the
lead of most pencils is composed of this, mixed with
other ingredients.   Visitors on entering the mill are
shown every stage by which the rough block of cedar is
transformed into the smooth and varnished pencil, and
in a few minutes they can have delivered to them pencils
with their name cut in them in gold or colours.   No
charge is made for admission, but a small purchase will
generally be made in acknowledgment of the courtesy
of those who go round the mill and explain the different operations.   There are similar mills in the town,
which compete with this mill in gaining the tourist's
attention.

The next object to be visited is MR. FLINTOFT'S
MODEL of the Lake District.   It is exhibited in the
Town Hall, a large church-like building in the middle
of the market square.   The charge is 1s. each.   Most
persons, on entering, will be disappointed.   At first
sight the model looks like a large table of unsightly
plaster, but a few minutes' study of it will give the
tourist a better knowledge of the whole Lake District
than he can obtain from a month's study of the maps.
It is on a scale of 3 inches to 1m., and its dimensions
are 12 feet 9 inches by 9 feet 3 inches.   It is the result
of many years of unremitting labour, and has been
pronounced by leading scientific men to be the most
finished specimen of geographical modelling that has
ever been constructed in England.   It ought to be seen
as often as possible, and after the first visit, admittance
is free for the remainder of the season.   Correct and
disinterested information may there be obtained, enabling
the tourist to make the best use of his time.

Pettitt's Picture Gallery, in the upper part of the town,
is free, and well worthy of a visit.

Near St. John's Church is the *Keswick Library and
Reading Room*, containing 3000 volumes.   Visitors,
upon payment of 2s. 6d., can obtain a ticket which will

entitle them to the use of the room and books for one month.

Crosthwaite's Museum now no longer exists. It was sold and dispersed during the year 1870.

Castle Hill.—In order to gain a knowledge of the geographical position of the mountains surrounding the vale of Keswick, it is desirable to walk to the summit of Castle Hill, which is ½m. from the town, and only 529 feet above the sea level. The view there is considered superior to any other which can be had from so low an elevation in the Lake District. It is sometimes called Castle Head, and Castelette.

Leave the market square by the Borrowdale road. When passing Atkinson's Lake Hotel, a road will be seen branching to the right, and another to the left; the one to the right leads to the boat-landings on the Derwentwater Lake, and to Friar's Crag. Avoid these branch roads and go straight forwards. After passing all the houses, a carriage-road to left is seen leading to the St. John's Church, and opposite to which there is a gate; and a foot-path through a field conducts to the Lake road. Passing these, and two other field-gates on the left, a small wicket-gate will be found. Go through this, and keep along the well-defined path, which soon takes a turn to the right. From a rock a few feet below the highest point, there is an opening in the trees which allows of one of the most lovely views of the town of Keswick.

Most of Bassenthwaite Lake, a portion of Derwentwater Lake, the whole of the intervening valley, and Skiddaw, are seen. St. John's Church, and the beautifully green and wooded grounds of the Parsonage, Crosthwaite Church, the Railway Station, and the Keswick Hotel, also add greatly to the view.

On arriving at the summit, the whole of the lovely lake of Derwentwater, with its wooded bays and islands, is spread below, and surrounded by a fine assemblage of mountains. To the N. there is Bassenthwaite Lake, and on the right of it Skiddaw. The trees hide Blenca-

thara.   To the E., over Castlerigg, peer White Pike and
Great Dodd, some of the Helvellyn range; and next to
them, but much nearer the lake, Wallow Crag presents
a beautifully-coloured and well-wooded front; and at
its foot are the Deer Close Cottage and Stable Hills
Farm, in the midst of woods and cultivated fields.
Beyond Wallow Crag the bold, bare Falcon Crag is seen
overhanging the lake, and then Gowder Crag, Barrow
House, Lodore Hotel and Waterfall, and Shepherd's
Crag; above which, Brund Fell appears to be assisting
the low conical hill, Castle Crag, in guarding the E.
side of Borrowdale, and it hides Bow Fell, but permits a
portion of Hanging Knott to come into view.   Great
End, Scawfell Pike, and Scawfell are clearly seen in the
distance.   To the W. are Maiden Moor, and the Cat
Bells, close to the lake.

Over the highest point of Cat Bells a little of Hindscarth is visible, and then the bold front of Robinson;
on the right of which is the Newlands Valley, and in
the distance High Stile and Red Pike, which are on the
farther side of Buttermere Lake.   Rowling End,
Causey Pike, Eel Crags, and Grisedale Pike, stand out
boldly, and allow Barrow, Swinside, and Silver Hill to
act as stepping-stones to the lake.   N.W. the Whinlatter Fells, Lord's Seat, Barf, and Wythop Fells run
along the side of Bassenthwaite Lake; and on a clear
day, to the right of these, the summit of Criffel, in
Scotland, may be seen.

Returning by the road taken in ascending, it is
advisable, on arriving at the first house, to go through
the gate leading to the church, in order to have the
view from the churchyard, which is much admired;
and then the foot-path can be taken, above referred to,
leading to the lake.

Friar's Crag and Derwentwater Lake.—Walk past
the boat-landings for about 300 yards to the Friar's
Crag, where there is a seat, and a view of the lake and
surrounding mountains which is perhaps unsurpassed.
This crag is a favourite resort of the Keswickians, and

truly the view from it ought to be to them "a thing of beauty," and "a joy for ever," for it would seem almost impossible to conceive one that could be more harmonious and truly beautiful. It is unnecessary to name the mountains which can be seen from this point, for they were all in view on Castle Hill.

The lake is 238 feet above the sea level, and its greatest depth is 81 feet. It is about 3m. long, and 1½m. broad at the widest part, being the broadest lake in the district; and it is most symmetrical in shape. Nine-tenths of the visitors to the Lakes consider Derwentwater the most beautiful of all, and many persons who have visited the lakes of foreign countries say that nowhere is there one more lovely.

It is fed by the river Derwent, which has its source in the Sprinkling and Sty Head tarns, near the Scawfell range of mountains. At Rosthwaite, in Borrowdale, the Derwent is joined by a stream which comes down the Longstrath Valley, from Angle Tarn, near Bow Fell. It enters the lake near Lodore, and leaves it at Portinscale. About 100 yards from the lake the Derwent is joined by the river Greta. The Greta is formed by the confluence of the Glenderamakin River, and the St. John's Beck, a short distance below Threlkeld; and is afterwards joined by the Glenderaterra, from Skiddaw Forest, and the Naddle Beck, from the Naddle Valley. The Glenderamakin rises at the Scales Tarn, on the E. end of Blencathara, and the St. John's Beck, after leaving Thirlmere Lake, flows through the vale of St. John. The Greta winds through a beautifully-timbered valley at the foot of Latrigg, where it is crossed many times by the railway, and then passes at the back of Greta Hall, and under Greta Bridge, at the low end of Keswick. In some Guide Books it is erroneously stated that this is the Greta mentioned in 'Rokeby.' The Greta of that poem is in the north of Yorkshire. The Derwent, after being fed by tributary streams from the Newlands and Coledale valleys, flows through Bassenthwaite Lake, and past

Cockermouth, to the Irish Sea at Workington. At Cockermouth it is joined by the river Cocker, which flows through the vale of Lorton, from the Buttermere, Crummock, and Loweswater lakes.

The tourist, from his position on Friar's Crag, will see on the right Derwent Isle, on which is seated the residence of H. C. Marshall, Esq., of Leeds. St. Herbert's Island is to the S.W., and upon it are the remains of a cell, which, it is said, was occupied, during the seventh century, by a hermit of the name of Herbert, who was a contemporary of St. Cuthbert, of Farn Island, off the Northumbrian coast. Bede says that St. Herbert left his cell once a year to visit St. Cuthbert, and "receive from his lips the doctrine of eternal life." It is said that they prayed that they might depart hence into heaven together, which petition was granted them, both expiring at the same moment. Wordsworth writes :—

> " Though here the hermit numbered his last day,
> Far from St. Cuthbert, his beloved friend,
> Those holy men both died in the same hour."

The island directly in front is Rampsholme. The larger one, to the left, containing a rookery, is Lord's Island. Upon it are the foundations of a mansion once occupied by the Earls of Derwentwater. The island is said to have been originally a peninsula, and was severed from the mainland by a deep artificial cut, which served as a fosse, and was spanned by a drawbridge. It was from this island that Lady Derwentwater is said to have escaped, taking with her the family jewels, in order to assist in the attempt to procure the release of the Earl, who was imprisoned in the Tower of London, for having taken part in the rebellion of 1715. A cleft in Wallow Crag, now called the Lady's Rake (rake being a provincial term for a miniature pass amongst rocks), is said to have been scaled by her when she effected her escape. All her efforts, however, proved useless; the Earl was beheaded, and the family estates in Northumberland,

Cumberland, and Durham having been confiscated, were granted to Greenwich Hospital. The property around Keswick now belongs to the Marshalls, of Leeds.

Besides these four principal islands there are three or four very small ones, and it is said that at irregular intervals of a few years a piece of ground, called a Floating Island, rises from the bottom to the surface of the water, near Lodore. Gas escaping from decayed vegetable matter is supposed to be the cause of this singular phenomenon.

Round Derwentwater in a Boat.—Before returning to the town, after visiting Friar's Crag, the tourist will do well to hire a boat, and row round the lake, calling at the bays and islands, and the Barrow and Lodore waterfalls. A few hours cannot be spent more agreeably on a fine hot summer's day than in thus leisurely visiting the bays and promontories, under the shade of the trees which clothe the margin of this lovely sheet of water.

The charge for a boat is 1s. per hour, and 5s. per day. For boat and boatman, 2s. for the first hour, and 1s. 6d. for every succeeding hour. For boat and boatman from Keswick to Lodore and back, no less a charge is made than for three hours. Fishing party with boatman, 10s. per day. Trout, pike, perch, eel, and occasionally salmon, frequent the lake. Unsuccessful attempts have been made to introduce char. There is an Angling Association for the protection of the fish in the lake and rivers near Keswick. Strangers can obtain tickets from the Association which will give them the privilege of fishing over the whole of the lake, as well as most of the rivers near Keswick. The tickets are, for one day, 1s., and for a week, 3s.; and they can be procured at Bowe's and Glover's fishing-tackle shops, or from the Secretary, Mr. A. Gibson.

As soon as the visitor leaves the landing-stage, and enters the boat, he will be pleased to find that the town, though so near, is completely hidden by the green round knoll of Crow Park.

Skiddaw appears to rise, in all its majesty, from within
a stone's-throw of the shore, and it continues to be an
attractive object during most of the excursion.

On skirting Friar's Crag, and making for the east
side of Lord's Island, Scawfell Pike, the highest mountain in England, comes in sight .at the head of Borrowdale. When near the island, the spectator suddenly
finds himself in a most charming position, where the
depression between Skiddaw and Blencathara is apparently filled up by the wooded rock of Castle Hill. The
western mountains, Cat Bells, Causey Pike, Grisedale
Pike, and Barrow, present, along with other heights,
grand outlines on the western shore. In front are the
wild cliffs, Wallow Crag and Falcon Crag, and behind
stand Derwent Isle and Friar's Crag, beautifully clothed
with wood.

Row round the next headland, and enter Scarf Close
Bay, keeping near the shore. By this means Wallow
Crag and Falcon Crag are seen to the greatest advantage; and very imposing and beautiful they look, the
trees hiding their base, and making them appear to
rise from the water's edge. Portinscale village now
comes charmingly in sight at the very foot of the
lake. Occasionally the castellated tower of Crosthwaite Church appears, and the spire of St. John's adds
greatly to the view during almost the whole circuit.
Blencathara has gradually disappeared, and the Causey
Pike range is hidden by Cat Bells, except the knob-like
summit, which now and then peers above the latter
height. Looking to the head of the lake, a fine jagged
lot of ˙hills present themselves, rising height above
height from the Lodore Crags, over Grange, Brund, and
Castle Crags, to the lofty summits of Great End, Scawfell Pike, and Scawfell.

Derwentwater is the broadest lake in the district, and
the tourist is now looking across its broadest part.

When Barrow Bay is entered, a landing must be
effected at a small boat-pier, and the *Barrow Fall*
visited. An excellent view is had of Derwentwater from

the pier. The waterfall is situated behind Barrow House, in the private grounds of S. Z. Langton, Esq., and may be seen on application at the lodge. The water makes two leaps, in all 122 feet. The fall is very pleasing, and well worth visiting. It presents a pleasant contrast to the wild neighbouring fall at Lodore.

On again entering the boat, and rounding the Barrow promontory, some fine cliffs clothed with trees are passed, and then Lodore Hotel and Fall are reached. Here is a long wooden pier a few yards up the river, and if the water be too low to allow of this being reached, a landing may be effected a few yards nearer the cliffs.

The *Lodore Fall* is close behind the Hotel. Except after heavy floods, a scanty stream of water descends between its perpendicular cliffs. After heavy rains the water tumbles down with a tremendous roar, which is heard at a great distance; and at those times the fall is surpassed by few in Britain. It is, however, at all times well deserving a visit, owing to its wild and rocky character. The water forms an innumerable number of small cascades when finding its way over, and amongst, a number of huge boulders, thrown together in wild confusion, and on each side rises an immense perpendicular cliff, Shepherd's Crag being on the right, and Gowder Crag on the left, both clothed in parts with wood. When thoroughly explored it is found to be as wild a bit of scenery as is to be met with in the district. For any stranger to pass without going through the grounds, and scrambling a short distance up the fall, would be an oversight to be regretted in future years.

Southey has immortalized the place in the following lines:—

> " ' How does the water
> Come down at Lodore? '
> My little boy asked me
> Thus, once on a time;
> And moreover he task'd me
> To tell him in rhyme.

Anon at the word,
There first came one daughter,
And then came another
To second and third
The request of their brother,
And to hear how the water
Comes down at Lodore,
With its rush and its roar,
As many a time
They had seen it before.

" So I told them in rhyme,
For of rhymes I had store:
And 't was in my vocation,
For their recreation,
That so I should sing;
Because I was Laureate
To them and the King.

" From its sources which well
In the tarn on the fell;
From its fountains
In the mountains,
Its rills and its gills;
Through moss and through brake,
It runs and it creeps
For awhile, till it sleeps
In its own little lake.

" And thence at departing,
Awakening and starting,
It runs through the reeds,
And away it proceeds,
Through meadow and glade,
In sun and in shade, -
And through the wood-shelter,
Among crags in its flurry,
Helter-skelter, hurry-skurry.

" Here it comes sparkling,
And there it lies darkling;
Now smoking and frothing
Its tumult and wrath in,

Till in this rapid race
On which it is bent,
It reaches the place
Of its steep descent.

" The cataract strong
Then plunges along,
Striking and raging,
As if a war waging,
Its caverns and rocks among :
Rising and leaping,
Sinking and creeping,
Swelling and sweeping,
Showering and springing,
Flying and flinging,
Writhing and ringing,
Eddying and whisking,
Spouting and frisking,
Turning and twisting,
Around and around
With endless rebound !

" Smiting and fighting,
A sight to delight in ;
Confounding, astounding,
Dizzying and deafening the ear with its sound.

" Collecting, projecting,
Receding and speeding,
And shocking and rocking,
And darting and parting,
And threading and spreading,
And whizzing and hissing,
And dripping and skipping,
And hitting and splitting,
And shining and twining,
And rattling and battling,
And shaking and quaking,
And pouring and roaring,
And waving and raving,
And tossing and crossing,
And running and stunning,
And flowing and going,
And foaming and roaming,

    And dinning and spinning,
    And dropping and hopping,
    And working and jerking,
    And guggling and struggling,
    And heaving and cleaving,
    And glittering and flittering,
    And gathering and feathering,
    And whitening and brightening,
    And quivering and shivering,
    And hurrying and skurrying,
    And thundering and floundering;
Dividing and gliding and sliding,
And falling and brawling and sprawling,
And driving and riving and striving,
And sprinkling and twinkling and wrinkling,
And sounding and bounding and rounding,
And bubbling and troubling and doubling,
And grumbling and rumbling and tumbling,
And clattering and battering and shattering.

" Retreating and beating and meeting and sheeting,
Delaying and straying and playing and spraying,
Advancing and prancing and glancing and dancing,
Recoiling, turmoiling, and toiling and boiling,
And gleaming and streaming and steaming and beaming,
And rushing and flushing and brushing and gushing,
And curling and whirling and purling and twirling,
And flapping and rapping and clapping and slapping,
And thumping and plumping and bumping and jumping,
And dashing and flashing and splashing and crashing,
And so never ending, but always descending,
Sounds and motions for ever and ever are blending,
All at once and all o'er, with a mighty uproar,
And this way the water comes down at Lodore."

An extra hour is pleasantly spent in clambering, in
the rear of the hotel, up the face of the Shepherd's Crag
height, called on this side Ladder Brow. By walking a
few yards along the road, until round the rocks, an
easier ascent might be made. Capital views are had
from the top. By following the course of the water for
few yards the High Lodore Fall is reached. It is

separate from the lower fall, and of a different character; but it is considered one of the best in the district.

On re-entering the boat, pass round the low ground on the W. of the river, and enter the large bay at the extreme end of the lake.

Here the Grange and Brund Fells, Shepherd's Crag, and Gowder Crag, with the Borrowdale Hotel below, form a scene eminently picturesque. Two or three pleasant little bays are now skirted, in one of which is Otter Isle, and then comes Brandelhow Lead Mine, which is now closed. The lake looks much larger at this point than at any other. The whole of the western shore is well wooded, without overhanging cliffs; the Cat Bells receding too far to be very imposing. Continuing along, near the shore, an islet called Otterbield is passed, and then *Derwentwater Bay* is entered. This is a lovely and secluded nook; perhaps the most charming that the lake affords. Visitors will be interested in discovering places in or near the bay where good echoes are obtained. A few yards from the bay, and almost invisible to the tourist, is situated the residence of Sir John Woodford, a veteran of Waterloo, to whom belongs the chief portion of grounds on this side of the lake. Soon after emerging from the bay, two or three islets, called Lingholme, and the Rose-trees and Faw Park Villas, are passed. A mountain cluster surrounding the vale of Newlands is now seen, consisting of Causey Pike, Robinson, Hindscarth, and Cat Bells. Greta Hall also appears to the N.E. Sailing past the Nickol End Landings, and the houses Derwent Bank, Derwent Lodge, and Roodlands, a landing-pier will be found a few yards down the river; and a path through the grounds in front of the Derwentwater Hotel leads to the pleasant village of Portinscale.

Another day the stranger will enjoy sailing round St. Herbert's Island, or down the middle of the lake, to Lodore and back.

Druids' Circle (706).—If the tourist be in want of an appetite, and desire an easy, gentle walk of about 4m., with good prospects and a healthy breeze, he cannot do better than visit the Druids' Circle, which is about 1½m. from Keswick, in a field adjoining the old Penrith road.

Leave Keswick by the Penrith road, having the river Greta on the left, and after passing under the railway, through the Brigham toll-gate, and then over the railway, by the side of the Brewery, take the second turning on the right.

The road for ½m. makes a gradual ascent to the crown of the hill, and just before the descent on the other side commences, a lane will be observed on the right, a few yards beyond which a stepping-stile leads into the field in which stands the circle of stones.

The circle is formed of 48 stones, the largest of which is upwards of 7 feet high and several tons in weight; and on the eastern side, within the circle, there is a small group of 10 other stones. This monument of an unknown past is in a good state of preservation, and will always be of interest to the thoughtful visitor. If, as is popularly believed, it was a Druidical temple, its commanding position must have served to impress a feeling of solemnity on the devotees. Near at hand are the towering heights of Helvellyn, Blencathara, and Skiddaw, and in the distance to the W. an imposing array of mountain-tops. Mell Fell, like a huge tumulus, stands in the eastern plain; and at the feet of the spectator lies the vale of Naddle, the Naddle Fells hiding the vale of St. John.

Leaving the field by the stile, the return journey may, for the sake of variety, be made along the lane above referred to, which enters the Ambleside road about 1½m. from Keswick. The views from the road during the descent to Keswick are very beautiful, and are said to be superior to those from any other coach-road in the kingdom.

Parties desiring to extend the walk may visit Wallow Crag by taking the first lane on the left hand, after entering the Ambleside road, in the direction of Keswick. See next page.

Ascent of Wallow Crag (1234).—The distance from Keswick to the top of Wallow Crag, and back by the ravine between Wallow Crag and Falcon Crag, is 5m. If a pony be taken, the return journey must be extended 1m. over Falcon Crag to Ashness Bridge.

Leave Keswick by the Ambleside road, and after passing the toll-gate, take the first turn on the right, and along a lane leading to some farm-houses. At the last of these, cross the stream and keep the wall on the right, until the trees are in sight which crown the height of Wallow Crag. Here incline to the left and make for the highest part of the wall, which runs along the fell, behind the trees.

A shepherd's house will be seen on the bleak moorland track at the foot of Bleaberry Fell.

Cross a wooden stile and go straight through the wood to the edge of the rock. The trees hide the view, and therefore it is desirable to descend until the precipice be overlooked, which position can be attained without danger. It was to this point that Southey loved to take his visitors, and the view is singularly grand. In the foreground is one of the finest woods in the district. The lake, with its islands, is extremely lovely, and it is backed by a multitudinous array of mountains, which are generally reflected in the crystal lake as if in a mirror. Bassenthwaite is displayed to the N., and Skiddaw rises imposingly out of the valley in which Keswick nestles as if in a terrestrial paradise.

By walking along the top of the crag a few yards to the S., the cleft called the Lady's Rake will be found; and some adventurous tourists will delight in descending where Lady Derwentwater clambered when she effected her escape from Lord's Island.

After returning to the stile and leaving the wood, a descent may be made by continuing southwards with the wall on the right until the Cat Gill Stream is reached. The Borrowdale Mountains appear singularly well grouped from this point, rising from Grange village

height above height to the summit of Great Gable and
Scawfell Pikes. On gaining the stream, a deep gorge,
in which the water forms some pretty cascades, will
appear to debar the passage, but by keeping near to the
wall a steep and rugged, but attractive, descent may be
made, and many tourists will be interested in learning
that this was one of Southey's favourite walks. When
two-thirds of the way down, cross the torrent, and walk
along the fell-side, under Falcon Crag, to a gate in the
wall. Here the Borrowdale road is entered 1½m. from
Keswick.

Ascent of Latrigg (1203).—The distance from Keswick to the top of Latrigg and back again, is 5m., and
the journey may be taken with pony or on foot.

See page 182, and follow the road which leads to
Skiddaw, until the western shoulder of Blencathara
comes into view. A winding road, overgrown with
grass, will be seen by the side of a straggling thorn
fence. Keep along this and it will lead without difficulty to the top of Latrigg, from which point there is a
delightful prospect.

The town of Keswick, and Derwentwater Lake, look
beautiful, surrounded by the Coledale, Newlands, and
Borrowdale mountains, and the rugged heights near
Lodore. The Greta and Derwent rivers are seen taking
a tortuous course along the valley to the Bassenthwaite
Lake, a strip of which is visible. The slope of Castle
Rigg is charmingly ornamented with wood, and on the
top of it the Druids' Circle is very prominent; beyond
is the Naddle Valley, backed by the mountain range of
Helvellyn. On the N., majestic and alone, stands Skiddaw, with its ravines fully exposed to view, and its base
graced with wood, and dotted here and there with hamlets and homesteads.

A descent may be made in a direct line with Keswick,
until one of the terrace roads be entered, and then by
walking a short distance to the right, the proper path
will be gained.

The Buttermere Excursion from Keswick, returning by the Vale of Newlands.

Barrow Fall, 2m.; Lodore Fall, 3m.; Bowder Stone, 5m.; Rosthwaite, 6m.; Seatoller, 7m.; Gatesgarth, 12m.; Buttermere, 14m.; Keswick, 23m.

The principal hotel proprietors in Keswick and the neighbourhood advertise a coach to leave their hotels every week-day, at about 9.30 A.M., for Buttermere, allowing tourists to see the Barrow and Lodore waterfalls, the Bowder Stone, Borrowdale Valley, Honister Pass, Buttermere and Crummock lakes, Scale Force, and the Newlands Valley. The charge is 5s., and 1s. for the driver; and this charge includes everything. The conveyances are usually open waggonettes. This is certainly the best and cheapest drive in the Lake District, and ought to be taken by every one. Even pedestrians are recommended to throw aside their knapsacks for one day, and indulge in this cheap circular tour of 23m.

Leaving Keswick by the Borrowdale road, Castle Hill is passed on the left, and on the right a portion of Derwentwater Lake is seen, and also Cat Bells, Causey Pike, Grisedale Pike, and the surrounding mountains. A retrospective view is obtained of Skiddaw, Latrigg, and Blencathara. On the left Wallow Crag rears its bold front, and the road now passes for about ¾m. through the thick wood at its base. Before ascending the steep part of the road, a small but pretty waterfall is seen to the left; and, on emerging from the wood, Falcon Crag overhangs grandly on the same side, claiming to be considered one of the best of the smaller rocks in the district. The road continues for 2m. along the eastern margin of the lake, allowing of fine views of Derwentwater and Skiddaw. Maiden Moor and Cat Bells, on the opposite side, appear to slope down close to the water's edge; and an old lead mine, now closed, is seen at their base. The Borrowdale Mountains, with Great End and Scawfell Pike, appear in front. After passing a branch road leading to Watendlath, a picturesque mountain

hamlet, the Barrow Lodge is reached, and a mile farther the Lodore Hotel, adjoining which is the Lodore Fall.
Both this and the Barrow Fall were mentioned in the
description of the journey round the lake in a boat; but
if they have not already been seen, it is advisable to visit
them now.   Gowder Crag, on the left, and Shepherd's
Crag, on the right of the Lodore Fall, are fine bold rocks,
clothed with wood.   The Borrowdale Hotel is ½m. beyond
Lodore; and here, by leaving the conveyance and walking through the hotel garden and a field, the Troutdale
Fish-breeding House may be visited.   No charge is
made, but tourists will willingly give a trifle to the man
in attendance for showing them the thousands of fish, of
all ages, which are being reared there for the market and
for stocking rivers and private fish-ponds.   The road
can be regained near the Grange Bridge, where the conveyance will be in waiting.   At Grange Bridge geologists
will be much interested in seeing a large stone which
lies on the opposite side of the river, at the back of the
houses, close to the water.   It is, perhaps, the best specimen to be met with in the district for showing the action
of ancient glaciers in smoothing and grooving the rocks.
After having had the mind awakened to the fact that at
some remote geological period glaciers occupied every
valley, the eye will be ready to notice the smooth and
scratched character of most of the surrounding rocks.

Borrowdale is now entered; and if an old story be
true, here ought to be the remains of a wall as famous
as the Roman Wall in Northumberland, or the Great
Wall of China.   It is said that the inhabitants of Borrowdale, believing that spring would last for ever if they
could keep the cuckoo in their valley, determined to
build a wall across the entrance at Grange.   The plan
failed, but it was the popular creed that success would
have been attained if the wall had been built one course
higher.

Borrowdale is generally considered one of the finest
valleys in Britain.   The rocks at its entrance are thrown
together in wild confusion, and barely leave room for the

road at the edge of the river. At some stone and slate quarries a path branches to the left, leading to the Bowder Stone; but it is advisable not to take this turn, as the views on the side of the river are extremely beautiful. A little farther on a foot-path leads to this far-famed Bowder Stone. Tourists who take the road leading past the slate-quarries will be interested in visiting the Fairy Cavern. It is a large and ancient underground quarry, now partly filled with water, and is reached by walking a few yards to the left after passing the main working. A rather awkward descent of a few feet leads to a platform, and a hole about 10 feet high and 6 feet wide will be seen, which is the opening to this wonderful Plutonic region. If a large stone be thrown into the cavern, it falls into the water and causes wonderfully impressive and weird-like sounds. The waves are distinctly heard some time after, rumbling in a narrow and distant part of this dark, mysterious region. The sounds resemble in a slight degree those heard in Fingal's Cave, on the island of Staffa.

The Bowder Stone is an immense detached block which has fallen from the adjacent crags, and rests on so small a base as to allow persons on its opposite sides to shake hands through a hole under it near the ground. Its length is 62 feet, height 36 feet, circumference 89 feet, and it has been computed to weigh 1971 tons. The following lines in the third book of Wordsworth's 'Excursion,' describing a large stone in Little Langdale Valley, are by many writers erroneously thought to refer to this Bowder Stone :—

" Upon a semicirque of turf-clad ground,
The hidden nook discovered to our view
A mass of rock, resembling, as it lay
Right at the foot of that moist precipice,
A stranded ship, with keel upturned, that rests
Fearless of winds and waves."

The summit is reached by a ladder affixed to the stone, and for the privilege of using which the occupant of a house close by will look for a small gratuity. The stone

L

will by many be considered a huge, vulgar nuisance, but fortunately all will be repaid for the visit by the beauty of the surrounding scenery. The Bowder Crag, from which the immense block has fallen, is directly above; and on the other side of the valley rise Gate Crag and Castle Crag. It is generally supposed that on the last-named rock there was a Roman fortification, some traces of which are said to have existed a few years ago. After regaining the carriage and proceeding a few yards, a gate crosses the road; and to the left will be seen a pony-track which winds over the hill to Watendlath.

In the middle of the valley, about 1m. from the Bowder Stone, is the pleasant village of Rosthwaite, containing two hotels, and lodging-houses. A short distance farther, a road on the left leads to Stone-thwaite, where there are two branch valleys; one, the Greenup Valley, leading by Easedale to Grasmere; and the other the Longstrath Valley, leading by the Stake Pass to Langdale. Some yards before arriving at Sea-toller, a road branches to the left, which takes by Sea-thwaite to Sty Head Pass, Great Gable, Scawfell Pike, and Wastwater.

Immediately after leaving Rosthwaite, the fine rugged heights of Glaramara are seen in front, separating the Seathwaite Valley from the Greenup and Longstrath valleys; and it almost completely hides the latter valley, which is on the E. side; but the bold Eagle Crag, which separates the Greenup and Longstrath valleys, stands commandingly on the left. At the head of Seathwaite Valley the Sty Head Pass depression is visible, and the stream which issues from Sty Head Tarn, but this must be distinguished from the Sour Milk Gill stream, issu-ing from the hollow above Seathwaite village, near the plumbago mines. The mountain beyond Sty Head Pass is Lingmell, a portion of the Scawfell range, and to the right of it is Great Gable. Arriving near Seatoller, Lingmell is lost to sight, and Great End appears.

At Seatoller the traveller must ascend the steep, rugged road leading up the Borrowdale Hause to the top of the Honister Pass. If there be one or two ladies who prefer remaining in the conveyance, they can of course do so, but all who can walk should do so for a distance of at least a mile and a half. Many tourists will prefer to walk two, or even three, miles. The beautiful mountain stream which flows close to the road on the left is well worth exploring. It contains many lovely miniature cascades, and will be found to beguile the traveller so as to make the toil of the way comparatively light. The pass is 1190 high, and the worst carriage-road in the Lake District, although during the summer months it is more frequented than any other. During the ascent Helvellyn comes into view, over the low range of hills between Borrowdale and Wythburn, and the jagged outline of Glaramara looks very fine.

On arriving at the summit of the pass, Honister Crag, the grandest in the district, rears its front on the left. Some of the best roofing-slate to be got in England is obtained from the quarries which are seen tier above tier along its perpendicular front. After a whistle from the driver, visitors are often astonished at seeing a man come sliding down the mountain, dragging a sledge behind him with some cwts. of slate upon it. A small sum is generally given to the man for his performance. During the wild and rapid descent to the Buttermere Valley, there is on the right Yew Crag, which would be considered very fine if it were not dwarfed by its grand compeer on the left. Many times ought the tourist to look back during the descent, and the best view of this King of Rocks will be obtained about half-way down.

As soon as the best part of the pass is left behind, the mountains surrounding the Buttermere Valley command attention. To the right is Robinson, and in front, in the distance, is Mellbreak. On the opposite side of the Buttermere Lake stand Red Pike, High Stile, and High Crag; and on passing Gatesgarth, the farm-house at the head of the lake, the Scarf Gap Pass, leading over to the head of Ennerdale Valley, and thence over the

Black Sail Pass to Wastwater, is seen winding along the hill-side, on the left of High Crag. To the left of the Scarf Gap Pass are the Hay Stacks and the Green Crags, with Great Gable above and beyond them.

Soon after leaving Gatesgarth, the road touches the lake, at its head, and continues near its margin its whole length, passing Hassness, the pretty residence of F. J. Reed, Esq., until the village of Buttermere is reached, which is situated on the strip of land between Butter-mere and Crummock lakes. Here are two good hotels, the Fish and the Victoria, and at one or the other the conveyance generally remains for about three hours, allowing tourists time for luncheon, and for a visit to Scale Force, where the water has a fall of 156 feet. This is generally considered the finest fall in the district, with the exception of Stanley Gill, in Eskdale, which attains its pre-eminence owing to its surroundings of wood and rock.

Buttermere Lake is 1¼m. long, ½m, broad, 93 feet deep, and 331 feet above the sea level.

Crummock Lake is 3m. long, ¾m. broad, 132 feet deep, and 321 feet above the sea level.

Both lakes contain char and trout. There are boats on Crummock, but not on Buttermere.

Passengers by the coaches from Keswick are taken by boat to the landing for Scale Force and back for 1s. each. A private party can have boat and boatman for 3s. 6d., and for this the boatman will accompany them to the waterfall if desired. The charge for boat and boatman from one end of the lake to the other is 5s., and 6s. if a visit to Scale Force be included. Boat and boatman for fishing, 5s. per day. The smaller boats will hold six, and the larger, ten people.

A cold luncheon is usually in readiness at both hotels when the conveyances arrive. Tourists are recommended to partake of this at once, and then walk a few hundred yards past the Fish Hotel to the boat-landings on Crummock Lake. A row of ten or fifteen minutes will take them to the landing-place for Scale

Force. The mountains seen from the bosom of the lake are very fine. At the head, surrounding Buttermere, are Buttermere Moss, Robinson, Honister Crag, Fleetwith, Hay Stacks, High Crag, High Stile, and Red Pike. On the W. of Crummock, Mellbreak rises from the very edge of the water, and at the foot of the lake are Low Fell and the Lanthwaite Woods. On the E., Whiteside, Grasmoor, Ladhouse, Whiteless Pike, and Rannerdale Knott look extremely wild and bold.

It is a .rough, stony walk of about ⅜m. to the Force. During the busy part of the season there is often difficulty in obtaining a boat without delay, and therefore some tourists will prefer walking from the inn to the fall, a distance of 2m. They must wind to the left of the Fish Inn, and then through the meadows to the bridge—crossing the stream flowing from Buttermere to Crummock. This path, after going over the bridge, is often very wet and disagreeable. It continues along the side of Crummock Lake until an islet is passed, and a wall is observed to run down the hollow near the S.E. shoulder of Mellbreak, and to meet the lake at the point where tourists are landed from boats. Some 600 yards from the lake there is a gate in the wall. Following the course of the streamlet, the waterfall will be noticed in a ravine on the left, about ⅜m. from the lake, and near to a new iron-ore mine. The quantity of water is not considerable, except after heavy rain; but the deep, secluded gorge, hemmed in by high perpendicular rocks of syenite, clothed with shrubs and trees, imparts to the on-looker a feeling of pleasing solemnity.

Before leaving Buttermere, tourists ought to visit Hartley Hill, and the Knotts, both of which stations command charming views. For Hartley Hill, take through the farm-yard below the church, and three minutes' walk leads to the top of this small rounded grassy knoll. The whole of Buttermere Lake is in prospect, and also a little of the head of Crummock Lake. Sour Milk Gill Fall is directly opposite.

The Knotts are reached by passing the clergyman's residence, and turning to the right at the last farmhouse. After two or three minutes' climb, the whole of Buttermere Lake comes in sight, and about half Crummock Lake. Another ten minutes' climb, with the Buttermere Hause road seen winding along the valley on the right, brings to the foot of Whiteless, and enables the tourist to look down the small glen of Rannerdale, at the back of Rannerdale Knott, with the foot of Crummock and the whole of Loweswater Lake spread to view.

It is advisable to state here that Loweswater Lake is situated in the western depression between Mellbreak and Low Fell, and the water from it, after flowing about ¾m., enters the Crummock Lake. It is 1m. long, less than ½m. broad, 60 feet deep, and 429 feet above the sea level. It is, perhaps, less visited than any other lake in the district. Its higher end is tame, and it is an exception to the general rule that the best view of a lake is obtained when looking from the lower to the higher end. It contains trout, pike, and perch, but there are no boats upon it. There are no islands on either Buttermere, Crummock, or Loweswater lakes, except one or two very small ones on the margin of the higher end of Crummock.

The return journey from Buttermere to Keswick is through the Newlands Valley. Leaving the little church on the left, the road takes up the steep ascent of Buttermere Hause, along the side of Buttermere Moss, for 1½m. Sail Beck flows below at the base of mountains presenting smooth, green, sloping sides. On the left is Whiteless Pike, and at the source of the stream the Sail. Knott Rigg is directly in front. Most persons will walk to the summit of the pass, which is 1096 feet high. During the whole of the ascent the mountains around look very beautiful, and form a pleasant contrast to the rugged Honister, passed during the morning's ride. On glancing back occasionally, portions of the Buttermere and Crummock lakes are seen, with the opposite mountains towering above. In the hollow, between Red Pike and High Stile, is situated Bleaberry Tarn, from which issues the Sour Milk Gill stream, flowing down the face of the mountain.

On gaining the summit of the pass, Robinson rises wild and precipitous on the right, with Robinson Fall streaming down its side. Blencathara is seen in the distance. The barren and desolate-looking valley immediately in front, along which the road winds for more than 1m., is the Keskadale portion of the vale of Newlands. This is the most uninteresting part of the day's drive, but after passing the first farm-house, new charms are revealed at every turn, and the mountains, Robinson, Hindscarth, and Dale Head, at the higher end of the valley, look beautiful and imposing. 4m. from Buttermere a small country inn stands a few yards off the road on the right, called the Mill Dam; leaving which the road winds along the side of Rowling End, the beginning of the Causey Pike range, and commands pleasing views up and down the valley, and across to Keswick and Derwentwater. The first turn must be taken on the right, and after passing the Newland's Beck, at "Stair," glimpses on the N. are obtained of Bassenthwaite Lake. Passing the hamlet of Swinside, the hill of that name is kept to the left. Portinscale is soon reached, and, 1m. farther, Keswick.

The Buttermere Excursion from Keswick, returning by the Vale of Lorton and Whinlatter Pass.

Buttermere, 14m.; Scale Hill Hotel, 18m.; Summit of Whinlatter Pass, 24m.; Keswick, 28m.

Parties who drive from Keswick to Buttermere independently of the public coaches, are recommended to lengthen the excursion from 23m. to 28m., and return by Scale Hill Hotel, the Lorton Valley, and Whinlatter Pass, instead of Buttermere Hause and Newlands Valley. This is more especially advisable, if it be intended to take the Wastwater excursion over the Sty Head, Black

Sail, and Scarf Gap passes, for then the return journey
from Buttermere to Keswick will be by the Newlands
Valley.

On arriving at Buttermere, take a boat for Scale Force,
and arrange for the carriage to meet the boat at the
Hause Point, which is on the E. side of Crummock Lake,
1m. from Buttermere. Those who desire to sail the entire length of the lake, can send the carriage to Scale
Hill Hotel, which is situated in the midst of the Lanthwaite Wood, about ½m. from the N. end of the lake.
It is a good hotel, and if luncheon has not been had at
Buttermere, it ought to be taken here.

From Buttermere to Scale Hill Hotel is 4m. The road
is on the margin of Crummock Lake, and at the foot of
some grand mountains. Opposite the ravine between
Grasmoor and Whiteside, near to a farm-house, a road
strikes to the left, through the woods, for Scale Hill
Hotel, and at this point the wild craggy front of Grasmoor is very imposing. A walk hence to Keswick,
along the ravine between Grasmoor and Whiteside, is
a great favourite with pedestrians.

Those who visit the hotel, and have half an hour to
spare, should walk to the " Station," a height situated in
the Lanthwaite Wood, commanding a magnificent view.
The reason it is called the " Station," is that it was
one of West's favourite stand points. It is situated
300 yards from the inn. After entering the plantation
at a gate near the S. end of the house, and walking a
few yards, a foot-path on the left will be seen, which
winds to the top of the hill. Below is spread almost the
whole of Crummock Lake, with Mellbreak, Red Pike,
High Stile, and Rannerdale Knott rising from its shores.
To the E., Grasmoor and Whiteside exhibit bold scarred
fronts, and the vale of Lorton is well displayed to the N.
Loweswater Lake is out of sight, but its surrounding
mountains—Low Fell, Burnbank, Carling Knott, Black
Crag, and Hen Comb—are visible.

If a visit to Scale Hill Hotel is not contemplated,
keep along the road at the foot of Grasmoor and White-

side, at the back of the wood. A road from the hotel soon joins it on the left, and a short distance farther a turn to the right must be taken. Two narrow paths are passed, which branch off to farm-houses on the right, and a short distance farther another road branches to the left. The fell-side is now attained, and the road winds round the shoulder of the Swinside Mountain, commanding an extensive view, embracing the village and valley of Lorton, and past Cockermouth and Maryport to the Solway Firth and the Scotch mountains. Some tourists may prefer extending the journey 2m., by driving from Scale Hill Hotel along the road leading through the vale, and past the village of Lorton, where is situated the celebrated Yew Tree, of which Wordsworth writes :—

> " There is a yew-tree, pride of Lorton vale,
>   Which to this day stands single, in the midst
>   Of its own darkness, as it stood of yore :
>   Not loath to furnish weapons for the bands
>   Of Umfraville or Percy ere they marched
>   To Scotland's heath ; or those that crossed the sea,
>   And drew their sounding bows at Agincourt—
>   Perhaps at earlier Crecy, or Poictiers.
>   Of vast circumference and gloom profound
>   This solitary tree ! a living thing,
>   Produced too slowly ever to decay ;
>   Of form and aspect too magnificent
>   To be destroyed."

Those who now visit this tree will be inclined to think that Wordsworth was not infallible, for Time is doing its work, and this relic will soon be a thing of the past. Few visitors will feel repaid for going out of the way to see it.

The road along the side of the mountain, and the road through the valley, meet a little way up the Whinlatter Pass; and after climbing along the sides of the Whinlatter Fells for 2m., with Swinside and Grisedale Pike on the right, the summit of the pass is attained, at a height of 1043 feet. Skiddaw once more rears its fami-

liar head, and at its base is seen the whole of the vale of
Keswick, with portions of Derwentwater and Bassenthwaite lakes.   Another 4m. conducts past Braithwaite
village, and through Portinscale to Keswick.

Tourists having plenty of time ought to return from
Buttermere down the Newlands Valley, and another day
drive up the valley to Buttermere, and return by Lorton
and Whinlatter. The Newlands Vale will well repay
driving both up and down it.

Keswick to Watendlath.

With conveyance, pony, or on foot.   Gate at Barrow, 2m.; Ashness
Bridge, 2½m.; View over Lodore, 3m.; High Lodore Fall, 3¾m.;
Watendlath, 5m.; Rosthwaite, 7m.; Bowder Stone, 8m.;
Grange Bridge, 9m.; Lodore Hotel, 10m.; Keswick, 13m.

This is the best short excursion from Keswick.   It is
one which should be taken on a fine day, and without
hurry. Conveyances can be hired to Watendlath, but
unfortunately the hotel proprietors of Keswick have not
yet so far studied their interests, and the comfort of
their patrons, as to make a road over the 2m. of hilly
ground between Watendlath and Rosthwaite, in Borrowdale, although such a road could be formed with very
little labour and expense.   Until this is effected the
carriages must be sent back to the gate at Barrow, and
thence to Rosthwaite, a distance of 7m., whilst the
tourists are walking the 2m. to Rosthwaite.   Ponies
can, of course, travel the whole distance.   Some parties
will merely go direct from Keswick to Watendlath, and
return without proceeding to Borrowdale; but all are
recommended to ascend the hill, as the views thence
obtained of the mountains surrounding Borrowdale are
very fine. When descending to Borrowdale, visitors who
are not expecting a carriage to meet them at Rosthwaite
can save a mile by making for the Bowder Stone, at the
gate mentioned in page 146.

Pedestrians may get a lift some portions of this journey
by availing themselves of the Lodore Hotel or the Bor-

rowdale Hotel omnibus from Keswick to the Barrow Gate, or on the return journey from either of those hotels to Keswick. The charge is 6*d*. each way. A boat might be taken from Keswick to Barrow, or from Lodore to Keswick.

Leaving Keswick, the first 2m. of the road travelled over have been described in the excursion to Buttermere, see page 143.

Immediately after entering the Watendlath road the traveller is recommended to climb a short distance up the hill to the left, until a glimpse can be obtained of Bassenthwaite. Here the view of Derwentwater and Skiddaw is very striking. Returning to the road which runs by the side of a wall, along the Barrow grounds, the tourist, after an ascent of ½m., will reach Ashness Bridge, which spans the torrent that enters the private grounds and forms the Barrow Fall.

The view from this bridge is a great favourite with artists. It is a little improved by taking a few steps up the side of the hill until St. Herbert's Island is in sight; then all the islands, and the wooded promontories of Friar's Crag and the isthmus help to add a grace and charm to the lake, which they appear to form into a number of pretty bays. Keswick, the two churches, and houses dotted here and there, are seen in the valley, at the foot of Skiddaw, which rears its majestic head. On the N.W., Swinside and Silver Hill, besides displaying their wooded slopes to the view, also render another service by hiding the low-lying lands at the head of Bassenthwaite, which lake adds to the distant prospect all that can be desired.

After crossing the bridge a plantation is entered through a gate, leaving which, and passing through a second gate, a little valley must be traversed, containing a few green fields. To the left is Ashness farm-house, the road to which must be passed. Having left the valley, enter another wood, and after walking 170 yards farther, a track to the right, some 20 yards long, leads to the edge of the rocks, from which the Lodore Hotel

and the marshy grounds at the head of the lake are seen
below.   From this point walk to the right, along the
edge of the cliffs, for 60 yards, and a most glorious view
will be obtained of the Borrowdale Mountains, with
Lodore Fall and woods as a foreground.   Regaining the
road by the same way, and walking 40 yards farther,
another track to the right leads to a tree at the edge of
the rock, and here will be obtained a *coup d'œil*, which is
considered by some tourists the finest in the Lake District.   The whole of Derwentwater and most of Bassenthwaite, with Skiddaw and the vale of Keswick, are seen,
and to the W., Swinside, Cat Bells, Maiden Moor, and
Grisedale Pike.   Lodore Hotel and Fall are immediately
below.   On emerging from the wood, and passing through
a gate which crosses the road, the little secluded valley
of Watendlath is in front, with fine rocks on either side,
and the Lodore stream flowing through its green fields
like a miniature river.   A knoll on the left in the middle
of the valley hides the hamlet.

Looking to the right a small wooden bridge is seen to
cross the stream just where it enters the wood.   The
tourist should leave the carriage and go over this bridge;
he must not be tempted to enter the wood through which
the stream flows, but should keep the path, having the
wall to the right.   Passing through a gate, continue a
few yards, and then turn to the left.   Here the two lakes
are, as it were, set in a frame, with Gowder Crag on the
right and Shepherd's Crag on the left, and the Lodore
stream is seen descending between them.   Stepping
down to the stream, Bassenthwaite is lost to view, but
Skiddaw and a portion of Derwentwater make a scene of
perfect beauty.   A hundred different subjects for the
pencil may be had here by varying the position only a
few yards.   Those who are fortunate enough to visit
this spot on a fine day will in future years think of these
lovely vistas in the spirit so finely portrayed by Wordsworth in the following lines respecting some daffodils
he saw on the margin of Ullswater Lake :—

❋   ❋   ❋   ❋

" I gazed, and gazed, but little thought
  What wealth the show to me had brought.

" For oft when on my couch I lie,
  In vacant or in pensive mood,
  They flash upon that inward eye
  Which is the bliss of solitude;
  And then my heart with pleasure fills,
  And dances with the daffodils."

Taking to the right a few yards up the stream, the High Lodore Fall, which, though not large, is one of the most beautiful in the district, meets the eye just where the water issues out of the wood.

Return by the same way to the road, avoiding a stile leading into the wood, unless time be no object.

The road continues along the middle of the valley, by the side of the stream, for about 1½m. Just before the hamlet is reached a little gate on the right leads to some small cascades, amongst which there is one rounded rock filled with water, called the Devil's Punch Bowl. At the first house, milk, lemonade, tea and oat cake, &c., can be obtained by the tourist.

The Watendlath Tarn, at the foot of which the hamlet is situated, is ⅔m. in circumference. It contains pike, perch, eels, and a few trout. There is no boat upon it. The water flows from a Blea tarn (one of the many of that name) distant amongst the hills 2m. S.E. By the route over the hills to the E. it is 2m. to Armboth House, on Thirlmere Lake; and 4m. to Wythburn, at the foot of Helvellyn.

After crossing the little rustic bridge, and ascending the hill, Dale Head comes into view on the W., and next to it is the Honister Pass depression, over which peers a little of the Pillar Mountain, in Ennerdale. To the left of Honister Pass stand Brandreth, Green Gable, and Great Gable, and beyond the Sty Head Pass is Lingmell, close to Great End and Scawfell Pikes; and Glaramara is also very prominent. To the E. the summit of Helvellyn is seen over the Watendlath Fells.

The path is well defined to the village of Rosthwaite nestling in the valley below.

When about half-way down the hill, a few yards before a rill is crossed, there is an opening in the wall to the right. Those who wish to descend to the road near the Bowder Stone, without visiting Rosthwaite, must go through this opening, and continue along an irregular path, having a wall on the right, until another wall joins it at right angles. Here there is a small gate. Go through this, and keep the wall to the left, walking in the direction of Castle Crag, which stands in the valley on the opposite side of the river, with Gate Crag towering above it. The road is joined at the point mentioned in page 146, where will be found a full description of the remaining 5m. which has to be travelled before reaching Keswick. If the return journey be made by the W. side of Derwentwater the distance will be increased by 2m.; the route being indicated at page 181.

The Wastwater Excursion from Keswick, by Sty Head, Black Sail, and Scarf Gap Passes.

Seathwaite, 9m.; Sty Head Pass, 12m.; Wastdale Head, 14m.; Gatesgarth, 20m.; Buttermere, 22m.; Keswick, 31m.

This excursion will be taken by all visitors of both sexes who are not afraid of a little hard work. It embraces much of the wildest scenery in the district, and two of the best passes.

It is usual to take a conveyance to Seathwaite and send it round by the Honister Pass to Buttermere, or to Gatesgarth, the farm-house at the head of Buttermere Lake, whilst tourists proceed over the Sty Head Pass to Wastdale Head, and then over the Black Sail and Scarf Gap passes to the Buttermere Valley. The time required for the whole journey is about twelve hours, and it is advisable to leave Keswick early in the morning. The driver must be specially instructed to wait at Gatesgarth, otherwise he will probably be at one of the inns at Buttermere, thus necessitating a walk of 2m. farther than is needful.

Seathwaite is a small hamlet, without an inn, and if ponies are wanted, they must be sent in advance from Keswick, or tourists must bring them with them; and this renders the excursion more expensive than any other; but few will begrudge the expense when they learn that no other single day's excursion in the Lake District can bear any comparison with this one for variety of sublime and beautiful scenery. Some tourists, in order to lighten the cost, will drive to Seathwaite, and leaving the conveyance, put saddles upon the horses, and take them over the Sty Head Pass to Wastdale Head, with the driver as guide, and return the same route; but by doing so, some of the grandest scenery is missed.

The road for the first 7m., from Keswick to Seatoller, is the same as that described in the Buttermere excursion. See page 143.

Turning to the left a few yards before arriving at Seatoller, a rough cart-road, of about 2m., leads along a picturesque valley to Seathwaite, noted for being the wettest place in England. At the head of the valley stands the perpendicular front of Great End; Glaramara is on the left, and Esk Hause depression between the two. A little to the right, under Great End, is Sprinkling Fell; and to the right of that, Sty Head Pass and Base Brown Mountain. Half-a-mile before arriving at the hamlet, a path, with the river on the left, can be taken to the famous yew trees of which Wordsworth, after commemorating the celebrated yew at Lorton, says :—

" Worthier still of note,
Are those fraternal four of Borrowdale,
Joined in one solemn and capacious grove ;
Huge trunks ! and each particular trunk a growth
Of intertwisted fibres serpentine
Upcoiling, and inveterately convolved—
Nor uninformed with phantasy, and looks
That threaten the profane ; a pillar'd shade,
Upon whose grassless floor of red-brown hue,
By sheddings from the pining umbrage tinged

Perennially—beneath whose sable roof
Of boughs, as if for festal purpose, deck'd
With unrejoicing berries, ghostly shapes
May meet at noontide—Fear and trembling Hope,
Silence and Foresight, Death the skeleton,
And Time the shadow—there to celebrate,
As in a natural temple, scattered o'er
With altars undisturbed of mossy stone,
United worship; or in mute repose
To lie and listen to the mountain flood
Murmuring from Glaramara's inmost caves."

Continuing by the side of the stream, and passing the world-renowned Borrowdale Lead Mine (see page 127) and the Sour Milk Gill Fall, which issues out of Giller-combe, a wooden bridge conducts to Seathwaite.

The path continues for 1m. by the side of the stream to Stockley Bridge. The valley in front, at the top of which is Great End and Esk Hause, is called Grains Gill, and the Sprinkling Fell separates it from the Sty Head Pass. The waterfall on the right, which descends from the Sty Head Pass, is called Taylor's Gill Fall. The most direct way for pedestrians to the summit of Scawfell Pikes is up Grains Gill, but the path by Sty Head and Sprinkling tarns, and under Great End, is the more interesting. After crossing the bridge and passing through a gate, leave the stream and climb the hill along a zigzag path, in the direction of Taylor's Gill Fall. The rocks on either side are very wild, and on looking back Blancathara is seen. When the level part of the pass is attained, Lingmell comes into view, and then the Scawfell Pikes and Great End. On the right are Green Gable and Great Gable. The Sty Head Tarn lies very secluded at the summit of the pass, and it receives the water from Sprinkling Tarn, which is situated ½m. to the left, under Great End. Both these tarns contain trout. From the top of the pass (1600), Wastdale, with its green fields and half-dozen houses, is observed below, surrounded by bulky, towering mountains. On the left, Lingmell, Scawfell Pikes, and Great End, look wild and rocky, with deeply-scarred and precipitous sides; and on the right, Great Gable looks even wilder, with overhanging rocks thrown together in wild confusion. Next to Great Gable is Kirk Fell, adjoining Mosedale Valley, on the farther side of which is Red Pike, and directly in front, Yewbarrow, with portions of Middle Fell and Buckbarrow on the left of it. A glimpse of the sea is caught in the distance, but Lingmell hides Wastwater Lake.

The path during the descent is very steep and stony.* When the valley is reached, about 1m. of green and smooth ground has to be traversed to the inn; and during the last ½m. the lake is in sight, with the Screes on the left of it, and the small height of Latterbarrow at its foot. The first sight of the lake is not impressive, but after ordering luncheon at the inn, it is well to walk 1m. farther to the head of the lake, and if time permit, row to the foot and back again. It is 3½m. long, ½m. broad, 204 feet above the sea level, and 270 feet deep, being the deepest lake in the district, and it has never been frozen over. It contains char and trout.

The charge for man and boat down the lake and back again, is 5s. A boat, without the man, is 1s., and including the man, 2s. 6d., per hour.

The lake is solemn and gloomy, destitute of islands, bays, or promontories. The mountains at its head, and on the W. side, rise to a great altitude, and look grand and imposing. The Screes, going sheer down into the

---

* Before descending, the tourist is recommended to ignore the regular beaten track, which is so detestably stony that no attention can be given to the wild scenery through which it passes. A pleasant and easy descent may be made by branching a few yards to the left from the cairn. An old, grass-grown track will be found, which conducts by the side of the torrent, and joins the regular path at the foot of the pass. After heavy rains care must be taken to cross to the Great Gable side of the stream as soon as the valley is reached. If time will permit, Piers Gill and Greta Waterfall ought by all means to be visited during the descent. See pages 274 and 275.

M

lake on the eastern side, form an extraordinary feature in the landscape.

In order to see the lake and Screes properly, some tourists who have not time for a sail will take a car or waggonette at the inn, and whilst luncheon is preparing, drive half-way down the W. side of the lake to Bowderdale and back; or to Strands, situated at the foot of the lake. There are two inns at Strands, and the distance from Wastdale Head is 6m.

The charge for the waggonette, which carries seven persons, is 1s. 6d. per mile, and for the car, which holds four persons, 1s. per mile; the driver's fee being additional. The charge for car to Bowderdale and back is 3s.

If any traveller should feel that the return journey over Black Sail and Scarf Gap passes would be too fatiguing without help, they can obtain ponies and guides at Wastdale Head.

Mr. William Ritson, at the inn, is a well-known and original character, a good sample of the genuine, honest dalesman. He has been brought into personal contact with most of the greatest men of this and the past generation, and many will consider it a privilege to have a "crack" with him. The writer was delighted with a vivid description which he once gave of a wrestling match he had had with the late Professor Wilson— a rather tough opponent, as Ritson himself acknowledged. Both stripped and went to work in right down earnest; in the first round Ritson threw the Professor, then the Professor threw Ritson, but in the third round Ritson came off conqueror.

At the first house reached after descending the Sty Head Pass, where lives Ritson's nephew (his brother John being dead), tourists can have good accommodation; and also at Mr. Tyson's, the house which stands nearer Black Sail Pass than the inn.

Leaving Wastdale Head, the stream must be followed for some distance up the Mosedale Valley. In front is the Pillar Mountain, and on the right Kirk Fell. The path winds up by the side of the branch stream on the right, to the top of Black Sail Pass (1750), which is the depression between Kirk Fell and the Pillar. On the left are Yewbarrow and Red Pike, and at the head of the valley between the Pillar and Red Pike a portion of the steeple comes into view. Looking back, are Lingmell and Scawfell, and a little of the Screes.

On arriving at the top, everything looks wild and solitary, and many persons will consider this finer than the Sty Head Pass. On the right are the craggy and waterworn sides of Kirk Fell. Commencing at the head of Ennerdale Valley, are the Great Gable, Green Gable, Brandreth, Hay Stacks, Scarf Gap Pass, and High Crag. Over the low part of the Hay Stacks are Fleetwith and Honister Pike; and farther distant, Dale Head. Over the highest portion of the Hay Stacks a little of Robinson can be seen.

After descending a short distance, the path runs by the side of the streamlet which was seen leaping down the deep cleft in Kirk Fell. Following the course taken by the water to where it enters the Liza, a wooden plank will be found acting as a bridge over the river, which is sometimes swollen after heavy rains. When at this bridge, the Pillar Rock is seen peering over a portion of the Pillar Mountain. The valley, which is extremely wild and desolate, will be preferred by many tourists to any other valley in the district, but others will gladly hurry from it to the prettier vale of Buttermere. The small rounded heaps of moraine matter will interest the geologist, and cause him to picture in his mind ancient glaciers descending Great Gable, the mountain which stands so nobly at the head of the valley.

After passing an old unoccupied building, the path winds up the hill to the right, and presently a lovely peep is had of Ennerdale Lake. During the whole of the ascent the Pillar Mountain, with its imposing and majestic front, stands prominently on the opposite side of the valley. The immense rock, which rises almost

M 2

separate from the main bulk of the mountain, has been
climbed by very few persons, and the ascent is difficult
and dangerous.   Wordsworth refers to it in his poem of
'The Brothers.'   He says :—

> " You see yon precipice; it almost looks
> Like some vast building made of many crags;
> And in the midst is one particular rock
> That rises like a column from the vale,
> Whence by our shepherds it is called the Pillar."

The descent from the top of Scarf Gap Pass (1400) to
Buttermere Valley is along a rough stony path.   The
Gatesgarth farm-house is seen below, a short distance
from the head of the lake.   The mountains and the
Buttermere Lake form a combination superbly beautiful.   The Hay Stacks, Green Crags, Fleetwith, and
Honister Pike make a grand amphitheatre; and the
Buttermere Lake lies calm and beautiful, at the foot of
the dark towering heights of High Crag, High Stile,
and Red Pike.   Mellbreak and Rannerdale Knott are
at the foot of the lake, and on the N.E. side of the
valley are Robinson, Hindscarth, and Dale Head; on
the right of which is Honister Pass, leading to
Borrowdale.

Arrived at Gatesgarth the carriage will be in waiting;
and the scenery of the next eleven miles to Keswick,
through Buttermere and Newlands, is described in the
Buttermere excursion.   See page 148.

Keswick to Wastwater, by Carriage.

Scale Hill Hotel, 10m.; Lamplugh Cross, 16m.; Egremont, 24m.;
  Calder Bridge, 28m.; Strands, 34m.; Wastdale Head, 40m.

The Sty Head Pass is, to some tourists, an insur-
mountable barrier, and to visit Wastwater they must
either take a carriage by Lorton Vale, Loweswater, and
Calder Bridge; or the train to Seascale or Drigg,
and hire a carriage from thence to Wastwater.

The distance by train, passing Cockermouth, Workington, Whitehaven, and St. Bees, is 40m.; and from Drigg or Seascale to Westdale Head, is 12m.

A railway route may be travelled by changing trains at Marron Junction, which is between Cockermouth and Workington, and again joining the coast line at Sellafield, the next station to Seascale.

With a carriage the right-hand road is taken at Portinscale, and 1½m. farther Braithwaite is passed. Here the stream from the Coledale Valley is on the left for a few yards, and the road winds to the right, and ascends the Whinlatter Pass (1043). During the ascent beautiful prospects are had of Derwentwater, Bassenthwaite, Skiddaw, and the Derwent Vale. A toll-gate, 5m. from Keswick, stands at the top of the pass, overshadowed by the Whinlatter Fells and the Grisedale Pike. 1m. farther the road branches to the left (the straight road takes about 2m. farther, passing through Lorton village), and crosses a rivulet. After making a slight ascent it continues round the Swinside Mountain, where charming views are had of the vale of Lorton, the Solway Frith, and the Scotch mountains. Low Fell stands on the opposite side of the valley, and hides Loweswater. Mellbreak is very prominent, and between it and Low Fell is an amphitheatre of smaller heights. Dodd, an offshoot of Whiteside, stands on the left, and then appear Whiteside, Grasmoor, and Red Pike. After going through two gates on the fell-side, a descent is made into the valley, and when a lane on the right, and two narrow lanes on the left, are passed, the main road is entered.

A short distance farther a road branching to the left, leads direct to Buttermere. After this is passed, Scale Hill Hotel is reached, the river Cocker crossed, and a view obtained of both the Crummock and Loweswater lakes.

Surrounding Crummock, appear Mellbreak, Red Pike, High Stile, High Crag, Scarf Gap Pass, Hay Stacks, and Rannerdale Knott. To the E. rise Grasmoor and Whiteside, wild and majestic. The road runs along the margin of Loweswater, with Carling Knott and Burn-bank on the opposite side.   The retrospective views are good, Mellbreak especially presenting a bold ap-pearance.

When the lake is passed, a climb is made, and at the top of the hill a guide-post informs the traveller that the distance to Keswick is 14m., to Workington 9m., and to Whitehaven and Egremont each 11m.   The left-hand road must be followed.

The Scotch mountains and the sea are now seen, and gradually Blake Fell and Knock Murton come into view on the left.

Lamplugh Hall and Church are passed 5m. from Scale Hill, and 1m. farther Lamplugh Cross Inn.

If it be intended to go direct to the Anglers' Inn, situated on the shore of Ennerdale Lake, the first left-hand turn must be taken after passing Lamplugh Church.

Beyond Lamplugh Cross Inn the first road on the left leads to Ennerdale Bridge; and it is the nearer but most hilly way to Calder Bridge.   The hamlet of Ennerdale Bridge, in which stands two small inns, and the church, the scene of Wordsworth's poem, 'The Brothers,' is 1½m. from the lake; but during the journey glimpses are had of that sheet of water and its grand mountain scenery, amid which the Pillar soars conspicuous.   Be-tween Ennerdale and Calder the road rises along the high mountain tract of Cold Fell, and descends close to Calder Abbey.

The highway from Lamplugh Cross to Calder Bridge is by Frizington, Cleator, and Egremont, a district rich in iron ore, and fast becoming thickly populated.   This road does not command a view of Ennerdale Lake; but by taking the second turning on the left, after leaving Lamplugh Cross, the lake may be seen in the distance, about a mile will be saved, and the main road again entered 1½m. from *Egremont*.   This is a clean, ancient market town of 2500 inhabitants, situated on the river Ehen, which flows from Ennerdale Lake.   The Globe and other hotels are very comfortable. The ruins of the castle stand on an eminence, surrounded by a moat, and belong to Lord Leconfield. They are not of great extent, but when seen from a short distance they look like an acropolis, and much enhance the beauty of the town. The Castle was built about the time of the Norman Conquest. There is a legend connected with it which is the subject of one of Wordsworth's poems, entitled, 'The Horn of Egremont Castle.' A horn was always suspended over the gateway, which could only be sounded by the true Lords of Egremont. Sir Eustace de Lucy, Lord of Egremont, and his brother Hubert, rode forth together to join the crusade in the Holy Land: but before parting Sir Eustace blew the horn, saying to his brother, "If I fall in Palestine, return and blow this horn, and take possession, that Egremont may not be without a Lucy for its Lord." When away, Hubert became ambitious of his lordship, and hired ruffians to drown his brother in the river Jordan; and he believed that his murderous commands were carried out. He returned to England and took possession of the Castle, not venturing to blow the horn. While giving a banquet to his retainers, he suddenly heard a blast from that horn which he well knew none but Sir Eustace, his brother, could have sounded. He started from his seat and fled, while Sir Eustace entered at the gate, and resumed his rights. Long afterwards the wretched Hubert came to ask forgiveness from his brother; and, having obtained it, retired to a convent, where he practised penance till he died.

The distance to Calder Bridge is 4m., along an excellent road, which allows of occasional glimpses of Seatallan and the Scawfell Mountains.

About 1½m. from Egremont, near the village of Beckermet, a small mound on the right, upon which stands a summer-house, bears the name of Wotobank. The derivation of this name is assigned by tradition to the following incident :—

A Lord of Beckermet, with his lady and servants, were

one day hunting wolves.   In the course of the chase the
lady was missing.   After a long and painful search her
body was found on this hill or bank, mangled by a wolf,
which was discovered in the act of tearing it to pieces.
In the first transports of grief, the husband exclaimed,
" Woe to this bank ! "

> " ' Woe to thee, Bank ! ' were the first words that burst,
> ' And be thy soil with bitter offspring curst !
> Woe to thee, Bank, for thou art drunk with gore
> The purest heart of woman ever bore ! '
> ' Woe to thee, Bank ! ' the attendants echoed round,
> And pitying shepherds caught the grief-fraught sound."

Calder Bridge is a good resting-place, the Stanley
Arms being a comfortable hostelry.   The village is
situated on the river Calder ; and within a few yards is
Ponsonby Hall, a pleasant mansion in a beautiful park,
the residence of William Stanley, Esq.

Calder Abbey is in a lovely situation in the grounds
of Captain Irwin, 1m. farther up the river, and the walk
to it along the banks of the beautifully-wooded stream
is charmingly picturesque.   It was founded in 1134, and
was affiliated to Furness Abbey.   The ruins are not
extensive, but have considerable beauty ; and the site
is thoroughly monastic, surrounded by hills and embowered in stately trees, with the music and sparkling
ripples of the Calder close at hand.

Leaving Calder Bridge, the sea is visible, and also the
mountains of Black Combe, Birker Moor, Muncaster
Fells, Coniston Old Man, The Screes, and Scawfell.
Two miles farther the road intersects the village of
Gosforth, and passes close to the churchyard, in which
stands a celebrated cross, of British or Danish origin,
14 feet high.   It is sculptured with figures of men and
animals, the meaning of which has given rise to much
archæological discussion.

Beyond Gosforth a steep rise is made, and then the
hollow in which Wastwater lies is seen in front, but the
lake is not yet visible.   The distance from Gosforth to

Strands is 4m., and to Wastdale Head 10m.; but by
leaving Strands on the right, and taking a rather hilly
road, close under the bold, craggy height of Buckbarrow,
about 1m. can be saved. After crossing the streamlet
which descends from Greendale Tarn, situated between
Buckbarrow and Middle Fell, the shore of the lake is
attained, and the road entered which runs from Strands
to Wastdale Head. The Screes, which rise on the opposite side of the lake, sheer out of the water, almost per-
pendicularly, to a height of 1800 feet, look imposing
and majestic; and the shingle lying in the different
hollows of the mountain adds a pleasing variety of shape
and colour. At the head of the valley are seen Scawfell,
Scawfell Pike, Lingmell, Great Gable, and Yewbarrow,
—a noble array of mountain masses, presenting a com-.
bination of the sublime and beautiful that is, perhaps,
unsurpassed by any other district in Great Britain. No
tourist is justified in believing that he has seen the Lake
District unless he has travelled by the shore of this lake
from Strands to Wastdale Head, and thereby received a
full impression of the grandeur of the scenery. After
passing Middle Fell, a peep is had up Bowderdale, with
Seatallan and the Haycock at its head.

When the stream is crossed which brings down the
water from Scoat and Low tarns, Yewbarrow presents a
graceful and imposing rocky peak. On rounding Yewbarrow, Kirk Fell comes into view; and the peaceful
and secluded vale of Wastdale Head is spread in front,
with its half-dozen houses, and modest church, and the
Mosedale Branch, on the left, closed in by the Pillar
Mountain.

Keswick to Wastwater, by Railway Route.—If, in
visiting Wastwater from Keswick, the tourist take the
train by the W. coast to Seascale or Drigg station, he
will pass Cockermouth, where Wordsworth was born, and
which contains the ruins of a castle, 8m. farther the sea
is reached at *Workington*. This town, which contains
7970 inhabitants, is surrounded by collieries and iron-
works. The principal hotels are the Green Dragon and

the 'Station Hotel. On a rising ground clothed with
wood, close to the town, stands the fine old mansion of
Workington Hall, the seat of the ancient family of the
Curwens. When Mary Queen of Scots fled to Eng-
land, she was hospitably entertained at this house by
Sir Henry Curwen, till the pleasure of Elizabeth was
known, when she was removed, first to Cockermouth
Castle and then to Carlisle.

From Workington the railway follows the coast line,
and 5m. farther it passes through *Whitehaven*, a sea-
port containing 17,000 inhabitants, and which sends
one member to Parliament. The principal inns are
the Globe, Golden Lion, Black Lion, and the Albion.
Hutchinson, in his 'History of Cumberland,' says that
in 1566 there were only six fishermen's huts, and one
small barque of about nine tons burden, in the creek
where now stands this large and thriving town. This
change is to be attributed, in a great measure, to the
munificence of the Lowther family, and to the existence
of valuable deposits of coal and iron in the district.
The coal-mines of Whitehaven are most interesting, and
extend a considerable distance under the bed of the
ocean. Packets leave the town two or three times a
week for Liverpool, Belfast, Dublin, and the Isle of
Man. Whitehaven Castle is a plain modern mansion,
occasionally occupied by the Earl of Lonsdale.

Leaving Whitehaven, the next station is *St. Bees*, 4m.
distant. This town is much resorted to for sea-bathing.
The Sea Cote Hotel is close to the sea; and in the town,
about ½m. distant from the shore, are the Royal Hotel
and Queen's Hotel; also many comfortable lodging-
houses.

The W. coast of Cumberland is generally flat and uninteresting, but here it is well worthy of being explored.
The cliffs are very fine, and composed of masses of red
sandstone, with vast blocks lying below, exposed to the
action of the tides.

St. Bees Church is built of red freestone, and is said
to be on the site of an abbey which was founded in

650 by St. Bega, an Irish female saint. A college was established here in the early part of this century for the education of young men proposing to enter into Holy Orders, but who do not intend finishing their studies at Oxford or Cambridge. The students are required to be well versed in the classics before admission.

The distance by railway from St. Bees to Seascale is 6m., and to Drigg 8m.

At either station a conveyance can be had for Wast-dale Head, the distance being about 12m. from both villages. Seascale possesses a comfortable hotel and a few lodging-houses. The sands are good, but otherwise the place is not inviting.

Keswick to the Vale of St. John and Thirlmere Lake.

Point of departure from Penrith road, 3m.; Enter main road in St. John's Vale, 4m.; King's Head Inn at Thirlspot, 7m.; Armboth House, 7¾m.; Enter Keswick road at Smaithwaite, 11m.; Keswick, 15m.

Travellers who enter Keswick by the coach from Ambleside, or who intend to travel from Keswick to Ambleside, often object to take the drive through the vale of St. John, as it involves going over 5m. of ground a second time; and more especially as they have a view of the Castle Rock, and a peep into the valley from the coach.

The usual drive is one of only 12m., the return journey being commenced at the point where the St. John's road meets the coach-road, between Ambleside and Keswick.

In order to render the drive a favourite, and one that all tourists may find it worth while to take, it is advisable to go from the vale of St. John to the bridge crossing the middle of Thirlmere Lake, and to proceed along a rather rough road on the W. side of the lake to Smaithwaite, and thence to Keswick. Thirlmere is best seen in this way, and some of the views obtained on the N.W. side are much and deservedly admired.

Leave Keswick by the Penrith route, and after passing under and then over the railway, three roads appear. That on the left hand is the new Penrith road, and the one to be pursued, unless it be intended to include a visit to the Druids' Circle; then take the old Penrith road, which is the middle one. See p. 140. The two roads unite 1½m. farther on, directly after which the Naddle Beck, flowing from the Naddle Valley, has to be crossed. A few hundred yards farther there is a road to the right, opposite the third milestone. Entering this, the valley and St. John's Beck are crossed, and then the main road is reached at right angles. Turn to the right, up the valley. White Pike and Great Dodd, portions of the Helvellyn range, are on the left; and the Wanthwaite Crags—wild and perpendicular—overhang the road. From one point these rocks look especially fine, being severed by a deep, wide cleft.

The tourist now stands on classic ground, this valley being the scene of Sir Walter Scott's poetical romance of the 'Bridal of Triermain.' The Castle Rock, which stands detached and alone, at the head of the valley, will, in some states of the atmosphere, assume the appearance of a castle, and remind the looker-on of Scott's words describing the visit of King Arthur:—

> " With toil the King his way pursued
> By lonely Threlkeld's waste and wood,
> Till on his course obliquely shone
> The narrow valley of Saint John,
> Down sloping to the western sky,
> Where lingering sunbeams love to lie.
> Right glad to feel those beams again,
> The King drew up his charger's rein ;
> With gauntlet raised he screen'd his sight,
> As dazzled with the level light,
> And, from beneath his glove of mail,
> Scann'd at his ease the lovely vale,
> While 'gainst the sun his armour bright
> Gleamed ruddy like the beacon's light.

" Paled in by many a lofty hill,
The narrow dale lay smooth and still,
And, down its verdant bosom led,
A winding brooklet found its bed.
But, midmost of the vale, a mound
Arose with airy turrets crown'd,
Buttress, and rampire's circling bound,
   And mighty keep and tower ;
Seem'd some primeval giant's hand
The castle's massive walls had plann'd
A ponderous bulwark to withstand
   Ambitious Nimrod's power.
Above the moated entrance slung,
The balanced drawbridge trembling hung,
   As jealous of a foe ;
Wicket of oak, as iron hard,
With iron studded, clench'd, and barr'd,
And prong'd portcullis, join'd to guard
   The gloomy pass below.
But the gray walls no banners crown'd,
Upon the watch-tower's airy round
No warder stood his horn to sound,
No guard beside the bridge was found,
And, where the Gothic gateway frown'd,
Glanced neither bill nor bow.

" Beneath the castle's gloomy pride
In ample round did Arthur ride
Three times ; nor living thing he spied,
   Nor heard a living sound,
Save that, awakening from her dream,
The owlet now began to scream,
In concert with the rushing stream,
   That wash'd the battled mound."

On arriving near the rock where the road crosses the
streamlet

" That wash'd the battled mound,"

there is a pretty view, embracing the bold perpendicular
rock, and a few picturesque buildings, in the midst of
wood and water, in the foreground. The rocks overhanging the river on the opposite side, the towering

height of Raven Crag, and the Great Howe, the round wooded hill in front, are also very fine; and looking back, Blencathara, with its ridgy front, hems in the valley on the N.

Here the tourist may rest awhile, and then with the following lines take his leave of this enchanted ground:

> " The Monarch, breathless and amazed,
> Back on the fatal castle gazed—
> Nor tower nor donjon could he spy,
> Darkening against the morning sky !
> But on the spot where once they frown'd
> The lonely streamlet brawl'd around
> A tufted knoll, where dimly shone
> Fragments of rock and rifted stone.
> Musing on this strange hap the while,
> The King wends back to fair Carlisle;
> And cares, that cumber royal sway,
> Wore memory of the past away."

The coach-road between Ambleside and Keswick is soon joined, and ½m. farther stands the King's Head Hostelry, at Thirlspot.

Passing by the inn, take the road on the right, and proceed by Dale Head Hall. Cross the lake at the bridge, leave Armboth House, a cottage, and a farmhouse on the left. The road now winds up the side of the hill, and, at the highest point it attains, pursues its course through a gate, conducting to a wood. A little to the right, before entering the wood, is the best position for obtaining a view of the whole of Thirlmere Lake; the part on the S. of the picturesque bridge looking extremely beautiful. Emerging from the coppice, and passing the towering height of Raven Crag, the lake and river are left in the rear, and a short distance beyond a farm-house the Ambleside and Keswick road is entered, in the Naddle Valley, about 4m. from Keswick.

From this valley the descent by Castle Rigg into Keswick is a satisfactory conclusion of a most enjoyable drive.

Keswick to (Ullswater Lake) Patterdale.

Troutbeck station, 9m.; Dockray, 13m.; Ullswater Lake, 14½m.; Patterdale (Ullswater Hotel), 17m.

Ullswater is generally visited either from Ambleside and Windermere, or from Keswick. See p. 26.

Some tourists who enter the district at Windermere and desire to leave at the same place, take the coach-road to Keswick *viâ* Grasmere and Thirlmere lakes, and then return to Ambleside *viâ* Ullswater, or *vice versâ*.

Private carriages leave Keswick by the Penrith road, and pass the village of Threlkeld, and along the base of Blencathara to Troutbeck railway station (which must not be confused with the Troutbeck near Windermere), and thence by the coach-road to Ullswater.

There are no public coaches from Keswick to Patterdale, but the railway company issue through tickets, which include the train to Troutbeck station, and coaches thence to Ullswater Hotel in Patterdale. The fares for the single journey are: 1st class, 4s. 2d.; 2nd class, 3s. 8d. Tickets available for return on the same or following day: 1st class, 6s. 3d.; 2nd class, 5s. 6d. Picnic parties, of not fewer than six 1st or 2nd, or ten 3rd class passengers, are booked at the following fares for the double journey: 1st class, 5s. 5d.; 2nd class, 4s. 11d.; 3rd class, 4s. 7d., returning on the same or on the following day. At Troutbeck station coaches meet the trains which leave Keswick at 9.26 A.M. and 4.10 P.M., and return to Troutbeck in time for the rail arriving in Keswick at 6.25 P.M.

Conveyances may also be obtained in connection with the train leaving Keswick at 12.40 P.M. on previous application to the station-master at Keswick.

Persons who take a railway ticket only to Troutbeck can go forward by coach from Troutbeck station to Patterdale for 2s. 6d., preference being given to travellers who have booked from Keswick. As slight alterations are sometimes made in these arrangements, it is well to inquire at the station.

Troutbeck station is seated in the midst of a wild moorland tract, one of the most uninteresting places near the Lakes; and therefore it is to be regretted that a circular tour is not arranged which would prevent this desolate piece of ground from being traversed both going and returning.

The better course would be to issue a circular-tour ticket, allowing tourists to go from Keswick to Penrith by train, then a round of 6m. by coach to Pooley Bridge, at the foot of Ullswater, passing Brougham Castle, Brougham Hall, Arthur's Round Table, Maybrough, and Yanwath Hall. The steamer from Pooley Bridge would meet the coaches at Patterdale for Troutbeck station, and thence by train to Keswick.

Leaving the inn at Troutbeck station, Mell Fell is passed to the left, and then a descent is made into Matterdale, where there is a small but interesting church by the roadside. The village of Dockray, containing a comfortable wayside inn, stands on the stream which soon afterwards forms the Aira Force, and separates the Glencoin and Gowbarrow Parks. After entering the Glencoin Park, the road makes a steep descent to the lake, with Aira Force out of sight to the left. During the descent there are superb views of a portion of the higher reach of Ullswater, with Place Fell and Birk Fell on the E. side, and the High Street range above and beyond. In the distance the Red Screes tower to the right of the Kirkstone Pass. On the W., Stybarrow Crag separates the Glencoin and Glenridding valleys; and beyond Hall Bank, the low wooded height which separates the Glenridding and Grisedale valleys, stands St. Sunday Crag. The head of the lake, with its three islets, looks extremely beautiful at every glimpse which is obtained of its surface during the descent through a sylvan and romantic district. On arriving at the lake, to the left stands Lyulph's Tower, in Gowbarrow Park, where leave may be obtained to visit Aira Force.

The road continues along the margin of the lake for 2½m. to the Ullswater Hotel, and 1m. farther up the valley to Patterdale Hotel and village. The stream issuing from Glencoin Valley divides Westmorland and Cumberland; and at this point the first and second reaches of the lake are in sight. The coaches usually arrive in Patterdale soon after 11 o'clock, and leave for Troutbeck station at 4.30 P.M.

The steamer sails from Patterdale at 2 P.M. for Pooley Bridge, at the foot of the lake, and arrives at Patterdale again about 4 P.M., in time for the coaches. For further particulars respecting Ullswater, see p. 28.

Round Bassenthwaite Lake, by Carriage-road.— Bassenthwaite Lake commences about 3m. to the N. of the foot of Derwentwater. It is 4m. long, and its mean breadth is nearly ¾m. The greatest depth is 78 feet, and the surface elevation above the level of the sea is 226 feet. It contains pike, perch, and a few trout. Salmon also pass through it.

The river Derwent, which carries the waters from the Derwent and Thirlmere lakes, enters it at its head, and leaves it at its foot, flowing past Cockermouth and into the sea at Workington. At some remote geological era this lake appears to have been joined to Derwentwater; but it would seem that they have since been divided by the deposit brought from the mountains by the streams which converge in the low-lying lands now separating these two sheets of water. Even now, occasionally, the heavy rains in winter are apt to flood the land between the two lakes, and actually unite the waters.

Bassenthwaite Lake is diversified on the E. side by the three promontories of Bowness, Braidness, and Scarness, but it does not contain a single island. Skiddaw overshadows its eastern shore. On the W. side the Barf and Wythop fells come down to the water's edge, and are well clothed with wood. At its foot, the mountains subside into small hills and an undulating and almost level tract of country.

Lying on the northern outskirt of the Lake District, away from the wild and lofty peaks, this lake is not often visited by tourists. The excursion round it is a distance

N

of 18m., and there is a good road all the way. On its western shore the road and railway both pass near the margin, but on the eastern side the road is in some parts more than 1m. from the edge of the lake. The best route is to go down the W. side, and return by the E.

After passing Portinscale, a good view is had of the Newlands and Coledale mountains; and then the road continues by the feet of beautifully-wooded heights of the Thornthwaite Fells, with the Derwent Vale spread below on the right, and Skiddaw on its opposite side.

On arriving at the Swan Inn, near the head of the lake, the Barf Mountain rises boldly on the left, and is wild and striking. From the Swan Inn to the Pheasant Inn, a distance of 4m., the road runs near to the lake, but is separated from it by the railway, and is boldly overhung by wooded fells, and commands here and there most lovely glimpses of the bays and promontories on the opposite side of the water.

The Pheasant Inn is pleasantly situated about 100 yards from the lake, and the same distance from the railway station. Boats can be had, and some capital pike-fishing. After passing the inn, the road crosses the railway, and then the river Derwent at Ouse Bridge, just where the water leaves the lake. A few yards E. of the bridge the finest view of Bassenthwaite is to be obtained. The whole length of the lake is seen, with beautifully-wooded heights on its W. side, Skiddaw on the E., and at the head Swinside, Wallow Crag, and Helvellyn.

Armthwaite Hall, the seat of John Bowstead, Esq., is passed on the left, and then the Castle Inn is reached. The inn commands a good view of the lake, and is very comfortable and well managed. The distance hence to Keswick is 8m. The road turns away from the lake, and presents nothing of particular interest until Mire House, the seat of H. A. Spedding, Esq., is passed.

The pedestrian, after leaving the Castle Inn, might have some capital views by taking the first turning on the right, and walking along the road until the margin of the lake be reached. The beautiful tree-fringed pro-

montory of Scarness is a good station. After passing
the little church of Bassenthwaite, the main road is
again entered near Mire House, and the mountains surrounding the Newlands Vale and Derwentwater begin
to be finely grouped. The small haycock-like peak in
the distance, to the S., is Pike O'Stickle, one of the
Langdale Pikes.

If the hamlets of Millbeck and Applethwaite have
not been already visited, it is advisable to take the
turning on the left at a farm-house near the third milestone from Keswick. This road runs along the base of
Skiddaw, and commands exceedingly beautiful views of
Derwentwater and the vale. The main road is again
entered about 1m. from Keswick.

Tourists who do not wish to make the circuit of the
lake, nor intend to visit it during the descent from Skiddaw (see p. 184), can take the train to Bassenthwaite station, and at the Pheasant Inn obtain a boat, and have a
sail on the best part of the lake. They can return by
the train, or walk along the E. side to Braithwaite or
Keswick. The distance from Keswick to the Pheasant
Inn and the railway station is 8m.

Those who are fond of visiting old castles will take
the train 5m. farther to

COCKERMOUTH,

a town which contains 5115 inhabitants, and sends one
member to Parliament. Isaac Fletcher, Esq., of Tarn-
bank, is the present member.

The principal hotels are the Globe, Sun, and Apple
Tree.

Cockermouth was the birthplace of Wordsworth. The
house in which the poet was born, in 1770, appears to
have been at that time one of the principal buildings in
the town ; and it has been very little altered since. It
stands in the main street, and the gardens at the back
extend to the river Derwent.

Cockermouth Castle is said to have been built soon
after the Norman Conquest, but there is nothing in the

present appearance of the building that can be assigned
to an earlier time than the end of the thirteenth or the
beginning of the fourteenth century. It was a place of
great strength, and was garrisoned during the Civil
Wars for Charles I., and stood a siege of about a month
in 1648, but was then captured and dismantled. It was
never restored, and, excepting a small portion fitted up
as a residence, it continues to be a ruin. The castle
belongs to Lord Leconfield.

Wordsworth was fond of exploring the ruin in the
days of his boyhood; and on visiting the scene when in
his sixty-third year, he wrote the following sonnet, representing the Spirit of the castle as thus addressing him :—

"Thou look'st on me. Dost fondly think,
    Poet! that stricken as both are by years,
    We, differing once so much, are now compeers,
    Prepared, when each has stood his time, to sink
    Into the dust? Erewhile a sterner link
    United us—when thou, in boyish play,
    Entering my dungeon, didst become a prey
    To soul-appalling darkness. Not a blink
    Of light was there; and thus did I, thy tutor,
    Make thy young thoughts acquainted with the grave,
    When thou went chasing the wing'd butterfly
    Through my green courts, or climbing, a wild suitor,
    Up to the flowers whose golden progeny
    Still round my shattered brow in beauty wave."

Round Derwentwater Lake, by Carriage-road.

Barrow Fall, 2m.; Lodore Fall, 3m.; Grange village, 4m.; Portinscale, 9m.; Keswick, 10m.

This is a most delightful excursion, and may be taken
in a carriage, on horseback, or on foot.

If the Bowder Stone and a peep into Borrowdale be
included, the distance will be 12m.

The road, on the eastern side of the lake, from Keswick to Grange, is described in the Buttermere excursion. See page 143.

Grange village is a favourite subject with artists, and
is very picturesque. In former years stores of grain

were laid up in it, when the lands of Borrowdale belonged to Furness Abbey.

Leaving the village, the road for a short distance is not particularly interesting. On the right are some old buildings, in one of which is a saline spring whence salt was formerly procured by the monks of Furness.

When Manesty, the last farm-house, is passed, it is well for the pedestrian to walk along an old grass-grown road, a little higher up the hill than the one now in use. It commands far better views. At one place it appears to be lost for a few yards, a wall having been built along it. The path over the hill to Newlands Valley can be distinctly traced. Near to the old Brandelhow Lead Mine the new road is again entered, and on rounding a small knoll, which stands upon the right, a superb prospect of Derwentwater bursts suddenly into sight. Immediately below is a well-wooded foreground. The low, marshy land at the head of the lake is hidden by the copse-clad knoll, but almost the whole of the rest of the lake, with its wooded islands and headlands, is fully displayed. Keswick, the two churches, and houses scattered here and there, half-concealed by trees, in the vale of Keswick, add a charm to the scene. In the background, Skiddaw, Latrigg, and Blencathara add all that can be desired to what we have no hesitation in pronouncing one of the finest views that is to be had in the Lake District.

On leaving this spot, the trees on the right shut out the prospect for some distance, and therefore the tourist is advised to climb on the left to an old road, which commands exquisite views, and joins the lower road at the end of Cat Bells.

Descending a little, a gate is passed through, and the carriage-road crosses the valley. At the point where it enters the road from Newlands to Keswick, fine retrospective views are obtained of the Newlands Mountains.

The pedestrian, after passing through the gate at the foot of Cat Bells, can go through a wicket-gate on the right, and a few yards farther, a path on the left leads through the woods, having a hedge on the right hand all the way.

Portinscale will be reached without difficulty, and 1m. farther, Keswick.

Ascent of Skiddaw (3058), from Keswick.—Skiddaw has in past seasons been ascended by more tourists than any other mountain in the Lake Country, and in the future it will probably maintain this pre-eminence, although the view from the summit is less grand than that from some other heights. Its proximity to Keswick, and the ease with which ponies reach the summit, render it a very tempting excursion for those who desire to attain one of the highest points with the least possible labour.

The distance from Keswick to the top is generally considered to be 6m., but 5½m. will be the more correct measurement. The time occupied by the whole journey —there and back—is from 3½ to 5 hours, according to the capability and inclination of the tourist. The charge for a pony is 6s., and guide 6s. A carriage may be taken 2½m. to the back of Latrigg.

Quitting Keswick by the Railway Station Road, take the turn to the right, wind round the base of the Keswick Hotel Gardens, and under the railway. A few yards past the station-master's residence (which is the only house seen on the farther side of the railway), incline to the left, and after continuing for 200 yards, a lane, bearing the euphonious cognomen of Spooney Green, is seen on the right.

Tourists may also arrive at this point by proceeding down the main street of Keswick, and over the Greta Bridge. Just beyond the toll-gate, turn to the right, and then to the right again, and under the railway, some 50 yards distant from the Spooney Green Lane.

Go up the lane, pass a cottage on the left, and through a gate which fronts the road. On the left of the path there is a hedge extending for a short distance, after which the road is continued through a gate at the N.E. corner of the field. Here are good views of Keswick, Derwentwater, the Coledale, Newlands, and Borrowdale mountains. Having gone through the gate, keep to the hedge on the left. When behind Latrigg, there is a small valley on the left, and a road is seen on the opposite side of the valley. After rounding the head of the valley, enter a road through a gate, and proceed to the right for 50 yards to where the road is terminated by a wall, containing a gate, through which pass, and turn to the left. A portion of Blencathara, the two Mell Fells in the plain, and the Helvellyn range are now in prospect. The wall on the left is seen to continue up the mountain-side, close by a small wooden hut, where refreshments may be had. This is the steepest part of the whole ascent. A short distance before the shed is reached the path passes through a gate, and then the wall is on the right. Resting awhile at the hut, it is well to note the mountains which are in sight.

Commencing at Bassenthwaite Lake, a very small portion of which can be seen, we have Barf, Lord's Seat, and Whinlatter fells; beyond the Whinlatter Pass depression, Grisedale Pike, the Coledale Valley, and the long range, commencing at Grasmoor and continuing past Eel Crags, Sail, Scar Crags, Causey Pike, and Rowling End to the Newlands Valley. The near hills below these are Outerside, Barrow, and Swinside. Surrounding the Newlands Valley, are Cat Bells, Maiden Moor, Eel Crags, Dale Head, Hindscarth, and Robinson; to the left of Robinson the Pillar Mountain, beyond Ennerdale Valley, and to the right, High Stile, beyond Buttermere. In the distance, to the left of Dale Head, is Great Gable, and then Scawfell, Scawfell Pikes, Great End, Hanging Knott, Bow Fell, Coniston Old Man, and Wetherlam; and Pike O'Stickle, one of the Langdale Pikes. Below these are Castle Crag, in Borrowdale, Brund Fell, Glaramara, High Raise, Armboth, and Watendlath fells, and Wallow Crag. Keswick and Derwentwater are immediately beneath, looking very beautiful. To the left of Latrigg are the Naddle and St. John's valleys, and the Naddle Fells between; and the small Tewet Tarn. A portion of the Castle Rock can be distinguished at the head of the St. John's Valley.

Great How and Raven Crag hide Thirlmere Lake;
beyond, on the right of Dunmail Raise, is Steel Fell,
and on the left, Fairfield, Seat Sandal, and the Helvellyn range.

A few yards past the hut, take the path which leaves
the wall and winds a little to the left. It soon ends, and
a grassy table-land has to be traversed. Continue climbing to the left, and presently the two peaks of Skiddaw
Low Man appear in front. Make for these, but when at
their base, go through a gate to the right, in the wire
fencing. A good path is now entered (leading to the
summit of Skiddaw) which winds round the Low Man
for about ½m., with the wild moorland tract of Skiddaw
Forest on the right. The forest is surrounded by Skiddaw, Blencathara, and the Caldbeck and Carrock fells;
and in the middle of it there is the gamekeeper's house.
To the astonishment of many tourists, it does not contain
a single tree.

After passing the hollow between the Low Man and
Skiddaw, another climb has to be made; and on arriving
at the first cairn, which is the highest point of the
mountain seen from Keswick, Derwentwater and Bassenthwaite are both in sight, and close to the E. side of
Bassenthwaite, Longside, an offshoot of Skiddaw. The
summit is ½m. farther N., at the fourth cairn. The
mountains in view from this point are almost the same as
those mentioned during the ascent, but they are too distant to allow of that glorious effect which is witnessed
when a near view is obtained of their craggy precipices
and beautifully-coloured slopes. Some tourists will think
this is amply compensated by the extensive view northwards, of the plain, the sea, and the Scotch mountains.

It is usual to return by the same route, but some
visitors will prefer winding round the foot of Bassenthwaite Lake to the railway at the Bassenthwaite Lake
station, a distance of 7m., and thence 7m. by train to
Keswick.

Continuing due N. to the fifth cairn (here Little Tarn
and Overwater Tarn are seen), and then descending to a

smooth green part of the mountain, two ways present themselves. By descending to the right, into the forest, and then bearing a little to the left, the road is entered, leading from the gamekeeper's house to Bassenthwaite village, past the Dead Crag and the Dash Fall (see page 224). If the descent be to the left, the Bassenthwaite road will be entered after passing the end of the Longside ridge. Practised mountaineers will perhaps prefer descending due W. from the summit, which part of the mountain is steep, but not dangerous. Two miles before arriving at the Bassenthwaite railway station the Castle Inn will be passed. It is clean, comfortable, and well managed. Close to the station is the Pheasant Inn, most pleasantly situated in its own well-arranged grounds, where boats can be had for a row on the lake.

Those who do not desire to descend to Bassenthwaite Lake can make for the depression between Skiddaw and Skiddaw Low Man, and then descend to the right, to Millbeck hamlet, down a perfectly safe, but wild and stony, part of the mountain. Or, commencing at the depression, they can cross the front of the mountain, along a narrow track, and descend by Carlside and the White Stones to Millbeck. If the Low Man be ascended, a direct descent can be made down a steep green slope to Applethwaite village. A few good mountaineers will wish to walk from Skiddaw to the summit of Blencathara. The distance is about 6m., and the ground in some places very wet and boggy. The best method is to pass near the gamekeeper's house.

Although the prospect from the summit of Skiddaw is not so good as that from many other mountains, yet if the tourist have time to visit its wild and beautiful recesses, he will be ready to exclaim with Wordsworth :—

> " What was the great Parnassus' self to thee,
> Mount Skiddaw? In its natural sovereignty,
> Our British hill is nobler far; he shrouds
> His double front among Atlantic clouds,
> And pours forth streams more sweet than Castaly."

Ascent of Blencathara (2847), from Keswick.

Threlkeld village, 4m.; Scales Toll-gate, 5½m.; Top of Blencathara, 8m.; Keswick, 14m.

This mountain is often called Saddleback, owing to
the rocks on its eastern side presenting the appearance
of a saddle, when seen from the neighbourhood of
Penrith. Its northern and western sides are smooth
grassy slopes, but to the S. and E. it presents steep
precipices, and long narrow ridges, which give it a place
amongst the representative and characteristic mountains
of the district.

The best plan is to ascend from Scales Toll-gate,
which is 5½m. from Keswick, on the Penrith road, and
1½m. past Threlkeld village. Ponies can go the whole
journey, or a carriage may be taken to Scales, and thence
sent back to an inn at Threlkeld, to wait until the tourist
descends the mountain; but most persons will take the
train to Threlkeld, a distance of 3m.

On the left of the road, close to the Threlkeld side of
the toll-gate, there is a square waste bit of ground.
Enter this, and pass through the gate in front, leading
out upon the mountain. Turn to the right, due E., and
continue along the side of the wall until the shoulder of
the mountain be rounded, and the wall begins to descend;
then leave it, and climb to the left, nearly due W., until
the bold perpendicular rock overhanging Scales Tarn is
in sight, with Sharp Edge declining from it. Continuing the ascent, and bearing a little to the left, a view
will presently be obtained of the southern ridges of the
mountain, and glimpses of the Thirlmere and Derwentwater lakes; and Bow Fell, Scawfell, Great Gable, and
Newlands Mountains come into prospect. Keeping
along the ridge, with the steep rocky hollows on the left,
it is impossible to make any mistake during the remainder of the ascent.

To the right, under the enormous perpendicular
rock called Tarn Crag, is Scales Tarn, which by some
fanciful writers is said to reflect the stars at noon.

Sir Walter Scott refers to this in his 'Bridal of Trier-main':—

> " Never sunbeam could discern
> The surface of that sable tarn,
> In whose black mirror you may spy
> The stars, while noontide lights the sky."

The dark, lofty, precipitous crags which overhang the tarn always impart to it a gloomy and solemn appearance, and pedestrians who are not afraid of a little extra toil will be amply repaid by descending to its shore, and there enjoying the deep solitude of what may be truly called one of nature's temples.

The hollow in which the tarn lies was formed, according to the dictum of recent geologists, by the scooping action of ancient glaciers, which descended from the rocks above, and with moraine matter produced the eastern embankment; but formerly it was supposed to be the crater of a volcano. In Hutchinson's 'History of Cumberland' it is stated that around the tarn lava is unquestionably to be found in large quantities.

It is amusing to read in the same History an account of an ascent of Blencathara made in 1793, by a party of gentlemen and a guide. They had not walked more than 1m., when one of the party, " on looking around, was so astonished with the different appearance of objects in the valley beneath him, that he declined proceeding."

Another had not gone much farther when "he was suddenly taken ill, and wished to lose blood and return." Only one of the party and the guide reached the summit.

Sharp Edge, the ridge of the right of the tarn, is all but inaccessible. Mr. Green, in describing the ascent which he and Mr. Otley made, says:—

" We had not gone far before we were aware that our journey would be attended with perils; the passage gradually grew narrower, and the declivity on each hand awfully precipitous. From walking erect, we were reduced to the necessity either of bestriding the ridge or of moving on one of its sides, with our hands lying over the top, as a security against falling into the tarn on the left, or into a frightful gully on the right, both of immense depth. Sometimes we thought it prudent to return, but that seemed unmanly, and we proceeded, thinking with Shakspeare, that ‘dangers retreat when boldly they're confronted.’   Mr. Otley was the leader, who, on gaining steady footing, looked back on the writer, whom he perceived reviewing at leisure from his saddle the remainder of his upper course.”

Leaving the tarn, and climbing along the green slope on the left, the top of the mountain is attained without much exertion; and whilst the tourist is enjoying what Southey considered “ one of the finest mountain scenes in the country,” he may repeat to himself the following lines from the pen of S. T. Coleridge :—

“ On stern Blencathara's perilous height ·
   The winds are tyrannous and strong ;
  And flashing forth unsteady light
  From stern Blencathara's skyey height
   How loud the torrents throng !
 Beneath the moon in gentle weather
 They bind the earth and sky together ;
  But, oh ! the sky and all its forms how quiet !
 The things that seek the earth how full of noise and riot ! ”

The view to the N. and N.W. is obstructed by the Carrock and Caldbeck fells, and Skiddaw; but on the right of Skiddaw a glimpse is to be obtained of the Solway Firth and the Scotch mountains, and on the left the Irish Sea, near Whitehaven, is visible.   Then stands forth a grand array of mountains, including Grisedale Pike, Grasmoor, Red Pike, High Stile, Pillar, Kirk Fell, Great Gable, Scawfell Pikes, Hanging Knott, Bow Fell, Crinkle Crags, Coniston Old Man, Steel Fell, Helvellyn, St. Sunday Crag, and High Street; and to the E., Cross Fell, and the two Mell Fells in the plain. There is also a peep of Thirlmere Lake, but the most lovely object in sight is Derwentwater.

The ridges on the S. side of the mountain are wild and romantic, and experienced mountaineers will take a pleasure in descending the narrowest and most rocky of them, which strikes off direct from the summit. Others will prefer walking along the top of the mountain, with its deep gorges, and stern precipices on the left.

On arriving at the western shoulder, which is smooth and rounded, a descent must be made in a direct line with the centre of Derwentwater Lake, until a farm-house is seen below, on the eastern side of the stream, the Glenderaterra, which flows southwards between Blencathara and Skiddaw.

Tourists intending to descend to Threlkeld must now incline to the left, and the village will be reached without difficulty.

In order to walk to Keswick the stream must be crossed by a foot-bridge behind the farm-house, and a path will lead round the eastern end of Latrigg, into a rough cart-road, which runs through Brundholme Wood, along the southern side of Latrigg, parallel with the Greta. This road affords delightful views, and leads direct to Keswick, passing Greta Bank, the residence of J. J. Spedding, Esq.

Ascent of Helvellyn (3118), from Keswick.

King's Head Inn at Thirlspot, 5½m.; Top of Helvellyn, 8½m.; Nag's Head Inn at Wythburn, 11m.; Keswick, 19m.

Helvellyn is ascended, as we have already stated, from Grasmere, Patterdale, Wythburn, and Thirlspot. The King's Head Inn at the latter place is the best starting-point for tourists sojourning in Keswick. It is situated on the Ambleside road, 5½m. from Keswick, and either a private carriage or the Windermere coach might be taken for that distance. The coach fare is 1s. 6d., and the driver expects a small fee. If the descent be made to Wyth-burn, which is 8m. distant from Keswick, a return coach might possibly be secured, but during the busy part of the season it would not be desirable to trust to this, for

the coach is often full.   Conveyances are to be had both
at Thirlspot and Wythburn, and at the latter place
a supply of ponies, but at Thirlspot only one pony
is obtainable.   Guides can always be procured.   If a
private carriage be hired at Keswick, the St. John's
Vale, and the W. of Thirlmere Lake might be visited on
the same day.   See page 171.

Commence the ascent at the back of the King's Head
Inn at Thirlspot, and on arriving at the last wall on the
left, keep alongside of it until the Fisher Place stream
is reached.

As the stream is a few hundred yards nearer to
Keswick than the inn, parties may save a short distance
by leaving the road at the fifth mile-post, and turning
up a lane to the farm-houses.

During the first part of the ascent keep the stream on
the left, and remain as near to it as possible, in order to
observe the numerous wild and romantic falls which the
water makes during its descent.   Sometimes the water
is confined to a single narrow stream which leaps to a
great depth, and at other times it diffuses itself and
descends gracefully along the front of the rock.   The
charms of this stream will beguile the tourist and
diminish the toil of the ascent, and before he is aware
he will have spread below him the Thirlmere Lake and
the St. John and Naddle valleys, with Blencathara and
Skiddaw to the N., and Raven Crag, High Seat, and
Armboth Fells to the W.   When at the principal fall
Great Gable is seen peering over the Armboth Fells,
and then at every succeeding step mountain after
mountain starts into view to the W. and S.W.; the
Pillar standing more bold and prominent than any
other.   To the left of Skiddaw part of Bassenthwaite
Lake, with the sea and the Scotch mountains, are visible.
When the stream becomes uninteresting, and just
before the point is reached where it branches into two
rivulets, leave it and take to the right, up a rocky knoll.
Then cross some disagreeable ground, covered with long
grass and bog.   The rock on the N. side of Helvellyn is

now beheld, and a smooth-rounded mountain height is on the left. Walk round to the S. side of the latter height, without scaling it, and without making any descent. The pony-path will soon be entered which leads from Patterdale to the summit of Helvellyn, and conducts up what looks like a narrow ridge, but the track is not in the least dangerous. Ullswater Lake, Place Fell, High Street, and Cossfell ranges are in sight; and immediately below are Keppelcove Tarn, in the Glenridding Valley, and the fine precipitous ridge of Catchedecam and Swirrel Edge. After climbing for a few minutes more, the Helvellyn Low Man is reached, and from this point six lakes are visible, Bassenthwaite, Thirlmere, Ullswater, Coniston, Esthwaite, and Windermere. At one particular place, about half-way down the N. side of the mountain, more or less of each of these six lakes, and also a small strip of a seventh, Grasmere, may be seen. Descending a few feet from the Low Man, and continuing along, with the precipice on the left, the summit is quickly attained—the view from which is described at page 96, as well as particulars of the descent to Wythburn, where carriages sent forward from Thirlspot will wait. Pedestrians may return along the western side of Thirlmere Lake, or cross over the fells to Watendlath, and thence to Keswick.

Ascent of Scawfell Pike (3210), from Keswick.

Seathwaite, 9m.; Sty Head Tarn, 12m.; Esk Hause, 13¼m.; Scawfell Pike, 15m.

Scawfell Pike being the highest mountain in England, most tourists are anxious to reach its summit.

The prospect which it commands is remarkably grand, although generally considered inferior to that which may be had from Great Gable. Owing to the rugged character of the mountain, and to the chaotic state of its bare rocky summit, the climb is especially interesting and exciting, and ought, if possible, to be undertaken by all lovers of mountain work. It is generally ascended from Keswick, *viâ* Borrowdale; from Ambleside, *viâ* Langdale; or from Wastwater.

The latter is the shortest but steepest route.

The one from Keswick is most travelled; the ascent from Borrowdale by Sty Head Tarn being easier and more gradual than from Langdale by Rossett Gill.

The Scawfell mass consists of the three Scawfell Pikes, and Scawfell, Great End, and Lingmell. The most northerly part is Great End, which looks towards Borrowdale. Behind Great End are the three Pikes, the remotest from Great End being the loftiest point in England. To the south of the highest Pike is Mickledore Chasm, on the opposite side of which rises Scawfell (3162), the second height in the district. Lingmell is a kind of buttress to the Pikes on the Wastdale side. To cross the Mickledore Chasm from Scawfell Pike to Scawfell, without making a *détour*, is considered—next to the dangerous ascent of the Pillar Rock—as the most difficult bit of mountaineering work in the Lake Country.

A carriage can reach as far as Seathwaite, in Borrowdale, and a pony to within 1m. of the summit of Scawfell Pike. Seathwaite is a small hamlet consisting of a cottage and one or two farm-houses, but it contains no inn. Carriages are allowed to remain at one of the farm-houses. If ponies are required, they must either be taken by the tourists or sent on in advance. Strangers to the district ought not to venture on the journey without the aid of a guide, as the summit of the mountain is most puzzling and dangerous, when enveloped in mist. Occasionally it will be arranged for the driver to act as guide, and loose saddles are then carried with the party from Keswick, to be put upon the horses when relieved from harness at Seathwaite.

The regular path by Sty Head Tarn is described at page 160, and it is the most interesting route; but a mile may be saved by branching off at Stockley Bridge, and following the course of the stream which descends from Grain's Gill and passes under the bridge. No mistake can be made by those using the Grain's Gill route, if they pursue the course of the torrent, and keep on the side of the right-hand fell. Great End is a fine object in front all the way up, and the retrospective view includes Skiddaw and Derwentwater. When near Great End, the stream flows through a broken, shaggy chasm, which must be kept on the right, and then crossed, so as to enter the track leading from Sty Head Tarn to Esk Hause. The track will be gained immediately under Great End, and at the point where a charming view is had of Derwentwater.

Those who take the regular route by Sty Head Pass will branch to the left after passing the tarn, and on arriving at the cairn on the summit of the pass. From thence the path can scarcely be traced for the first hundred yards, until a low, wet bit of ground is crossed. It is then entered again, and is found to lead under the north part of Great End, by the course of the rivulet which flows into Sty Head Tarn from Sprinkling Tarn. When this rivulet is reached, keep it on the left for a few hundred yards, and then pass over, with it to the right, until it is again crossed at the exact spot where it leaves the Sprinkling Tarn. This tarn lies amongst a number of low, rocky hillocks at the foot of Great End. The path skirts the shore for a few yards, and bends to the right, and mounts until directly under the huge perpendicular cliffs of Great End. This is one of the grandest and most imposing rocks in the district. At its base is a red-coloured chasm, down which a rivulet rushes to Stockley Bridge, and there joins the stream from Sprinkling and Sty Head tarns. This chasm must be kept on the left. When it is reached a most charmingly beautiful prospect will suddenly attract the tourist.

Derwentwater, with its lovely wooded bays and islands, is seen as if set in a frame. Castle Crag rises prominently in front; Skiddaw and Blencathara fill up the background; and on turning round the traveller is awed by the frowning mass of Great End.

When a few yards farther, a piece of wet ground may

o

be avoided by bending to the right and mounting the
green slope, so as to round to the back of Great End.
It is, however, advisable to proceed for a little distance
in the direction of the rivulet, until the Langdale Pikes
and Windermere Lake are seen.   Here incline to the
right, up a green slope, and presently the top of Esk
Hause is gained (2490), and a peep is had down into
Eskdale.

The view from the Hause is much admired.   Der-
wentwater and Windermere lakes and Sprinkling Tarn
are in sight.   Between Allen Crags, the beginning of
Glaramara, and Hanging Knott, in the direction of
Windermere, are, in the distance, Dolly Waggon Pike,
St. Sunday Crag, Fairfield, High Street, Scandale, Red
Screes, Ill Bell, and the Yorkshire Hills; and nearer
are High Raise, Sergeant Man, Langdale Pikes, and
Lingmoor.   In the direction of Eskdale are Hard Knott,
Harter Fell, Birker Moor, Black Combe, a strip of the
sea, and, to the right, a part of the Scawfell Pikes.
Between Allen Crags and Great End, in the direction
of Derwentwater, are Blencathara, Skiddaw, Maiden
Moor, Grisedale Pike, Dale Head, Robinson, Eel Crags,
Whiteless Pike, Grasmoor, Grey Knotts, Brandreth,
Base Brown, Sprinkling Fell, Green Gable, Great Gable,
and the Pillar.

After resting awhile, and enjoying the prospect, the
tourist must strike to the right, and aim for Great End.
When at the commencement of the bare, stony part of
the mountain, avoid ascending, enter the hollow on the
left, cross the rill, and follow a track which mounts
round a rock on the side near the hollow.   The track
bends to the left, and crosses a few yards of level grass
land.   Here the ponies must be left.   Some rocks are
now scaled, and a few heaps of stones will be found,
acting as good indicators all the way.

The Great Gable, Pillar, Grasmoor, and a host of
other heights to the N.W. now look extremely grand.
Bend slightly to the left, and pass over large stones
between two small rocky heights.   The hills to the E.

are now seen from Helvellyn to Coniston, and a view is had into the upper desolate part of Eskdale. Bend slightly to the right, and walk along a smooth grass track. The tourist is now on the first pike, a few rocks on the left being its highest point. The highest pike, with its well-constructed cairn, is prominent in front, and nearer is the second pike, with Lingmell appearing behind it.

A strip of Crummock Lake is visible between Great Gable and Kirk Fell. A slight descent, and then a climb leads to the second pike. Some rocks on the Eskdale side of the highest pike look very fine from this point. In the hollow on the right is seen Sty Head Tarn. Leaving the rocky summit a little to the right, a descent over large stones is made into a deep hollow, from which point are seen the grand masses of Great Gable, Grasmoor, Kirk Fell, High Stile, Pillar, and Lingmell, and on the left the rocky sides of the pikes.

The last climb is now commenced. A well-marked track up a narrow ridge leads to the large cairn on the summit, where an extensive and magnificent panorama is spread to view.

A large tract of sea is visible to the S. and S.W., with the Isle of Man in the distance, and it is said that on a very clear day the coasts of Ireland and Wales can be seen. The lakes in sight are Wastwater, Derwentwater, and Windermere, and the tarns Devoke, Sty Head, and Low Tarn. To the E. are Helvellyn range, Seat Sandal, St. Sunday Crag, Fairfield, High Street, Scandale, Ill Bell, Yorkshire Hills, and Wansfell Pike; and in front of these Ullscarf, High Raise, and Langdale Pikes; and nearer still a fine range, which commences at Hanging Knott, and includes Bow Fell, Crinkle Crags, Wetherlam, Coniston Old Man, and Seathwaite Fells. Close to, on the S., is Mickledore Chasm, with Scawfell on the other side, and then a bit of Eskdale, an extent of level country, and the heights of Birker Moor and Black Combe.

By turning round, and looking in an exactly opposite
direction, are Great End, High Seat, Castle Crag, in
Borrowdale, Wallow Crag, Blencathara, and Skiddaw.

Surrounding Newlands are Grasmoor, Whiteless Pike,
Eel Crags, Grisedale Pike, Causey Pike, Robinson, Hinds-
carth, Dale Head, and Maiden Moor. At the head of But-
termere, and to the left of that valley, are Green Gable,
Base Brown, Grey Knotts, High Crag, and High Stile.
The grandest heights are, however, those standing be-
tween Wastdale and Ennerdale: Buckbarrow, Seatallan,
Yewbarrow, Haycock, Steeple, Pillar, Kirk Fell, and
Great Gable.

" From this centre of the mountain region beautiful
and solemn is the aspect to the traveller. He beholds
a world of mountains, a hundred and a hundred savage
peaks, like giant spirits of the wilderness; there in
their silence, in their solitude, even as on the night
when Noah's deluge first dried. He gazes over those
stupendous masses with wonder, almost with longing
desire; never till this hour has he known Nature, that
she was one, that she was his Mother and divine. A
murmur of eternity and immensity, of death and of life,
steals through his soul; and he feels as if death and life
were one, as if the earth were not dead, as if the spirit
of the earth had its throne in that splendour, and his
own spirit were therewith holding communion."*

On leaving the summit, no difficulty will be found in
again descending to the first hollow. When scaling the
middle pike, the stranger, by using care, will be surprised to find that walking over large blocks of stone is
not a very fatiguing or dangerous pursuit. The top of
this pike is kept on the left, a large block with small
stones upon it is passed, and then the second descent is
commenced, and the path can be traced ascending on
the other side. The top of the last and lowest pike is
comparatively flat and smooth. A small rocky knob is,
however, seen on the right. When the level, smooth
part is gained, bend to the right, and pass, amongst

* Carlyle's ' Sartor Resartus.'

rough stones, between two rocks. A smooth descent is now found to the right-hand hollow, in the rear of Great End, which height might be visited without much extra labour, and a lovely view had of Borrowdale and Derwentwater, with Skiddaw in the background.

After crossing a rill, Esk Hause is reached. When Derwentwater and Windermere come in sight, incline to the left, and make for the red-coloured ravine below. A pleasant change on the return route may be had by following the course of the stream down Grains Gill. When it leaves the front of Great End, cross it, and keep it on the left for some distance. It flows down a picturesque chasm, which, when seen from below, with Great Gable above as part of the picture, is extremely fine. Derwentwater and Skiddaw are pleasing objects in front during the descent. The regular path is again entered at Stockley Bridge.

Another change in the return route may be made by descending from Esk Hause to Angle Tarn, in the direction of Windermere, and then following the course of the rivulet which issues from the tarn. It flows through the Longstrath Glen to Stonethwaite, and Rosthwaite, in Borrowdale.

Ascent of Great Gable (2949) from Keswick, by Sty Head Tarn.

Seathwaite, 9m.; Sty Head Tarn, 12m.; Top of Great Gable, 13m.

The view from Great Gable is generally considered one of the finest views to be had from any mountain in the district. The ascent is usually made from the Sty Head Pass. The road from Keswick to the Sty Head Tarn is described in the Wastwater excursion (see page 158).

The pass being 1600 feet, and Great Gable 2949 feet, there is a steep climb of 1349 feet, which may be accomplished with ease in about an hour. Good climbers will reach the top in about 40 minutes. Ponies can be taken some distance up the mountain, but not to the summit.

On arriving at the Sty Head Tarn, a hollow will
be seen on the right, between Great Gable and
Green Gable. The lower height, Green Gable, is
on the Borrowdale side, and Great Gable overlooks
Wastdale.

The ascent may be commenced from the tarn, and
care must be taken to avoid Green Gable on one side,
and on the other the cliffs overlooking Wastdale.
Perhaps the best plan is to walk beyond the tarn and
commence the ascent from the cairn at the top of the
pass, and then gradually incline to the right. About
half-way up the mountain Wastwater and the sea
appear to great advantage. It is almost impossible to
go astray during the ascent; a good steady pull must
necessarily land the tourist on the summit, where there
is a large cairn. If the day be fine, and the atmosphere clear, the prospect will be magnificent in the
extreme.

To the N. and N.E. are seen the Borrowdale Valley,
Blencathara, Skiddaw, Eel Crags, Dale Head, Hindscarth,
Robinson, Grisedale Pike, Causey Pike, and intervening
ridge to Grasmoor, Whiteless Pike and Rannerdale
Knott, Crummock Lake, the Solway Firth, and the
Scotch mountains. To the W., Low Fell, Mellbreak,
Herdhouse, High Stile, High Crag, Hay Stacks, Fleetwith, and Brandreth. The Rannerdale Valley lies
secluded at the foot of the mountain; a portion of the
Pillar hides the lake. Between Ennerdale and Wastwater are Kirk Fell, Pillar, Steeple, Red Pike, Yewbarrow, Middle Fell, and Seatallan; the Pillar towering
grandly above the others. The whole of Wastwater is
spread below, and beyond are the Irish Sea and the Isle
of Man. To the left of Wastwater appear the Screes,
Black Combe, and a strip of Burnmoor Tarn; but the
wild rugged masses of Lingmell, Scawfell, the three
Scawfell Pikes, and Great End, add greatly to the
splendour of this extensive panorama. Below Great
End is seen Sprinkling Tarn, and to the left of Hanging
Knott and Bow Fell, a portion of Windermere Lake,

with the Yorkshire Hills away in the distance. On the E. are the different ranges of Ill Bell and High Street; Fairfield, Seat Sandal, and Helvellyn; Langdale Pikes, Sergeant Man, Ullscarf, and Wallow Crag; and the bare rocky summit of Glaramara.

Before the visitor leaves this commanding position, his mind will revert to the melancholy fate of the Hon. Lennox Butler.

On the 2nd February, 1865, Mr. Butler left the Derwentwater Hotel, Portinscale, to spend a few days at Wastdale Head, knowing well that at no season of the year does this district look more beautiful than during winter. After making excursions on the Scawfell and other mountains, he quitted Mr. Ritson's inn on the 8th, with the intention of ascending Great Gable, and going thence to Portinscale. The mountains were covered with a thick mantle of snow and ice. When on the top Mr. Butler had evidently thought of again returning to Wastdale Head, and with that intention entered a gully a little on the Wastwater side of Kirk Fell, full of ice and snow. Here he is supposed to have slipped, and before he could regain his footing, to have been precipitated over a perpendicular cliff of 300 feet. His skull was broken, and death must have been instantaneous.

Mrs. Bell, of the Derwentwater Hotel, became uneasy at his long absence, and wrote to Mr. Wm. Ritson. On the 16th, eight days after the accident, a very arduous search was made, and the body, which was shrouded in snow, was discovered by one of the dogs belonging to the searching party.

Tourists who look upon English mountaineering as dangerous must remember that almost all accidents amongst these heights have occurred when the ground was covered with snow and ice.

At other times, with ordinary care, little or no danger need be apprehended. By one well acquainted with the district, most of the mountains may be visited, even in the depth of winter, without much risk, and the glorious

scenes then beheld are well worth the extra exertion
required.

> " And now I am a Cumbrian mountaineer;
>   Their wintry garment of unsullied snow
>   The mountains have put on, the heavens are clear,
>   And yon dark lake spreads silently below;
>   Who sees them only in their summer hour
>   Sees but their beauties half, and knows not half their power."
>
> *Southey.*

The writer once ascended Helvellyn alone, when it
was covered with snow, and on the top encountered a
snowstorm. After pacing to and fro on the summit for
half an hour, waiting for a view, the storm was succeeded
by masses of silvery-lined clouds, which cast deep
shadows over hill and dale, and the whole district
appeared like an Alpine region. At another time, on a
bright winter's day, when all the mountains were covered
with frozen snow, he has stood under the immense perpendicular cliff of Great End, and seen it ornamented
with countless numbers of icicles, hanging from the
snow-covered rocks, and glittering in the sun. He has
then scrambled to the summit of Great Gable, over
which a magician's wand appeared to have been waved,
the cairn and every bit of rock being covered with
frozen snow, which had taken fantastic shapes, as
though of a fairy world. Coming suddenly on this
wonderful scene the eye was so entranced as to dis-
regard for a moment the glorious panorama that was
spread out before it.

The writer would recommend those in robust health
to visit the Lake District for a few frosty days in winter
after a fall of snow, and to climb, in company with a
guide, some of the mountains; or, at all events, to cross
the passes, and spend a few happy days in skating on
Derwentwater.

The reader must excuse this slight digression, and
now prepare for the descent from the summit of the
mountain.

In returning to Keswick, a pleasant change in the route may be had by pursuing the direction of Honister Pass. Avoiding the precipice on the Ennerdale side of Great Gable, a descent must be made along a rough rocky ground to the depression between Great Gable and Green Gable. To this point the ponies can ascend from Sty Head Pass, and be of service during the whole of the return journey. The top of Green Gable is quickly gained, and no error can be made in descending on the other side if care be taken to avoid dropping into Ennerdale on the left, or into Gillercombe on the right.

When off Green Gable, and before Brandreth is reached, at the point where are two pools of water, a descent might easily be made into the desolate-looking hollow on the right, called Gillercombe. It is the source of the Sour Milk Gill stream flowing to Seathwaite hamlet; and if its course be followed, the old workings and *débris* of the Plumbago, or Borrowdale Lead Mine, might be visited.

It is, however, not desirable to take this course, for presently, on attaining the top of Brandreth, a most charming view is had of Buttermere, Crummock, and Ennerdale lakes. During the whole walk, by looking back, Great Gable is seen, presenting a noble and precipitous front; and on the left the Pillar towers above all the neighbouring heights. Over the Black Sail Pass there appears to be a deep, dark den, with the Steeple and other mountains on the opposite side. If the rocks on the top of Brandreth be ascended, a capital view is had of a number of fine mountains, including the Pillar, Great Gable, Great End, Bow Fell, Grasmoor, and High Stile; but the most lovely bit of scenery is that including the Buttermere and Ennerdale valleys, and the lakes of Buttermere, Crummock, and Ennerdale.

When crossing Brandreth, two detached blocks of stone are passed, and then a low part on the right of Fleetwith and Honister Pike must be aimed at.

Avoid descending too far into the hollow leading to Buttermere, and go immediately under and to the left of

the rocks stretching from Grey Knotts. Presently the
slate-quarries on the side of Dale Head appear, and also
the road leading from them to the top of Borrowdale
Hause. Make for the right-hand end of the road, and a
slight descent will lead to the summit of the Honister
Pass.

Pedestrians may save 1m., and have an interesting
change in the route, by leaving the road a short distance
below the top of the pass. At some sheepfolds, or at a
point a little lower down, where a gate crosses the road,
branch to the left, and walk along the side of the mountain. Pass just above a small plantation, and go through
an opening in the wall, then keep the wall on the right
until a rivulet is reached, on the opposite side of which
is seen a cart-road leading to Grange village, from some
slate-quarries situated near the top of the mountain.
Cross the stream, enter the road, and follow its course
to Grange. Rosthwaite is seen below on the right; and
when passing the wild, rocky ground between Castle
Crag and Gate Crag, a charming view is had of Derwentwater, with Skiddaw in the background. During
the descent the path is rough, but there are few bits in
the district more beautiful, rock, wood, stream, lake,
and mountain, all forming a happy combination.

The tourist who may wish to descend from Great
Gable to Buttermere should take the route above described as far as the two detached blocks of stone on
Brandreth. Then let him drop into the hollow in front,
and follow the course of the streamlet; keep the marshy
ground on the right, and avoid getting entangled amongst
the rocks on the left. Cross the rivulet a few hundred
yards below a lot of slate *débris*, and enter the road leading from an old slate-quarry to Buttermere.

Green Crags and the Hay Stacks now look wild and
rocky, with the Pillar above and High Crag in front.

The road, which is uncommonly rough and stony,
descends the rocky side of Fleetwith Mountain, and on
the left the stream dashes along a rugged course in a

deep cleft of the rock. Presently, at a sharp turn in the road, Buttermere and Crummock lakes come in sight, with the hills Mellbreak, Rannerdale Knott, and Grasmoor.

Although the scenery here is singularly fine and wild, the traveller will have his attention distracted by the rough, stony nature of the path, and he will be relieved when he reaches the soft, green turf at the foot of the mountain.

The road rounds the end of Fleetwith, and enters the Honister Pass road at Gatesgarth, 2m. from Buttermere village.

Ascent of Great Gable (2949), from Keswick, by Honister Pass.

Rosthwaite, 6m.; Top of Honister Pass, 10m.; Green Gable, 12m.; Great Gable, 13m.

Although Great Gable is generally ascended from the Sty Head Tarn, it may be reached as expeditiously, and with as little exertion, by commencing at the top of Honister Pass. Ponies can be taken as far as the summit of Green Gable.

Pedestrians may have a pleasant variation in the route to Honister Pass, and save 1m. by crossing the bridge at Grange, and following a rough cart-road on the W. side of the stream. The road mounts the hill and passes between Castle Crag and Gate Crag, in the midst of wild and beautiful scenery. Looking back, a lovely vista includes Derwentwater and Skiddaw. After gaining the highest point, Great End is in front, at the head of the Seathwaite branch of Borrowdale, and on the left are Rosthwaite, Stonethwaite, Eagle Crag, and Greenup Gill. The road now winds to the right, and mounts steeply by the side of a torrent to some slate-quarries. The tourist must leave the track, descend a few yards, cross the torrent, scale a wall, and turn round a grass-covered mound to a gate in another wall, which runs up the hill. He will then keep a stone-fence on the left, and round the shoulder of the mountain to the de-

pression in front, in a direct line with the Seathwaite
Glen.   When a view is had down to Seatoller, go through
an opening in a small sheepcot, and incline to the right,
at the back of a plantation.

Avoid descending, and presently the road over Honister Pass will be entered, 1m. from the summit.

Here roads leading to slate-quarries branch right and
left, and a miner's hut is situated in a small recess.
Follow the left-hand road for 150 yards, then mount
the hill along a grassy slope by the side of a rill.   After
a short climb, incline to the left and pass under some
rocks connected with the height called Grey Knotts.
A hollow will be observed on the right in the rear of
Honister Pike and Fleetwith Mountain.   By avoiding,
on the one hand, ascending the rocks on the left, and on
the other descending into the hollow on the right, an
ill-defined track will be followed.   High Stile, High
Crag, Hay Stacks, Pillar and Kirk Fell, gradually come
in sight, and presently Buttermere and Crummock lakes
appear, with Mellbreak apparently rising sheer from the
shore of the latter.   Continuing a few yards farther,
the Ennerdale Lake and Vale are seen over the back of
the Hay Stacks, and then the three lakes, the valleys,
and surrounding mountains present a charming prospect.

On passing the rocks on the left, called Grey Knotts,
a gradual ascent must be made over grass and loose
stones to Brandreth, in the direction of two large detached blocks standing in front.

When these are reached, Great Gable rises nobly at
the head of Ennerdale Glen, presenting a fine perpendicular front.   Green Gable is on the left, and Kirk Fell
on the right of it.   Here a slight descent is made, and
the tourist has the choice of routes.   He will see a
narrow track a few yards below on the right.   It winds
round the base of Green Gable, crosses the head of
Ennerdale, and passes under the front of Great Gable,
and over the hollow between Great Gable and Kirk Fell,
and then descends into Wastdale Head.   It was formerly

used for carrying slates from Honister quarries. This track may be followed until the rivulet is met which descends between Green Gable and Great Gable. Then a climb must be made to the top of the hollow between those two mountains. It is a delightful walk, with the towering and precipitous crags of Great Gable directly overhead, and the Ennerdale Glen and mountains behind. During the last few yards a rather rough bit of ground has to be scrambled over. The ascent is, however, gradual and easy. When the top of the hollow is reached, the Sty Head Tarn is perceived below, and a short way above it Sprinkling Tarn is visible.

If the track here described be not followed, the ascent of Green Gable must be made after leaving Brandreth. A good view will be obtained, and then an easy and quick descent leads to the hollow between Green Gable and Great Gable. From this point a rough steep part of Great Gable has to be scaled. By inclining to the left, in order to avoid the precipices overhanging Ennerdale, the summit of the mountain is quickly attained; the prospect from which is given at page 198.

Ascent of Bow Fell (2960), from Keswick.—Bow Fell ought to be ascended from Langdale, but some tourists may wish to visit it from Keswick. They might have a pleasant day's excursion by climbing the mountain from Esk Hause, then descending to Angle Tarn, and following the course of the stream down the Longstrath Glen to Stonethwaite.

Between Esk Hause and Bow Fell is a mountain called Hanging Knott (2903), which can be scaled from the top of the Hause in about twenty minutes. The summit is uneven, and covered with loose stones and bare rocks.

The prospect from Hanging Knott is extensive. To the N. are Derwentwater Lake, Skiddaw, and Blencathara; and to the left of these the Grasmoor and Newlands mountains. Nearer are Great Gable, Green Gable, Great End, Steeple, Scawfell Pikes, and Scawfell. To the S. are the sea, Devoke Water, Black Combe,

Birker Moor, Harter Fell, Duddon Estuary, Walney
Scar, Coniston Old Man, Dow Crags, Seathwaite Fells,
Wetherlam, and another strip of the sea.   To the S.E.
are the Crinkle Crags, Bow Fell, Windermere Lake,
Langdale Valley, Lingmoor, and the Langdale Pikes.
At the foot of the mountain is the Longstrath Glen,
with Glaramara on the left, and High Raise and Ullscarf on the right.   Beyond these are the Helvellyn
range, High Street, St. Sunday Crag, Fairfield, Red
Screes, Ill Bell, Loughrigg, Wansfell Pike, and Yorkshire Hills.
   A descent is made to a slight depression called Ewer
Gap, and then a scramble up bare rocks leads to the
summit of Bow Fell.   The view is described at page 66.
On again descending to Ewer Gap, Angle Tarn is quickly
reached, and no error can be made of the course if the
streamlet be followed down Longstrath to Borrowdale.

Ascent of Glaramara (2560), from Keswick.

Rosthwaite, 6m.; Top of Glaramara, 9½m.; Keswick, 19m.

   Glaramara is a long rugged mountain of great bulk,
but not one of the highest.   It rises out of the Borrowdale Valley, and stands between the Seathwaite and
Longstrath glens; its southern end, called Allen Crags,
reaching to Esk Hause.   It is seldom ascended, although,
owing to its . central position, and proximity to the
highest and most rugged heights, a very fine view is to
be had from its summit.   Tourists desirous of making the
journey as light as possible might drive to Rosthwaite
and back, and take a pony to within a few yards of the
top of the mountain.   One of the best guides in the
district is to be had at Rosthwaite.   If the whole distance be walked the time required will be seven or eight
hours.
   After leaving Rosthwaite and passing the Stonethwaite road, a gate on the left will be found, near to a
small stream which flows from the Combe—the large
opening scooped out of Glaramara.   Having crossed a

field, pass through another gate, and also an opening in the wall on the left. Continue along the fell-side for some distance until a building used as a corn-mill is reached. Walk by the side of the stream, and some beautiful cascades will be found in a secluded recess of the mountain. Here the writer and a friend once saw a heron, a hawk, and a raven at one time. These birds are occasionally to be seen in the solitary parts of the district.

Climbing by the side of the stream, a small gate leads through a wall, and presently a sheepfold is reached. Here those who desire to visit Tarn-at-Leaves during the ascent will strike up the mountain on the left, and after reaching the tarn, a rather tedious climb to the right, due S., with the Longstrath Glen on the left, will enable them to gain the summit of Glaramara; but the tarn is very small, and scarcely worth the extra labour. It contains trout.

The easier plan is to cross to the S.W. side of the stream at the sheepfold, and strike boldly up the mountain. A hollow below a large crag will appear to be an impediment, but by bearing to the right until Seatoller and the Seathwaite Glen are seen, an easy and gradual ascent will be found, which allows of grand retrospective views of Derwentwater and Skiddaw. The Honister Crag is also very prominent. On arriving at a cairn standing on a height to the right, the Borrowdale Lead Mine is seen directly opposite, and Great Gable, Lingmell, Scawfell Pike, and Great End are well defined. The craggy height of Glaramara is observed to be at some distance, requiring a toilsome climb. The ascent must be made on the right side of the crag. The view from the summit is magnificent, and will convince many tourists that the most enjoyable prospect in a mountain district is not always from the highest point.

On the N. are Borrowdale and the Derwentwater Lake; and beyond the vale of Keswick, rise Skiddaw and Blencathara. On the E. is the whole of the Helvellyn range, with Seat Sandal and Fairfield; and nearer, the

low ridge running from Wallow Crag to the Langdale
Pikes; Dock Tarn and the hamlet of Watendlath being
visible.   To the S.E. is Morecambe Bay and the low
ranges of hills near to Windermere Lake.   Turning
to the W. there is a cluster of heights, including the
Newlands, Grasmoor, and Grisedale Pike ranges; and
to the left the sea and the Scotch mountains.   Then
come the hills surrounding the Buttermere and Ennerdale valleys; the Pillar and Great Gable being, as usual,
very distinct and characteristic.   On the S. are Lingmell, Great End, Scawfell Pikes, Hanging Knott, Bow
Fell, and the Coniston Old Man and Wetherlam mountains.   The nearer heights are very wild; and altogether
the scene is one of impressive grandeur.

Some tourists will walk due S. along the top of the
mountain to Esk Hause.   It is a rough and fatiguing
route, and should not be undertaken by those who
already feel tired with the ascent.   From Esk Hause the
descent to Borrowdale may be made by Angle Tarn and
the Longstrath Valley, or by Great End and the Sty
Head Pass to Seathwaite.

Keswick to Grisedale Pike (2593), Grasmoor (2791), and Causey Pike (2000).

Braithwaite, 2½m.; Grisedale Pike, 5½m.; Grasmoor, 8m.; Newlands Valley, 13m.; Keswick, 17m.   Time, 7 or 8 hours.

This is one of the most delightful of mountain excursions, but hitherto it has been very little known.   Ponies
will accomplish the whole journey, but there are a few
yards of difficult ground shortly before the summit of
Grisdale Pike is reached, and again when descending
Eel Crags in returning from Grasmoor.   These obstacles
might be removed if a man were employed for a day or
two in making a path.   The walking distance might be
shortened 2m. by taking the train to Braithwaite station,
and then walking to the village; or a carriage might be
taken to Braithwaite, 2½m.

Starting from Keswick, and crossing Greta Bridge,

the road goes through Portinscale, where it turns to
the right, and after passing Braithwaite village, with the
Coledale stream on the left, and the Coledale Valley
in front, it deviates to the right. About 150 yards
farther commence climbing the hill on the left. A
smooth grassy path runs N.W., in the direction of the
road, for a hundred yards, and then turns to the left.
Continue this course, and it will soon be found to branch
due W., with a wall on the right, and the Coledale
Valley on the left. After climbing, ½m. of level ground
has to be traversed, and then there is another steep
ascent over burnt heathery ground, and here it is advisable to incline a little to the right. When the top of
the ridge is reached a combe is observed below, with a
smooth side of Grisedale Pike rising almost perpen-
dicularly, and farther N. are Lord's Seat and the Whinlatter Fells, at the foot of which is the road leading
to Lorton Valley. From the very commencement of the
climb the views of Derwentwater, Bassenthwaite, Keswick Valley, and Skiddaw, are very picturesque. The
Coledale Valley on the left, besides being a good guide,
is also interesting. At its head the Force Crag looks
extremely diminutive, when compared with the wild
rocky front of Eel Crag towering above it. On the
opposite side of the Coledale Valley the comparatively
small mountains are Barrow and Outerside, with Causey
Pike above and between them. At the head of the Coledale Valley a portion of the smooth summit of Grasmoor
is in sight.

A very steep and rather narrow ridge has now to be
scaled, and gradually the Scawfell and surrounding
mountains come into view, one after the other, with
magical effect. From no other place are the different
heights of the Scawfell range so well defined.

Having attained the summit, a most extensive prospect is disclosed. To the N.E. and N. are Blencathara,
Skiddaw, Lord's Seat, Whinlatter and Lorton fells; a
portion of Bassenthwaite; and beyond is a small tarn,
called Overwater.

P

On the N.W. there is a large tract of level country,
with the sea and the Scotch mountains in the distance.
Within a stone's-throw are the Hobcarton Crags,
Whiteside, Grasmoor and Eel crags, all fine bold mountains. Looking to the E., the Mell Fells stand in
the plain like huge tumuli, with the Crossfell range
beyond.

Derwentwater is in sight, and near the foot of the
lake a number of mountain ranges seem to converge.
The most distant is the Helvellyn range, commencing
with White Pike and ending with Fairfield. Catchedecam peers over to the left of the top of Helvellyn.
The next range begins with Wallow Crag, and ends at
Pike O'Stickle, one of the Langdale Pikes. Then there
are the Cat Bells and Newlands mountains, and nearer,
the Causey Pike chain, with Barrow and Outerside
below, and close to the Coledale Valley. In the distance, to the S., portions of Glaramara are to the right
of Pike O'Stickle, and then Bow Fell, Hanging Knott,
Great End, Scawfell Pikes, and Scawfell; and in front
of Scawfell Pikes, Great Gable and Green Gable; and
Kirk Fell to the right of Scawfell.   .

In descending to the Coledale Pass, in order to reach
Grasmoor, keep to the S.W., with the wall to the right.
After going a few yards downwards, a small climb has
to be made, and then a farther descent, until the wall
ends. Here there is a precipice, and the best view which
is to be had of the Hobcarton Crags. Turn to the left,
and make for the stream which has its source between
Eel Crags and Grasmoor, and is seen to flow down between Grasmoor and Whiteside, in which direction
Loweswater Lake presently appears. On arriving at
the stream it will be seen to divide, some of the water
being diverted eastward through the Coledale Valley,
that it may be of use at the Force Crag mine. The water
is quite pure, and therefore it will be wise to rest awhile
and have luncheon. Here the tourist will not fail to
admire the Whiteside Crags, which for beauty of shape
and colour are perhaps unsurpassed except by the Ho-

nister Crag. Some tourists, indeed, do not hesitate to give them the first place of honour.

After luncheon, keep up stream for a short distance, then turn to the right, and commence climbing Grasmoor. If the mountain be clear of mist, it is well to incline to the right, and walk along the northern edge of the mountain, with the Whiteside Crags in sight. On that side of Grasmoor there are also some bold precipices well worth observation; on the long flat top of the mountain all is covered with moss, and as smooth and soft as a carpet.

The view from the summit will vie with that from any one of the Lake mountains. On the N. are Blencathara, Skiddaw, Grisedale Pike, Whiteside, Lord's Seat, and Lorton Fells; the Lorton Valley and Cockermouth; and beyond, the sea and the Scotch hills. Loweswater, Crummock, and Buttermere lakes are seen immediately below. On the right of Loweswater is Low Fell, and on the left Blake Fell and many smaller heights. On the W. of the two other lakes are Mellbreak, Herdhouse, Red Pike, High Stile, and High-Crag; and beyond them the mountain range on the farther side of Ennerdale Valley, including the Haycock, Steeple, and Pillar. Over Scarf Gap and Black Sail passes is seen one of the heights on Birker Moor, separating the Esk and Duddon valleys, and to the left of those passes are the Hay Stacks, Kirk Fell, Great Gable, and Green Gable. In the distance, Scawfell, Mickledore Chasm, Scawfell Pikes, Great End, Hanging Knott, Bow Fell, and Wetherlam, a portion of the Coniston Old Man range. To the E. are Helvellyn and Fairfield; and nearer, the Langdale Pikes, Glaramara, High Raise, Ullscarf, Eagle Crag, Eel Crags in Newlands, Dale Head, Hindscarth, and Robinson.

Returning along the S. side of the mountain, Rannerdale Knott is seen rising from Crummock Lake, and Whiteless Pike, between it and Eel Crag Mountain. Catchedecam, with its pointed summit, peers over the depression on the left of the highest point of Helvellyn.

A bit of hard work is now required in ascending the smooth slope of Eel Crags (2749), which name seems a misnomer when the mountain is seen from this side. The toil is forgotten when the highest point is attained, for a magnificent view rewards the traveller. There is a multitudinous assemblage of mountains, all finely grouped, and the Newlands Mountains are most pleasingly coloured. Derwentwater, Keswick, and the valley at the foot of Skiddaw appear like a perfect fairyland. On the left, the road and stream wind along the Coledale Valley, at the base of Grisedale Pike, and through the valley on the right the Sail Beck flows to Buttermere. Here also the carriage-road from Buttermere to Newlands Valley and Keswick is seen winding along the side of Buttermere Moss, an offshoot of Robinson Mountain; and nearer, the Knott Rigg and Aikin Knott ridge has a beautifully green slope. After a steep descent along a narrow ridge, a rise is made to the Sail (2500). Looking back to the left when on the Sail, Eel Crags, Whiteside, and Grisedale Pike are very grand. As soon as the summit is crossed, the Newlands Valley is in sight, and the watershed on the right is passed—Rigg Beck flowing down to the Newlands Valley. Persons who do not desire to continue on the heights over Causey Pike can descend here, to the right, and follow the stream to a small inn called the Mill Dam. When on the next mountain, Scar Crags (2205), a retrospective view on the right will reveal some fine crags, and solve what hitherto will have been a mystery, viz. why this height should be named Scar Crags, its northern part being so smooth and green. A road in the small valley to the left, originally made to a cobalt mine which is now closed, can be taken by those who are tired and anxious to reach Keswick.

Having attained the highest point of Causey Pike (2000), before descending, and leaving this glorious panorama, it is well to stay awhile and let the eye rest on the matchless beauties of Derwentwater. It is unnecessary to enumerate the mountains seen from hence,

as the tourist will now be familiar with almost every
height. The Newlands Valley, with its green fields,
hamlets, and homesteads, looks very quiet and beautiful. Many travellers will be glad to see on the right a
small inn, by the side of the stream; but those who
are in haste to reach Keswick will save a little time by
descending on the left, and taking the road which crosses
the Newlands Beck. The distance is about 4m., through
Portinscale and Keswick.

Persons who are anxious to visit Grasmoor, but consider the route above described too laborious, may take
ponies, without any difficulty, to the top, by going along
the rough cart-road which runs to the Force Crag Mines,
along the base of Grisedale Pike, up the Coledale Valley.
When at Braithwaite, the road is distinctly seen on the
hill-side, with the Coledale stream below and on the left
of it; and it continues for 2½m. to the head of the valley.
A car might be taken to this point, a distance of 5m.
from Keswick. The Force Crag, at the head of the
valley, with the bold and irregular Eel Crags towering
above it, has an imposing effect, and at first sight it
appears to present an impassable barrier. On the right
is the long wooden trough connected with the mine, and
in the middle of the crag a beautiful silvery stream leaps
from ledge to ledge, whilst on the left is another stream
by the side of which the tourist must ascend. Ponies
should be taken across the valley, so as to have the
stream on the right, but pedestrians may ascend on
either side. On arriving at the top of the crag, bear a
little to the right, so as to avoid some wet ground, and
make for the top of the pass, which is to the right of
Eel Crags. When its summit is attained, Whiteside is
seen on the right and Grasmoor on the left, and the
directions given to pedestrians who first ascended Grisedale Pike will apply to the remaining part of the ascent.

If, after visiting Grasmoor, and again arriving on the
Coledale Pass, travellers desire to ascend Grisedale Pike
with ponies, they must ride due N. for a few hundred
yards, until a wall is reached.

Here there is a precipice, and on the left the Hobcarton
Crags.   Let them then climb to the right, having the
wall on the left, and after passing over a rather difficult
height, and following the direction of the wall, another
effort will bring them to the summit of Grisedale Pike.
In descending take to the N., with the wall on the right,
for a short distance, and then branch to the left, and
make for the Whinlatter toll-bar, which will be seen
below.   The distance from the toll-gate to Keswick is
4½m., and the road passes through Braithwaite and
Portinscale.

Keswick to Cat Bells (1482), Maiden Moor (1887),
Eel Crags (2143), Dale Head (2473), Hindscarth (2385),
and Robinson (2417).—This is a most agreeable mountain excursion of about 17m., and will occupy seven or
eight hours.   A pony may be taken.   It may, however,
in many ways be much shortened if desired, but each
height will repay the journey.   A boat may be taken
across Derwentwater Lake to a bay at the foot of Cat
Bells, and by detaining it there for the return trip, 4m.
of walking will be saved.   Tourists who think the whole
distance too tiring would enjoy a walk along the tops of
Cat Bells, Maiden Moor, and Eel Crags, returning by
the Dale Head branch of the Newlands Valley, which
is walled in by massive cliffs, and is the wildest and
most secluded valley to be found near Keswick.   It
contains a beautiful stream which in one place forms a
fine mountain fall.   Should the walk not extend even so
far as this, but merely over Cat Bells, the views will be
found exceedingly good, and scarcely to be surpassed.

Those who walk the entire way must, on reaching
Portinscale, take the left-hand turn in the village, and
1½m. farther, along a path through the woods, on the
western side of the lake, will lead to the foot of Cat
Bells.

Sir John Woodford, a Waterloo officer, who lives in a
secluded part of the wood, has made a good zigzag path
to the summit of the lower height.   Immediately the
ascent is commenced, Derwentwater begins to spread

beautifully below; its islands looking remarkably well shaped when seen from this point. Bassenthwaite Lake is soon in sight, and on arriving upon the ridge, the Vale of Newlands and its surrounding mountains burst into sight, and add new charms to a view which has before appeared to be well-nigh perfect.

Continuing along the ridge, the Borrowdale Valley and its jagged mountains also claim attention. Leaving the lower height of the Cat Bells the shaft of an old lead-mine is passed, and then a steep climb leads to the top of the higher Cat Bells. Descending a little, a foot-track between Newlands and Borrowdale is crossed, and a gradual ascent is made to Maiden Moor. The top of this mountain is in some places very wet, but much of the disagreeable ground may be avoided by inclining to the right until the Newlands Valley is overlooked.

Before the highest part of the mountain is attained, a small cairn is passed, which stands in a position commanding a capital view of Derwentwater and Bassenthwaite, with the heights of Skiddaw and Blencathara on the N.; Grisedale Pike, Causey Pike and Grasmoor range on the W.; and on the E. the Helvellyn range, ending with Fairfield and Seat Sandal; and the High Seat range ending with Pike O'Stickle. Rising from the Stonethwaite branch of the Borrowdale Valley is Glaramara, and in the distance, to the S., are the heights of Wetherlam, Bow Fell, and Hanging Knott.

Continuing the walk along the top of the mountain, Great Gable is seen in front, and Dale Head, Hindscarth, and Robinson on the right; with the Dale Head branch of the Newlands Valley immediately below, most charming in aspect.

Between Maiden Moor and Eel Crags the mountain narrows, and allows, on the left, a glimpse of Grange village, the Bowder Stone, Rosthwaite, and Borrowdale.

The geologist, in walking from one height to the other, will notice the transition from the blue to the green slate, and if he afterwards climb Dale Head and Hindscarth, he will again pass from one formation to the other.

On scaling the first part of Eel Crags, a height on the left, crowned with a cairn, commands a splendid prospect. To the N. are Derwentwater and Bassenthwaite, and the surrounding heights well displayed, Grange and Borrowdale are below, and in the distance the mountains Wetherlam, Coniston Old Man, Bow Fell, Hanging Knott, Great End, Scawfell Pikes, Scawfell, Great Gable, and the Pillar. The nearer heights also look wild and rugged.

During the remainder of the ascent craggy precipices are on the right descending into the Dale Head Valley, and on arriving at the well-built cairn, the prospect is magnificent. Derwentwater is hidden, and only a glance is had of Bassenthwaite, but this is amply compensated by the complete circles of nearer and distant heights; the Newlands Mountains being especially well grouped.

The descent must be made to a small sheet of water called Dale Head Tarn; and here the tourist has the option of returning either by descending to the right, down the Dale Head Valley, or to the left down a rugged cart-road leading from some slate-quarries into Borrowdale, and past Castle Crag to Grange; or he can continue past the tarn in a straight line with Great Gable, and enter the Honister Pass. If he be not too fatigued, a more desirable course is to ascend Dale Head Mountain, and then Hindscarth and Robinson can be visited without much extra labour.

During the ascent the Honister Pass and Honister Crag are on the left, and above the High Crag, High Stile, and Red Pike range, the Pillar Mountain stands out prominently.

On arriving at the cairn on the summit, a portion of Bassenthwaite Lake is seen, but not Derwentwater. The view of the mountains is excellent. Eel Crags, rising out of the Dale Head Glen, are very rugged; and beyond the Newlands and Derwent valleys, Skiddaw and Blencathara are fully displayed. To the W. is a fine

group, including Causey Pike, Grisedale Pike and Gras-
moor. To the E. is the Helvellyn ridge, and below the
one commencing with Wallow Crag and ending with the
Langdale Pikes. The outer circle to the S. includes
Bow Fell, Hanging Knott, Great End, Scawfell Pikes,
Great Gable, Kirk Fell, Yewbarrow, Middle Fell, and
Pillar; and nearer are Glaramara, Brandreth, Fleetwith,
Honister Crag, Hay Stacks, High Crag, High Stile,
Red Pike, and a portion of Mellbreak.

During the walk from this height to Hindscarth,
glorious views are obtained on the right, of the Newlands and Derwent valleys, with every height from
Helvellyn to Grasmoor; and on the left the Honister
Pass and Crag, and the Buttermere Lake, with the
loftiest and wildest mountains in the district, the Pillar
mountain especially presenting a wild craggy front, and
being finely displayed.

In order to reach the summit of Hindscarth, a *détour*
of about ½m. must be made to the right; but as the view
is similar to that from the other heights, some tourists
will pass it, and begin to explore Robinson.

In ascending this latter mountain, it is advisable,
after climbing a short distance, to incline to the left
until a wall is reached, and a view is obtained of Buttermere, Crummock, and Loweswater lakes; and then, by
bearing to the right, the summit is attained. Buttermere Lake is now invisible; but by walking a few yards
to the N.W., Derwentwater comes into view, and allows
of the three lakes, Crummock, Loweswater, and Derwentwater, being seen from one point. The sea is
beheld on the N.W., and in the hollow between Red
Pike and High Stile a glimpse is caught of Bleaberry
Tarn. Around Crummock and Loweswater lakes are
Rannerdale Knott, Mellbreak, Herdhouse, Blake Fell,
and Low Fell; and over the Black Sail Pass stands
Black Combe. All the other heights will by this time
be familiar to the tourist.

In descending, make for the hollow between Robinson and Hindscarth, at the point where the streamlet is

observed to fall under a low rocky knob of the latter
mountain. The water forms some pretty cascades,
which, with the high, precipitous rocks overhanging,
give to the glen a wild character, and make it well
worth visiting. After passing an old reservoir, a track
on the W. side of the stream will lead to the Newlands
Valley, and past the chapel to the Mill Dam Inn. The
remaining 4m. to Keswick are described at page 151.

Ascent of Lord's Seat (1811) and Barf (1536), from Keswick.

Comb Beck, 3m.; Lord's Seat, 6m.; Barf, 7m.; Keswick, 12m.

The tourist may save 4m. of this journey by taking
the train to Braithwaite station and back; or he may
add to the interest of the route by walking from
Barf for 4m. along by the side of Bassenthwaite Lake
to the Bassenthwaite station, and there catch the
train.

If it be intended to walk from Keswick, the right-hand
turn must be taken at Portinscale, and a few hundred
yards short of Braithwaite the road again turns to the
right. On passing the third mile-post, the Thornthwaite
church is seen on the right; and in the Comb Gill on
the left are a number of houses, and one or two large old
buildings. Pass through a field on the south side of the
beck, and then cross the stream, keeping it on the left.
The walk up the Gill is delightful; wood, rock, and
stream forming a pleasing combination.

When a large plantation, standing in front, is reached,
a tedious ascent must be made up the heath-covered hill
on the right. On arriving at the top, High Seat will be
seen to the north. Although the loftiest of this range
of hills, it is low when compared with its neighbours,
Grisedale Pike and Skiddaw. The view is tolerably
good, but will not bear comparison with many others.
Some wire fencing crosses the top of the mountain, and
by descending in the direction of the fencing, taking
almost due east, Barf is quickly reached. This moun-

tain presents a fine appearance when seen from the road below, and the view from its summit is good. Perhaps from no other height does Bassenthwaite Lake look so well. The wooded acclivities on the W. side descend close to the water's edge; and the promontories of Bowness, Braidness, and Scarness are seen diversifying and beautifying its eastern shore.

The easiest descent is by a gill on the S. side of the mountain, down which flows a streamlet forming some pretty waterfalls. The road is entered near to the Swan Inn, 4m. from Keswick, and the same distance from the Bassenthwaite station.

Ascent of Skiddaw Dodd (1612).—There are many hills in the district known by the appellation of Dodd, and they are generally small, and attached to large mountains. The Skiddaw Dodd is no exception. It is an infant Skiddaw, nestling under its parent, on the south-western side, and close to the head of Bassenthwaite. It is, in places, clothed with wood; and a few years ago a *soi-disant* hermit built on its side a kind of bird's-nest, on the rocks and trees, with an umbrella, or movable cover, as the only protection from storm. Here he lived through two or three winters with very scanty clothing. Being regarded as a trespasser, he was not allowed to remain. His rookery has since been removed.

The distance from Keswick to the summit is about 4m. The most practical ascent is from Dancing Gate farm-house, 3m. from Keswick, where the Bassenthwaite and Skiddaw Terrace roads meet. The ascent is steep, but not difficult; and on the summit there is an excellent prospect, including Derwentwater and Bassenthwaite; Keswick vale, the sea, and the Scotch mountains. The Helvellyn range, and lower heights, extending from Wallow Crag to Pike O'Stickle, are on the left of Derwentwater; and at the head of that lake are Glaramara and the Borrowdale summits. Surrounding Newlands are Cat Bells, Maiden Moor, Dale Head, Hindscarth, and Robinson; and in the centre of the vale stand

Swinside. On the right rises Rowling End, the beginning of the long ridge, which includes Causey Pike, Scar Crags, Sail, and Eel Crags. The other eminences on the W. are Grisedale Pike, Lord's Seat, Barf, and the Wythop Fells. To the right of Bassenthwaite stand Longside, Skiddaw, Carlside, White Stones, and Latrigg.

In returning to Keswick the tourist may have a very delightful walk by crossing to the White Stones, and then taking along the breast of Skiddaw; or he might descend from the White Stones to Millbeck, and walk by the terrace road, past Applethwaite and Ormathwaite. The views of Derwentwater and the vale, from the terrace road, are most enchanting. Southey thought very highly of the landscape from the hamlet of Applethwaite and from other points in front of Skiddaw. He says, " The old roofs and chimneys of that hamlet come finely in the foreground, and the trees upon the Ormathwaite estate give there a richness to the middle-ground which is wanting in other parts of the vale. I know not from which of the surrounding heights it is seen to most advantage, any one will amply repay the labour of the ascent; and often as I have ascended them all, it has never been without fresh delight."

Parties who are not able to take the walk here described, and who do not visit Millbeck and Applethwaite when driving round Bassenthwaite Lake, may have a pleasant drive of 7m. from Keswick and back, round by the Terrace road at the base of Skiddaw. It is undoubtedly one of the finest short drives from Keswick.

Ascent of Castle Crag (900).—This hill stands prominently in the centre of the jaws of Borrowdale. It is said to have been crowned with a Roman fortress, but of this there are no traces. Near its summit is a large excavation, where slate has been got in former years; and on its southern side, which is the only side on which it can be scaled, there is strewn a large quantity of slate *débris*. The ascent may be commenced either from Grange or Rosthwaite. Perhaps the best plan is to ascend from Rosthwaite, and descend to Grange. Take from the former village along the lane opposite the inn. The Borrowdale Beck will be crossed either at some stepping-stones or at a bridge, and the tourist will have no difficulty in making out for himself a way of ascent. The slates will not trouble him, as they are tolerably well fixed together. When on the summit, a lovely view is had of the whole of Derwent-water, backed by Skiddaw, and in the foreground Grange village and the river winding in the valley. Gate Crags, overhanging on the left, are very grand. To the N.E. and E. are Blencathara and Helvellyn; and turning southwards there are the Borrowdale Valley and the heights of Eagle Crag, White Stones, Glaramara, and Base Brown; and farther distant, Great End, Scawfell Pikes, and Scawfell.

Rounding the slate-quarry a descent may be made to a rough cart-road which passes under Gate Crags, and by the side of the river to Grange village, from which place the tourist can return to Keswick by either side of the lake.

Ascent of Swinside (803).—Swinside is a low, detached hill, situated near the junction of the Newlands and Derwent vales, and commands an exceedingly pleasant prospect.

From Keswick to the summit and back again is 5m.; but 2m. of walking may be saved, if a boat be taken across the lake to the Nickol End Landings. Those who walk the entire distance must take the left-hand road at Portinscale, and 1m. will bring them to the foot of Swinside, which is the first hill on the right.

The ascent is best made either from a well, called Howkeld, which will be seen on the roadside, or from the hamlet of Swinside, on the S. end of the hill. From the top there is a charming prospect of the lakes Derwent and Bassenthwaite, and the Newlands and Derwent vales. The heights in view on the N.E. and E. are Skiddaw, Latrigg, Blencathara, Mell Fell, portion of Helvellyn range, and the low ridge extending from

Wallow Crag to Pike O'Stickle. Surrounding the New-
lands Vale are seen the Cat Bells, Maiden Moor, Dale
Head, Hindscarth, portion of Robinson, Rowling End,
Causey Pike, Whinlatter Fells, and Barf.

The tourist will be able to descend, and return to
Keswick, without directions.

Ascent of Barrow Mountain (1494).—Barrow is a
small mountain which rises out of the Newlands Valley.
As seen from Keswick, it is the one which stands at the
back of Swinside.

Tourists who make a long stay in Keswick can have
a pleasant four hours' walk to the top of this mountain
and back, a distance of 9m.

The best plan is to go through Portinscale to Braithwaite, and there commence the ascent. 2m. might be
saved by taking the train to Braithwaite station. The
climb is easy, and the view from the top is good, though
less commanding than from higher summits.

Derwentwater and its islands, Bassenthwaite Lake,
the Keswick Vale and town, and a portion of Newlands,
are seen below, surrounded by a fine group of mountains.
To the N. and N.E. are Skiddaw, Latrigg, Blencathara,
and Mell Fell. To the E. are the Helvellyn range, with
the summit of Catchedecam, and the range extending
from Wallow Crag to High Raise. Rising from the
Newlands Valley are Cat Bells, Maiden Moor, Dale Head,
and Hindscarth. Only a portion of Robinson is in
sight. The nearer heights are Rowling End, Causey
Pike, Scar Crags, Sail, Eel Crags, and Outerside. On
the N.W. are Grisedale Pike, Whinlatter, Barf, and
Binsey.

The descent can be made into Newlands, and the beck
crossed at Stair Bridge, 3m. from Keswick

From Keswick, up Ashness Gill, to High Seat (1996), and back by Shoulthwaite Gill.

Ashness Bridge, 2½m.; High Seat, 4½m.; Ambleside Road, 7m.; Keswick, 10m.

The road to Ashness Bridge is given at p. 154. From the bridge follow the watercourse for ½m., until a bold rock stands commandingly in front. There is a deep gorge on each side of the rock, and down the one on the right the water leaps from ledge to ledge, and makes a series of fine falls. After enjoying this wild scene, the fell on the S. must be scaled, with the gill kept on the left. When upon the broad fell-top, incline to the right, and ascend a height crowned with a well-built cairn. Bleaberry Fell is on the N., and to the E., High Seat. To reach the latter height, the wet, heathery moor must be crossed, with a slight inclination to the right. During the climb, the mountains to the S. come grandly into view, and on attaining the top of High Seat, a complete circle of towering heights is beheld, below which break on the sight portions of Derwentwater and Thirlmere Lakes, and the whole of Bassenthwaite. Descending due E., the Shoulthwaite Gill stream will be met with, which flows northwards down the ravine. If the tourist have time, and be not too weary, it is well to cross the stream, and ascend the height of Raven Crag, which overlooks the northern portion of Thirlmere, and commands a lovely view of the whole of the lake. Returning to the stream, and descending, with it on the left, those who are fond of archæological pursuits will be interested in examining a bold rocky height overhanging the ravine on its E. side, which is partially surrounded by three trenches, and is supposed by some antiquaries to have been a Roman fort. If it were ever used as a place of strength, the more feasible hypothesis is that the native inhabitants fled thither for concealment and security from the observation and onslaught of the enemy.

When a plantation is reached, a wall and the stream

must be traversed, and a foot-path will be found leading to the Ambleside road.   The distance thence to
Keswick is 3m.   See page 59.

A Walk through Skiddaw Forest.

Back of Latrigg, 2½m.; Gamekeeper's House, 5½m.; Bassenthwaite
Station, 12m.

Tourists who are pleased with wild moorland scenery,
will enjoy a walk through Skiddaw Forest (a treeless
forest).   The road to the back of Latrigg is described
at page 182.

Just before arriving at the place where the steep climb
to the hut commences, a smooth, grassy path must be
taken which branches to the right at the last gate passed
through.   It crosses the stream, which descends the
ravine at the back of the hut.   It then rounds the Lonscale Fell, the most eastern offshoot of Skiddaw, and
runs due N. into Skiddaw Forest, having the Glenderaterra stream and valley beneath, with Blencathara on
the opposite side.

On looking back, the Naddle and St. John's valleys
are in sight, and in the distance the Dunmail Raise
Pass.   The Lonscale Crags, towering overhead on the
left, look black and frowning.   On entering the forest, a
wall is seen running from W. to E.; where it ends, go
through a gate, and walk in the direction of the gamekeeper's house, which is now observed standing a short
distance higher on the left.   The path is, in some places,
wet and ill-defined.   Pass close to the wall in front of
the house, and a good road will be found leading due N.
out of the forest to Bassenthwaite village.   The round,
dark, conical hill on the right is called Calva.   After
leaving the forest, in front is Binsey, a low, outlying
hill, and to the right of it the small sheet of water called
Little Tarn.

When descending from the forest, the Dead Crags on
the left appear wild and impressive; and on the right
the Dash stream forms some fine mountain falls.   The

distance from this point to Bassenthwaite station is 5m. Keswick is 8m. distant by the road at the foot of Skiddaw on the eastern side of the lake.

Tourists who are fond of geology would be interested in tracing the course of the river Caldew, which rises near the gamekeeper's house, and flows due E. through the forest. In and near the bed of the river will be found the Skiddaw granite, a compound of grey quartz, light-coloured felspar, and black mica. It is also found in Syningill, at the back of Blencathara. Some portions have undergone considerable decomposition. On arriving at the first farm-house, a small rill will be observed issuing from a hollow in the mountain, situated on the S. side of the river. A few minutes' climb will enable the hollow to be visited. It contains Bowscale Tarn, which is not only one of the best tarns to be met with for illustrating the action of ancient glaciers, but which tradition asserts is inhabited by two immortal fish. Wordsworth, in his poem of the 'Feast of Brougham Castle,' represents these fish as waiting on the good Lord Clifford in the days of his shepherd life in the mountains :—

> " Both the undying fish that swim
> In Bowscale Tarn did wait on him ;
> The pair were servants of his eye
> In their immortality :
> They moved about in open sight,
> To and fro for his delight."

The Carrock Fells, which stand on the other side of the river Caldew, opposite Bowscale Tarn, possess interest to the mineralogist and geologist, and are, according to an old Cumberland proverb, worth all England besides. They contain veins of copper and lead, and are principally composed of syenite, which is here usually a compound of felspar, quartz, and hornblende. On the top of the eastern end are the remains of stone walls of unknown antiquity, and almost in the shape of a square.

Keswick to Patterdale, by Mountain-road to Dockray.

St. John's Vale, 4m.; Dockray, 10m.; Patterdale, 15m.

This road is not often travelled, and it is rather uninteresting. The part between Keswick and the St. John's valley is described at page 172.

After crossing the St. John's Beck and entering the main road, turn to the right, and a few yards farther another turning must be taken on the left, leading past the out-buildings of a farm. The road is good, but rather steep. It winds round the N. end of the Helvellyn range, bends to the right, and continues for about 4m. along the base of the mountain, with a swampy, unattractive moorland track on the left. The monotony of the walk is, in some measure, relieved by the good view which is obtained of the ridges and ravines of Blencathara, after the ascent is made from St. John's Vale, and also of the High Street and Ullswater mountains when they become visible on the S.

On arriving at some farm-houses, the road descends rapidly, at first by the side of a wall, and then by the Aira stream, to the village of Dockray, where there is a pleasant little inn. For the remaining 5m. to Patterdale, see page 176.

Keswick to Patterdale, by Styx, or Sticks Pass.

Legberthwaite, 5m.; Top of Pass, 7m.; Patterdale, 11m.

Although this is the shortest way from Keswick to Patterdale, it is not the most interesting. If time permit, it is advisable to extend the walk a few miles, and cross over the top of Helvellyn.

The first 5m. are along the highway between Keswick and Ambleside. At the point where the road branches for the Vale of St. John, pass through two fields to a farm-house. After climbing a few yards behind the house, cross a small bridge, and take up the winding path, having the stream and ravine on the left. When a sheepcot is reached, the path is difficult to trace, but no error can be made if the tourist keep ascending with a slight inclination to the right, and the Naddle Valley and Bassenthwaite Lake in a straight line behind. When the shoulder of the mountain is rounded, a stream is seen in a hollow to the right, and, without descending to this, the path continues along the mountain-side until the top of the pass (2450) is reached, near where the right-hand stream takes its rise. The track, during the descent, is well-defined as far as a reservoir and some buildings connected with the Greenside Lead Mines. Keep the reservoir on the right, and a rough cart-road will be found leading past the mines, and through Glenridding Valley, to the Ullswater Hotel, and thence to the Patterdale village.

Keswick to Armboth House (Thirlmere Lake), by Watendlath.

Watendlath, 5m.; Armboth House, 7½m.

The road from Keswick to Watendlath is described at page 154.

Two deeply-worn watercourses will be seen running down the hill on the eastern side of the hamlet. Climb between these, and when at the top, cross the right-hand stream above a few trees, and walk nearly due E., inclining rather to the right for a short distance. Wet ground covered with bog and heather will be seen to the S., with the Coldbarrow Fell rising above the hollow where, though out of sight, is situated Blea Tarn.

When the highest part of Helvellyn is seen directly in front, keep to the left, until some rising ground is attained, upon which will be found a heap of stones, forming a kind of semicircle, or arm-chair. From this point some low peaty ground lies on the right, and in front a few peat-stacks and a hollow, which is the beginning of a ravine down which rushes a stream to Armboth. Make for this hollow, keeping the N. side of the peat-stacks, and when the stream is reached, have it

Q 2

on the right. The wall which runs along the side of
the fell may be passed through at a gate close to the
sheepfold, a few yards on the N. side of the stream, and
then a direct descent will lead to Armboth House.

If the descent be made on the S. side of the ravine a
gate will be found in the wall about 200 yards from the
stream.

Tourists who have time ought to travel southwards by
the side of the wall for ½m., at the back of Fisher Crag,
to the head of Launchy Gill. Descending with the
Launchy Gill stream on the left, some gloriously fine
peeps are had of wild secluded falls, overhung by towering crags. The many beauties of this stream are well
worth travelling miles purposely to see. Before the
Thirlmere Lake is reached,. a stone curiously perched
will be observed on the right. Though not so large as
the famous Bowder Stone it is almost as great a curiosity,
and from the rock upon which it rests there is a splendid
prospect of Thirlmere Lake and the surrounding mountains.

Keswick to Wythburn, by Watendlath, Blea, and Harrop Tarns.

Watendlath, 5m.; Blea Tarn, 7m.; Harrop Tarn, 8m.; Wythburn, 9m.

The road to Watendlath is described at page 154.

The fells between Watendlath and Wythburn are wet
and full of bog, and the tourist must therefore expect a
toilsome and in some respects a disagreeable walk.

On arriving at the hamlet of Watendlath, take up the
fells which stand due E. at the back of the buildings.
Climb between the two deeply-worn watercourses, and
bear to the S., crossing the right-hand stream just above
a wall and a few trees. Keep near the wall for a short
distance, and then strike to the S.E., being careful not
to descend into the low ground on the right. There will
be no difficulty in finding Blea Tarn if it be borne in
mind that the water from it flows down the valley on the
right into the Watendlath Tarn, and that it is situated

high up in a hollow at the foot of Coldbarrow Fell, which is the highest near hill on the right.

During the ascent Helvellyn comes into view due E.; behind are the mountains encompassing Borrowdale, and at the head of Longstrath Valley are Hanging Knott, Bow Fell, and the Crinkle Crags. The top of Eagle Crag is seen to the right of Coldbarrow.

· Blea Tarn is reached after about three-quarters of an hour's walk from Watendlath. Leaving the tarn well on the right, some very wet, peaty ground has to be crossed, and then a short climb must be made, with a rock on the right and a small knoll on the left. Some travellers, to avoid crossing the bog, will make the circuit of the S. side of the tarn, at the base of Coldbarrow Fell.

Fairfield and Seat Sandal come into view, and also immediately afterwards Harrop Tarn, and at the foot of Helvellyn two or three farm-houses, while the inn is out of sight. Make for the tarn, and cross the stream emerging from it. Descending by a winding path, having the stream on the left, some farm-houses are reached; a cart-road crosses the valley and enters the highway between Keswick and Ambleside, a few hundred yards from the Nag's Head Inn.

· If the tourist be going to Grasmere, and does not wish to visit the inn at Wythburn, he can, on descending from Harrop Tarn, keep on the side of the fell, behind a stone wall, until a farm-house is reached. Here he will enter a cart-road which passes two other houses, and joins the main road a few hundred yards below the summit of Dunmail Raise Pass.

Keswick to Grasmere, by Borrowdale, Greenup Gill, and Far Easedale Valley. Distance 14m.

The road to Borrowdale is given at page 143. After leaving Rosthwaite take the first turn on the left, and on arriving at the hamlet of Stonethwaite the second road on the left will lead over the beck. Keep the stream on the right hand all the way up the Greenup Gill. When

the Longstrath Valley and Eagle Crags are passed,
several heaps of terminal moraine matter are met with,
and then a fine prominent rock, called Lining Crag, will
be seen on the left, near the top of the pass. A little to
the right of the head of the valley there are some inferior
crags called Long Crags. Climb on the left of Lining
Crag, and when the top is reached a capital view is had
of Bassenthwaite Lake, and the mountains from Skiddaw to Bow Fell. Crossing the summit of the pass the
White Stones and High Raise heights are on the right;
and on the left there are a few rocks and strewn stones.
Pass to the right of these low rocks, and presently Helvellyn, Seat Sandal, and Fairfield appear, with the nearer
and lower heights of Steel Fell and Helm Crag. To the
right of Helm Crag a strip of Grasmere Valley is seen,
and beyond, stands Wansfell Pike.

In descending, incline to the right and walk round
the base of White Stones and High Raise. Tourists
sometimes err by inclining to the left down the valley,
through which flows the Wythburn Beck to Wythburn
and Thirlmere Lake, at the foot of Helvellyn. This
mistake is easily made, as all the drainage from this
valley is to Wythburn; but on climbing a low ridge,
after walking with an inclination to the right, the Far
Easedale Valley is seen below, and on the right are the
craggy heights of Sergeant Man, and on the left the
low ridge ending with Helm Crag.

Immediately the descent is commenced, a few rocks on
the right are passed, on one of which there is a small
tree; and here it is desirable to turn a little to the right,
and walk down the valley with the stream on the left.
Sometimes the tourist will see fit to walk at a distance
from the stream, and then again along its banks, in
order to avoid wet ground. On arriving at the bottom
of the valley the path winds by some smooth rocks,
and when the first building is passed, Sour Milk Gill
Fall is observed on the right. The water forming it
flows from Easedale Tarn. A cart-road is here entered
which leads to Grasmere.

Keswick to Langdale (Dungeon Gill), by the Stake Pass.

Rosthwaite, 6m.; Top of the Stake Pass, 11m. Dungeon Gill, 14m.

The road from Keswick to Rosthwaite is given at page 143.

After leaving Rosthwaite, take the first turn on the left, and along a rough cart-road which leads past the hamlet of Stonethwaite, round the end of Glaramara, and enters the Longstrath Valley. The stony road may be avoided for a short distance, when the hamlet is passed by pursuing a path leading through the fields. Eagle Crag stands prominently forward guarding the valley on its E. side, and at the back of it is the Greenup Valley, along which is the nearest way to Grasmere.

Longstrath is a wild and desolate glen, without a single habitation, and almost bare of trees. To the geologist its terminal moraine matter will be interesting. At its head stands Bow Fell, with its peaked summit, and bared craggy front, and Glaramara guards the whole of the western side. On the E. are the Eagle and Bull crags, and the high ridge terminating in the Langdale Pikes.

When at the foot of Eagle Crags the tourist must cross the Longstrath Beck by a narrow wooden bridge. A rough foot-track will be found which takes up the valley, at the base of Eagle and Bull crags, and under a large perched stone. When the projection is rounded upon which the stone rests, another similar projection will be seen a little farther up the glen. After passing this, the tourist will notice, on the left hand of the low height at the head of the valley, water running down a seam in the mountain, and he will be surprised to learn that the path over the Stake Pass is one seen zigzagging on the right hand of the streamlet. The glen continuing on the right, at the base of Glaramara, leads to Angle Tarn, which lies at the foot of Bow Fell and Hanging Knott. On arriving at the streamlet, near where it enters the Longstrath Beck, a little wooden bridge will be found near to a post, and a few diminutive trees. Cross the bridge and climb the hill, having the streamlet a few yards on the left hand. The water, during its descent, forms a series of small cascades.

On arriving at the top of the pass (1576), some wet, uninteresting ground, has to be got over. The Pike O'Stickle on the left, one of the Langdale Pikes, will be recognized. Its bare rounded summit looks like a large haycock, and will disappoint the tourist who is acquainted with its more pleasing aspect from the Windermere district. During the descent to the Langdale Valley, Bow Fell is most imposing, and the Crinkle Crags and Pike O'Blisco are on the left of it. On each side of Pike O'Blisco portions of the Coniston Old Man range are in sight. Looking down the valley, Lingmoor is in front, with the road leading to Little Langdale Glen and Blea Tarn distinctly traced, and on the left the Pike O'Stickle becomes more characteristic, and shows to greater advantage at every step. The path descends by the side of a streamlet, and when the valley is entered one cannot err in travelling to the Old Dungeon Gill Hotel, at the base of Pike O'Stickle, or 1m. farther, to the New Dungeon Gill Hotel, at Millbeck, situated by the side of the stream which issues from Stickle Tarn, and near to the Dungeon Gill Fall.

Keswick to Scale Hill Hotel (near the foot of Crummock Lake), by the Coledale Pass.

Braithwaite, 2m.; Top of Coledale Pass, 5½m.; Scale Hill Hotel, 8m.

This excursion can be made on pony or on foot, and embraces some magnificent crag and mountain scenery. It is the route which is recommended to pedestrians who, having previously taken the Buttermere trip, are desirous of walking from Keswick to Wastwater, by Ennerdale.

The road from Keswick to the top of the pass is described at page 213.

Those who have not climbed Grasmoor, are recommended to do so before descending the pass. Many parts of the N. and W. sides of the mountain are extremely precipitous, and therefore it is advisable to return to the pass, or to within a short distance of it.

The stream descending between Grasmoor and Whiteside is the only guide required. The best course is to keep along the base of Grasmoor for some distance, and then to descend to the stream, and walk along a narrow track at its northern side, and round the base of Whiteside.

There is another, but narrower, track on the Grasmoor side of the stream.

During the descent the Whiteside Crags are seen to great advantage, and the towering mass of Grasmoor, with its rugged side, is wild and imposing. Loweswater Lake appears below, and on emerging from the ravine, the sea, and portions of Crummock Lake, are in sight. The Lorton Valley is on the right, and Scale Hill Hotel —invisible from this point—is on the opposite side of the low wooded height in front.

The road from Buttermere through Lorton Valley to Cockermouth and Keswick is seen below. Make for this, at the point where it passes the second farm-house from Crummock Lake. Close to the house there is a direction-board to the Scale Hill Hotel. The road thither leaves the main road at right angles, and after crossing one or two fields enters the wood, through which it continues for about ½m. to the hotel.

Keswick to Scale Hill Hotel (near the foot of Crummock Lake), by the Coledale Pass, and along the summit of Whiteside.—The road from Keswick to the summit of the pass is described at page 213.

When at the top of the pass, Grasmoor is seen on the left, and Whiteside on the right, of a deep ravine, with Loweswater Lake at the bottom. It is intended to walk along the ridgy top of Whiteside, and in order to do so, an ascent must be made to the right; not, however, inclining too much in that direction, which leads to

Grisedale Pike. After climbing a short distance, an inclination must be made to the left. At one point a glorious peep is had on the right, down the Hobcarton Crags. Crummock Lake soon comes in sight on the left, with a portion of Mellbreak, and then to the N.W. appear the Lorton Valley, Cockermouth, the sea, the Scotch mountains, and a wide extent of level country. The long offshoot of Swinside branches due N. from the E. end of Whiteside. Skiddaw, Grisedale Pike, and the valleys and heights around Whinlatter, are most beautiful. When the ridge is commenced, the Whiteside Crags, Grasmoor, and Eel Crags, look uncommonly wild and grand, and the silvery rivulet is seen flowing down the deep, dark ravine, at the foot of Whiteside. The ridge is in some places narrow, but not dangerous. The writer has travelled along it during winter, without difficulty, when it has been covered with snow and ice, and in the face of a high wind. A ramble along the top of this mountain will always be an especial favourite with mountaineers. Besides the great contrasts in the views—all being on one side dark and wild, and on the other bright and beautiful—there is the feeling of adventure and danger, with sufficient of security to take away fear; and this, combined with the great height and healthy breeze, imparts to the tourist a joyous and exhilarating feeling.

Before descending, the Loweswater Lake comes in sight, and the Ennerdale Mountains and Red Pike.

Scale Hill Hotel is visible in the valley at the foot of a small hill, a short distance from Crummock Lake, and the tourist will be able to mark out the best and most direct way to it. In descending the mountain it is advisable to incline to the left, and to cross the stream which flows down the ravine.

Keswick to Dacre Castle, Pooley Bridge, Patterdale, and back over Helvellyn.

Penruddock Railway Station, 10m.; Dacre Castle, 13m.; Pooley Bridge, 15m.; Patterdale, 25m.; Helvellyn, 29m.; Keswick, 37m.

Pedestrians will find this a pleasant day's excursion. Take the early train (7.45 A.M.) from Keswick to Penruddock. When through the village, a guide-post at the third road branching to the right directs to Dacre. It is, however, more agreeable to go down the second road, where another guide-post points to Hutton John. The tourist soon reaches Hutton John, the fine old mansion of the Huddlestones, and a foot-path will be found which passes in front of the building, and through a pleasant park to Dacre village and castle.

Bede mentions a monastery which stood here, but no vestiges remain.

King Athelstan is stated by Malmesbury to have held a congress at Dacre in the year 930, and to have received the homage of the kings of Scotland and Cumberland, after having achieved a victory over their combined forces. The congress would probably be held in the monastery, although there is a room in the castle called to this day " The Room of the Three Kings." The only occupants of the castle are some poor people who show visitors the towers and dungeons, and attend to an adjoining farm. The moat is almost extinct, the outworks having disappeared, and only four square embattled towers, with connecting walls, remain of what was once a magnificent fortress of the fierce Barons of Dacre.

1½m. farther, Ullswater Lake is reached, on the W. side of Dunmallet, at the point where the landing-pier for the steamer is situate.

Pooley Bridge is near the foot of the lake, ¾m. distant. The steamer generally leaves for Patterdale at 11.20 A.M. The distance by the road on the N. side of the lake is 10m.; but if a boat be taken across to How Town, the

distance thence to Patterdale, by a pleasant foot-path on
the S. shore, is 6m.; or up the Boredale Glen, 5m.

The description of the route from Patterdale to Wythburn or Thirlspot, over Helvellyn or the Sticks Pass,
will be found in other parts of the book.

If the tourist be tired after descending Helvellyn, he
might catch the coach from Ambleside, at Wythburn or
Thirlspot, and arrive in Keswick a little after 8 P.M.

Keswick to Penrith, by Railway.—Penrith is a
pleasant market-town, containing 8317 inhabitants, and
has several good hotels, the principal of which are the
Crown and the George.

It stands on the outskirts of the Lake District, and on
the main line of railway from London to Carlisle and
Scotland. Its immediate neighbourhood abounds in the
seats of the nobility and gentry, and is rich in antiquarian remains. As most visitors to the Lakes enter at
Windermere and leave the district at Penrith, the latter
town is either entirely neglected in the haste to get
home, or it is only *cursorily* glanced at. When Pater-
familias is homeward-bound by train from Keswick, he
is anxious to avoid all intermediate stoppages; and therefore it is advisable to make a separate excursion from
Keswick to Penrith and back.

When at Penrith, the day might be pleasantly occupied by taking one or more of the excursions hereafter
described.

The distance from Keswick to Penrith is 18m. The
first 3m., a most charming sylvan glen, called the Greta,
at the foot of Latrigg, is passed through, in which the
river Greta is crossed eight times. On emerging from
the glen, the Glenderamakin River is crossed, and Threlkeld station reached. On the right is the lower part of
the Vale of St. John, with the Naddle Fells on the W.,
and the beginning of the Helvellyn range on the E. side.
Threlkeld village rests at the foot of the beautiful ridgy
front of Blencathara.

There is a rather steep gradient over a wild desolate
moorland tract to the next station, which is called Trout-

beck, owing to its being situated near to a streamlet and half a dozen houses bearing that name. Visitors often mistake this for the Troutbeck between Kirkstone and Windermere.

Ullswater Lake is 5½m. distant, and Patterdale 9m. Coaches generally meet the trains here.

The round, conical hill on the right is Mell Fell, behind which comes in sight a part of High Street.

On leaving the next station, Penruddock, the line makes a curve, and the mountains appear to change their relative positions.

Greystoke village and castle are seen about 2m. distant on the left.

Greystoke Castle stands in a park of 5000 acres. It is the seat of Henry Howard, Esq., and was formerly the property of the Dukes of Norfolk, who still retain the title of Baron of Greystoke. A few years ago the picture-gallery, armoury, and many valuable parts of the building, were destroyed by fire. It is a modern structure, and stands on the site of a more ancient castle, a very small part of which still remains.

Another station, Blencowe, is passed, and nothing worthy of note meets the eye until Penrith is reached. The geologist will have noticed the transition from the Skiddaw slate to the limestone, and now again to the new red sandstone, upon which, and with which, Penrith is built.

Close to the railway station stand the ruins of *Penrith Castle*. They are not extensive, but have a noble appearance when seen from the E. side of the town. Richard III., when Duke of Gloucester, is said to have resided in the castle, and to have acquired great popularity in the district by his magnificent style of living. It is said to have been built in the reign of Edward IV. It continued after Richard's time in the possession of the Crown, until it was besieged and dismantled by the adherents of the Commonwealth.

The parish church is a large, plain structure, built of red sandstone. In the churchyard is the *Giant's Grave,*

a monument of antiquity which has long excited the
curiosity of antiquaries. It is supposed to be the burial-
place of Owen Cæsarius, a man of great courage and
colossal stature, who ruled Cumberland with regal sway
in the Saxon times. Another venerable monument,
called the *Giant's Thumb*, stands in the churchyard.' It
is an upright stone, 6 feet high, with a rude representa-
tion of a cross. Sir Walter Scott never passed through
Penrith without visiting these mysterious remains ; and
on his last mournful journey to the S. in quest of health,
he could not be induced to leave them unnoticed, although he had seen them many times before.

On a small hill to the N. of the town is a square building, called the *Beacon*, which was formerly a good station
for obtaining an extensive view of the surrounding
country. The view is now, however, entirely obstructed
by trees. The hill upon which the beacon-tower stands
was one of those whereon fires were lighted, in former
times, to give warning of the approach of an enemy.

Drive from Penrith to Pooley Bridge, by Brougham Castle, Brougham Hall, Arthur's Round Table, and Maybrough.

Brougham Castle, 1½m.; Brougham Hall, 2¼m.; Arthur's Round
    Table, 2½m.; Maybrough, 2¾m.; Pooley Bridge, 6m.

Parties who take this drive might sail up Ullswater
Lake to Patterdale, and there catch the coach for Troutbeck station, and thence by train to Keswick. Those
who do not desire to extend the drive to Pooley Bridge,
can return from Maybrough to Penrith, and thus have
only a 4m. drive.

Brougham Castle stands on the site of a Roman station,
near the junction of the rivers Eamont and Lowther. It
was one of the strongest of the Border fortresses. The
ruins now present a venerable and majestic appearance,
and give evidence of the former strength and magnificence of the structure. The outer walls are in a good
state of preservation, but the whole of the interior is in

ruins. The first historical notice of the castle is in the reign of William the Conqueror. It passed successively into the hands of the Veteriponts, Cliffords, and Tuftons, and is at present the property of Sir Henry Tufton. James I. was entertained within its walls for three days on his last return from Scotland in 1617. The stranger can saunter in and around the ruins without asking permission of anyone, and no guide is required.

Brougham Hall, the seat of Lord Brougham, stands in a charming situation, about ⅜m. from Brougham Castle. It is a lofty castellated edifice, commanding extensive prospects, and was originally fortified. The property belonged at an early period to his lordship's ancestors, and it then passed to a family of the name of Bird, from whom it was repurchased in 1727 by the grandfather of the late ex-Chancellor, Lord Brougham.

Arthur's Round Table is ¼m. from Brougham Hall, in a field adjoining the main road at Eamont Bridge, and at the point where the Pooley Bridge road is entered. It is a small circular plot of ground, and entered by two opposite approaches. Many have been the conjectures as to the purpose for which it was used. It certainly was not designed for a place of strength, and it is evidently too small to have been used for tournaments. It might, however, be the arena upon which athletic contests were exhibited.

Another ancient monument, enshrouded in even greater mystery, is *Maybrough*, situated ¼m. from the Round Table, in a field on the opposite side of the Pooley Bridge road. It is a circular area of meadow ground, 100 yards in diameter, surrounded by a mound of pebble stones, 12 feet high, with an entrance on the E. side, 12 yards in width. The space thus enclosed is now encircled with trees. In the middle of the area stands a large block of unhewn stone, 11 feet high and 22 feet in girth. In old histories of Cumberland and Westmorland, it is stated that formerly there were other similar stones, three forming, with the present one, a square, and four at the entrance, one on each

exterior, and one on each interior corner. It is supposed
to have been either a court of justice or a Druidical
temple.

Yanwath Hall, an old castellated mansion, now used
as a farm-house, is seen a few hundred yards distant.

The tourist may now follow in the footsteps of one of
Sir Walter Scott's characters in the 'Bridal of Triermain.'

> " He pass'd red Penrith's Table Round,
> For feats of chivalry renown'd ;
> Left Maybrough's mound, and stones of power,
> By Druids raised in magic hour,
> And traced the Eamont's winding way,
> Till Ulfo's lake beneath him lay."

Before reaching Ulfo's Lake (Ullswater), the Friends'
Meeting-house at Tirril will be passed, and many lovers
of mountaineering will glance with interest into its little
burial-ground, on learning that here were interred the
remains of Charles Gough, who lost his life in attempting the ascent of Helvellyn, see page 93.

Drive from Penrith to Lowther Castle, Hawes-water, and Mardale Green.

Askham, 5m.; Lowther Castle, 6m.; Bampton, 10m.; Mardale
Green, 16m.

If Brougham Castle and Brougham Hall have not
been visited they might be included in this drive by in-
creasing the distance only 1½m.

Arthur's Round Table and Maybrough must necessarily be passed, whichever route be taken.

At Mardale Green, a secluded district at the head of
Haweswater, is some very fine wild scenery. Haweswater is perhaps less visited than any other of the lakes,
owing to its lying away from the main road of tourists,
and to the deficiency of hotel accommodation at Mardale
Green, there being only one small inn, called the Dun
Bull.

Pedestrians generally reach this lake by crossing the

mountains from Ullswater or Windermere. Carriages can only approach from Ullswater, Penrith, and Shap.

When 1m. out of Penrith the river Eamont is crossed, and the traveller passes from Cumberland into Westmorland. After passing Arthur's Round Table and Maybrough, there is nothing worth special notice until the pretty village of Askham is entered.

There is a pleasant walk to this village along the bank of the river Lowther from the bridge near the Round Table.

Lowther Castle, the seat of the Earl of Lonsdale, is ¾m. from the village, and the stranger can either walk this distance or take the carriage. It is a splendid palace, situated in a noble park, and all the year round it is open to strangers six days a week. The interior is fitted up in a style of great splendour, and will well repay a visit, more especially to all lovers of painting and sculpture; the picture-gallery being rich in some of the *chef-d'œuvres* of the Old Masters.

The next 6m. from Askham is rather uninteresting. When, however, about 1½m. past Bampton, a village which possesses a large inn, the lower part of the *Haweswater Lake* appears, with the wooded fell of Wallow Crag on the opposite side. The lake is 3m. long, ½m. broad, and height above the sea 694 feet. It is the property of the Earl of Lonsdale, and contains trout, char, and perch. If a boat, or a day's fishing, be desired, application must be made to the steward at Lowther Castle.

The Measand promontory, a broad tract of flat meadow-land, which approaches to within 250 yards of the opposite shore, appears to cut the lake in two. The lower half is not particularly striking. When, however, the Measand Beck and hamlet are reached, the road skirts the shore, and at the head of the lake is seen a cluster of lofty mountains, including Harter Fell, High Street, and Kidsty Pike. The beautiful view from this point will win the admiration of the tourist. On arriving at the head of the lake there are some fine crags on the

right.   The interesting little church is seen half screened
by yew trees, and a view is had up Riggindale, with
High Street and Kidsty Pike at its head, the latter on
the north side.

The one small inn, the Dun Bull, rests at the foot of
Branstree, near the top of the glen, which is closed in by
Harter Fell.   The Nan Bield Pass and the Small Water
and Blea Water tarns are in the hollows to the right of
the latter mountain.

Few travellers will visit this out-of-the-way district
without being pleased with its wild beauty and seclusion.

Penrith to Shap, Shap Abbey, Bampton Grange, and (Haweswater) Mardale Green.

Shap, 10m.; Shap Abbey, 12m.; Bampton, 15m.; Mardale Green,
21m.

Mardale Green (Haweswater) is occasionally visited
by taking the train to Shap railway station, and then
driving 11m. by Shap Abbey and Bampton Grange.

Shap is a straggling village, containing many hotels,
the principal of which are the Greyhound (close to the
station) and the King's Arms.

There is also a large, well-furnished hotel 4m. to the
S.E. of the village, at what is called Shap Wells, where
exist medicinal springs, saline and sulphurous, the latter
waters resembling those of Harrogate, but milder.

Shap Abbey may be visited in the drive to Haweswater, by making a *détour* of ½m. from the regular road.
It is situated on a head-stream of the river Lowther; the
only part left standing is a ruined tower.   It was founded
in the twelfth century, and is believed to have been extensive and magnificent.

Before arriving at Bampton Grange, a part of Haweswater comes in sight, and the High Street range of
mountains.   For a description of the road from Bampton to Mardale Green, see page 241.

Drive from Penrith to Eden Hall, and Long Meg and Her Daughters.

Eden Hall, 4m.; Druids' Circle, 7m.

Eden Hall is the seat of Sir George Musgrave, Bart. It is a noble edifice, recently rebuilt, and is seated in the centre of well-timbered grounds, which slope down to the river Eden.

The Musgraves came to England with the Conqueror, and were afterwards a famous border clan.

This mansion is celebrated for containing a curious old drinking-glass, called the *Luck of Eden Hall*, which is preserved with almost superstitious care, and is only brought out on rare occasions. It is thought to be an ancient and rare specimen of Oriental workmanship. It is not known how or when the family became possessed of the goblet. The tradition of this mystic glass is narrated in an old ballad to be found in the Percy Collection. It has also formed the subject of a German ballad which has been translated by Longfellow. The legend connected with it is that the butler having gone one day to a fountain called the Fairy Well, which is situated in the park in front of the Hall, surprised a party of fairies dancing. In their flight they left this glass behind, which the butler seized. One of them returning, found it in his hand, and on his refusing to restore it, she flew away, saying,

> " If e'er that glass should break or fall,
> Farewell the luck of Eden Hall."

The church is a beautiful edifice, with a low embattled tower, and stained windows.

It contains several marble monuments of the Musgrave family.

Long Meg and Her Daughters is one of the finest Druidical remains in England. It stands on an eminence on the E. bank of the river Eden, and consists of sixty-seven large blocks of unhewn stone, forming a circle 350 yards in diameter. *Long Meg* is a large upright stone fixed about 17 yards without the circle. Wordsworth writes—

> " A weight of awe not easy to be borne
> Fell suddenly upon my spirit, cast
> From the dread bosom of the unknown past,
> When first I saw that sisterhood forlorn ;
> And her, whose strength and stature seemed to scorn
> The power of years, pre-eminent, and placed
> Apart, to overlook the circle vast.
> Speak, Giant-mother ! tell it to the morn,
> While she dispels the cumbrous shades of night ;
> Let the moon hear, emerging from a cloud,
> When, how, and wherefore, rose on British ground
> That wondrous monument, whose mystic round
> Forth shadows, some have deemed, to mortal sight
> The inviolable God that tames the proud."

Penrith to Carlisle, by Railway, 18m.—Carlisle, a fine old border city, stands at the junction of the Eden and Caldew rivers, 8m. from the Scottish border, on the main western line from London to Scotland. The principal hotels are the County, close to the station, the Coffee House, the Bush, Crown, White Hart, Mitre, and Victoria.

It contains 31,049 inhabitants, sends two members to Parliament, and is the capital of Cumberland. It dates back to the time of the Romans, and was in close proximity to the wall of Hadrian.

In the wars between England and Scotland it took position as a place of great consideration.

A defensive wall was early built round the city, the circumvallation enclosing a triangular area. The walls were encircled by a moat, and had three gates severally toward the N., the W., and the S.E., called the Scotch, the Irish, and the English gates. A small part of the W. wall, above the river Caldew, is now the only remaining portion.

The *Castle*, a stronghold of the first importance in the Scottish and Civil wars, is said to have been built by William Rufus, on the site of a more ancient fortress.

Mary Queen of Scots was imprisoned here for two months in 1568, but the tower she occupied has recently been pulled down.

The *Cathedral* stands in the centre of the city. It was partially sacked in the time of the Civil Wars, and many additions have been made to it during the present century. It does not take a foremost rank among English cathedrals, but its E. window is said to be the largest and finest in the kingdom, superior even to the famous W. window of York Minster.

The stranger, on visiting Carlisle, will be disappointed on finding that the old border city has retained so few evidences of its past character and history. Its walls and gates have disappeared, and its streets are now wide and clean, with an entirely modern aspect.

If it be intended to return to Keswick, new ground may be travelled by taking the Maryport and Carlisle Railway through the N.W. part of the county, *viâ* Cockermouth.

Keswick to Windermere, by Coach.

Wythburn, 8½m.—fare, 2s.; Grasmere, 12½m.—fare, 3s.; Ambleside, 16½m.—fare, 4s.; Windermere Railway Station, 21½m.—fare, 5s. 6d.

These fares do not include the coachman's fee, and extra charge is made for seats inside the coach.

Coaches leave Keswick for Windermere railway station every day during the year, at 9.10 A.M. and 4.45 P.M., and during the summer months extra coaches are run, one generally starting about mid-day. This drive is considered one of the best in Britain. The coach-office is opposite the Town Hall, and the coaches call at the Keswick Hotel and the railway station.

To avoid a steep ascent a short distance from Keswick, a *détour* is often made by taking the Penrith road for ½m. by the side of the river Greta, and then, *viâ* Castle Rigg, joining the Ambleside road at the toll-gate, 1m. out of the town. Another climb brings to the top of

Castle Rigg; and here a prospect of unrivalled beauty presents itself.

All Derwentwater, and a portion of Bassenthwaite, are spread below, with Keswick apparently at the very feet of the spectator; and between the two lakes lies the Keswick Vale, like a garden of the Hesperides, with villages and hamlets, two churches, and gentlemen's seats, farmsteads, and cottages, placed in most picturesque positions in the midst of woods and cultivated fields.

The rivers Derwent and Greta, and tributary streams, are seen meandering in their course to the lake; and mountains entirely encircle this most happy and truly perfect scene.

Skiddaw, Latrigg, and Blencathara stand to the N. On the opposite side of Bassenthwaite Lake are Wythop Fells, Barf, and Lord's Seat. Between Grisedale Pike and the Causey Pike range are the lower heights of Swinside and Barrow. Rising from the Newlands valley are Cat Bells, Maiden Moor, Hindscarth, and Robinson; and to the right of Robinson the heights High Stile and Red Pike, which stand on the farther side of Buttermere. At the head of Derwentwater are the Borrowdale Mountains, with Castle Crag conspicuous; and in the distance, Great Gable, Great End, and Scawfell Pike. Falcon Crag and Wallow Crag, with Castle Rigg, complete the circle.

The poet Gray, who visited this district in 1769, in writing a description of his journey from Keswick to Ambleside, says, the view from this position was so enchanting, that he " had almost a mind to have gone back again;" and few tourists will leave without entertaining a similar feeling of regret.

A steep descent leads into the Naddle Vale, and the road is rather uninteresting for 2m. or 3m., thus allowing the traveller to contemplate for a few minutes on the beauties of Derwentwater before the mind is attracted by new and pleasing prospects, which are unfolded at every turn, after arriving at the head of the St. John's Valley. During the journey through the Naddle Vale,

Blencathara is fully displayed; the long, bulky mass of the Helvellyn range is in view to within a few feet of the summit; and Raven Crag gradually comes in sight, on the opposite side of a large, low-lying tract, consisting of peat bog and morass.

The round, wooded hill in front, at the foot of Helvellyn, is Great Howe.

At a sharp turn in the road, the river which flows from Thirlmere Lake down the Vale of St. John, is crossed, and then on the left stands Castle Rock, the enchanted castle of Sir Walter Scott's 'Bridal of Triermain.' At the point where the road branches to the left for the Vale of St. John, a glorious peep is had down the valley, and Blencathara is seen, standing like an immense mountain barrier, right across at the other end.

On the left a track, called the Sticks Pass, winds by the side of a stream, and takes over the fells to Patterdale. The next stream, leaping down the mountain, is seen forming a number of good cascades. After passing the King's Head Inn at Thirlspot, the road slightly ascends, and then Thirlmere Lake is immediately below, with a picturesque bridge dividing it into two parts at a point where it narrows considerably.

Armboth House stands close to the bridge, and a little to the left of it are Fisher Crag and Launchy Gill. Raven Crag is again seen at the N. end of the lake. After rounding a knoll, the road continues along at the foot of Helvellyn, and on the margin of the lake.

The opposite shore is charmingly diversified with bays and promontories, over which stand the wild, craggy precipices of the Armboth and Wythburn fells. Right in front are Steel Fell and the Dunmail Raise Pass, between which and the head of the lake are a few fields and farmsteads. A lead mine is observed on the side of Helvellyn, but the road is too close to that mountain to allow of more than half of its height being seen. Tourists who only make an acquaintance with the mountain during this drive will be disappointed, and be apt to

consider Scott's expression, "The mighty Helvellyn," too
far-fetched; but when it is ascended, and the long ridge
of wild, perpendicular crags and deep recesses is observed
on its eastern side, the feeling of disappointment is
turned to that of wonder.

Nearly in front of the lead mine, on the opposite side
of the valley, stand five houses bearing the distinguished
name of "The City."

The stream flowing down the hill, behind "The City,"
has its source in Harrop Tarn, which lies in the hollow
above, and is in the route often taken to Keswick by
pedestrians. A few yards farther, the Nag's Head Inn
at Wythburn is passed. From Wythburn the shortest
and steepest climb is made to the summit of Helvellyn.

Opposite the inn stands

> " Wythburn's modest house of prayer,
>   As lowly as the lowliest dwelling."

An ascent is now made to the top of Dunmail Raise
Pass, 783 feet above the sea.

A stone fence is seen to descend Steel Fell on the
right, cross the summit of the pass, and ascend Seat
Sandal by the side of a torrent. This marks the division between the counties of Cumberland and Westmorland.

Close to the road, by the side of this fence, lies a heap
of stones, which is said to indicate the spot where Dunmail, the last king of Cumberland, was defeated by
Edmund, king of England, A.D. 945.

On descending the pass, the little peaceful lake and
vale of Grasmere look charming below, backed by
Loughrigg Fell, and encircled by hills, the most distinguished of which, though not the highest, is Helm Crag.
One rock on the summit of this hill draws the attention
of the traveller by its presenting the appearance of a
mortar throwing shells.

To the N. of Helm Crag is the Greenburn Valley, and
to the S. Easedale Valley and the height of Silver Howe.
Beyond Seat Sandal the whole of the eastern side of the

Grasmere Vale is bounded by the mountain mass of Fairfield and Nab Scar.

When the Swan Inn is reached, the road continues 1m. farther direct to the Prince of Wales Hotel. Another road branches to the right, and makes a slight *détour* to the village, passing the Red Lion Hotel and the church, and then joins the main road at the Prince of Wales Hotel, which is situated on the margin of the lake.

The shore of Grasmere Lake is skirted for a short distance, with the single green island full in view; and on rounding a rocky, wooded knoll, Rydal Lake comes in sight, resting at the feet of Nab Scar and Loughrigg.

The pretty ivy-covered cottage standing close to the water was formerly the residence of Hartley Coleridge. After traversing the margin of the lake, the charming village of Rydal is passed, and a glimpse is caught of Rydal Mount, where Wordsworth lived for many years.

Rydal Hall, the large mansion seen standing in the midst of Rydal Park, is the seat of General Le Fleming. The beautiful vale of Rothay is now passed through, and a peep had of Fox How, the residence of the late Dr. Arnold. The Knoll, where Miss Martineau resides, stands almost out of sight, behind a Methodist chapel, on the right of the road just before entering Ambleside. On leaving Ambleside, Wetherlam and Oxenfell are seen on the right, and the Windermere Lake is reached at Waterhead.

The road now continues along the shore for some distance, with the lake full in view as far as Belle Isle and Bowness.

Wray Castle is a prominent and pleasing object on the opposite bank. Coniston Old Man, Lingmoor, Crinkle Crags, Bow Fell, and the Langdale Pikes now appear to the W. Soon after leaving the Low Wood Hotel the road gradually bends from the lake, and after passing Troutbeck bridge, and a number of large mansions charmingly situated in the midst of a well-timbered country, the Windermere station is entered.

BUTTERMERE SECTION.

—◆◇◆—

BUTTERMERE.

THE hamlet of Buttermere is delightfully situated on the strip of land separating the two lakes, Buttermere and Crummock. It consists of about half a dozen houses, a small church, and two hotels, the Fish and the Victoria. Both hotels have lately been enlarged, and are now very comfortable. There is also one private lodging-house, which is connected with the Fish Hotel. The Scale Hill Hotel, situated 4m. from Buttermere, and about ½m. from the foot of Crummock Lake, is also a capital resting-place for visitors. Loweswater Lake lies 1m. to the N.W. of the foot of Crummock, and between the two lakes are a few houses, one of which is a private lodging-house, and another is a small, but clean inn, called the Kirk Stile Inn, and having the sign Hounds and Hare.

The Buttermere Valley is enclosed by lofty mountains, and is a most secluded and charming retreat for the tourist. The lakes at times look solemn, but always beautiful.

The story of Mary, the beauty of Buttermere, which has been told in verse by Southey, is familiar to most readers. She was the daughter of the innkeeper at the Fish, and waited upon the guests. Being possessed, it is said, of considerable personal attractions, she was much admired, and many suitors in vain sought her hand. At last a stranger named Hatfield arrived, of gentlemanly exterior and address, who called himself the Honourable Colonel Hope, brother of Lord Hopetoun. He won Mary's heart, and married her. Soon after the marriage he was apprehended on a charge of forgery, surreptitiously franking a letter in the name of a member of Parliament, tried at Carlisle, convicted, and

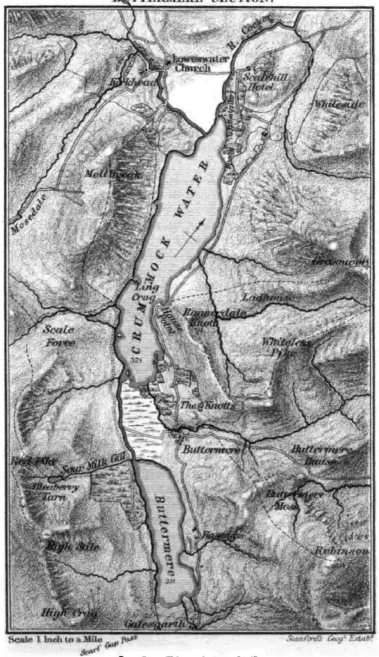

Scale 1 Inch to a Mile

Stanford's Geog.l Establ.

London: Edward Stanford.

hanged. It was discovered during the trial that he had a wife and family, and had fled to these sequestered parts to escape the arm of the law. Mary married again, a respectable farmer of Caldbeck, and died about forty years ago.

Many tourists merely visit this valley for a few hours, in a day's drive from Keswick (see p. 143); but so quiet and lovely a spot is well deserving a more lengthened stay.

Round Buttermere Lake, 4½m.—After passing the church, the road runs along by the Buttermere Lake, at a short distance from the shore. Rising from the opposite bank of the lake is the towering and rugged mass consisting of Red Pike, High Stile, and High Crag. The white streak of water running down the face of the mountain is Sour Milk Gill, which issues from Bleaberry Tarn, situated in the hollow above. At the head of the valley stands a fine amphitheatre, consisting of the Hay Stacks, Green Crags, Brandreth, Fleetwith, and Honister Pike; with Great Gable and Green Gable showing their summits beyond them. A portion of Kirk Fell peers over the Scarf Gap Pass, between High Crag and the Hay Stacks. The hollow of Honister Pass is directly in front. On the left hand of the road Robinson Mountain presents some interesting clefts and crags. A retrospective view embraces Whiteless Pike, Grasmoor, Rannerdale Knott, and Mellbreak, with a portion of Crummock Lake.

After passing the pretty villa of Hassness, the residence of F. J. Reed, Esq., the road touches the head of the lake, and then the farm-house of Gatesgarth is reached. Here the gate in front of the house must be passed through, the stream crossed at the bridge, and the fields entered. The Scarf Gap Pass is the depression to the right of the Hay Stacks, and the zigzag path can be distinctly observed commencing at the foot of High Crag. Two fields must be traversed, with the hedge kept close on the right hand. The view which is to be had in these meadows is of a very high order.

The whole of the lake is in sight, encompassed by mountains finely grouped, and the amphitheatre on the left is especially grand.

Some planks lead over a small stream, and then a rough track will be found running by the side of the lake, at the foot of the Red Pike range of mountains. The torrent descending from between High Crag and High Stile forms some pretty cascades, and the rocky peak of High Crag frowns grandly overhead. A plantation may be passed by keeping close to the edge of the lake; but the regular path enters the wood a few yards above the shore; and at the point where it emerges the whole of Buttermere and most of Crummock are seen, with the huge mass of Grasmoor on the right. After passing Sour Milk Gill stream, the remainder of the path is often very wet; but the bridge over the river, flowing from Buttermere to Crummock Lake, is only a few hundred yards distant, and a short walk through the meadows leads to the hotels.

Round Crummock Lake, 9m.—This is a delightful trip, embracing a variety of picturesque views of lake and mountain.

Leaving the Victoria Inn, the road, after passing the clergyman's residence and two or three farm-houses, makes a slight ascent, and then the head of Crummock Lake is seen, with Rannerdale Knott on the right, and Mellbreak opposite, rising sheer out of the water; both mountains being bare of trees, but beautifully coloured. On the left is the Red Pike and High Stile range, with Sour Milk Gill stream flowing out of the crater-like hollow above, where rests Bleaberry Tarn. Looking back, the amphitheatre stretching from Honister Crag to the Hay Stacks is remarkably grand, with the characteristic stream flowing down its centre. Beyond, rise Green Gable, Great Gable, and Kirk Fell. Descending a little, the shore of the lake is reached, and here an old grass-covered road branches to the right, round the end of Rannerdale Knott. This was formerly the regular road, but discontinued when the lower one was made.

On arriving at the Hause Point, where the road rounds
the rocky knob of Rannerdale, a view is had of the whole
of the lake, with Low Fell and the Lanthwaite woods at
its foot. A few yards farther, the lofty and massive
bulk of Grasmoor is seen towering on the right, and on
rounding the beautiful rocks of Rannerdale Knott, Ladhouse and Whiteless Pike are observed rising out of a
pretty little glen. A farm-house and a cottage are
passed, and then there is no habitation for 1½m., but a
succession of fine views greets the eye. The whole of
Mellbreak is seen rising sheer and beautifully out of the
water, and the rocky perpendicular front of Grasmoor
is gradually displayed. When the tourist is close under
the wildest part of this mountain, he will doubtless consider it the most noble object in the Buttermere district.
The road makes a slight rise, and leaves the lake some
distance on the left. Carling Knott and other smaller
heights come into prospect on the opposite side of the
valley. On the right is Whiteside, separated from Grasmoor by a deep hollow. Pedestrians often pass to
Keswick between these two mountain masses. At the
second farm-house, a guide-post directs to Scale Hill
Hotel, along a road through the woods on the left. The
hotel is 1m. distant, and stands a few yards on the E.
side of the bridge, crossing the river Cocker. Whether
or not it be intended to visit the hotel, it is advisable to
proceed through the wood, along the road conducting to
it. When over the bridge, take the second turning on
the left, by a blacksmith's shop. On proceeding a few
yards farther, a view is obtained of Loweswater Lake.
Close to the church is a small inn. At the inn follow
the left-hand road, and after passing two or three farm-
houses, the base of Mellbreak is reached, and the path
runs along the margin of Crummock Lake. On making
a slight ascent, a glimpse is caught of Buttermere Lake,
and all Crummock is visible, with Whiteside, Grasmoor,
Whiteless Pike, and Rannerdale Knott on the opposite
side. In front stand the Red Pike range, and the mountains at the head of Buttermere.

From a rocky knoll, called High Ling Crag, which rises at the foot of Mellbreak, near a low promontory projecting into the lake, called Low Ling Crag, an excellent prospect is had of both lakes and the surrounding mountains. The fine amphitheatre at the head of the valley appears to ascend sheer from the head of Buttermere, and Honister Pike rises nobly from the hollow of the Honister Pass. Opposite are Robinson, Rannerdale, Whiteless, Ladhouse, Grasmoor, and Whiteside, and at their feet a few beautifully-green fields. The water is seen descending the Scale Force cleft, and the Red Pike range appears to make a graceful ascent from the shore of Buttermere.

The same mountains are seen from the promontory, but Buttermere is hidden by the wooded knolls at the head of Crummock, and the amphitheatre appears to rise almost from the shore of the latter lake.

Crossing the stream flowing from Scale Hill Force, at the point where parties are landed from boats, the wall is passed over at a stile. The Scale Force cleft is plainly seen on the right. The geologist will be interested in observing the sudden change in the nature of the pebbles on the shore of the lake. At the promontory, they are of the clay slate formation, and on passing the landing-place for Scale Force, almost all of them consist of syenite. The hollow at the end of Mellbreak is the division between these two kinds of rock. Mellbreak is Skiddaw, or clay slate, and Red Pike is syenite. After crossing some wet ground, and arriving at a clump of holly bushes, a stony path will be entered leading to the bridge which spans the stream flowing from Buttermere to Crummock.

A cart-track through two fields leads to the village of Buttermere.

Round Loweswater Lake, 3m.—After crossing the river Cocker from Scale Hill, and arriving at the smithy, the excursion round Crummock Lake may be lengthened 3m. by taking round Loweswater Lake. The road runs close to the shore, and on arriving at the head of the lake, a foot-track will lead across the meadows to a farm-house. Here a rough road is entered which takes through a plantation, parallel with the bank, and crosses the fields at the foot of the lake. In this plantation is a fine fall, called Howe Force, formed by the streamlet which flows between Carling Knott and Burnbank.

The lake is tame when compared with most others in the district, but a fine view is obtained from the high end, with Mellbreak and Grasmoor in the background.

Buttermere to Bleaberry Tarn.—Bleaberry Tarn, resting in the hollow between Red Pike and High Stile, is not a large sheet of water, but it well deserves a visit, owing to the wild seclusion of the situation. It is full of trout, which are usually in very poor condition. The distance from the village to the tarn and back is 3m. The principal ascent is at the point where the Sour Milk Gill stream enters the lake.

Here a rough track will be found striking to the left, and where it terminates it is advisable to incline to the right and climb until a wall is reached. The wall is difficult to get over with safety, but by continuing to the right, along the side of it, as far as the gill, it can be easily passed; and then, if the direction of the water be taken, no mistake can be made during the rest of the walk.

The most interesting ascent is close by the side of the stream. About half-way up the hill, the water flows between wild, overhanging rocks; and few tourists will visit the place without being tempted to have a romantic scramble between the crags, along the course of the stream.

The views during the ascent are extremely beautiful. The two lakes, Buttermere and Crummock, with the vale and village, are seen spread below, surrounded by a grand panoply of mountains; including Honister, Robinson, and Grasmoor ranges; Rannerdale Knott, Low Fell, and Mellbreak.

The tarn is small in size, but this defect, if it be one, is amply compensated for by the grand rocky amphitheatre

From ~ Red Pike and High Stile
rises ? the tarn without much extra
proje to Buttermere is easily made.
cell ...nerdale **Knott** (1160), from Butter-
m Knott juts into Crummock Lake on
vr It is not of great elevation, but com-
, ...pect superior to that gained from many
...points. An easy and pleasant walk of about
...ducts to the summit. A few yards beyond the
...Inn, at the last farm-house, turn to the right,
...the Knotts, and keep climbing, with the Buttermere Hause road in sight, until the base of Whiteless
Pike is reached, and then incline to the left. Here a vista
through the Rannerdale Glen reveals Loweswater Lake.

Continuing along the whole length of the mountain,
superb views are obtained of the three lakes, and lofty
heights rise on every side.

From the summit, the mountain amphitheatre at the
head of the valley, the Red Pike range, and Mellbreak,
Grasmoor, and Whiteside, are especially fine. A descent
may be made to the road on the shore of the lake, at the
place called Hause Point.

Ascent of Grasmoor (2791), **from Buttermere.**—
The shortest ascent is from behind Rannerdale Knott,
up the side of Ladhouse, but this is very steep. A more
gradual course, and one commanding better prospects, is
over Whiteless Pike. A pony can be taken the whole
journey.

On passing the clergyman's residence, turn to the
right, at the last house, ascend the Knotts, and continue
climbing, with the road over Buttermere Hause in sight
on the right. When at the base of Whiteless a peep
reveals Loweswater and the foot of Crummock Lake.
Great Gable and Kirk Fell are observed overlooking the
Hay Stacks and Scarf Gap Pass. It is a steep climb to
the top of Whiteless, but the ascent of Whiteless Pike
is still steeper, and necessitates a little hard work. The
view from the summit of Whiteless Pike embraces the
three lakes and a grand mountain array. A slight

descent must now be made, and a rather narrow ridge. crossed, with a few picturesque rocks on the right; and on the left, within a stone's-throw, are the steep sides of Ladhouse and Grasmoor.

After travelling some distance along a grassy table-land, an easy climb, with an inclination to the left, leads to the flat, broad summit of Grasmoor, the view from which is given at page 211.

Some pedestrians will make a direct descent down the steep side of the mountain, in the direction of the point where Rannerdale Knott juts into the lake.

Ascent of Robinson (2417), **from Buttermere.**— Robinson is the mountain which stands on the E. of Buttermere Hause. From almost every point of view near Keswick it is a very attractive object. A pony can reach the top from Buttermere without difficulty, and the ascent is commenced at once on leaving the hotel. The distance to the summit is 2½m.

Follow the Newlands road for some hundred yards past the church, and at a solitary tree on the roadside commence mounting the smooth slope on the right. The climb is somewhat steep, along a winding grass-covered track, which was formerly used by those bringing down peat from the mountain.

During the ascent, Buttermere, Crummock, and Lowes-water lakes come into view, and the mountains rising from their shores, especially the High Stile range, are fine objects. The heights on the left of the Keswick road also present smooth slopes beautifully tinted. On attaining the top of the western offshoot of Robinson, called Buttermere Moss, the summit of the main mass of the mountain is seen on the opposite side of a wet, flat tract of ground. There is also a grand array of mountain masses to the S., including Red Pike, High Stile, High Crag, Pillar, Hay Stacks, Kirk Fell, Scaw-fell Pike, and a portion of the highest part of Scawfell, Great Gable, Green Gable, Brandreth, Fleetwith, and Honister Pike.

To the left of Robinson a part of Derwentwater Lake is

s

seen beyond the Newlands Valley, and the grand mountain ridge from Causey Pike to Grasmoor. Tourists who are travelling from Buttermere to Keswick would enjoy ascending to this point, and then making for the top of the Buttermere Hause.

Those who continue the ascent must bear to the right, cross the wet ground, and then climb in the direction of the wall, which is observed rounding the southern end of the mountain. The summit is then quickly attained, the prospect from which is good, and fully described at page 217.

Ascent of Fleetwith (2126) and Honister Pike, from Buttermere.—The Honister Crags are so celebrated that they have almost robbed of its proper name the mountain Fleetwith, on which they are situated. In order that strangers may not be misled, the writer has often, when referring to Fleetwith, also mentioned Honister; although Honister Pike is merely a rocky knob above the Honister Crags, and part of the Fleetwith Mountain.

After travelling the 2m. between Buttermere and Gatesgarth, the ascent may be made in three ways. The most direct course is up the steep ridge leading direct from Gatesgarth to the summit. Another plan is to follow the cart-road branching to the right at Gatesgarth, and which, after rounding the shoulder of the mountain, ascends amongst rough stones, in a tortuous course, until directly above the ravine, down which tumbles the stream, forming so prominent an object at the head of the valley, as seen from Buttermere village.

The third, and better plan, is to take the car-road to the top of Honister Pass, and there commence mounting the hill from the track which leads to the quarries.

The prospect from the summit is of a high order. Buttermere, Crummock, and part of Loweswater look charming, with the surrounding heights, Mellbreak, Red Pike, High Stile, High Crag, Grasmoor, Whiteless Pike, Rannerdale Knott, and Robinson. On the opposite side of the deep hollow of the Honister Pass, Dale Head and Hindscarth present beautifully-coloured sides. To the left of Hindscarth are Causey Pike and part of Skiddaw. Looking eastwards are Helvellyn, Ullscarf, High Raise, and Glaramara. Over the neighbouring heights, Grey Knotts and Brandreth, appear Bow Fell and Hanging Knott. Great Gable is bold and prominent, and to the left of it are Green Gable, Great End, and strips of the Scawfell Pikes; and to the right Scawfell. Over the Hay Stacks stand the lofty mountains Pillar and Kirk Fell, with Yewbarrow between them, in a line with the Black Sail Pass depression. Beyond Mellbreak are the lower heights, Blake Fell and Low Fell.

If the top be gained from Honister Pass it is well to go down by the course of the torrent on the N.W. side of the mountain, and to follow the rough road to Gates-garth. Fine views are had all the way down.

Ascent of Great Gable (2949), from Buttermere.— Follow the regular road from Buttermere to Gatesgarth. When through a gate a few yards past the last building enter a cart-road which branches to the right, and is partly overgrown with herbage. It rounds the end of Fleetwith, and approaches the grand amphitheatre of rocks consisting of Fleetwith, Green Crags, and the Hay Stacks.

A stream flowing down the centre of the rocks forms a number of pretty cascades. The road ascends a rough, stony part of the mountain, and winds round to the point where the stream descends the cleft between Green Crags and the side of Fleetwith. The scenery during the ascent is extremely wild, the perpendicular cliffs of the Green Crags and Hay Stacks looking uncommonly fine. On glancing back the Buttermere and Crummock lakes are spread to view with Mellbreak rising apparently sheer from the shore of the latter lake. The stream on the right careers musically down a rough, stony channel, forming fine cascades during the whole length of its descent. When the lakes are lost to view the Pillar appears over the Hay Stacks. The *débris* of an old slate-

quarry comes in sight; and also the rocky summit of
Grey Knotts, which rises out of the hollow in front.
Here leave the path, cross the torrent, and wind round
the rocky knob which is on the other side, keeping it
on the right hand. Avoid the boggy hollow, and make
for the stream where it is seen to form a small cascade
higher up the hill. Brandreth is the height observed in
front, and from it the stream takes its source. If the
day be clear two large blocks of stone will be observed at
the top of Brandreth, apparently about two yards apart.
Follow the course of the stream, and make for these
stones, avoiding the rocks on the right. The remainder
of the walk is described at page 204.

Ascent of Red Pike (2479), from Buttermere.—Red
Pike, High Stile, and High Crag constitute the moun-
tain mass opposite Buttermere, which runs from Scale
Force to the Scarf Gap Pass.

Red Pike is the round peak on the right of Sour Milk
Gill, and it is the only mountain from which can be
seen the five lakes, Buttermere, Crummock, Loweswater,
Ennerdale, and Derwentwater. It is composed of a
species of granitic rock called syénite. The ascent can
be made from Bleaberry Tarn, by taking the course of
Sour Milk Gill, or from the head of Crummock Lake;
but the easiest route is from Scale Force.

Pedestrians who have only a short time in the district,
and who are walking from Keswick to Wastwater by
Buttermere, are recommended to cross over this mountain from Scale Force, and descend into the Ennerdale
Valley.

Visitors who are remaining in Keswick will be amply
repaid by driving up the Newlands Valley to Buttermere,
specially for the ascent of this mountain.

After visiting Scale Force, a steep ascent must be
made, with the ravine on the right, and then a gradual
climb, with an inclination to the left, will bring to the
summit of the mountain.

Buttermere, Crummock, and Loweswater lakes are
seen; also most of Ennerdale Lake, and a strip of

Derwentwater. There is also a fine group of mountains. Between the Newlands and Lorton valleys are Blenca‑ thara and Skiddaw; the range from Causey Pike to Grasmoor, with the head of Grisedale Pike peering above; and nearer are Aikin Knott, Whiteless Pike and Rannerdale Knott; and a portion of Whiteside appears beyond Grasmoor. Between the Lorton and Ennerdale valleys are Mellbreak, Low Fell, Carling Knott, Blake Fell, Knockmurton, and Herdhouse; and beyond are visible the sea and the Scotch range of summits. On the opposite side of the deep, dark hollow of Ennerdale Valley stand the Haycock, Steeple, and Pillar; and then the Black Sail Pass depression. The nearer height of High Stile hides Kirk Fell, Great Gable, and Green Gable; on the right of it are Scawfell, Mickledore Chasm, and Scawfell Pike: and on the left Honister Pike, Fleetwith, portions of Glaramara, Eagle Crag in Borrowdale, Ullscarf, Helvellyn, Dale Head, Hindscarth, and Robinson. Looking over the Buttermere Hause are seen Cat Bells, Derwent Island, Castle Hill, and Wallow Crag; and some houses around Keswick. In the hollow immediately below the spectator, lies visible Bleaberry Tarn. Leaving Red Pike a magnificent walk may be had by continuing on the tops over High Stile (2643) and High Crag (2443), and descending by the Scarf Gap Pass. When High Stile is reached Kirk Fell, Great Gable, Green Gable, and Brandreth come into view. During the walk the Pillar Mountain presents a wild aspect, and on the left are passed some dark precipitous crags. If it be intended to return to Butter‑ mere either side of the lake may be taken. For Wast‑ water the Black Sail Pass must be crossed.

The whole distance here described is 10m.

Ascent of Mellbreak (1676), from Buttermere.— Mellbreak is the mountain on the N.W. side of Crum‑ mock Lake. The preferable ascents are either from near Scale Force, or from the point on the shore of the lake at which tourists going to the waterfall are landed from boats. Starting from the latter place, make for

the hollow between the main part of the mountain and
the southern projecting knob.   The climb is at first
steep, over smooth and grassy ground, whence charming
views of the two lakes and surrounding mountains repay
the toil of the ascent.   Soon after passing the wire
fencing, Herdhouse, and then Hen Comb come in sight
on the W., and also the pass at the head of the Mosedale Valley, leading to Ennerdale Lake, past Floutern
Tarn.   A few minutes' more hard work enables the
tourist to attain the summit, which he finds is much
broader than it appears as observed from below.

In places it is dry and covered with grass, and in
other parts are heather, and marshy ground.   Keeping
along the E. side, the Buttermere and Crummock lakes
are observed lying calm and lovely below, with grand
mountains rising from their shores, while to the N. is
spread the Lorton Valley.

After walking some distance along the top, there is a
slight depression which appears to divide the mountain
in two.   On crossing this and attaining the highest
point, Loweswater Lake bursts into view, and then the
plain, the Solway Firth, and the Scotch hills.   Mosedale
Valley is on the left, and the comparatively low heights
of Hen Comb, Black Crag, Blake Fell, Carling Knott,
and Burnbank.   Low Fell stands between Loweswater
Lake and the Lorton Valley.   Whiteside, Grasmoor,
and Whiteless Pike, are extremely fine; and also
Robinson, Honister Pike, and Red Pike, surrounding
Buttermere Lake.   The best point of observation is
found by continuing a few yards N.E.   The three lakes
Buttermere, Crummock, and Loweswater, are there in
prospect, with mountains beautiful in shape and colour
rising majestically from the shores.   If the descent be
made on the N., the hamlet of Buttermere may be
reached by taking either side of Crummock Lake; or
up the Mosedale Valley, and past Scale Force.

Ascent of Blake Fell (1878), from Buttermere.—
Blake Fell is the highest of the hills which stand
between Loweswater and Ennerdale, at the back of

Mellbreak. Those who stay at Buttermere or Scale Hill for a few days, will be anxious to make acquaintance with this range of hills, which is rarely visited. They will be amply repaid for the journey, the views being good, and owing to the close proximity to the sea the walk along the smooth grassy tops is most exhilarating. An interesting ascent is made from the point on the western shore of Loweswater, where the stream from Carling Knott Gill enters the lake, in the middle of Holme Wood.

The stream, during its course through the ravine. between Carling Knott and Burnbank, forms some fine falls. A few yards from the lake a small bridge which spans the stream is a good position for seeing the whole in one view. The water makes five or six long leaps in its descent. The ravine is clothed with wood, but wants overhanging rocks to give effect; the scene, however, is very pleasing, and will reward the visitor for climbing up along a winding path by the side of the gill. The fall near the top is peculiar, the rocks causing the water to be thrown up a few feet, and the water then makes a regular bend in its descent. At the top of the plantation a hole will be found in the wall, close to the stream, leading out upon the mountain. By following the water to its source the top of Blake Fell would be reached in the most expeditious and direct way, but the best ascent is by Carling Knott. Quitting the stream, a good steady climb to the left, along a grassy slope, leads to the top of Carling Knott, which commands an extensive view of level country to the N. and N.W., and also of the sea and Scotch hills. Loweswater Lake, the foot of Crummock, and the Lorton Valley, are seen. Skiddaw, and the mountains around the Buttermere Vale, are also very grand.

After continuing along the top of this mountain, a slight descent has to be made, and a little wet ground crossed. Mockerkin Tarn is on the right, lying away from the hills, and on the left are Black Crag, Gavel Fell, Hen Comb, the Mosedale Valley, and Mellbreak, with

Herdhouse and the Ennerdale Mountains beyond. After some exertion the top of Blake Fell is reached, and here beyond Knockmurton Fell is observed the Cleator District, covered with coal and iron mines and smelt furnaces. The prospect embraces a part of the three lakes Buttermere, Crummock, and Ennerdale, and many high and rugged mountains. The return journey may be made in a direct line with Scale Force and Buttermere, but the easier course is between Carling Knott and Black Crag into the Mosedale Valley, and then to the Loweswater Church.

Ascent of Low Fell (1336), **from Buttermere.—** This mountain, though of low elevation, is well worth ascending. The easiest way up is from the foot of Loweswater Lake. The view from the summit is very fine, and superior to that which is had from many higher mountains.

Loweswater, Crummock, and half of Buttermere are seen; also the Lorton Valley, a great extent of level country, the sea, and the Scotch hills. To the E. are the Lorton Fells, Skiddaw, Swinside, and the top of Grisedale Pike. The great swelling masses of Whiteside and Grasmoor are directly opposite, and then there stands a vast array of heights, including Whiteless Pike, Rannerdale Knott, Robinson, Honister Pike, Fleetwith, Brandreth, Hay Stacks, Great Gable, Green Gable, High Crag, High Stile, Red Pike, Mellbreak, Herdhouse, Hen Comb, Blake Fell, Carling Knott, and Burnbank. For the descent no instructions are required.

Buttermere to Wastwater, by Scarf Gap (1400) and Black Sail (1750) Passes.

Time, 3½ hours. Distance, 8m.

The road from Buttermere to the foot of the Scarf Gap Pass is given at page 251.

After passing Gatesgarth, and crossing the meadows and the stream, the ascent of the pass must be com-

menced. During the first half of the way a dilapidated
wall is on the left; and when the track leaves the wall,
the High Stile Crags are above on the right, and on the
left the Hay Stacks. The cleft through which the path
runs is very distinct to the right of the latter rocks.
Before the top of the pass is reached, another wall is
passed through at a small gate, and then the path becomes very rough and stony. On looking back, fine
glimpses are caught of the head of Buttermere Lake,
with Grasmoor Mountain beyond. When a peep is had
into Ennerdale, the great towering mass of the Pillar
Mountain will be seen opposite, stretching away to the
right. Great Gable is at the head of the valley, and
between it and the Pillar stands Kirk Fell.

Tourists often find it difficult to make out which is the
Black Sail Pass when crossing from Buttermere to
Wastwater, owing to the track being ill-defined and the
hollow being hid by a strip of the Pillar Mountain;
therefore, before descending into the Ennerdale Valley,
it is well to trace clearly the route which has to be
taken. The error which is naturally made is that of
supposing the depression at the head of the valley,
between Great Gable and Kirk Fell, to be the Black
Sail Pass; whereas it is to the right of Kirk Fell.
Directly opposite the Scarf Gap Pass stands a lower
part of the Pillar, with a smooth round top; and a ridge,
gradually lowering, stretches from that point to the left.
Over the lowest part of this ridge will be seen a dark
cleft in Kirk Fell, with a white streak of water flowing
down to the river Liza. The direction of this cleft
must be taken. When descending into the valley, a
remarkably fine view is had of Ennerdale Lake, the
Angling Crag promontory making the water take a beautiful curve. The English Matterhorn, the Pillar Rock,
is also finely displayed in front of the Pillar Mountain.
After descending the Scarf Gap Pass, walk a little distance up the valley, passing close in front of an old
building. Threading through a few of the innumerable
rounded moraine heaps, a wooden plank crosses the

river Liza a few yards above a sheepcot. Here the
streamlet from the cleft in Kirk Fell enters the river,
and will be a good guide for the tourist during the ascent
of the Black Sail Pass. The climb must be made with
the streamlet on the left hand. When a solitary tree is
passed, the path winds round some small rocks; and at
a second tree, where the rill is observed descending the
deep cleft, the path zigzags to the right, and the top of
the pass is only a few yards distant.

During the whole of the ascent, and when at the top
of the pass, the craggy front of Kirk Fell looks imposingly grand.

Descending into the Mosedale Valley, the Pillar is on
the right, and in front the Steeple, Red Pike, and Yewbarrow; and between the two latter a little of Middle
Fell is seen. Following the course of the stream, Lingmell, Scawfell, and a part of the Screes come into view,
and also the far-famed inn at Wastdale Head.

Buttermere to Ennerdale Lake, by Scale Force and Floutern Tarn, and thence to Wastdale Head, by Windy Gap.

Floutern Tarn, 4m.; Ennerdale (Anglers' Inn), 6m.; Windy Gap,
13½m.; Wastdale Head, 16m.

Take the road on the left of the Fish Inn for a few
yards, and then over a stile, and through two fields to
the bridge which spans the beck flowing between Buttermere and Crummock lakes.

After crossing the bridge turn to the right, and a
rough path, often rather wet, will be found, which runs
along by the side of the beck, and then near the shore of
Crummock Lake.

After an islet is passed, a wall will be seen running
down the hollow near the S.E. shoulder of Mellbreak;
at the point where it touches the lake tourists are
landed, who take a boat across the water to visit Scale
Force. After passing through a gate in the wall, about
600 yards from the lake, follow the course of the stream-

let for about ½m., and it will lead to the waterfall, which
is in a ravine on the left, near an iron-ore mine. The
fall has a leap of 156 feet, between two perpendicular
rocks, which are in part covered with trees and vegetation, and impart to the spot a character of wild picturesque beauty.

Leaving the fall, take by the side of the wire fencing,
until another similar fence is met at right angles; then
keep straight along by the side of the hill on the left,
to avoid some swampy ground.

The Mosedale Valley on the right, at the back of Mellbreak, leads to Loweswater Lake and Scale Hill Hotel,
which is situated near the foot of Crummock Lake.
Herdhouse is the last rocky height seen on the left, and
in a hollow at its base is Floutern Tarn; and as that is
the source of the stream flowing down the Mosedale
Valley, the tourist will find the tarn without difficulty.
Near the second sheepcot cross the stream, and take
over the wire fencing; a similar fence will be passed at
a third sheepcot. A small climb, with a slight inclination to the left, leads to the tarn. It is in shape long
and narrow, but not a large sheet of water. After it is
passed, keep near the base of Herdhouse, and a streamlet
will presently be found flowing down to Ennerdale Lake.
Following the course of the streamlet, a house will
presently be reached, and then a road entered which
branches to the right, and runs near the shore of the
lake to the Anglers' Inn. The inn is comfortable, and
pleasantly situated close to the water.

Ennerdale Lake is about 2½m. long, and 1½m. broad.
It is 369 feet above the sea level, and its greatest depth
is 80 feet. The river Liza enters it from the Ennerdale
Valley, and the Ehen flows from it to the sea. It is
well stocked with trout, and with an inferior kind of
char.

Lying away from the ordinary route of tourists, this
lake is rarely visited. Most strangers merely catch a
glimpse of part of it when crossing the Scarf Gap Pass,
between Wastdale and Buttermere. It is, however, wild

and romantic, ánd well deserving of a special visit.
Few trees adorn the shores, and it is without islands,
with the exception of a small pile of stones which appears
a few feet above the water near the centre of the lake.
From the shore, opposite the inn, Angling Crag promontory, Revelin, and Iron Crag rise sheer and bold out
of the water. On the N. side is the Herdhouse mountain, with the Bowness promontory at its base, round
which the lake makes a beautiful curve. At the head
is a grand mountain group, consisting of the Pillar,
Steeple, and Haycock.

Two miles from the Anglers' Inn, and about 1m. from
the foot of the lake, is Ennerdale Bridge, a hamlet containing a small inn. The churchyard will be glanced at
with interest by those who are able to pay it a visit. It
is the scene of Wordsworth's pathetic poem, ' The
Brothers.'

> " . . . . . In our churchyard
> Is neither epitaph nor monument,
> Tombstone nor name—only the turf we tread
> And a few natural graves."

On leaving the Anglers' Inn for Wastdale Head by
Windy Gap, a foot-path may be followed by the shore of
the lake, or by following the cart-road past one or two
farm-houses the base of Herdhouse and the beautiful
cliffs of Bowness Knotts are skirted. The road then
continues pleasantly for 2m. by the shore of the lake,
allowing of a view half-way up Ennerdale Glen. The
sloping sides of Red Pike range being on the left, and
on the right the Haycock, Steeple, and Pillar. Windy
Gap is the depression between the two latter heights.

After leaving the lake, the road continues for some
distance by the side of the river Liza to Gillerthwaite,
where there are a few fields and two farm-houses, one of
which is not occupied. Just before arriving at the first
walled enclosure, cross the river at a long wooden foot-
bridge, close to a small plantation of larches and Scotch
firs. Wend away up the glen with the river on the left,
and climb to the right up the gap, in front of the Pillar,

1m. beyond Gillerthwaite. On passing the plantation a
brook has to be crossed, and sometimes it is rather
swollen. If it be difficult to cross, a bridge may be
found by walking a few yards to the right.

Before leaving the river and commencing the long
climb to Windy Gap, a clump of trees is passed, which
is observed growing a short distance above on the side
of the hill; and on the left a pool of water containing a
few tiny islets covered with bushes. Ennerdale Lake is
a beautiful object on glancing back.

Do not climb until a torrent is reached which descends
from a combe in the Steeple. This is crossed at a tiny
foot-bridge close to some shrubs. After ascending by
the side of the torrent for a few yards, a fine waterfall
will be found in a pleasant wooded dell, the water having
a descent of about 80 feet.

Continuing by the side of the ravine, many more
pretty cascades will be observed, and near the top are
two or three larger and very beautiful ones. Passing
through a wall, leave the stream, and incline to the left.
The wild front of the Steeple is observed directly above.
Aim for the Steeple, bearing in mind that Windy Gap
is to the left, and between it and the Pillar. On arriving
at a streamlet, cross it near its source, and then mount
by the side of the Pillar. The Steeple rocks look very
fine from this point. A wide extent of sea is visible,
also the Scotch Hills and Ennerdale Lake. A long,
gradual climb leads to the narrow summit of the pass
without fear of error. The Mosedale Glen lies immediately below, with a rivulet winding along to the inn at
Wastdale Head, which is visible. Red Pike and Yewbarrow are on the right, and in front Lingmell, Scawfell, Mickledore, Scawfell Pike, Great End, Bow Fell,
part of the Screes, and Burnmoor and Eel tarns.

From this point the tourist has the choice of three
routes. He may climb some steep rocks on the left, and
thus reach the summit of the Pillar Mountain in about
thirty minutes. Then walk to the other end of the
mountain, keeping the cliff-line on the left, and descend

by the Black Sail Pass. Another plan is to climb to the
right from Windy Gap, ascend the Steeple, and then
continue over the tops round the head of the Mosedale
Glen; and descend by Dore Head, close to Yewbarrow.
The third way is to make a direct descent from Windy
Gap. The ground at first is steep, but discovered to be
free of all difficulties when the tourist boldly ventures
down. On entering the glen, follow the course of the
streamlet, keeping it on the left, and it will lead to
the inn, which is 2m. distant.

Scale Hill Hotel to Ennerdale Lake, by Mosedale Valley and Floutern Tarn.

Kirk Stile Inn, 1m.; Floutern Tarn, 4m.; Ennerdale Lake (Anglers'
Inn), 6m.

Leaving the Scale Hill Hotel, cross the river Cocker
at the bridge, and take the second turn on the left, at a
blacksmith's shop. By proceeding a few yards farther,
a glance is had of Loweswater Lake. Near the church
is a small inn. Take the road on the right of the latter.
It conducts up the Mosedale Valley, on the W. of Mellbreak, by the side of some wire fencing, and with a
stream below. At the point where the valley is entered
Loweswater is spread to view on the right. When the
fencing turns to the right, the road divides; the left-
hand branch leading to Buttermere. Follow the track
which crosses the valley, and continue on the road,
winding round the base of Hen Comb. The dark steep
front of Herdhouse is now in sight, at the foot of which
lies Floutern Tarn, the source of the stream. Make for
the low hill to the right of Herdhouse, keeping the
stream well to the left. The road continues for some
distance up the pass, but in some places it is not easily
traced. By inclining to the right, however, no mistake
can be made. When the road goes through some wire
fencing, close to a sheepfold, keep a small hollow on the
left, and a slight climb will lead to the top of the pass,
with Floutern Tarn below on the left hand. A streamlet

will presently be found flowing down to the Ennerdale
Lake. Follow its course until a house is reached, then
make for the inn which stands on the shore, near the
foot of the lake.

If the tourist has not seen Scale Force, he ought to
walk from the Kirk Stile Inn, along the E. side of Mellbreak, on the shore of Crummock Lake, and at the S.
end of the mountain a streamlet will be met issuing
from the fall. From this point the route described at
page 266 must be followed, where will also be found
directions for walking over Windy Gap to Wastdale
Head.

From Buttermere, or the Scale Hill Hotel, to Keswick, by the Coledale Pass.

From Buttermere, 11½m. ; from Scale Hill Hotel, 8¼m.

The road from Buttermere for the first 3½m. is on the
eastern margin of Crummock Lake, and at the foot of
lofty mountains.

On reaching the second farm-house, after leaving the
lake, a road will be observed branching to the left for
the Scale Hill Hotel; and opposite, on the right, is the
ravine between Grasmoor and Whiteside. Travellers
from Scale Hill will climb the small hill at the back of
the hotel, and make for this point. Two very narrow
tracks will be observed leading up the ravine; one by
the side of Grasmoor, and the other round the base of
Whiteside. It is recommended to cross the stream, and
commence with the latter path, in order that the high
and precipitous side of Grasmoor may be in sight. The
track runs amongst rocks, a small height above the
stream, for about ¾m., and then vanishes. Here the
tourist should cross to the Grasmoor side of the stream,
where he will have a fine view of the wild and beautiful
rocks of Whiteside. A good steady climb, with the
rivulet a short distance on the left hand, will enable the
tourist to reach the top of the pass without the possibility of a blunder. The streamlet will be observed to

flow from between Grasmoor and Eel Crags, and some
of the water being diverted by miners down the Coledale
Valley, no trouble will be experienced in crossing the
pass, if the course of the diverted water be taken. After
commencing the descent, it is well to incline a little to
the left, in order to avoid some marshy ground at the
foot of Eel Crags. When a little way down, an inclination must be made to the right to the course of the
stream. A steep descent now leads to the Coledale
Valley, where a cart-road from some barytes mines takes
to Braithwaite village, which is 2½m. from Keswick.

Ennerdale Lake (Anglers' Inn) to Scale Hill Hotel, by Floutern Tarn and Mosedale Valley.

Floutern Tarn, 2m.; Kirk Stile Inn, 5m.; Scale Hill Hotel, 6m.

Floutern Tarn lies under the cliffs of Herdhouse, and
will be found without difficulty, if the climb be made by
the course of the ravine at the base of that mountain.
Near the summit of the pass a grassy peak stands in
front, which must be kept on the left. The tarn will
be observed on the right, and the water from it flows
in the direction which has to be taken. Descending,
with the stream at some distance on the right, a gate is
found leading through wire fencing, near to a sheepfold. A road is now entered which rounds the end of
Hen Comb Mountain, and runs down the Mosedale
Valley, with Mellbreak on the right, and Low Fell in
front, and takes direct to the inn and the Loweswater
Church. Just before the valley is left, Loweswater Lake
is seen on the left, and then Crummock Lake comes in
sight, with the mountains Grasmoor and Whiteless
rising from the opposite shore, and a noble mountain
group is observed standing at the head of the Buttermere Valley. After passing the church and a blacksmith's shop, an inclination to the right leads to the
bridge over the Cocker, flowing from Crummock Lake;
Scale Hill Hotel stands on a rising ground a few yards
distant.

On leaving Floutern Tarn, some travellers will prefer going in the direction of Scale Force. (See page 288.) From the fall they can follow the stream to Crummock Lake, and continue along the shore, at the base of Mellbreak, to the Kirk Stile Inn, and thence to Scale Hill Hotel.

T

WASTWATER SECTION.

WASTDALE HEAD.

WASTDALE HEAD lies secluded, at the foot of the most wild and lofty mountains in the district. It is a favourite retreat of the lover of mountaineering. Here he may remain for weeks, and still find plenty of work.

There is only a plain inn in the valley, and this, until recently, was merely a farm-house. Mr. Wm. Ritson, the proprietor, is a well-known character—a genuine specimen of the dalesmen of the district. Comfortable private lodgings are to be had at two other farm-houses. The young Ritsons know the neighbouring mountains well, and make excellent guides.

At Strands, 1m. from the foot of the lake, are two cosey inns, the Strands Inn and the Strands Hotel. Occasionally during the busy part of the season, when the houses are full at Wastdale Head, parties are taken down the lake in a boat, or by the side of the lake in a conveyance, to Strands.

Piers Gill.—There is, perhaps, nothing grander in the district than this dark, rugged fissure, with its wild, impending cliffs. It is worth travelling many miles purposely to see, and it is an unpardonable neglect for any tourist to remain a day at Wastdale Head without visiting it. It lies on the N. side of Lingmell, and can be reached after two miles' walk up the glen from the inn.

Of course the cleft is seen when descending Sty Head Pass; but this is of little account. To inspect it properly, the stranger must enter it, and walk some distance up the bed of the torrent, until irregular vertical cliffs are on either hand, rising grandly one above another; and right in front at the head stands nobly above the rest the lofty, perpendicular front of

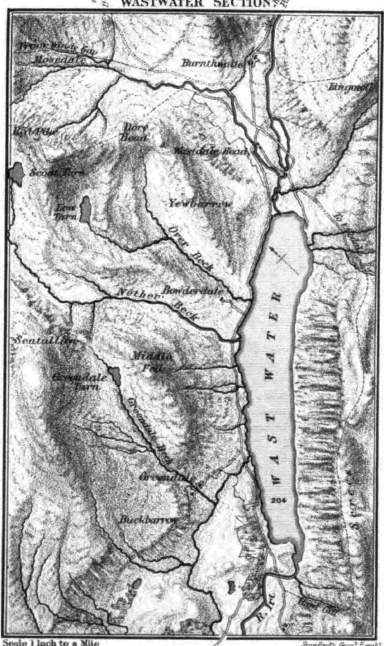

Scale 1 Inch to a Mile

Strands

London: Edward Stanford.

Lingmell (2649). When the traveller has reached a point where he is, as it were, estranged from the rest of the world, the scene is found to be indescribably grand, and so imposing that some will not dare to proceed more than a few yards. For this reason it is advisable not to go unaccompanied.

Greta Waterfall.—This waterfall, which is, perhaps, the largest and most magnificent in the district, is formed by the streamlet which descends the W. side of the Scawfell Pikes, and joins the one from Piers Gill. It may be seen by walking to a large detached block a few yards on the N. side of the stream. The water descends along a fissure in the rocks for hundreds of feet, forming a series of large wild mountain falls. On every side are bare rocks and precipices. It is well also to cross to the S. side of the stream, in order to obtain a view of the twin, but more hidden, ravine to the N. The whole of this side of the Scawfell Pikes is deserving exploration, and a day ought to be set apart specially for it.

Ascent of the Screes (1978), **from Wastdale Head.** —The Screes, when seen from the opposite shore, near the foot of the lake, are grand and beautiful objects, but they look far more picturesque and weird-like when viewed from above. The tourist is therefore strongly advised to walk from one end of the mountain to the other. During the journey he will have an extensive prospect of the sea, the level country bordering the coast, and the neighbouring mountains; but these he will little notice after gaining the first enchanting view of the lake and the crumbling, weather-beaten cliffs immediately at his feet. In some places the rocks assume most fantastic shapes, quite different in character from anything of the kind seen in other parts of the district. The ascent is best made by crossing the beck and valley near the head of the lake, and following the path which leads to Boot, in Eskdale, beyond Burnmoor Tarn, between Scawfell and the Screes. When a little way up, leave the path, bend to the right, and a gradual

T 2

climb over green, sloping ground will lead to the summit of the mountain. From the highest point are seen Buckbarrow, Seatallan, Middle Fell, Haycock, Red Pike, Pillar, and Yewbarrow. Beyond Black Sail Pass is Robinson, and then Kirk Fell, Brandreth, and Great Gable. On the opposite side of the Sty Head Pass are Lingmell, Scawfell Pike, Scawfell, Crinkle Crags, Coniston Old Man, Harter Fell, Birker Moor, and Black Combe.

Having arrived at the S. end of the mountain, an interesting descent may be made down Hawl Gill, a deep ravine formed by the decomposition of the felspar of the granite rocks. It has a very peculiar appearance, the rocks being finely coloured and shaped into miniature peaks; but it has nothing of the wild grandeur presented by Piers Gill at Wastdale Head, or Crinkle Gill in Langdale. Near the foot of the ravine the stream which descends breaks into three most beautiful cascades. The rocks are charmingly covered with mosses, and the dell is well timbered. There are few prettier bits of scenery than the one formed by these three cascades, when the tourist gains a point where he can see them all collectively. On reaching the valley the river Irt may be crossed at a small bridge. Strands is 1m. and Wastdale Head 5m. distant.

Some adventurous tourists may desire to walk to Wastdale Head by the E. side of the lake at the foot of the Screes. It is possible to do so, but most of the journey has to be accomplished close to the water, over bare, rough blocks of stone. The writer undertook the walk, in company with one of the Ritsons, of Wastdale Head, but he found the journey rather monotonous, and not worth the labour. In one or two places there is a little danger of the stones rolling into the dark and deep waters of the lake.

Ascent of Scawfell Pike (3210), **from Wastdale Head.**—Scawfell Pike may be ascended in many ways from Wastdale. The most direct course is to cross the valley directly opposite the inn, and ascend the lower part of Lingmell by a distinct path close behind the highest wall. If the beck in the valley be swollen, this point may be reached by walking up the glen to the highest house, in the direction of Sty Head Pass, and then crossing the beck at a small stone bridge and descending to the wall. Another way is to cross the torrent at a wooden foot-bridge near the head of the lake, and over some rough, stony ground, to the foot of Lingmell. A gradual ascent will lead to the highest part of the wall; passing which, a steep climb conducts to the top of the southern shoulder of Lingmell, and the stiffest part of the toil is over. After walking some distance over a grassy plateau which makes a gradual rise, incline to right and leave some small rocks on the left. A wall is attained which leaves Lingmell some distance below the summit. Here the tourist must go over some smooth ground just above a little wet, boggy tract. The remainder of the ascent is over rough stones, with an inclination at first to the right, in the direction of Mickledore, and then again to the left.

The cairn on the summit of Scawfell Pike will now be a distinct object, and easily gained. During the ascent the rocky front of Scawfell and the cliffs surrounding the Mickledore Chasm look extremely wild; a fine view is had of Wastdale Head, Mosedale Glen, Wastwater Lake, and the sea.

Ponies can be taken to within a short distance of the summit, and the route which they travel, though rather circuitous, is one which is recommended to pedestrians, as it affords a closer view of the grand vertical cliffs overhanging Mickledore. The valley is crossed near the lake, and an ascent made by the side of Scawfell, just above the highest wall. Leaving Mickledore on the right, the green, level ground is reached where the wall descends from near the top of Lingmoor, and then the track previously mentioned is entered.

Another ascent for pedestrians is by the N. side of Piers Gill ravine. This involves a little harder work, but the ground travelled over is exceedingly interesting, and reveals some of the grandest rock scenery in the district.

Descent of Scawfell Pike (3210) to Wastdale Head.
—The most direct descent from Scawfell Pike to Wastdale Head is over Lingmell, the route generally taken by tourists; but much more interesting ways are by Mickledore Chasm and Piers Gill.

From the summit aim in the direction of the Mosedale Glen, seen close below to the N.W., with the Pillar mountain rising sheer from it.

After descending a short distance, with Scawfell and Mickledore on the left, Lingmell gradually comes in sight, directly in front, on the opposite side of a smooth grassy hollow. Make for the wall seen descending from Lingmell to the top of this hollow, and on reaching it pass some wet ground on the left, and walk by the side of Lingmell under a few low rocks.

A green slope will be reached, and a descent must be made along it in the direction of Wastwater Lake, until a wall is reached which runs from the valley, up the side of the mountain. Descend by the side of the wall, keeping it on the left.

To reach the inn a stream has to be crossed. After heavy rains the tourist will probably desire to avail himself of a bridge. He will find one ½m. farther up the glen, or another by descending near to the head of the lake.

If he desire to take the Mickledore route, he may aim for Scawfell, and quickly reach the narrow ridge which unites the two highest mountains. Here he will be in the heart of one of nature's most savage retreats. Desolate rocks and mountains are all around. The vertical cliffs of Scawfell, hundreds of feet high, frown in an oppressive and imposing manner. The ridge is 100 yards from end to end, but there is no danger in walking along it, as it is comparatively smooth and sloping, without precipices. The traveller might almost bestride it, and have one foot in Eskdale and the other in Wastdale. A descent can be made without difficulty into either valley. A good cragsman may scramble direct to the top of Scawfell from this spot, by first taking a long, dangerous step amongst the rocks on the left of the ridge, but a stranger will be unable to find the way without the aid of a guide.

Scawfell may be reached after descending some distance on either side of the ridge and rounding the cliffs. A method of ascent, as little circuitous as possible to be free from danger, is by the "Lord's Lake," a narrow cleft a short distance from the ridge, on the Wastdale side.

To reach Wastdale from Mickledore take boldly down the sloping screes, and follow the course of the streamlet. When a short distance down, a fine view is obtained of the magnificent overhanging cliffs.

Those who descend from Scawfell Pike by the side of Piers Gill must incline to the right on reaching the highest wall running from Lingmell. The head of Piers Gill is quickly gained, and then the descent is made with the chasm on the left. After walking a few yards, the water is heard descending a deep rugged gorge, and the visitor here and there selects safe stand-points whence he may look into the abyss. The wild cliffs of Lingmell frown grandly on the opposite side, and all around nature assumes her most noble and savage aspect. This journey should not be undertaken during misty weather. When half-way down, two or three small gullies are on the right, which must be passed at their head. Here it is recommended to leave the chasm for some distance, and branch to the right. After descending some rocks, make again for the gill. The best view during the descent is now obtained, and it is unequalled in sublimity by any other in the district. The traveller looks into a deep, savage chasm, and on either side rise wild and picturesque cliffs, height above height, to the summit of the bold, vertical front of Lingmell (2649).

The valley is entered a short distance below the Sty Head Pass. It is well to walk for a few yards by the side of the Greta Gill, which joins the Piers Gill stream, and thus get a view of the largest waterfall in the district.

Ascent of Scawfell (3162), from Wastdale Head.—Scawfell is easily ascended from Wastdale Head, but most tourists will prefer reaching it from Scawfell Pike. It is only 48 feet lower than its highest neighbour.

From the inn, walk down the valley and cross the river at a foot-bridge close to the lake, then ascend some distance behind a wall by the path leading to Burnmoor Tarn and Boot in Eskdale. When at some small buildings, leave the path, incline to the left, and wind up the long, sloping side of Scawfell. The way to the summit is unmistakable.

From the N. end there is a most extensive panorama, the mountains to the W. being finely grouped. The Yorkshire Hills are seen to the E., and the ranges of High Street, Fairfield, and Helvellyn; also the heights Bow Fell, Crinkle Crags, Wetherlam, Coniston Old Man, and Harter Fell. The sea stretches from a great distance S. of Morecambe Bay, round to the Solway Firth, with the Isle of Man and the Scotch Hills in perspective. Wastwater Lake and Burnmoor Tarn are at the feet of the spectator, with Miterdale, Eskdale, and a large extent of level country. Close at hand are the Screes, Buckbarrow, Seatallan, Middle Fell, and Haycock. The heights surrounding the Mosedale Glen look like a great mountain amphitheatre, and include Yewbarrow, Red Pike, Steeple, Pillar, and Kirk Fell. Over the Pillar is the High Stile range, and beyond, towers Grasmoor and the group of hills surrounding Newlands. Great Gable presents a wild and cone-like appearance. Near to it are Green Gable, Brandreth, and Maiden Moor. Scawfell Pike appears to be within a stone's-throw on the opposite side of Mickledore, and beyond it are High Seat and Wallow Crag, stretching away by the side of Derwentwater, which, from this point of view, is extremely beautiful. Skiddaw and Blencathara present a graceful outline in the distance.

From the cairn near the S. end of the mountain,

Derwentwater is lost to sight, but Devoke Water and Eel Tarn appear.

Ascent of the Pillar Mountain (2927), from Wastdale Head.—The Pillar Mountain, one of the finest heights in the district, is especially famed, as we have stated elsewhere, for the Pillar Rock, standing half-way down the side fronting into Ennerdale Valley.

The mountain is not in the least dangerous, and it is ascended without difficulty; but the rock has been scaled by very few, and it is exceedingly hazardous and foolhardy to attempt it.

On leaving the inn at Wastdale Head, proceed up the Mosedale Glen, with the stream on the left. Take by the side of Kirk Fell, just above the highest wall, and pass through a small gate in a corner. Another wall is observed to run across the head of the valley. Go through this at a gate, then bend to the right, and aim for the top of the depression between Kirk Fell and the Pillar. Walk for some distance, a rill being on the left; then cross it, keeping it on the right until the top of Black Sail Pass is reached. Here a peep is obtained down into Ennerdale. Commence ascending the left-hand ridge. When round a few small rocks, the mountains about Buttermere burst into view, including the High Crag and Grasmoor ranges, also a portion of Skiddaw. Two or three rather steep ascents have to be made before the summit is reached, and during the walk splendid views are had on either hand. The head of Wastwater, Burnmoor Tarn, and the sea are visible on the left, with Black Combe and Birker Moor range of hills; and on the right are wild rocks on the side of the Pillar and immediately at the feet of the traveller. On arriving at the Pillar Cove, a part of the famous Pillar Rock is in sight, and when the loftiest part of the mountain is attained, this rock is observed to stand about half-way down the Ennerdale side, prominent and separate, apparently rising sheer from the valley.

All Ennerdale is spread out to view, with the river Liza winding away to the Ennerdale Lake, which is fully

displayed, and looks charming; the Angling Crag promontory jutting into it, and causing it to take a fine
curve. Loweswater Lake is also beheld to the left of
Red Pike. A large extent of sea is visible from the
Solway Firth to Morecambe Bay, and a broad tract of
level land bordering on the coast. Many lofty heights
meet the eye. From the opposite side of Ennerdale
Glen rise Herdhouse, Red Pike, High Stile, High Crag,
and Hay Stacks; and beyond these are Brandreth,
Fleetwith, Robinson; Grasmoor, and Causey Pike
range; the Scotch hills, Skiddaw, and Blencathara.
To the E. are the long ranges of Helvellyn and Fairfield, and in front the lower heights of High Street,
Ullscarf, Sergeant Man, and Glaramara. At the head
of Ennerdale stand Green Gable and Great Gable, the
latter being very fine; between these and the spectator
is Kirk Fell. The Scawfell range, wild and bulky, includes Great End, Scawfell Pikes, Mickledore Chasm,
Scawfell, and Lingmell. To the right of Great End
rises the summit of Bow Fell. Southwards is a lower
range, including Harter Fell, Birker Moor, and Black
Combe; whilst nearer are the Screes, Yewbarrow, Red
Pike, Seatallan, Steeple, and Haycock.

A short, steep descent, leads to the top of Windy
Gap, the depression between the Pillar and the Steeple,
and from this point the tourist may either drop down to
Wastdale Head or to Ennerdale. A better course is to
ascend the Steeple and walk round the head of Mosedale, or the tops called Black Combe Head, and over
Red Pike and the Chair to Dore Head, whence an easy
descent conducts to Mosedale Glen. This is one of the
best walks that can be taken in the Wastwater district,
and it deserves a day being devoted to it.

Deep glens and lofty mountains are on every hand, a
wide extent of sea greets the eye, and the tourist rejoices
in a healthy breeze. When on the Steeple, which is
easily attained from Windy Gap, wild rocks are seen on
the Ennerdale side. By inclining to the left the tourist
arrives at Red Pike (2629). It is rather inconvenient

that this mountain bears the same name as one of the first heights near Buttermere.

From the summit are seen Grasmoor, Red Pike near Buttermere, Brandreth, Green Gable, Great Gable, Kirk Fell, and the Pillar. A charming view is had into the Mosedale Glen, and beyond are Great End, Scawfell Pikes, Mickledore Chasm, Scawfell, Lingmell, Coniston Old Man, Harter Fell, Birker Moor, Black Combe, Duddon Sands, Eel and Burnmoor tarns, the Screes, Middle Fell, Seatallan, Haycock, Scoat Tarn, and the Sea.

Travelling along the tops, with fine picturesque rocks below on the left, the "Chair" is soon reached, and here a pleasant stone-seat will enable the tourist to sit with comfort and enjoy a beautiful and extensive prospect. Close below are the Low and Scoat tarns. A fine view is obtained of the Wastwater Lake, with the Screes rising sheer and beautiful. Burnmoor Tarn, Eel Tarn, the Duddon Sands, and the Sea, are in sight, as well as most of the heights seen from Red Pike.

A quick descent is made to Dore Head, whence Yew-barrow (2058) may be scaled by a rather formidable-looking cliff. It is not advisable to attempt this without a guide.

A longer and easier ascent of Yewbarrow may be made by taking a slanting direction on the side of the mountain.

Ascent of Great Gable (2949), and Kirk Fell (2631), from Wastdale Head.—Great Gable may be ascended from Wastdale *viâ* the Sty Head Pass. (See page 197.)

A descent may easily be made to the depression between Great Gable and Kirk Fell, and thence into the valley; or the latter height may be scaled, and the Black Sail Pass reached.

Both these mountains can of course also be visited by ascending from Black Sail and returning by Sty Head.

Seatallan (2266) and the Haycock (2619) Mountains, and the Bowderdale and Greendale Tarns.—Few tourists who have walked on the mountain tops round the amphitheatre at the head of Mosedale Glen, commencing at Black Sail and ending at Dore Head, or Yewbarrow (see page 282), will feel disposed to make any further visit to the mountain cluster which stands between the Wastwater and Ennerdale lakes. The views to be obtained from Seatallan and the Haycock are not remarkably striking; they embrace a wide extent of sea and level country, but not much wild rock and mountain scenery. There are three lakelets lying amongst these mountains, Scoat Tarn, Low Tarn, and Greendale Tarn, all containing trout; but they are not particularly interesting sheets of water. From the first and second flow respectively Nether Beck and Over Beck, which enter the Lake at Bowderdale, on the N. side of Middle Fell; and from the third issues Greendale Beck, between Middle Fell and Buckbarrow. The tourist may ascend Yewbarrow, Haycock, and Seatallan, from Bowderdale. The latter mountain may also be scaled from Greendale Tarn, which is the best point whence to ascend Buckbarrow.

Wastdale Head to (Dungeon Gill) Langdale.

Top of Sty Head Pass, 2½m.; Top of Rossett Gill, 5m.; Top of Esk Hause, 4m.; Dungeon Gill, 9m.

Some pedestrians will desire to walk from Wastdale to Langdale, over Scawfell Pike, but if they have not seen the Sty Head and Sprinkling tarns, they ought to take that route and climb Scawfell Pike from Esk Hause, and then return to Esk Hause and resume the journey to Langdale.

From the inn the path may be seen winding up the side of Great Gable to the top of the Sty Head Pass. There are two or three ways leading from the inn to the remotest house up the glen. One leads past the church. The shortest path enters a field at a gate in front of the house next to the inn. After traversing some green smooth ground, the ascent is commenced by a well-defined, rough, stony track. Most of the lake is now in sight, but gradually vanishes behind Lingmell, and the sea appears before arriving at the top of the pass. During the climb Lingmell and Great End are fine objects on the right, and the Scawfell Pikes gradually come into sight between them. On the left are the wild and beautiful cliffs of Great Gable. When about three-fourths of the way up, the latter look remarkably picturesque.

Unfortunately the path is so disagreeably stony that the stranger can give little attention to the scenery during the climb. For this reason it is advisable to ignore the beaten path and mount by a smooth track on the side of the torrent.

From the cairn on the top of the pass (1600) strike to the right, cross a small plot of boggy ground, and enter a path which winds round Great End.

Sty Head Tarn is seen below on the left, and Sprinkling Tarn is reached without error, if the traveller will bear in mind that a streamlet flows from it into the Sty Head Tarn.

At first the streamlet is on the left, then it is crossed and kept on the right until the tarn is reached, where it is again passed over.

The path now runs directly under the majestic cliffs of Great End, and mounts Esk Hause by the side of a red-coloured ravine, the ravine being on the left hand.

Derwentwater, Skiddaw, and Blencathara, are seen in the distance. (See page 193.) Should a *détour* be made to Scawfell Pike, directions also will be found at that page for climbing the mountain and returning to Esk Hause.

When the top of the Hause (2490) is reached, a wide extent of country is seen to the S.E., and a part of Windermere Lake. The Langdale Pikes present a fine appearance.

On the right are the bare rocky heights of Hanging Knott and Bow Fell. A descent is made with the Longstrath Valley on the left and Helvellyn in sight in the distance, and then another slight climb leads to

Angle Tarn. The streamlet is crossed just where it leaves the tarn, and then the path winds to the right and mounts to the top of Rossett Gill (2002). From this point Mickleden Glen and the upper part of Great Langdale Valley are seen directly below. Bow Fell is on the right, and looks remarkably grand and wild.

To one unaccustomed to mountain work, a descent by Rossett Gill appears at first sight impossible. But by taking boldly down the rocky bed of the watercourse all difficulties disappear, and after some rather rough work the valley is reached. A long winding pony-track branches to the right from the top of the pass, and descends amongst the rocks on the side of Bow Fell. The pedestrian will find the watercourse considerably more direct, and only a trifle more rugged. When about a third of the way down the watercourse, some smooth ground appears a few yards to the right. Upon entering the valley the Old Dungeon Gill, and then the New Dungeon Gill hotel, is easily reached. The first is 2m. and the latter 3m. down the valley.

Wastdale Head to Ennerdale Lake, by Windy Gap; and thence to Buttermere, by Floutern Tarn and Scale Force.

Windy Gap, 2½m.; Ennerdale (Anglers' Inn), 10m.; Floutern Tarn, 12m.; Buttermere, 16m.

From the inn at Wastdale Head walk to the head of the Mosedale Glen on either side of the beck.

Near the inn the water forms a pretty cascade, which will repay a visit.

On the right are passed Kirk Fell, Black Sail Pass, and the Pillar Mountain; and on the left Yewbarrow, Dore Head, and Red Pike. In front is part of the Steeple, which on this side is known by the natives as Black Combe Head (locally Blackem Head). Between the Pillar and the Steeple is a slight depression called Windy Gap. The tourist will find it a steep toilsome climb to the top of the pass, and if he has not been on

the summit of the Pillar Mountain he is advised to
ascend by the Black Sail Pass and walk over the above
mountain to this point. (See page 281.)

Having reached Windy Gap, the sea, the Scotch hills,
and Ennerdale Lake come into sight; also the Anglers'
Inn, situated on the shore of the lake, and the farm-
house at Gillerthwaite, in the Ennerdale Glen. A long,
easy descent is made, with the wild perpendicular cliffs
of the Steeple on the left, and on the right, the Pillar
Mountain. When a part of the way down, bend to the
left, cross the rivulet, and aim for Gillerthwaite. The
lake from some points of view is attractive. In another
streamlet on the left will be found some pretty cascades.

The shortest cut to Buttermere is over the hills at the
back of Gillerthwaite, with Red Pike on the right. By
this route a descent may be made to either Scale Force
or Floutern Tarn.

The river Liza, in Ennerdale Valley, may be crossed
in dry weather above the farm-house, but after heavy
rain keep the river on the right, descend the valley to a
plantation, and there cross the stream by a wooden foot-
bridge. The cart-road is then entered just below the
last enclosure of the Gillerthwaite farm. The road runs
for 2m., first by the side of the river, and then above the
shore of the lake, the sea-like cliff of Angling Crag
making the latter take a fine curve. On rounding the
picturesque syenitic cliffs on Bowness Knotts, Herdhouse comes in sight, looking beautiful and lofty. By
bending to the left and passing a house, the tourist
comes again to the lake, and the shore is traversed to
the Anglers' Inn, which is ¾m. distant. The hostelry
may also be gained by continuing along the cart-road at
some distance from the lake. Those who do not desire
to halt, may climb at once by the side of Herdhouse to
Floutern Tarn. To arrive at the tarn from the inn
follow the cart-road in the direction of Herdhouse until
some farm-houses are gained, then incline to the left,
and climb in the direction of a ravine. By keeping
Herdhouse to the right no mistake can be made in

climbing to the summit of the pass, where tourists will have the mountains surrounding the Buttermere Valley in a direct line in front; the lofty mass of Grasmoor being very prominent. On the left is a small knoll, and on the right Floutern Tarn lies at the foot of the dark rocky front of Herdhouse. The water from the tarn flows down the Mosedale Valley, behind Mellbreak, and enters Crummock Lake, near its foot. The course of the stream has to be followed for some distance. It is well to keep it a few hundred yards on the right, until a sheepfold and a gate in some wire fencing are passed. After walking several yards farther incline to the right, and near a second sheepfold pass again over some wire fencing to the streamlet, and continue round the base of the hill on the right. By this means some very wet, swampy ground is escaped. The Low Fell Mountain, seen at the bottom of the Mosedale Valley, on the left, is situated near the Loweswater Lake, and Scale Hill Hotel.

When the head of Crummock Lake appears, some wire fencing has to be passed, and by following the direction of another fence, which leaves it at right angles, Scale Force will be reached. It is situated in a recess on the right. Leaving the fall, follow the course of the stream until within about 600 yards of the lake. Here, at a place where the wall makes a slight bend, pass through a gate and bear to the right. Cross another streamlet and a rough track will lead to the lake, and then by its shore, and by the side of the beck which flows from Buttermere Lake, until a bridge be reached. Cross the bridge, and after passing through two fields, a lane is entered leading to the Fish and Victoria Inns.

Those who desire to walk from Ennerdale to Scale Hill Hotel will find the route described at page 272.

Westdale Head to Ennerdale Lake (Anglers' Inn), by Black Sail Pass. Distance 11m.—The road from Wastdale Head, over the Black Sail Pass to the head of the Ennerdale Valley is given at page 163.

After descending the pass, cross the stream and walk

down the valley with the river Liza on the left hand. The path is in some places as smooth as a carpet, but occasionally it is rough and covered with large loose boulders.

This valley is one of the most wild and desolate in the district. From its head to Gillerthwaite, a distance of 5m., there are no trees or fields, and not a single habitation. Along the whole length of this stern and solemn Alpine glen flows the river Liza, over a stony bed, and on either side are lofty mountains.

The Pillar, especially, presents a dark and irregular front of stupendous and perpendicular rocks, superior to anything of the kind in the neighbourhood, and from no point does this wild mountain look more grand and impressive than when seen during a walk along the valley. The famous Pillar Rock is observed to stand very distinct and separate about half-way up the front of the mountain. The comparatively smooth mountain mass on the right consists of High Crag, High Stile, and Red Pike, which overlook Buttermere and Crummock lakes. After walking a mile or two down the valley, a glorious peep is had of Ennerdale Lake during most of the remaining part of the journey. When the Pillar is passed, the Steeple comes into view on the left, looking very sombre; and between these two mountains is Windy Gap, a route often taken by pedestrians travelling from Ennerdale Lake to Wastdale Head. In the next opening on the left stands the Haycock, and opposite, on the right, an easy ascent will lead to Scale Force and to Buttermere.

After passing Gillerthwaite, which consists of two farm-houses surrounded by a few fields, the whole of the lake becomes fairly displayed.

On the opposite side the Angling Crag looks like a great sea-cliff. The road continues for some distance by the eastern shore, then turns to the right, and after passing some beautiful rocks composed of syenite, and the Herdhouse Mountain, it again touches the lake near the Anglers' Inn.

U

Wastdale Head to Coniston, by Boot, Birker Moor, and Walney Scar.

Boot, 5½m.; Ulpha, 11½m.; Newfield, 14m.; Coniston, 19m.

From the inn at Wastdale Head follow the road within a short distance of the lake. Here cross the brook at a wooden foot-bridge, and walk over what appears like the dry bed of a torrent, to the opposite side of the valley. Then mount the hill by a rough, stony path behind a wall to the top of the depression between Scawfell and the Screes. Burnmoor Tarn now comes into view. It must be passed at the point where the water issues from it. After crossing the streamlet, slightly ascend by a smooth, grass track, leave the gamekeeper's house to the right, and continue in the direction of the brook to the hamlet of Boot. The distance traversed is a bleak, solitary, heath-clad moor. Eskdale, Harter Fell, Birker Moor, and other heights gradually appear. Follow the road in front of the Masons' Arms, at Boot, and when the main road is reached, take to the right down the valley. At the school-house, a few hundred yards distant, enter a road which bends to the left and crosses the river and valley to Dalegarth Hall. Here a guide can be obtained for the Stanley Gill Fall.

The road for Ulpha, after passing Dalegarth Hall, runs through a larch plantation, and mounts the hill, leaving the fall a short distance to the left. When the open fell is gained, a good view is had of Eskdale and surrounding mountains. Hanging Knott, Bow Fell, and Crinkle Crags present a wild appearance. The smooth sides of the Screes and Scawfell are seen, Kirk Fell being situated between them. When first entered, the moor is covered with heather and granitic rocks and boulders. Presently two or three farm-houses are reached, seated in the midst of verdant fields. After passing the first house, follow a car-track which bends to the right, and runs through some fields to another house. Shortly after passing the latter, the road is entered which leaves Eskdale at the King of Prussia Inn, 2m. below Boot. A bleak heath-clad moor is traversed, and during most of the walk lofty heights are visible. On the left, the crags of Harter Fell, and others at the base of that mountain, present pleasing outlines.

When the road begins to descend, hills appear to the S. Some green fields and a few houses are passed on the right, resting at the base of the smooth, sloping hill, called Hesk Fell. The mountains from which the tourist is travelling now gradually disappear, and the Coniston range comes in sight. After passing in the rear of a farm-house, a quick descent is made, and at one place, where the road takes a sharp turn, the Duddon Estuary, and the lower part of the Duddon Vale, present a charming picture. The first house reached in the valley is the Traveller's Rest, at Ulpha, a small, clean inn. After visiting the Ulpha church, a few yards distant (see page 122), the road will be followed which runs up the valley to Newfield.

Rocky hillocks are passed on every hand, and these divide the valley into a number of small vales, each containing a few green fields and houses embowered by trees. Low hills are on either side, and in front is the Coniston range of mountains. The road over Walney Scar can be traced running from a slate-quarry on the side of the hill. On reaching the Newfield Inn, the rocks around are very beautiful. The river flows through a deep ravine at the foot of Wallowbarrow Crag. The inn and church are delightfully situated. The tourist will enter the churchyard, and look at the "Wonderful Robert Walker's" grave. For 1m. beyond Newfield the valley, or rather series of valleys, is charmingly picturesque. At every point are beautiful craggy hills and bosses of finely-coloured rock.

The geologist will be interested in the many evidences of ice action. Almost every rock is smoothed and rounded, and perched stones are numerous.

About ½m. from Newfield a road branches to the left,

and crosses the Seathwaite Beck. Passing this, and continuing in a direct course, a peaceful valley is entered, and high above it, in a deep recess in the Coniston Mountains, lies Seathwaite Tarn, the source of the streamlet which flows at the feet of the traveller. The river Duddon is on the farther side of the valley behind some rocks. At the first house, enter the road which branches to the right and leads up the hill to near the slate-quarry, and thence over Walney Scar. When almost under the slate *débris*, the path divides. Take the left-hand branch, and leave the quarries on the right. The path is well defined, and during the last half entirely free of stones. The valley and neighbouring heights, and the more distant masses of Scawfell, with a long streak of the sea, form a grand prospect. When the summit is gained, the path is steep, and descends by the base of Dow Crags and the Old Man. The whole of Coniston Lake lies spread to view immediately below, and the head of Windermere is seen. The Furness and other fells to the S.E., and portions of the sea, are stretched out before the eye like a map. When a short way down, a peep is had of the wild recess in which rests Goats Water Tarn, at the foot of the Dow Crags. After rounding the base of the Old Man some combes in Wetherlam appear. A cart-track leads from the foot of Walney Scar, close by the base of the Old Man, to the town of Coniston. Before the town reveals itself, a view is had into the glen of Yewdale, which lies directly in front. On leaving the open fell, and passing through a gate, a lane is travelled for a few yards, and then a road is met at right angles. Here incline to the left. A steep descent is made by the side of a rill. Coniston bursts suddenly in sight at the feet of the traveller, and looks fresh and charming. Passing in the rear of the railway station and under an archway, the town is entered.

Wastdale Head to Esk Hause, by Boot and Upper Eskdale.—There is no part of the lake country less known than that situated between the Scawfell and

Bow Fell ranges, and none surpassing the desolate grandeur of the scenery which there meets the eye of the stray visitor.

Proceeding from Wastdale to Boot, and up Eskdale, the road turning to the left, ½m. beyond the Wool-pack, should be followed.

Before leaving the last farm-house, the tourist must take care to be prepared for a long, solitary walk. He will not meet with another building until he has traversed at least 10m. of rough, uneven ground.

Proceeding up the valley, the rocky bed of the river Esk is interesting, the stream tumbling musically amongst large boulders. Bow Fell and Crinkle Crags are directly in front, and the former is remarkably fine. From no other point does its peaked summit present so well-defined and characteristic an appearance. Rocks and huge blocks of stone are passed on every hand, as the traveller wends his way up the glen.

On reaching a picturesque little bridge which spans the stream, just where the latter separates into two streamlets, the *Esk Falls* are observed. The right-hand branch flows from Bow Fell and the Crinkle Crags, and the other from the Scawfell range. The waters in both tumble over numerous ledges of rock, and form dozens of cascades, infinitely varied and pleasing. By some travellers, this spot will in after years be remembered with more pleasure than any other. The rocks and mountains are placed as if to form a perfect picture; and those who are fortunate enough to visit the place are enabled to enjoy the scene in absolute seclusion.

The tourist will, no doubt, be loath to leave without exploring both streamlets. He ought to take the right-hand one first, and then return to the bridge, and track the other. Should he continue along, and not return, he might walk to the foot of Bow Fell, and cross over between that mountain and Crinkle Crags, and descend by Oxendale to Langdale.

After tracing the left-hand streamlet for a few yards, he will discover the *Irwin Force*, a mountain fall of

great beauty. The water, during its fall of about fifty
feet, is divided into two, and tumbles into a pool, in
front of which rises a rock most symmetrically and
infinitely varied, and resembling a group of castles
and church towers. Below are numerous other falls,
whilst above stand some rocks which harmonize with
the scene.

After reluctantly dragging himself away from this
sweet spot, the tourist passes by the side of the ravine,
and many are the subjects for the pencil observed at
every step. Presently fine rocks appear, and in front
rise the Scawfell Pikes and Scawfell, wild and majestic.
Here they are seen to advantage, more so than from
any other point. Attaining a station from which Bow
Fell and Crinkle Crags are also in view, the tourist
gazes on as wild and lonely a scene as the district can
present. He is surrounded by some of the highest
mountains, in their sternest and most rugged aspect.
Continuing a few yards farther, Esk Hause appears in
front, to the right of the Scawfell range. Boggy ground
is passed on the left, apparently the bed of an ancient
lake. During the whole of the walk by the course
of the streamlet, to the top of Esk Hause, the wild,
irregular cliffs of the Scawfell range are close to on the
left. When the top of the pass is gained, a descent
may be made to Wastdale, to Borrowdale, or to Langdale.

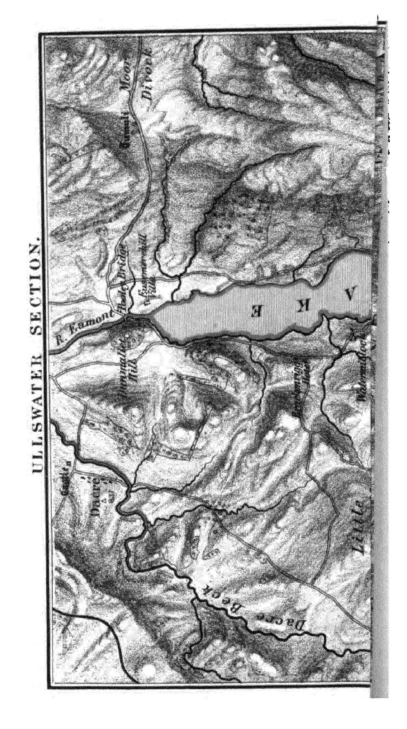

ULLSWATER SECTION.

PATTERDALE.

AT Patterdale are two large hotels—the Ullswater, charmingly situated close to the lake, and the Patterdale Hotel, a few hundred yards from the head of the lake. There is also in the village the White Lion, a small, comfortable house, and some good houses where private lodgings may be obtained.

Patterdale is a telegraph station. Here the tourist will be surrounded by some of the most beautiful scenery in the whole district. He may have boating and fishing on the lake, saunter into wild, secluded glens, or climb lofty, rugged heights. The more this neighbourhood is known, the more it will be appreciated, the scenery on every side being in the highest degree picturesque and beautiful.

Round Ullswater Lake.

Sandwick 4½m.; How Town, 6m.; Pooley Bridge, 10m.; Brackenrigg Hotel, 12m.; Lyulph's Tower, 16½m.; Patterdale, 20m.

This is throughout a most delightful excursion; more especially so from Patterdale to How Town, and from Lyulph's Tower to Patterdale.

There is a good carriage-road from Pooley Bridge to Patterdale, on the N. side of the lake, and also between Pooley Bridge and How Town, on the S. side; but merely a bridle-path between How Town and Patterdale. Those who do not desire to make the circuit of the lake, may travel a part of the journey, and for the remaining distance avail themselves of the steamer which plies between Patterdale and How Town and Pooley.

There are two bridges over the Goldrill Beck, near

the head of the lake. It is desirable to pass over the
one a few yards above the Patterdale Hotel and village.
After crossing the river and valley, a point on the fell-
side is reached where are two paths in opposite directions.   The right-hand one takes the shortest cut to
How Town; it ascends the hill at the back of Place
Fell, and crosses over Boredale Hause into the head of
Boredale Glen, which is a part of Martindale.   The
left-hand path is, however, the one which the tourist
must now take. It ascends a few yards, and goes by
some slate-quarries.   There is a path lower down; but
the higher one is preferable, and commands charming
prospects.   Looking up the valley, a glimpse is caught
of Brothers Water, with the Caudale Moor on the left,
and Dove Crag on the right; the Red Screes and Kirkstone Pass being at the head of the valley.   The whole
of Patterdale lies at the feet of the spectator, beautifully wooded, and with houses picturesquely grouped.
The first reach of the lake is in sight, with two of its
islets; but what adds greatly to the charm of this scene
is the display of the Deepdale, Grisedale, and Glenridding glens, with the heights which separate them.   The
path, which is smooth and covered with short grass,
runs for 1m. along the side of Place Fell, under wild
and exquisitely-coloured rocks.

After passing through a depression between Place
Fell and the projecting knob called Silver Hill, the
second reach of the lake is seen below, and on the other
side Lyulph's Tower, and the Glencoin and Gowbarrow
fells, with Mell Fell in the distance. After walking a
few yards farther, the House Holm islet and the Glencoin Glen appear.   The path now descends to Silver
Bay, and winds along the rocky base of Birk Fell, a few
feet above the shore.

The crags on the right are exceedingly wild and
picturesque.   The second reach becomes fully displayed,
the lower part having finely-wooded and indented
shores, but without overhanging cliffs.   When the
smooth part of the mountain is reached, and Birk Fell

rounded, Hallin Fell stands in front, with the High Street range in its rear. The path now bends from the lake round a plantation, and a rill is crossed, close to a pleasing cascade. On passing a farm-building a glimpse is caught of the lower reach of Ullswater, with Dunmallet, a round hill covered with wood, standing in a prominent position at its foot. On rounding a smooth, verdant hill standing on the right, called Sleet Fell, most of High Street range is in sight, and the small hamlet of Sandwick is gained. The beck is spanned by a bridge close to the hamlet, and a rough foot-path takes round Hallin Fell, along the shore of the lake to How Town. The regular, and in every respect better, road is secured by walking a few yards up the Boredale Beck to a second bridge, on crossing which a gate is entered, and an ascent made with another stream, called How Grane Beck, on the left. On passing a house, and through another gate, a road on the right is observed which leads up the Boredale Glen, and over the hills at the back of Place Fell to Patterdale. At a little bridge pleasantly situated, the How Grane Beck is crossed, and a view is had of the hills which enclose the secluded glens of Martindale. The Nab is very prominent, and also Beda on the right.

The tourist will enjoy a rest for a few minutes on the bridge, until he masters a little of the topography of this out-of-the-way district. If he succeed in having a chat with an intelligent native, he will learn that Martindale is a township in the parish of Barton, and includes the four glens Fusedale, Rampsgill, Bannerdale, and Boredale. The High Street range is on the E., and Place Fell on the W., of the Martindale heights. The Nab hill divides Rampsgill from Bannerdale, and at the lower end of these two glens, where they unite into one glen, it is called the How Grane Vale; the Beda hill is seated between Bannerdale and Boredale. The hamlet of *How Town* is situated at the bottom of Fusedale, and it is entered by ascending from the bridge, and taking round Hallin Fell.

Before descending to How Town, the lower reach of
Ullswater comes into view, looking most charming, with
its shores indented and divided into a number of pretty
bays, clothed with wood.   The hills subside into a level
country, but Dunmallet adds greatly to the prospect.
How Town, seen at the feet of the spectator, is a
pleasant resting-place.   The How Town Hotel is clean
and comfortable.   Boats can be had for a row on the
lake, which yields some good trout and perch fishing.
The charges for boats are 1s. for the first hour, and 6d.
for every succeeding hour.   Boat and boatman for
fishing, 5s. per day.   The post arrives daily at 9.30 A.M.,
and leaves at 1.30 P.M., and the steamer calls regularly.
Behind the hotel are the Steel Knotts, and to the E.
Swarth Fell, the beginning of the High Street range.
A good car-road leads to Pooley Bridge, situated at the
foot of the lake, but it runs at some distance from
the shore, and the surrounding scenery is comparatively
flat and unattractive.

Pooley Bridge contains two small inns, the Sun and
the Crown.   It is distant from Penrith 5m., Lowther
Castle 5m., and Dacre Castle 2m.   It is often made the
starting-point for a visit to Haweswater Lake.   Euse-
mere Villa, which stands some hundred yards distant,
on the shore of the lake, was formerly the summer
residence of the celebrated Thomas Clarkson, who took
an active part in the agitation for the abolition of negro
slavery.

On crossing the bridge over the Eamont, the road
skirts the margin of the lake at the foot of Dunmallet,
and after passing the point where passengers are landed
from the steamer, a good-sized hotel is reached, called
the Brackenrigg Hotel, standing on a slight eminence
by the roadside, 2m. from Pooley Bridge.   A part of
Helvellyn now comes in sight, and across the lake Place
Fell and the Martindale heights look very fine.   For the
next 2m. the road is at some distance from the lake.

After passing the straggling village of Watermillock,
the shore is regained at Hallsteads, the occasional

residence of Mr. Marshall, of Patterdale Hall; the scenery at this point, and during most of the remainder of the journey, is exceedingly beautiful.

The middle reach of the lake is now in view, with the heights of Hallin Fell, Birk Fell, and Place Fell on the opposite side. At the head stand the bulky mass of Helvellyn and the peaked summit of Catchedecam, with Stybarrow Crag, Glencoin Glen, and the Glencoin and Glenridding fells nearer the lake. At a gate which crosses the road the Gowbarrow Park is entered; and here the tourist will be disappointed if he expect to find large old trees and a green tract of park-land. The rocky fell stretches down almost to the level of the lake, and contains only a small quantity of timber. The park is well stocked with deer, and close in the rear of Lyulph's Tower is Aira Force (see p. 30). In speaking of Gowbarrow Park, Wordsworth says: "Here are beds of luxuriant fern, aged hawthorns, and hollies decked with honeysuckles, and fallow deer bounding over the lawns and through the thickets; these are the attractions of the retired views, and constitute a foreground for the ever-varying pictures of the lake." On crossing the Aira stream and leaving the park, a road on the right conducts to Troutbeck railway station and to Keswick. The highest and most beautiful reach of the lake is now displayed to the view, and the road continues close to its shore. On passing over the Glencoin beck, which divides Cumberland from Westmorland, a prospect is gained which embraces both the first and second reaches, and many pleasing vistas are had through the openings in the trees before Ullswater Hotel is reached. The Glenridding Beck flows close to the hotel, and the water is discoloured by the lead-washings at the Greenside mines.

The Patterdale Hotel and village are situated 1m. farther up the valley, and the road passes close by the Patterdale Hall and church.

Glencoin Glen.—This glen is the most northern offshoot from Patterdale Valley. To reach it the Keswick road must be followed for 1½m. beyond the Ullswater

Hotel.   At the point where Glencoin Beck enters the
lake go through a field to a farm-house, and ascend in
the rear of the house to some cottages.   A fine view
is had of the whole of the middle reach of Ullswater,
with Birk Fell rising sheer and bare out of the water
on the right, and on the left and in the distance beautifully-wooded bays.   When at the cottages, a large
mound is seen to run across the valley and divide the
glen into two parts, an upper and a lower.   This mound
is ascended by following a winding track by the side of
a wall.   When under Black Crag, the wall is passed
through at a gate.   Most of the lower reach of the lake
now comes in sight, and Cross Fell chain of hills beyond.
When the upper part of the glen is reached, it is found
to be a very secluded and picturesque little place, with
an amphitheatre of low, bare hills, and to command a
charming prospect.   By following the track which winds
to the left and rounds the hill, the Glenridding Glen and
Greenside mines may be visited.   The whole journey is
about 6m.

Perhaps the best plan is to go by the Greenside mines
and return by Glencoin.

Deepdale Glen.—Deepdale is wild and beautiful,
especially at the head of the glen, and will repay exploring.

Starting from the Patterdale village, walk nearly 1m.
up the valley, and enter a rough cart-road by the side of
the Deepdale Beck.   The farmsteads and trees are soon
left behind, and the tourist finds himself in a pleasant,
secluded glen, with the high end hid by a projecting
part of St. Sunday Crag.   A green path runs along the
side of the right-hand fell, with the Deepdale Beck a
few yards below on the left.   On looking back, a good
view is had of Place Fell and the hill down the side of
which trickles a rill having its source in Angle Tarn.
A long, low ridge on the left hides Dovedale.   St. Sunday Crag is on the right, and at the head of the valley
are the wild, vertical cliffs of Fairfield.   From no other
point does Fairfield present a more rugged appearance.

The depression between Fairfield and St. Sunday Crag bears the name of Deepdale Hause. It is the route often taken by the natives when going to Grasmere by Grisedale Tarn, and the tourist might ascend it, and then either descend into, and return by, Grisedale Glen, or ascend Fairfield or St. Sunday Crag.

The upper part of Deepdale is bare of trees, and thickly strewn with large stones, some of which rest upon smooth terminal moraine heaps—mute evidences of a glacial era. It is a place well adapted for a quiet stroll on a summer's afternoon.

Dovedale Glen, and Ascent of Dove Crag (2500).— Dovedale is one of the many beautiful glens branching to the W. from the Patterdale Valley.

It is little visited, though it is full of wild beauty, and will afford much delight to those who ramble up it, and stroll amongst its rocks and torrents.

It is reached by a cart-road which runs to Hartsop Hall, on the W. side of Brothers Water. A carriage may be taken as far as the Hall. The lower part of the valley is called Hartsop Park, and here the tourist sees the Kirkstone Pass road, and to the left of it, Low Hartsop Dodd and Caudale Fell; and to the right, Kelsey Chimney, Red Screes, Caiston Glen, and High Hartsop Dodd. Directly in front is a fine, rugged mountain-wall, of which Dove Crag forms part. An old lead-mine is passed on the right, and some distance farther up the valley the Dovedale Beck is crossed at a foot-bridge. Below Dove Crag stand three knobs, called the "Stangs," which hide the upper part of the glen. Having crossed the bridge, ascend, with the beck and a pretty cascade on the right. When a short distance up, go through an opening in a wall, and then pass through a gate in some wire fencing. Follow in the direction of the fencing and the torrent, and presently Dove Crag stands nobly in front. This is Dovedale proper, as secluded and rocky a glen as could be wished. A rough scramble to the right, past an old slate-quarry, or to the left, will land the traveller at the cairn on the top of

Dove Crag, where an extensive and beautiful prospect is obtained. To the S. are a large extent of the sea, Blelham Tarn, Coniston and Esthwaite lakes, and the whole length of Windermere, with its islands most charmingly displayed. Strips of Ullswater and Brothers Water are to the N.E., and mountain tops on every hand. If it be not intended to visit Fairfield or Deepdale, an easy descent may be made by striking due E. to the hollow at the foot of Red Screes. After rounding Hart Crag, which stands at the head of the Scandale Valley, take down Glaiston Glen to Brothers Water, and thence to Patterdale.

Ascent of Place Fell (2154), from Patterdale.— Cross over the bridge which spans the river, a few yards above the village. When the open fell-side is reached, follow the right-hand path. It mounts to Boredale Hause, the lowest part of the S. end of the mountain, and commands charming views of Brothers Water and the head of Ullswater; the Patterdale Valley, with the glens Deepdale, Grisedale, and Glenridding; and the heights from Kirkstone to Glencoin, including Caudale Moor, Red Screes, Fairfield, St. Sunday Crag, and Helvellyn.

When on the top of Boredale Hause, incline to the left, and by continuing a gradual ascent, the summit is reached without the possibility of losing one's way. On the E. the Martindale Fells come into view, and the perpendicular cliffs of Helvellyn are seen from end to end.

Standing at the cairn on the highest point, the tourist beholds on the N., Blencathara; on the W., the Helvellyn range, including Catchedecam, and Dolly Waggon Pike; in front of which are the Striding and Swirrel Edges, and the glens Glencoin, Glenridding, and Grisedale. Between the latter and Kirkstone Pass are St. Sunday Crag, Fairfield, Deepdale Glen, High Hartsop Dodd, Dove Crag, and Red Screes. On the E. side of Kirkstone are Caudale Moor, Low Hartsop Dodd, Ill Bell, Froswick, High Street, and the Martindale Fells. Patterdale Valley and Brothers Water are immediately

below, and in the distance Skiddaw, Carrock Fell, Great
and Little Mell Fell, Dunmallet, Hallin Fell, the higher
and lower reaches of Ullswater, and just a strip of the
middle reach.

A pleasant variation in the return route may be made
by descending on the E. side of the mountain into Boredale, and then pursuing the path from Sandwick round
Birk Fell, and by the shore of the lake.

Ascent of Fairfield (2863) and St. Sunday Crag (2756), from Patterdale.

Distance, 9m.   Time, 4 hours.

Fairfield is usually reached from either Ambleside or
Grasmere.   The ascent may, however, be made in many
ways from Patterdale, and much wild and interesting
scenery passed in the different routes.   The other height
—St. Sunday Crag—may justly be claimed as belonging
specially to the Patterdale district, and can be visited
on the return journey from Fairfield.   The easiest route,
and one quite practicable for ponies, is up the Grisedale
Glen, and past the tarn to the top of the pass, from
which point the wall is followed up the side of Fairfield.
Another ascent is from the head of Deepdale, by Deepdale Hause, and has been described in the account of a
walk up that glen.   A third mode is referred to in the
account of a visit to the glen of Dovedale.

Good pedestrians will prefer the round described
below, and they will not have much fear of the exertion
when they learn that the writer was accompanied during
the round by Mr. Walton, the Master of the Patterdale
Hounds, who is sixty-six years of age.

Fine views are had into the wild glens of Dovedale,
Deepdale, and Grisedale, and of the precipitous sides of
Dove Crag, Fairfield, and Helvellyn.

The tourist must walk from the Patterdale village
along the main road until the Deepdale Beck is crossed.
Then let him go through the first gate on the right, and
commence ascending amongst some scraggy trees.   On

emerging from the trees, the ascent for some distance is along a smooth, grassy slope, with a wall on the right hand. On the left are Brothers Water and the Kirkstone Pass, with a grand group of hills, including Low Hartsop Dodd, Caudale Moor, Gray Crag, and High Street. A retrospective view embraces the Patterdale Valley, with Place Fell on the opposite side, and a strip of Ullswater. On the right are St. Sunday Crag and Fairfield rising nobly at the head of Deepdale. On passing through an opening in a wall, a small rough crag has to be scaled, and then appear on the left High Hartsop Dodd and the Red Screes. On gaining the top of the rocks, on which is fixed a staff, Dovedale is seen on the left, and on the right Deepdale, with a grand amphitheatre stretching from Red Screes to St. Sunday Crag, the Dove Crag and the front of Fairfield being especially wild. Some uneven, hillocky ground has now to be crossed, and the S. end of Helvellyn range gradually appears over the Deepdale Hause, the hollow between Fairfield and St. Sunday Crag. The upper parts of the Dovedale and Deepdale glens are immediately below and fully revealed. In front, connected with the ridge upon which the tourist is travelling, stands a rocky height on this side, called Greenhow End, and on the S. side Rydal Head. Take round to the left of this. When on the summit-level, an extensive view is had to the S., and the lakes Windermere, Esthwaite, and Coniston are spread to view. Incline to the right, pass over Rydal Head, and descend to the hollow called the "Step." Another climb leads to the top of Fairfield, the view from which is described at page 45.

The ridge between Fairfield and St. Sunday Crag is in places very narrow, but not dangerous to one accustomed to mountain work. Those, however, who wish to avoid it can reach St. Sunday Crag by walking a few yards below the top of the ridge.

The small rocky height between Fairfield and St. Sunday Crag is called "Cofa Pike," and it commands one of the best prospects it is possible to obtain, the crags of Fairfield and those of Helvellyn being finely displayed. During the remainder of the gradual ascent of St. Sunday Crag the traveller is favoured with beautiful views on either hand. Perhaps from no point do Helvellyn and Fairfield look more imposing. Those who have only seen Fairfield from Ambleside or Grasmere, and Helvellyn on its W. side, will now be astonished at their wild, rugged character.

On reaching the summit of St. Sunday Crag, a charming prospect is had of the upper reach of Ullswater, with its three tiny islets and banks clothed with wood. Perhaps from no other mountain does this lake present a lovelier aspect. The heights seen to the E. and S. are Mell Fell, Birk Fell, Place Fell, Dunmallet, Cross Fell, High Street, Martindale Fells, Gray Crag, Low Hartsop Dodd, Caudale Moor, Ill Bell, Red Screes, Dove Crag, Rydal Head, and Fairfield, with Angle Tarn and Deepdale Glen. To the W. are Seat Sandal, Silver Howe, Sergeant Man, High Raise, Langdale Pikes, Pavey Ark, Pike O'Blisco, Crinkle Crags, Bow Fell, Hanging Knott, Scawfell Pikes, Great End, part of Great Gable, Pillar, Helvellyn, Striding Edge, Catchedecam, and part of Blencathara.

In descending, make for the first hollow, with a peaked part of St. Sunday Crag, called Gavel Pike, on the right, and then incline to the left, and Patterdale is quickly reached.

Ascent of Helvellyn (3118), from Patterdale.—Helvellyn is the principal mountain which is ascended from Patterdale. The easiest course, and the one generally taken with ponies, is up the Glenridding Valley, and back by the same route. The journey would be far more interesting if it were slightly lengthened by continuing along the top of the mountain from one end to the other, and descending by Grisedale Tarn and Grisedale Valley. A better plan still is to ascend by Grisedale and return by Glenridding. The whole journey thus extended is 12m., and will occupy five hours. Pedestrians generally

x

make for Red Tarn and then up Swirrel Edge.   Some
steady mountaineers ascend by Striding Edge.

Helvellyn is also ascended from Grasmere, Wythburn,
and Keswick, but the route from Patterdale is as interesting as any, and may, perhaps, be considered the
best.   It also requires as little exertion as any other.

Those who decide on the Glenridding route must
follow the cart-road which enters the main road at right
angles, at the back of the Ullswater Hotel.   After passing some cottages and through a gate, turn to the right.
Another ½m. leads to the Greenside Lead Mines.   On
the right are the Glenridding Dodd and Glenridding
Screes, fine bold rocks ; and on the left, rising from the
Glenridding Beck, are Hall Bank, beautifully wooded,
and Little Cove and Blea Cove, connected at the back
with the Helvellyn Mountain by the Striding Edge,
which is out of sight.   Some pedestrians will take to the
left at the gate just passed through, cross the beck,
ascend the Blea Cove height, and continue on the tops
and along Striding Edge; or descend to Red Tarn and
take up Swirrel Edge.   Others will cross the beck
and walk at the base of Blea Cove to the Greenside
Mines, and there join again the pony-track.   By making
this slight *détour* good views are obtained of the Lucy
Tongue Gill, in which the mines are situated.   The
Greenside Mines are worth a separate visit.   They are
nearly as large as any similar works in the country.
The metal is richly mingled with silver.   The visitor can
inspect the process of ore-crushing, washing, and smelt-
ing, and also the plan adopted for extracting the silver.
Near the buildings a lovely view is had of the higher
reach of the lake, with Place Fell rising on the opposite
side, and High Street in the distance.   A few yards past
the works, pedestrians who wish to ascend by Swirrel
Edge ought to cross the stream at a foot-bridge, and
make for the rivulet which flows from Red Tarn.

Beyond the mine the pony-track continues up the glen,
at the base of a low mountain ridge, with the stream on
the left.   Catchedecam rears its bold peaked summit, and

right at the head of the glen stands Helvellyn Low Man. When past the point where the stream from Red Tarn and that from Keppelcove Tarn join, at the E. end of Catchedecam, the pony-track branches to the right.

Pedestrians may go straight forward, and when a few yards past Keppelcove Tarn a steep ascent, with an inclination to the right, will enable the top of the depression between Helvellyn Low Man and Whiteside to be attained; and the regular path again entered.

Sometimes tourists who want to make this ascent, err by walking too far beyond the tarn, and attempt to climb up a steep part of the mountain on the left of the Low Man, at the very head of the glen. The writer has known tourists who have had to return after getting half-way up.

When the pony-track has made the above-mentioned turn it winds up the hill on the right. Whiteside soon appears in front, and the summit of Helvellyn comes into view with Swirrel Edge branching from it, and forming a junction with Catchedecam. The Keppelcove Tarn, which gradually reveals itself beneath, is very diminutive. It acts as a reservoir for the mines, and scarcely merits the name of tarn. Often in droughty seasons it is for some weeks nearly dry. The head of the glen is, however, wild and secluded. After the first steep ascent strips of the upper and lower reaches of Ullswater come into sight, and also Place Fell, and the whole length of High Street. St. Sunday Crag peers over the left of Catchedecam.

On completing the worst part of the ascent, and obtaining a westward prospect, Grisedale Pike, Grasmoor, Robinson, Red Pike, and a number of other heights are observed.

Rounding to the left, and attaining the top of Whiteside, the tourist, forgetting the toil, will begin to experience the invigorating and elevating effect of mountain air and prospect. Thirlmere Lake is beautifully displayed immediately at the feet of the spectator, and Bassenthwaite lies to the N., with Skiddaw rising from its eastern shore. To the right of Skiddaw is its companion, the ridgy-fronted Blencathara.

After descending a few feet a steep narrow ridge leads to the top of Helvellyn Low Man, where are seen the six lakes, Bassenthwaite, Thirlmere, Ullswater, Coniston, Esthwaite, and Windermere.

At a point some distance on the right down the mountain, more or less of each of these six lakes, and also a small strip of a seventh, Grasmere, may be seen.

Descending a few feet from the Low Man, and continuing along, with the precipice on the left, the summit is attained; the view from which is described at page 96.

Ascent of Helvellyn from Patterdale, by Swirrel Edge.

Distance to the top, 4m.   Time required for the ascent, 2 hours.

Ponies cannot go farther than Red Tarn by this route. If the Patterdale village or the Patterdale Hotel be the starting-point, the same route can be taken to Red Tarn as that described in the ascent by Striding Edge.

From the Ullswater Hotel proceed up the Glenridding Valley. After passing a few farm-houses and through a gate, the road branches.

The best views of the Glenridding Screes and the picturesque buildings at the Greenside Lead Mines are obtained by following the left-hand road. It passes over the Glenridding Beck, bends to the right at a point a few yards below the highest house, and goes through a gate leading on the side of the fell just above the highest wall. Proceed up the valley, keep the wall on the right, and avoid crossing the stream. On passing the Greenside Mines the peaked summit of Catchedecam appears in front, and at the head of the glen stands Helvellyn Low Man. Mount the fell on the left in a slanting direction, making for the eastern end of Catchedecam. The torrent which empties itself into the main stream on the right issues from Red Tarn, and, therefore, no mistake can be made if its course be pursued. The tarn, when discovered, is found to rest at the base of a grand amphitheatre of rocks, consisting of Catchedecam and Swirrel Edge on the right, the principal cliffs of Helvellyn in front, and on the left Striding Edge. It is a large sheet of water, and is higher above the sea than any other tarn in the Lake Country, and it contains fine trout. The situation is most wild and secluded. Another steep climb of 762 feet leads to the summit of the mountain; Helvellyn being 3118 and the tarn 2356 feet above the sea. The path will be seen running up the side of Catchedecam and along Swirrel Edge, a few feet below the top of the ridge.

Ascent of Helvellyn from Patterdale, by Striding Edge.

Distance to the top, 4m.   Time required for the ascent, 2 hours.

Ponies cannot go farther than Red Tarn.

Some tourists who start from the Ullswater Hotel will walk up the Glenridding Valley and reach Red Tarn by following the route described in the ascent by Swirrel Edge; or, after crossing the Glenridding Beck, they will ascend the hill at the back of the cottage, and keep on the summit of the ridge.

From Patterdale Hotel and village pass the Church and the Hall, then enter the Grisedale Glen, and cross the beck at the first stone bridge. Go up a field by the side of wire fencing, then through a gate at the corner of a plantation, and follow the track on the left which zigzags up the hill. When the top of the long ridge is attained, pass through a gate in a wall which has been in sight during most part of the ascent, and presently you will stand on the eastern end of the far-famed Striding Edge. On the left is the Grisedale Glen, with St. Sunday Crag and Fairfield on its opposite side, and wild rocks and hollows at its head. Looking to the right, Red Tarn is seen at the foot of the perpendicular front of Helvellyn, and from its northern shore rises Catchedecam, which is joined to Helvellyn by the narrow ridge called Swirrel Edge. The top of Striding Edge is in some places extremely narrow, and visitors generally consider a walk along its ridge to be as dangerous as any bit of mountain work in the district. The fate of Charles Gough (see page 93) must have given rise to this opinion, for there is really no danger to be apprehended by those who have a steady head, and accomplish the walk in fine weather. It must be remembered that when Gough's fatal accident occurred the mountains were covered with snow and ice.

After leaving the ridge, a few yards of steep, rough rock have to be scaled, and then the cairn on the summit of Helvellyn is reached by walking a short distance to the right.

Patterdale to Grasmere by Grisedale Pass.—The distance from the Ullswater Hotel, Patterdale, to the Prince of Wales Hotel, Grasmere, is 8m. A pony can be taken the whole journey.

Leaving either the Ullswater or the Patterdale Hotel, make for the bridge crossing the Grisedale Beck in front of Patterdale Hall. A few yards beyond, turn to the right, and after passing through a wood, with the stream flowing below, the valley is entered. A short distance farther another bridge is seen leading over the rivulet to a farm-house, and some tourists will there cross the valley and follow a path on the other side. The course generally pursued is to continue up the valley, with the stream on the right, for some distance past the highest farm-house. On the right is the Grisedale Fell, which is joined to Helvellyn by Striding Edge, and on the left the fine vertical cliffs of St. Sunday Crag.

Right in front, Helvellyn and Dolly Waggon Pike present a wild and sombre-looking mass of rocks and precipices, rising from the dark, solitary hollows of Nethermost, Ruthwaite, and Cock coves. A low, projecting knob descends from St. Sunday Crag, and runs half-way across the glen. At the base of this ridge cross the stream at a wooden bridge. From this point the head of the glen looks very stern and desolate.

The path leads past a miner's old hut, through a wall at a gate, and below a lead-mine, which is now closed. The stream on the left breaks into a series of cascades. On the right are the Eagle Crags, beautiful and wild, separating the Nethermost and Ruthwaite coves.

A small building is now passed which was erected by Mr. Marshall, of Patterdale Hall, and which is occasionally used by his guests, when they ascend the mountains.

The path is in some places steep and rough, and near the summit of the pass the Tarn Crag on the right overhangs, dark and frowning.

Grisedale Tarn lies very lonely at the feet of Seat Sandal, Fairfield, and Dolly Waggon Pike.

The stream is crossed at the point where it leaves the tarn, and then the track follows the shore and ascends to a wall, through a gap in which the tourist passes.

Grasmere and Coniston lakes now come into view, and gradually appear the Coniston and Langdale mountains, and a number of heights to the S. and S.W.

After descending a few yards bear to the right, and pass over some rocks by the side of Seat Sandal; then follow the course of a rill, which presently joins the Tongue Gill stream, which has its source near the Grisedale Pass. The path continues at some distance above the ravine, in which is situated the Tongue Gill Fall, and enters the main road 1m. from Grasmere.

Patterdale to Keswick, by Styx, or Sticks Pass.

Top of Pass, 4m.; Legberthwaite, 6m.; Keswick, 11m.

This is the most direct route from Patterdale to Keswick, and must be travelled with pony or on foot. Near to the Ullswater Hotel take the road leading up the Glenridding Valley, with the stream on the left which comes from Keppelcove and Red tarns. About 1m. from the hotel the works connected with the lead-mine are passed. At the last building, commence climbing the hill on the right, and make for the base of the left-hand rock, overhanging the ravine in which the mines are located. After passing under the rock, cross the valley above the ravine, and by keeping the reservoir to the left a path will be entered, running due W. to the top of the pass. During the first part of the descent on the other side of the mountain, a streamlet is seen in a hollow on the left, whence the path inclines to the N.W., and rounds the shoulder of the mountain, until a sheepfold is reached. During the remainder of the descent the path is steep, with a stream on the right.

After passing a farm-house, the tourist enters the coach-road between Ambleside and Keswick.

Patterdale to How Town, by Boredale Hause and Boredale Glen.

With pony, or on foot. Distance, 5m.

Cross the river Goldrill at the bridge, a few yards above the Patterdale village. On entering the open ground at the base of Place Fell, take the right-hand path. It winds up the hill, and commands a charming view of the vale, Brothers Water, and the head of Ullswater; the Glenridding, Grisedale, and Deepdale glens, and the heights which separate them. After traversing a few hundred yards of table-land over the low southern part of Place Fell, the whole of the secluded and peaceful-looking glen of Boredale is seen below.

Smooth, green hills are on every side of it. At the bottom of the glen is Hallin Fell, with a large cairn on the top. On the left is Place Fell, and on the right the height called Beda. A small stream winds through walled enclosures, and by two or three farmsteads, to the hamlet of Sandwick, and then flows into Ullswater Lake.

The path to be followed may plainly be traced at the foot of Place Fell. When about half-way down the glen, the road crosses the beck and takes over the end of the

right-hand hill, allowing a glimpse of the middle reach
of Ullswater. It then descends, and where a peep is
had of the Rampsgill Glen, crosses the bridge spanning
the How Grane Beck, and mounts a height from whence
is seen the lower reach of Ullswater. The How Town
Hotel and hamlet rest in a quiet nook immediately
below.

**Patterdale to Mardale Green (Haweswater), by
Hayeswater Tarn, High Street, and Kidsty Pike,
8m.**—This is the way usually taken by tourists on horseback. Those on foot may save 1m. by following the
path which goes past Angle Tarn. Another interesting
route is up the glen of Thrasthwaite Mouth.

Take the main road from Patterdale to Hartsop Pass
through the latter village, and enter a track leading up
the glen, with the Hayeswater Gill streamlet below on
the right.

Some lead-mines are seen standing at the entrance to
Thrasthwaite Mouth; and the view up that wild, rocky
glen is extremely picturesque. Cross the streamlet over
some flat stones, pass two farm-buildings, and continue
along a gradually ascending path which rounds the end
of Gray Crag height, and again approaches close to the
torrent. The water tumbles along a rugged, stony bed,
and forms a number of pretty cascades. Hayeswater is
soon reached. It is oblong in shape, and is one of the
longest tarns in the district. It is well stocked with
trout, and lies in a secluded situation, in a hollow
between High Street and Gray Crag. The pedestrian
may continue by the shore of the tarn, and climb High
Street by following the course of the rivulet.

Cross the streamlet 200 yards below the tarn, and pass
through a gate. Mount the hill by a winding path until
a wall is reached, which is observed to run up from the
tarn. A gate is passed through at the point where the
wall from the tarn joins another wall at right angles.

Avoid ascending a small round elevation on the right.
The summit of a part of High Street is quickly attained,
and here the tourist has a choice of routes. He can

follow the wall over the highest part of High Street, and descend by the Nan Bield Pass (see pages 315 and 320). If on foot, he may keep by the side of the wall for a few yards until a small gate is reached; then a steep descent can be made into the Riggindale Glen, at the foot of Kidsty Pike. The regular pony-track runs due E., with Riggindale on the right, and passes over Kidsty Pike, or rather a few yards in the rear of that mountain. On crossing High Street, a splendid prospect is unfolded, Ullswater Lake and the Martindale Fells being very beautiful, and quite a contrast to the savage-looking cliffs of Fairfield and Helvellyn.

After leaving Kidsty Pike, a pile of stones on the right indicates the point where a winding track is entered, which descends steeply and passes a sheepfold. A short distance beyond a farm-house, the road is entered near to the interesting little church.

The Dun Bull Inn is the highest house in the valley.

Patterdale to Mardale Green (Haweswater), by Angle Tarn, High Street, and Kidsty Pike, 7m.— Take over the Goldrill Beck at the bridge, a few yards above the Patterdale village, and cross the valley to a farm-house. Here follow the right-hand track which leads up the hill to the Boredale Hause depression, at the S. end of Place Fell, and then descends into Boredale Glen. All the way up beautiful views are had of the Patterdale Valley, Brothers Water, and the head of Ullswater. Also of the glens and mountains on the W. side of the valley, and the Kirkstone Pass, Red Screes, and Caudale Moor.

A few yards before the top of the Hause is reached, branch off to the right, pass a sheepcot, and continue for a short space at the back of a low hill, which hides Patterdale.

Where Brothers Water again appears, follow a track which passes close under the highest crag on the left. Presently Angle Tarn is reached, and the High Street range is seen beyond. Angle Tarn is irregular in shape, and is studded with one or two islets covered with heather. It lies in a solitary recess of the hills, but is without much beauty. It contains trout.

Leave the tarn on the right, and continue round the E. side, without descending close to the shore. A wall will be observed running from the S. end of the tarn. Its course may be followed, but it is well to leave it at some distance on the right, and after getting a view into Bannerdale on the left, meet it again higher up the hill, at the point where there is a small gate. When through the gate, continue along the wall, with the Martindale Glens on the left, and Hayeswater on the right. When the wall ends, and some wire fencing commences, the whole of Hayeswater is in sight, and a wall is observed to run from it, up the hill on the left, and to join another wall at right angles. At the junction is a gate, and this is the point for which the tourist must aim. The best course is to follow the wire fencing, and when it branches to the right, where the stone wall again commences, follow its course and avoid climbing Rest Dod, the round hill on the left. After crossing a plot of wet, boggy ground, and some wooden railing, a steep climb lands the tourist at the junction, previously mentioned, of the walls on the side of the hill directly in front.

For a description of the remainder of the journey, see previous page.

Patterdale to Mardale Green (Haweswater), by Thrasthwaite Mouth Glen, High Street, Nan Bield Pass, and Small Water Tarn, 10m.—Thrasthwaite Mouth Glen is parallel with, and to the E. of, the Kirkstone Pass. On its W. side is Low Hartsop Dodd and Caudale Moor, and on the E. Gray Crag. The depression on the head of it, called Thornthwaite Hause, leads into the vale of Troutbeck. The glen is reached by following the main road from Patterdale to Hartsop, and then entering the track which leads to Hayeswater Tarn.

Some works connected with a lead-mine stand at the entrance to the glen, and the tourist must get to the rear of these, and then follow the course of the stream which bears the name of Pasture Beck. The glen, when

first entered, has a severe and almost threatening aspect.
The fine wild rocks of Grey Crag are on the left, and
Raven Crag on the right, and large boulders are strewn
in every part. It is bare of trees and without a habitation. When about half-way up the glen, the rivulet
tumbles down a deep, rocky cleft, and forms a series of
small cascades. A short ascent is made, and then the
tourist reaches a wild, secluded cove, at the head of the
glen, enclosed by a rocky amphitheatre. Directly in
front is the Thornthwaite Hause Gap.

A steep climb leads to the top of this, and a view is
had down into the upper branches of the vale of Troutbeck, with Troutbeck Tongue between them. Windermere is in view, and looks most charming, all its bays
and islands being displayed to great advantage. On
looking back, Patterdale and the highest reach of Ullswater are in sight. By following the direction of the
wall to the left, a steep climb leads to the large cairn on
the top of Thornthwaite Crag.

From this point a good view is had of Helvellyn,
Fairfield, and other heights on the W. of Patterdale,
and during the remainder of the walk on the summit-
level, a fine prospect is had to the S., a large tract of
sea being visible in the distance. From the cairn follow
the wall, and then the wire fencing, until the wall is
reached, which runs along the summit of High Street.
Here take a S.E. direction. The upper part of Kentmere Vale is on the right, with Ill Bell and Froswick
rising sheer and wild from the hollow in which lies the
Kentmere Reservoir.

In a deep recess on the left will be seen Blea Water
Tarn. Continuing along the S.E. shoulder of High
Street, in the direction of Harter Fell, a slight descent
leads to the summit of the Nan Bield Pass, resting at
the foot of which is observed the beautiful and secluded
Small Water Tarn.

On reaching the shore of this lakelet, the course of
the rivulet must be followed to the Dun Bull Inn, the
highest house in the valley. See page 320.

Patterdale to Haweswater, by Pooley Bridge and Lowther Castle.

Pooley Bridge, 10m. ; Lowther Castle, 15m.; Bampton Grange, 19m. ; Mardale Green (Haweswater), 25m.

Persons staying at Patterdale, who object to an excursion over the hills, will sometimes drive to Haweswater by this route.

The road traverses the whole length of the N. shore of Ullswater. On leaving Pooley Bridge there is nothing of interest until the village of Askham is reached, ½m. from which is Lowther Castle. See page 241.

After visiting the Castle, 6m. of ordinary ground has to be gone over before a view is had of Haweswater. During the last 3m. of the journey to Mardale Green, the road skirts the western shore of the lake, and commands excellent views.

The journey between Patterdale and Pooley Bridge might be accomplished by steamer, and a carriage hired at the latter village.

ᐟ It it be not desired to visit Lowther Castle, 3m. may be saved by taking a rough road, which is practicable for a carriage, over Moor Divock, from Pooley Bridge to Bampton. The road gradually ascends to the top of the moor, and commands most beautiful views of the two reaches of Ullswater and the neighbouring mountains, Helvellyn filling up the background. When at the top of the moor the traveller will observe a small mound where stone coffins were found, also a tiny circle of stones, which some persons consider to be Druidical. A large solitary stone, standing at the point where the descent is commenced, is said to turn round when it hears a cock crow in the adjoining valley. The main road from Penrith to Haweswater is joined 2m. from Bampton.

Mardale Green (Haweswater) to Patterdale, by Kidsty Pike and Hayeswater Tarn.—This journey can be accomplished on horseback, and the distance is 8m.

A few yards beyond the church at Mardale Green go
through a gate on the left, and along a cart-road
through some fields to a farm-house. When in the rear
of the house it is well to note the position of the mountains. On the left is the Riggindale Ridge, and at the
head of the glen, which also bears that name, stands
High Street. Kidsty Pike is the highest point seen on
the right, and the tourist has to climb to the top of it.
A few yards from the house cross the streamlet at a tiny
bridge. Follow a path which winds up the right-hand
fell. It passes a sheepcot, and under some rocks, to a
pile of stones. When hills appear in front on the
farther side of a hollow, incline to the left, and a gradual
climb over a long grassy slope leads to the summit of
Kidsty Pike (2560). Here a capital view is had of the
High Street range, Nan Bield Pass, Harter Fell,
Branstree, and Riggindale. Beyond a large level cultivated tract, rise the Yorkshire Hills. To the N. are
Mell Fell, and Blencathara. To the W. Fairfield, Dove
Crag, Red Screes, Caudale Moor, Gray Crag, and the
sea in the far distance. Another easy ascent leads to
the top of a part of High Street, where a still more
extensive and splendid prospect is unfolded. Strips of
Ullswater are now in view, with Rampsgill Glen, the
Martindale Fells, and Place Fell. The Coniston Old
Man range appears to the S.W., and due W. are the
wild masses of Helvellyn and Fairfield, and the glens
branching from them.

A wall will be observed on the southern part of High
Street. It descends in the direction of the hills between
Martindale and Hayeswater. Incline to the left and
descend until the wall is reached. When it runs over a
small round hill, leave it a little on the left, and at the
point where it reappears on the other side of the hill,
a gate must be passed through. Here the pedestrian
who descends to Angle Tarn will branch to the right.
See next page.

The pony-track drops into the hollow on the left, in
which lies Hayeswater Tarn. Brothers Water and

Hartsop village are seen, and are good guides until
Hayeswater appears. Pass through a gate in a wall
200 yards below the tarn. Cross the stream and continue along a rough romantic road to Hartsop. The
torrent is a pleasing object all the way down the glen.
The water flows over a stony bed, and in places forms
some pretty cascades. The main road is entered at
Hartsop village, just below Brothers Water, and 2m.
from Patterdale village.

**Mardale Green (Haweswater) to Patterdale, by
Kidsty Pike, High Street, and Angle Tarn, 7m.—**
The same track must be followed as that described at
page 318, until the wall is reached which descends from
High Street.

On passing through the wall at the gate, avoid descending to Hayeswater on the left, or climbing to the
top of Rest Dod, the round hill on the right. After
crossing over some wooden railing, it is well to bear in
mind that if the left-hand wall, which runs by the side,
and then along the tops of the fells, be followed, it will
lead to Angle Tarn. A little ground is saved after
crossing the railing, by leaving the stone wall a few
yards on the left, until some wire fencing is reached,
which acts as a substitute for the wall for a short
distance. Follow the wire fencing, and when it ends,
and the wall again commences, continue in its course.

On passing through a small gate, leave the wall a few
yards on the left. A view is had into Bannerdale on the
right, and presently Angle Tarn comes in sight. Walk
round to the N. end, and avoid descending close to the
shore. Follow a track which winds round a hill and
passes over an uneven ground. At the sheepcot a path
is entered which leads from Patterdale to Boredale Glen,
and to the hamlet of How Town. After quitting Angle
Tarn, good views are had of Brothers Water and the
head of the Patterdale Valley, with many high mountains, including Helvellyn, Fairfield, and St. Sunday
Crag.

The tourist will probably have the pleasure of seeing

that noble animal the red deer run before him; it frequents most of the Martindale Fells.

Superb views are obtained during the descent to the Patterdale Village.

Mardale Green (Haweswater) to Patterdale, by Small Water Tarn and Nan Bield Pass, 10m.— Leaving the Dun Bull Inn, traverse the flat ground at the head of the glen. For some distance the road runs between stone walls, afterwards passing through a gate, and entering the open fell. Here the cart-road winds to the left, and passes between Branstree and Harter Fell, over the Gatescarth Pass, descending into the Long Sleddale Valley, and thence to Kendal, which is 15m. from Mardale Green.

On the right of Harter Fell are observed two rivulets. The one nearer that mountain descends from the Nan Bield Pass and Small Water Tarn; the other has its source in Blea Water Tarn, which lies in the hollow above, at the foot of High Street, and with the Riggindale Ridge on the right. After a romantic climb along a rough track, Small Water is reached. It is situated in a solemn recess of the mountain at the base of high cliffs. This lakelet and its neighbour Blea Water are the most wild and picturesque tarns in the district. Of the two, perhaps Blea Water ought to have the place of honour. The tourist will be amply repaid for a little extra labour if he ascend by the torrent which flows from Blea Water. He will then cross the small projecting ridge on the left to Small Water. From the latter tarn a path will be seen winding up the steep side of the mountain. Near the top it zigzags in the direction of Harter Fell. When the summit of the Nan Bield Pass is attained (2100), a peep is had into part of Kentmere, and immediately below is perceived the Kentmere Reservoir, with Froswick and Ill Bell rising from the western shore. The reservoir was formed for regulating the supply of water to the mills at Staveley. By inclining to the right, a short climb leads to a part of the broad, flat top of High Street, called Lingmell End. On the left is the hollow of the head of Kentmere Glen, and to the right a view is had of Blea Water. Haweswater is also seen over the Riggindale Ridge.

Continuing the walk, with a slight ascent along the smooth green summit, a wall is observed which runs along the top of High Street from S. to N. Here the traveller has a choice of three routes. He may scale the wall, and descend direct to Hayeswater Tarn, which will be seen lying immediately below, in the western hollow; then, by following the course of the stream for 2m., he will reach Hartsop village, in Patterdale. Or he may walk along the summit of High Street, by either side of the wall, until Riggindale and Kidsty Pike are passed on the right, and the wall leads to the left and begins to descend. Here the most direct pony-track from Mardale by Kidsty Pike to Patterdale is entered; and the rest of the journey is described at page 318.

The third plan is to walk from High Street in a S.W. direction, following the wall and some wire-fencing to a large cairn which stands on the height, called Thornthwaite Crag. At every step the tourist is delighted with new and charming prospects. Wild and lofty heights gradually appear on every hand. To the S., at the foot of the Troutbeck Vale, Windermere, with its cluster of wooded islands, looks most lovely, winding away to the sea, a large extent of which is visible.

From Thornthwaite Crag a good view is had of Helvellyn, Fairfield, and other heights, on the W. of Patterdale. The vale close below on the left is Troutbeck, and the one on the right Thrasthwaite Mouth. Caudale Moor is the near height opposite.

Following the wall to the depression of Thornthwaite Hause, a descent is quickly made into the cove at the head of the wild and solitary glen of Thrasthwaite Mouth.

A pleasant walk by the side of the torrent, with part of Ullswater in sight, leads down the glen to the works connected with a lead-mine.

Y

The beck may be crossed at the works, or at a small stone bridge a little lower down.

Hartsop village is passed through, and then Patter-dale is reached.

Shap to Mardale Green (Haweswater), by Shap Abbey and Swindale Glen.—Pedestrians will some-times enter the Lake District at Shap, and walk 7m. over the hills to Mardale Green at the head of Haweswater, and thence over High Street to Patterdale.

From the railway station at Shap, walk through the village, and at the N. end enter a road on the left, lead-ing to Bampton. A mile farther a guide-post directs down a lane on the left, to the Abbey, situated a few hundred yards distant in the dell through which flows the river Lowther. From the abbey follow a rough cart-road for a few yards. It leads to the open moor in the rear of the ruins. When crossing the moor leave a clump of trees on the right, and at some farm-steads keep above the highest wall on the fell-side, and a rough, grass-grown cart-road takes over to Swindale. The glen comes in sight at the feet of the traveller when about 1½m. from the Abbey. It is a quiet little glen, with a rugged streamlet flowing through it, and the wild front of Branstree Mountain at its head. It contains half a dozen farmsteads, and nearly its whole extent is covered with bare rocks, loose stones, and a few stunted trees. Avoiding too sudden a descent, follow a track which runs along the side of the left-hand fell, and crosses the beck at some stepping-stones close to the little church.

This is one of the smallest churches in the district, and its interior is undoubtedly the most primitive look-ing. There is no burial-ground attached to the building. Nearly 1m. beyond the church, at some farm-houses, commence ascending the hill on the right, with a gradual inclination to the left in the direction of Branstree. Some rough ground covered with heather has to be crossed before the descent to Mardale Green is com-menced. Good views are had of the Yorkshire Hills and the High Street range. The mountains at the head of

Mardale look extremely wild. The Dun Bull is the
farthest house from the head of the lake, and it will be
observed almost immediately below the hill down which
the traveller descends.

Ascent of Hallin Fell (1271), **from How Town.**—
From How Town, Hallin Fell is well worth ascending.
An easy climb of thirty or forty minutes will enable the
tourist to reach the top, where there stands a large
square pile of stones, erected by an enthusiastic admirer
of the late Lord Brougham. On one stone is cut H. B.,
1864, being his lordship's initials, and the date of the
cairn's erection. There is a stone seat on the S. side of
the pile, from which is obtained a fine prospect. Most
of the Ullswater Lake is seen at the feet of the spectator.
Hallsteads House and grounds are in front, and to the
left, Lyulph's Tower. More remote are Penrith, the
plain, Cross Fell, Blencathara, and Skiddaw. Helvellyn
range and Catchedecam are very prominent to the W.
Looking southwards are the Boredale and Rampsgill
glens, with the heights, Place Fell, Birk Fell, Beda, Nab,
High Street, and Swarth Fell.

**How Town to Haweswater and Mardale Green, by
Rampsgill Glen and High Street Mountain.**—If the
descent from High Street be by Kidsty Pike and Riggindale, the distance will be 8½m.; if by Nan Bield Pass
and Small Water Tarn, 10m.

On leaving the How Town Hotel, cross over the depression between Hallin Fell and Steel Knotts. Enter
the first road on the left, and when ⅞m. from How Town,
the mean-looking church, with its solitary yew tree, is
passed. The How Grane Beck is now crossed, and the
road continues at the base of some picturesque rocks on
the side of Beda Mountain. The valley in which stands
the church is called How Grane, but about 1½m. beyond
the church a round prominent hill, called the "Nab,"
divides the valley into two small glens, the one on the
left being Rampsgill and the other Bannerdale. Go
through fields in front of the Nab, and walk up Rampsgill by the side of the beck. The glen has a peaceful

Y 2

aspect. It is almost bare of trees, and without a single habitation. The hills on either side are smooth and green, and at the head stands a bold, rugged part of High Street.

On passing through the wall which crosses the glen near its head, make for the right-hand hollow. The climb will occupy from thirty to forty-five minutes.

When the summit is reached incline to the left, and ascend in the direction of a wall. Hayeswater Tarn is in the hollow to the S., and a wall runs up from it and meets the one by which the tourist is walking. At the point where they meet, the pony-track from Patterdale over High Street to Mardale is entered. For a description of the remainder of the journey see page 314.

How Town to Haweswater and Mardale Green, by Fusedale Glen and Measand Beck, 7½m.—Fusedale is the small glen at the back of How Town. On its E. side are Swarth Fell and Lade Pot, portions of the High Street range, and on the W. a long ridge called Steel Knotts.

Pursue the course of the Fusedale Beck, which enters the Ullswater Lake near the How Town Hotel, and keep it on the left until past the last walled inclosure. Then either side of the stream may be traversed, but perhaps the best plan is to cross the brook and walk up the E. side to the head of the glen. There is not much to interest the traveller. He is however in a tranquil dale, and on looking back a pleasant view is had of part of Ullswater. At the head of the glen is a stone building from which the pedestrian must follow a track winding up the fell to the left. Presently, on looking back, Blencathara is beheld rising over the Steel Knotts. When the Martindale Fells, Helvellyn, High Street, and other mountains appear, continue the ascent with a slight inclination to the right, taking care to avoid on the one hand dropping into the wet hollow, and on the other getting too far up the hill. A wall will be observed running from Steel Knotts, which, after passing an old building, ascends the hill along the course of a ravine.

When it reaches the top of the High Street chain, it bends due S., and goes along the middle summit-level of the mountain, as far as the eye can range. The tourist is advised to continue walking due S., gradually mounting the hill, until he arrive at the point where the wall bends on the top of the mountain. He must then incline to the left, and descend into the hollow along which flows the Measand Beck.

It will show how complete an isolation from large towns the traveller will feel on these heights when the writer states that in March last he saw at this spot seventy red deer. It is pleasant to know that the ground which is being gone over is the resort of so noble an animal. The dalesmen say that there are about 300 on the Martindale Hills. J. E. Hasell, Esq., of Dalemain, near Penrith, is the proprietor. Some strangers will need to be reminded that what is called a forest amongst these mountains is often a treeless space. There is scarcely a single tree on the fells included in this deer forest. Following the course of the Measand Beck, part of Haweswater is presently seen. The rivulet forms a few cascades and then flows into the lake, 1m. from its foot.

A good cart-road will be entered which traverses the shore, and leads to the Dun Bull Inn, at Mardale Green. It is 3m. distant, at the foot of Harter Fell, the high mountain seen standing at the head of the glen. The best view of Haweswater is from the Measand promontory, 1m. from the foot of the lake, and the walk thence to Mardale is remarkably fine. It is therefore advisable to take the route above indicated.

FINIS.

INDEX.

LONDON: PRINTED BY EDWARD STANFORD, 6 AND 7, CHARING CROSS, S.W.

Exhibited in the Town Hall, Keswick,

From 8.30 a.m. to 7.0 p.m. daily,

FLINTOFT'S

CELEBRATED

Model of the English Lake District,

Coloured to Nature, on a Scale of Three Inches to a Mile.

All the Mountains, Valleys, 16 Lakes, and 52 Tarns, Towns, Houses, Plantations, Rivers, Roads, and Mines, exhibiting an area of 1200 square miles. Distance 51 miles by 37.

"W. WORDSWORTH, Esq., of Rydal Mount, has examined this Model and greatly approves of it."—*July* 8, 1840.

JOHN DALTON, Esq., D.C.L.—"I have examined Mr. Flintoft's Model of the Lakes and Mountains in Cumberland and Westmorland, and have been much interested and pleased with it."—*John Dalton, D.C.L., Manchester, August* 17, 1840.

CHARLES MACKAY, Esq., LL.D.—"No traveller to the Lake District should omit paying a visit to a curiosity of art to be seen in Keswick— Mr. Flintoft's beautiful Model of the whole country."—"Scenery and Poetry of the English Lakes."—*Charles Mackay, Esq., LL.D.*

MISS HARRIET MARTINEAU.—"This Model is held to be a work of extraordinary correctness; and a leisurely visit to it should be an object to every traveller who cares to know where he is, and where he is going." —'The Land we live in.' Part XIII.—*By Miss Harriet Martineau.*

THE ASTRONOMER ROYAL.—"Mr. Flintoft's Model of the Lake District is the most beautiful work of that kind I have ever seen. Several years ago I was in the habit of not unfrequently examining it, and critically comparing its representations of special tracts (some of them not often visited) with the realities as I had seen them, and in every instance I found the Model to be surprisingly correct."—*G. B. Airey, Royal Observatory, Greenwich, May* 21, 1860.

MISS HARRIET MARTINEAU.—"Of the attractions of Keswick, the first is, undoubtedly, Mr. Flintoft's Model of the Lake District, which is within a few yards of all the principal Inns. That Model will beguile a sensible traveller of a longer time than he would suppose possible. Ten minutes would give him a better idea of the structure and distribution of the country than all Maps and Guide Books."—*Harriet Martineau, July,* 1852.

PROFESSOR SEDGWICK.—"Mr. Flintoft's Model is a work of very high merit, and ought to be studied by every one who wishes to be well acquainted with the Physical Geography of that beautiful country."— *A. Sedgwick, May* 31, 1860.

"Its real beauty is its truth, and its utility that accuracy of information which nothing but truth can give."—*Liverpool Journal.*

ADMISSION ONE SHILLING EACH FOR THE SEASON.

NORTH-EASTERN RAILWAY.

FARES for Monthly Tickets to Scarborough, &c., from the undermentioned Stations.

STATIONS.	SCARBOROUGH.			WHITBY.			FILEY.			BRIDLINGTON.			HORNSEA or WITHERNSEA.			HARROGATE.		
	1st	2nd	3rd	1st	2nd	3rd	1st	2nd	3rd	1st	2nd	3rd	1st	2nd	3rd	1st	2nd	3rd
	s. d.	s. d.	s. d.	s. d.	s. d.	s. d.	s. d.	s. d.	s. d.	s. d.	s. d.	s. d.	s. d.	s. d.	s. d.	s. d.	s. d.	s. d.
Alnwick	39 9	30 9	18 9	31 0	23 3	14 8	40 9	30 9	19 3	43 3	32 0	20 2	46 6	35 0	22 0	31 6	23 9	15 0
Arthington	18 9	14 0	8 9	22 3	16 6	10 2	21 0	15 3	9 3	21 6	16 6	10 2	19 3	14 8	8 9	—	—	—
Berwick	47 6	36 8	23 6	38 8	29 0	18 3	48 3	36 0	23 0	50 0	37 6	23 9	64 0	40 6	25 6	39 3	29 6	18 8
Bridlington	—	—	—	28 0	20 0	7 0	—	—	—	—	—	—	13 3	11 3	5 6	19 6	14 8	8 2
Carlisle	41 8	31 0	19 6	38 0	26 9	16 8	42 9	31 9	19 9	44 8	33 0	20 8	48 6	36 0	21 8	33 9	25 0	15 6
Doncaster (via Goole)	21 0	15 9	9 6	13 6	10 2	6 6	21 0	15 3	9 9	21 0	16 6	10 6	15 3	11 6	6 8	—	—	—
Darlington	19 6	14 8	9 2	16 6	12 6	7 9	20 3	15 3	9 9	22 0	16 6	10 6	26 0	19 6	12 3	11 3	8 6	5 6
Durham	25 6	18 9	12 0	65 6	49 6	30 0	28 3	19 9	12 6	29 0	21 0	13 2	31 9	24 0	15 2	17 3	12 9	8 2
*Edinburgh	75 6	57 0	34 6	—	—	—	—	—	—	—	—	—	—	—	—	65 0	50 0	30 0
Ferryhill	23 6	17 0	10 9	14 3	10 9	6 8	23 9	17 9	11 3	25 6	19 3	12 0	29 3	22 0	14 0	14 9	11 8	7 0
Filey	24 0	18 0	11 3	14 3	10 6	6 6	24 9	18 9	11 9	26 9	20 0	12 6	15 6	11 3	7 0	17 8	13 3	8 6
Hartlepool, East	17 0	13 0	8 0	10 9	8 0	9 0	17 8	13 3	8 6	19 6	14 6	9 2	30 6	20 3	14 5	15 9	13 0	7 2
Harrogate	14 3	12 0	8 0	10 9	15 0	9 0	12 0	9 0	5 6	8 3	6 0	4 0	18 9	14 3	9 0	—	—	—
Hull	21 0	16 0	10 0	24 6	18 6	11 3	12 0	9 0	5 6	6 0	4 6	2 8	20 8	15 0	10 0	13 9	12 0	7 6
Ilkley	63 0	39 9	25 2	44 6	33 6	21 0	54 0	40 6	25 6	56 6	41 8	26 6	68 0	44 8	28 3	45 0	33 9	21 3
Keso	18 3	13 6	8 6	23 9	16 9	10 8	19 0	14 3	9 0	19 0	14 3	9 0	16 9	12 9	8 0	12 6	9 6	5 6
Leeds, New Station, and Holbeck	34 3	25 9	16 2	25 0	19 2	12 0	35 0	26 3	16 8	38 3	27 9	17 5	36 3	27 6	17 3	20 3	19 6	12 6
Leyburn	22 9	17 3	10 9	21 9	16 3	10 0	23 6	17 3	11 0	23 6	18 0	11 0	26 3	20 0	12 6	21 9	16 6	10 3
Morpeth	18 0	13 6	8 6	12 0	9 0	5 9	18 9	14 0	7 9	18 6	13 6	8 6	16 0	12 0	7 6	—	—	—
Newcastle	20 8	15 6	9 9	17 3	12 9	8 0	18 9	14 0	9 0	21 6	17 8	11 0	27 3	20 6	13 0	8 3	6 0	3 8
Northallerton	16 3	13 0	7 9	16 6	12 6	7 0	17 0	12 9	8 0	18 6	14 0	8 9	23 3	16 9	10 6	12 9	9 6	6 0
Normanton	15 0	11 3	7 2	18 9	12 6	7 6	21 0	12 0	7 6	21 9	18 3	6 6	11 3	9 0	5 6	—	—	—
Richmond	23 3	21 9	13 8	30 8	18 6	9 0	28 6	21 9	14 2	32 0	24 0	15 0	33 9	6 9	17 0	21 0	15 0	10 0
Ripon	16 0	18 0	8 8	19 6	8 0	6 0	18 0	14 8	8 8	21 9	16 9	11 2	27 0	20 3	12 9	12 0	9 0	5 6
Selby	28 0	21 0	12 3	19 6	14 9	9 2	18 0	14 0	8 8	30 9	23 6	14 6	34 6	26 0	16 6	20 0	15 0	9 6
South Shields	31 3	23 6	14 9	23 6	17 6	10 6	23 3	24 6	15 3	33 9	19 6	16 2	38 0	28 6	18 0	23 3	17 8	11 0
Stockton	7 6	6 0	4 8	13 9	17 0	10 8	9 6	7 6	5 6	16 6	12 9	8 2	30 0	22 6	14 3	16 3	15 0	7 0
Sunderland	11 3	8 6	5 6	15 0	11 3	7 2	19 6	8 9	5 9	14 3	10 9	6 8	23 9	17 3	10 9	19 9	15 0	9 0

* Passengers leaving Edinburgh at 2.50 and 7.30 P.M. break the journey at Newcastle or York.

For General Conditions, see Programmes issued by the Company.

FIRST, SECOND, and THIRD CLASS MONTHLY TOURIST TICKETS are issued to the watering places of Ilkley, Ben Rhydding, Harrogate, Scarborough, Whitby, Filey, Bridlington, Hornsea, Withernsea, Boston, Redcar, Saltburn, Tynemouth, and Glaisdale, from any North-Eastern Station upwards of 29 miles distant from the particular watering place.

HENRY TENNANT, General Manager.

THE ENGLISH LAKE DISTRICT.

MAPS.

ORDNANCE MAP OF THE ENGLISH LAKE DIS-TRICT, constructed from the Government Survey under the direction of Major-Gen. SIR HENRY JAMES, R.E., F.R.S., and recently published. Scale, 1 inch to a mile, with the Mountains and Hills very carefully shaded, so that the eye immediately distinguishes the different mountain chains, with their precipitous and sloping sides, gorges, and gradually-descending valleys. The Mountain Passes are also very distinctly traced, and the altitude above the sea, in feet, of nearly every eminence is engraved.

With reference to the lower ground, the Main and By-roads and Lanes are distinguished; the Railways and their Stations; the names of County Towns, Market Towns, Parishes, Hamlets, Mansions, Parks, Large Farms, &c., are all suitably characterized; and lastly, a special style of letter is used to point out Roman, Old English, and other remains of antiquity.

Size, 39 inches square. Price, mounted on cloth to fold in case, plain, 12s. 6d.; or coloured, so as to more clearly distinguish counties, main roads, railways, canals, parks, lakes, mountain tarns, &c., 15s. 6d. The same may be had in six sheets; price, plain, 6s.; coloured, 9s.

The following can be obtained at the same prices, when specially demanded.

A separate edition of the above Map, with the Contours of Elevation shown by graduated shading.

Also an edition without the hills shaded, but with Contour Lines and Elevations marked.

MURRAY'S NEW HANDBOOK MAP OF THE LAKE DISTRICT: chiefly from the Ordnance Survey, and constructed especially with a view to the requirements of tourists. Heights of Hills, Lakes, &c., above the Sea are given in English Feet. Scale, 2 miles to an inch; size, 21 inches by 20. Price, mounted to fold in case, 3s. 6d.

GEOLOGICAL MAP OF THE ENGLISH LAKES and adjoining Country, with descriptive Pamphlet. By JOHN RUTHVEN. Mounted on cloth, in case, 5s.

Gratis on application, or per Post for Penny Stamp.

STANFORD'S TOURIST'S CATALOGUE,

Containing a List, irrespective of Publisher, of all the best Guide Books and Maps suitable for the British and Continental Traveller, with Index Maps to the Government Surveys of England, France, and Switzerland.

London:
EDWARD STANFORD, 6 & 7, CHARING CROSS, S.W.

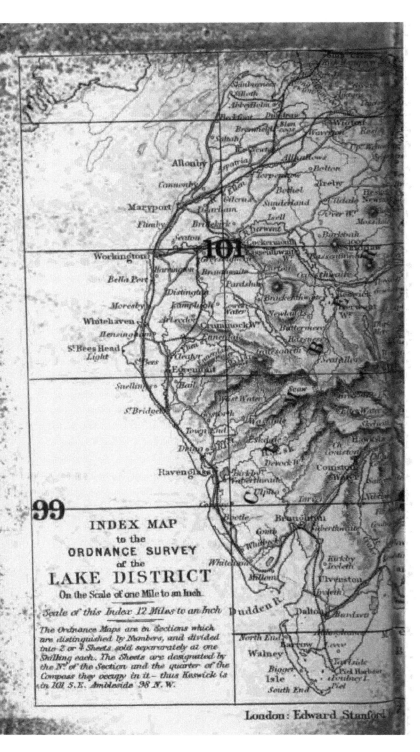

99

101

INDEX MAP
to the
ORDNANCE SURVEY
of the
LAKE DISTRICT
On the Scale of one Mile to an Inch

Scale of this Index 12 Miles to an Inch

The Ordnance Maps are on Sections which are distinguished by Numbers, and divided into 2 or 4 Sheets sold separately at one Shilling each. The Sheets are designated by the N.º of the Section and the quarter of the Compass they occupy in it.- thus Keswick is in 101 S.E. Ambleside 98 N.W.

London: Edward Stanford